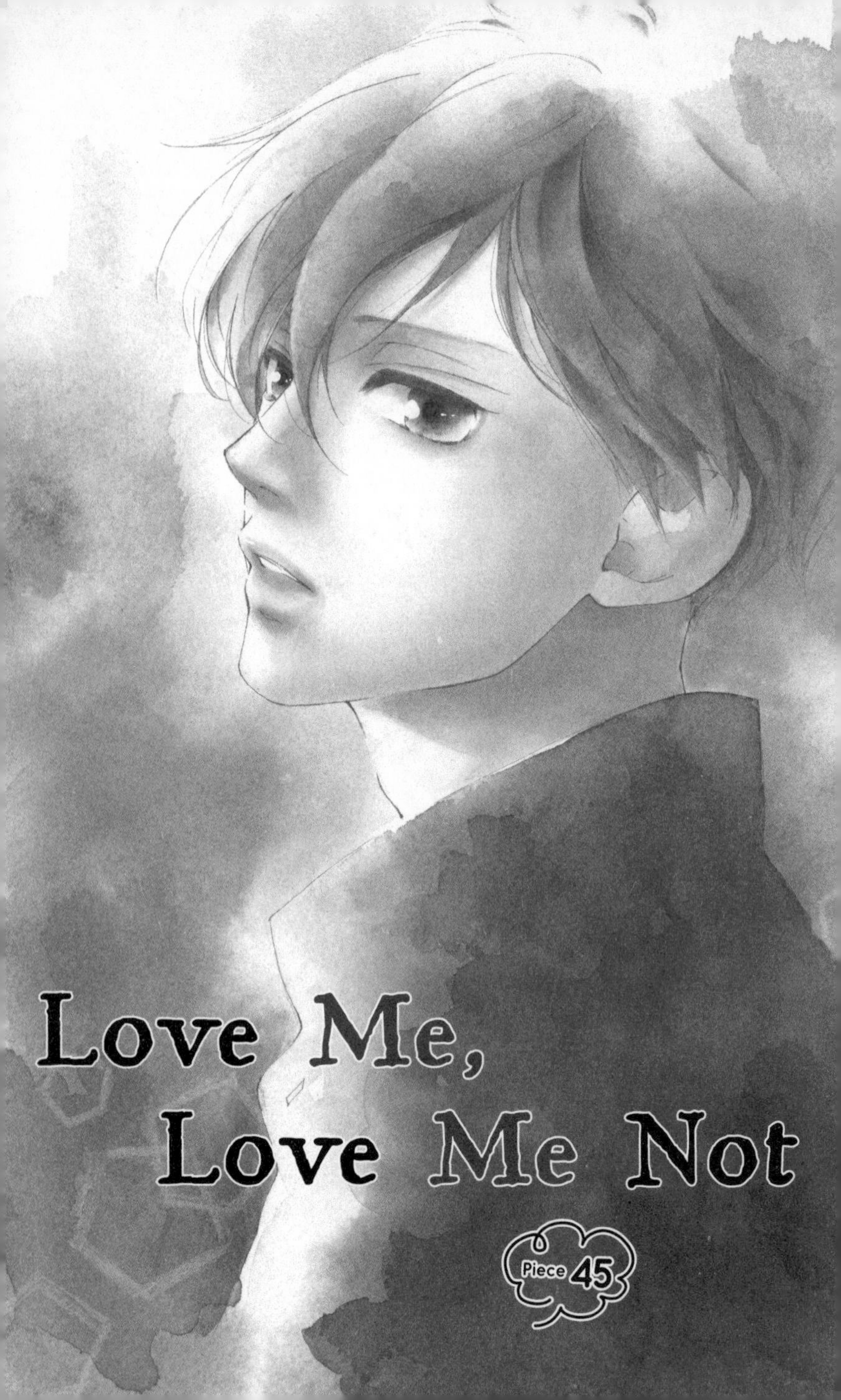
Love Me,
Love Me Not
Piece 45

Hello, I'm Io Sakisaka. Thank you so much for picking up volume 12 of *Love Me, Love Me Not*.

We've reached the last volume! The main characters in this series are Yuna and Akari. They are two girls who have very different values. I touched on this in the Greetings section of volume 1, but the reason why I made them both my heroines is this: Just because two people have different values doesn't mean they have to be in opposition to each other! I thought it would be great if my heroines could influence each other by taking a little of the other's differences. I thought it would be best if they were both main characters to portray that. As I was working on this manga, I became aware of the assumptions I held, and I had to stop and think more about the "shoulds" in life, like "You should do it this or that way," etc. Is it really something I truly believe or something I just say? If only for that, I think this was a very fruitful series for me. How was it for everyone else?

Please enjoy this final volume of *Love Me, Love Me Not*.

Io Sakisaka

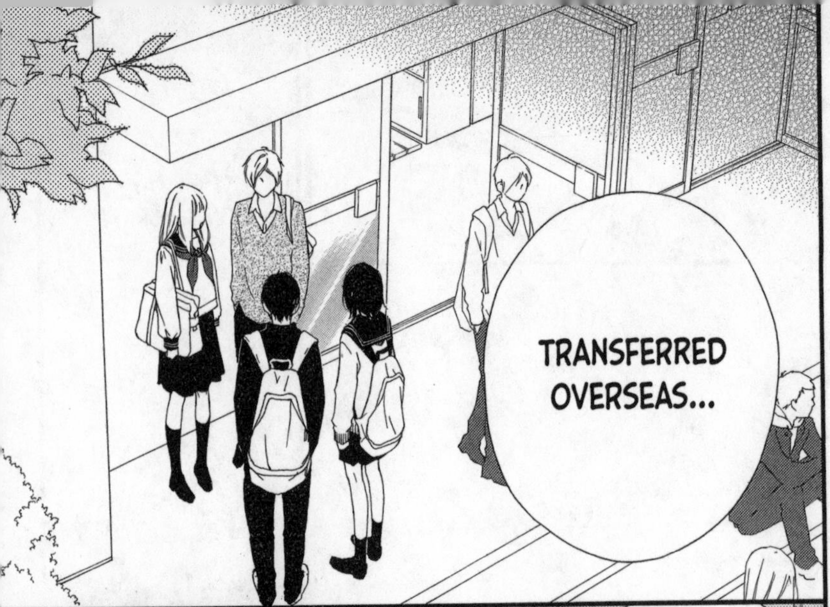
TRANSFERRED OVERSEAS...

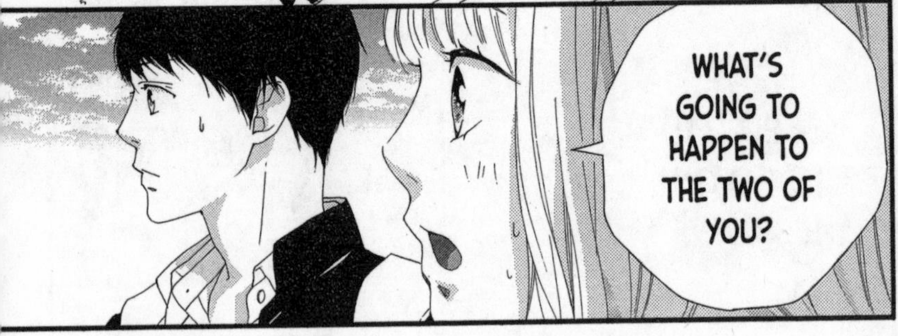
WHAT'S GOING TO HAPPEN TO THE TWO OF YOU?

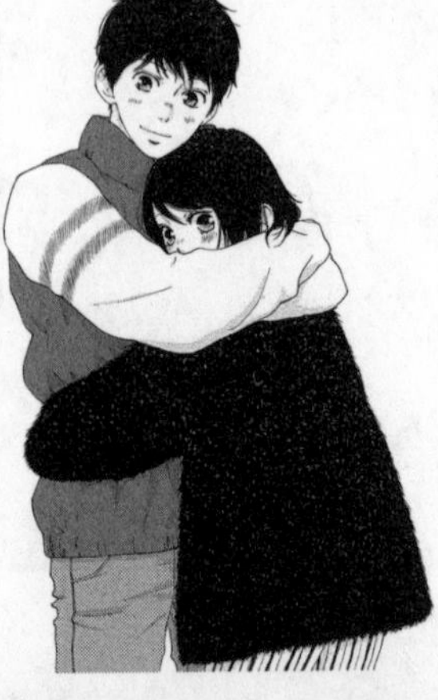

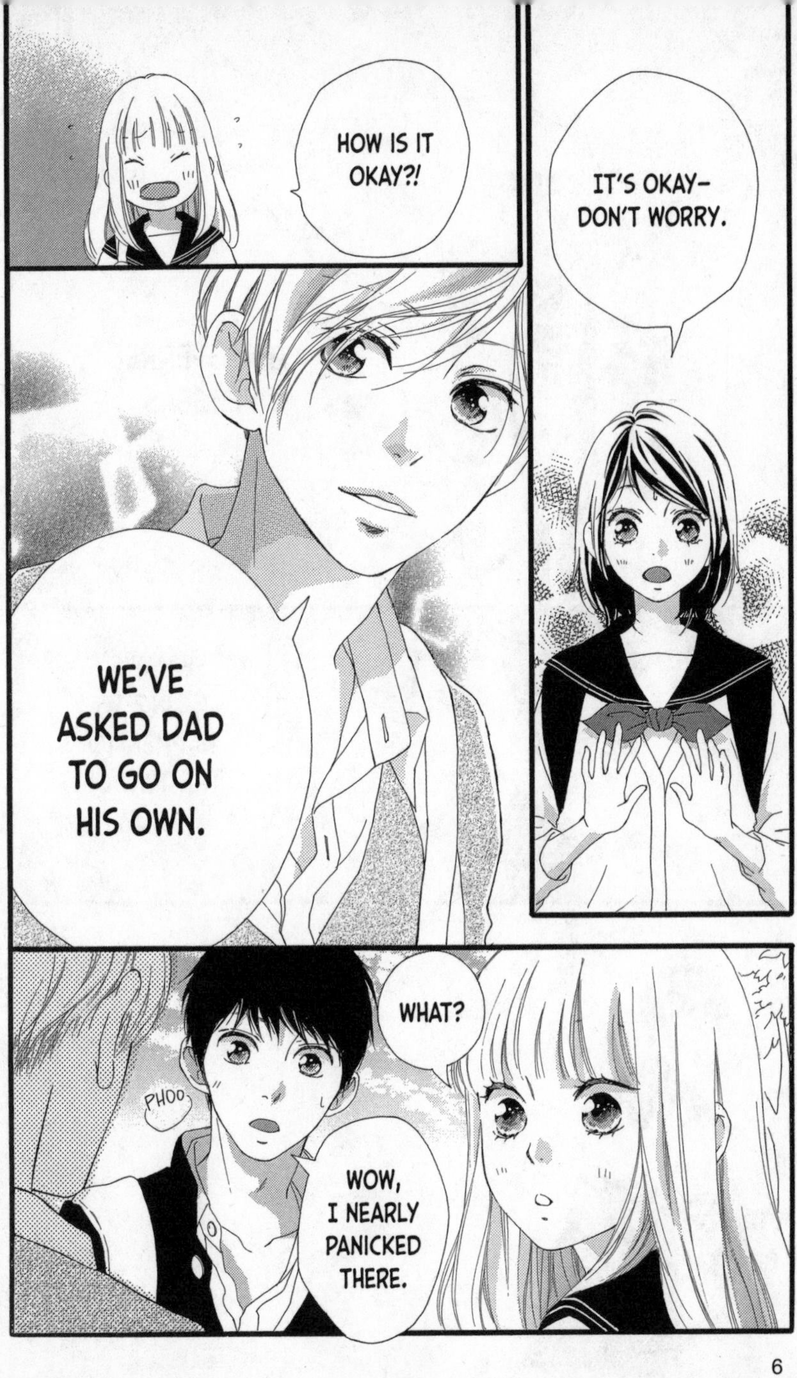
IT'S OKAY— DON'T WORRY.
HOW IS IT OKAY?!
WE'VE ASKED DAD TO GO ON HIS OWN.
WHAT?
PHOO
WOW, I NEARLY PANICKED THERE.

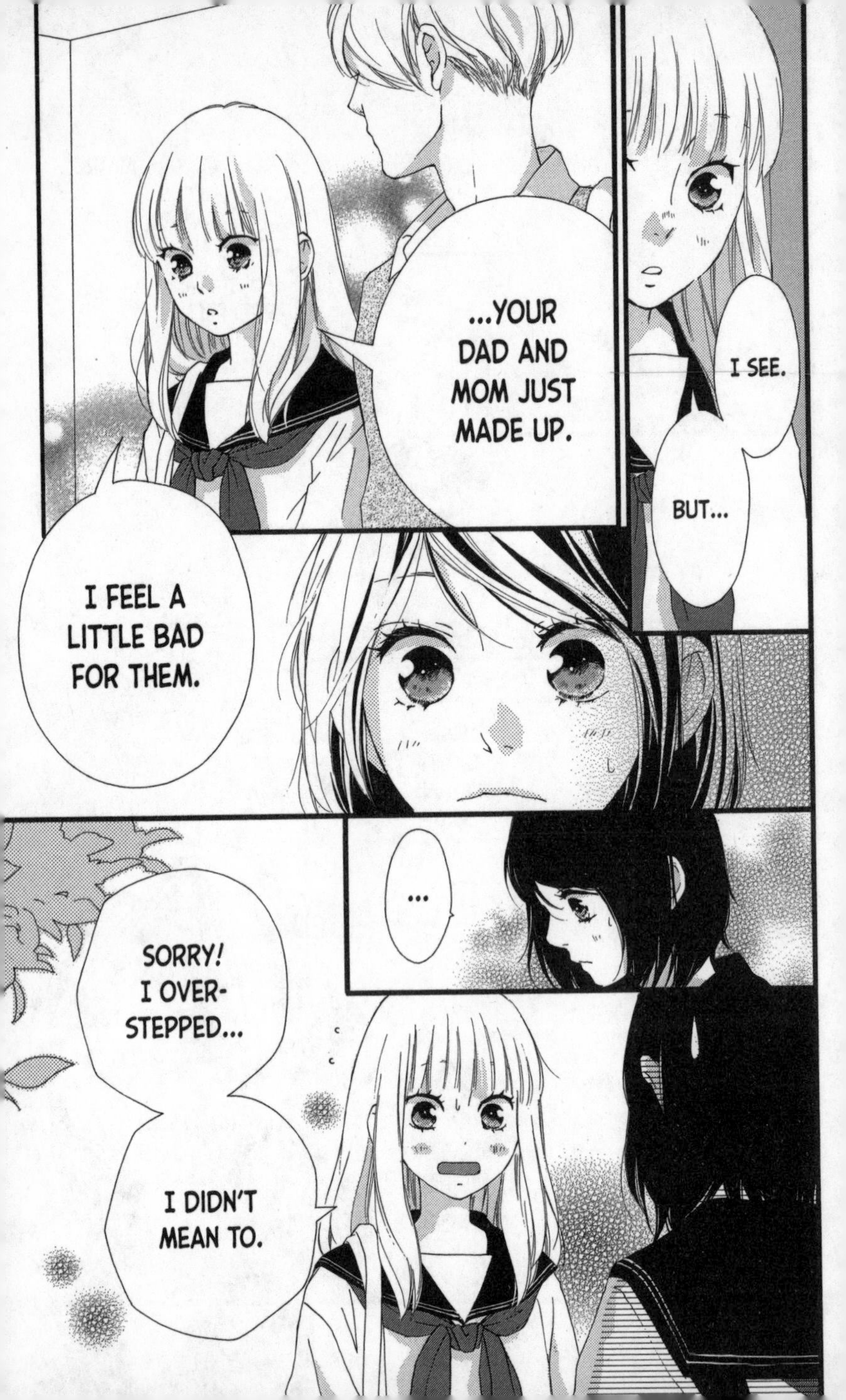
I SEE.
BUT...
...YOUR DAD AND MOM JUST MADE UP.
I FEEL A LITTLE BAD FOR THEM.
...
SORRY! I OVER-STEPPED...
I DIDN'T MEAN TO.

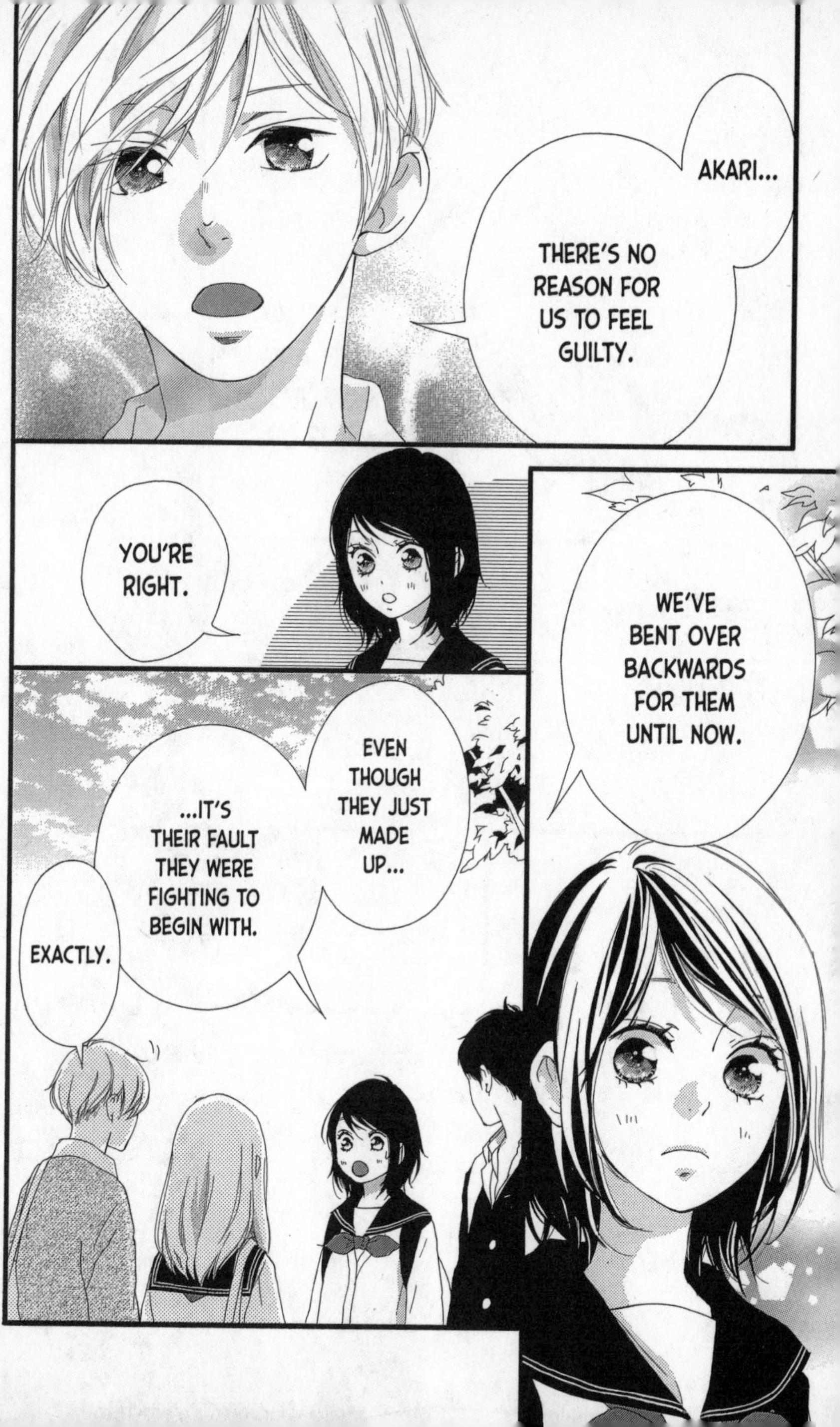
AKARI...
THERE'S NO REASON FOR US TO FEEL GUILTY.
WE'VE BENT OVER BACKWARDS FOR THEM UNTIL NOW.
YOU'RE RIGHT.
EVEN THOUGH THEY JUST MADE UP...
...IT'S THEIR FAULT THEY WERE FIGHTING TO BEGIN WITH.
EXACTLY.

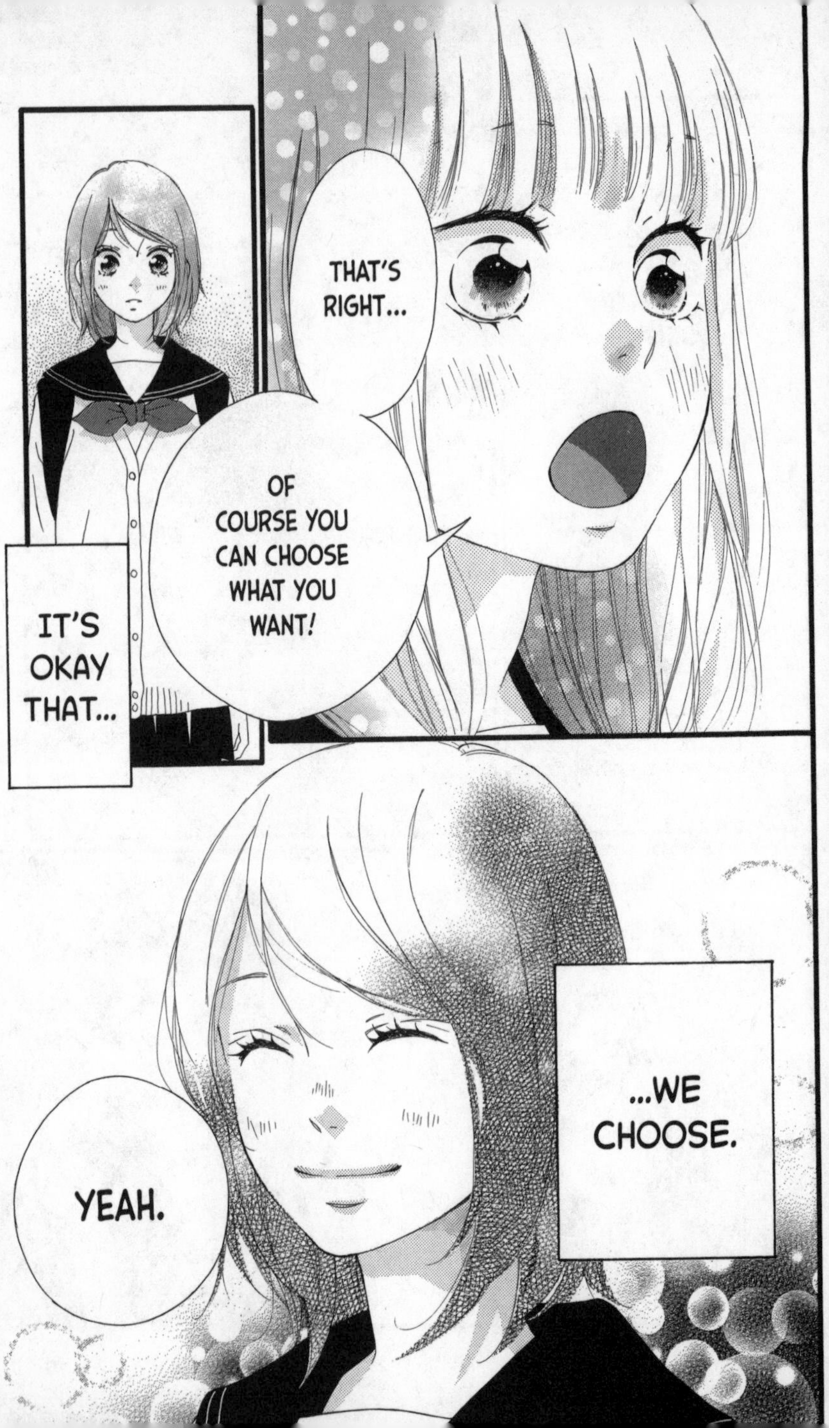
THAT'S RIGHT...
OF COURSE YOU CAN CHOOSE WHAT YOU WANT!
IT'S OKAY THAT...
...WE CHOOSE.
YEAH.

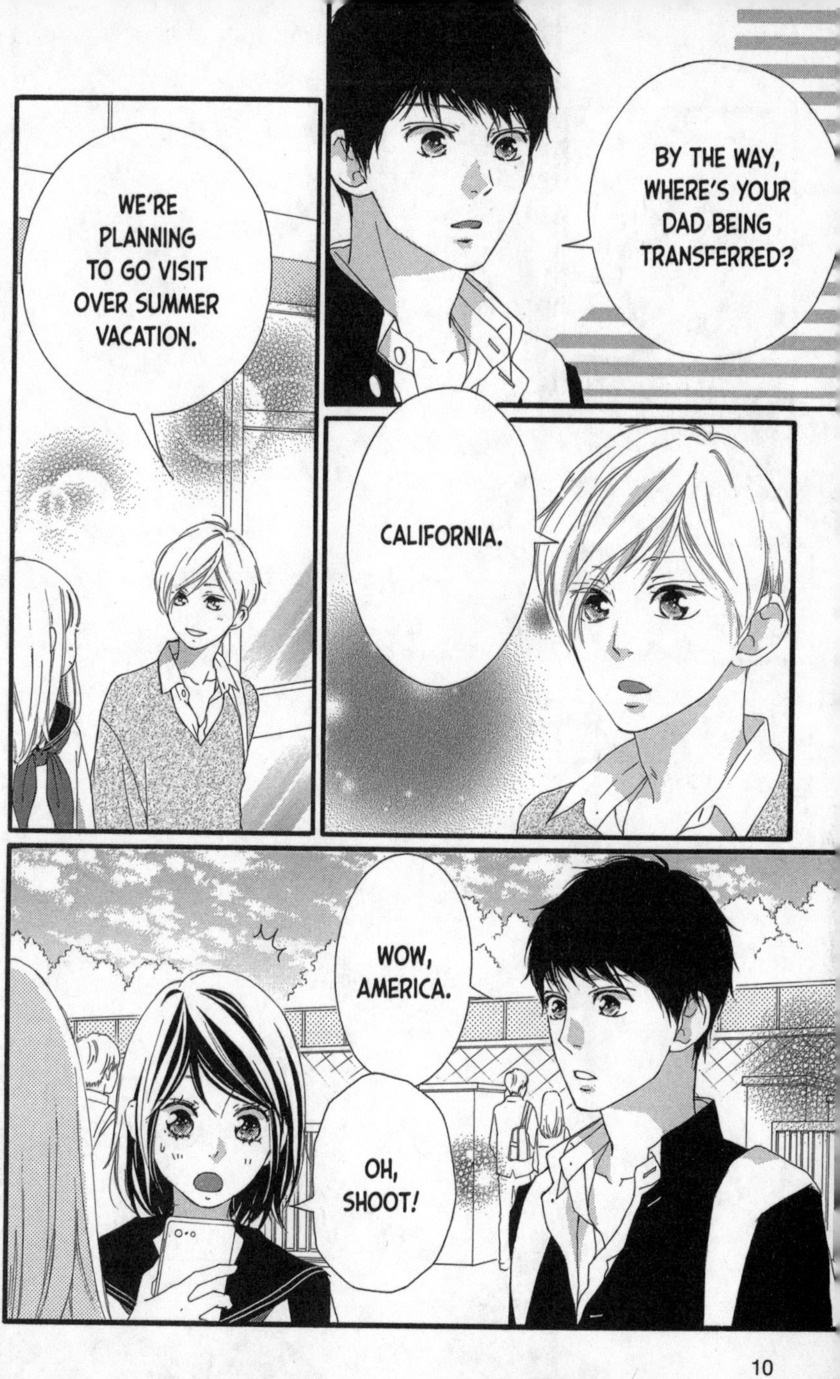
BY THE WAY, WHERE'S YOUR DAD BEING TRANSFERRED?
CALIFORNIA.
WE'RE PLANNING TO GO VISIT OVER SUMMER VACATION.
WOW, AMERICA.
OH, SHOOT!

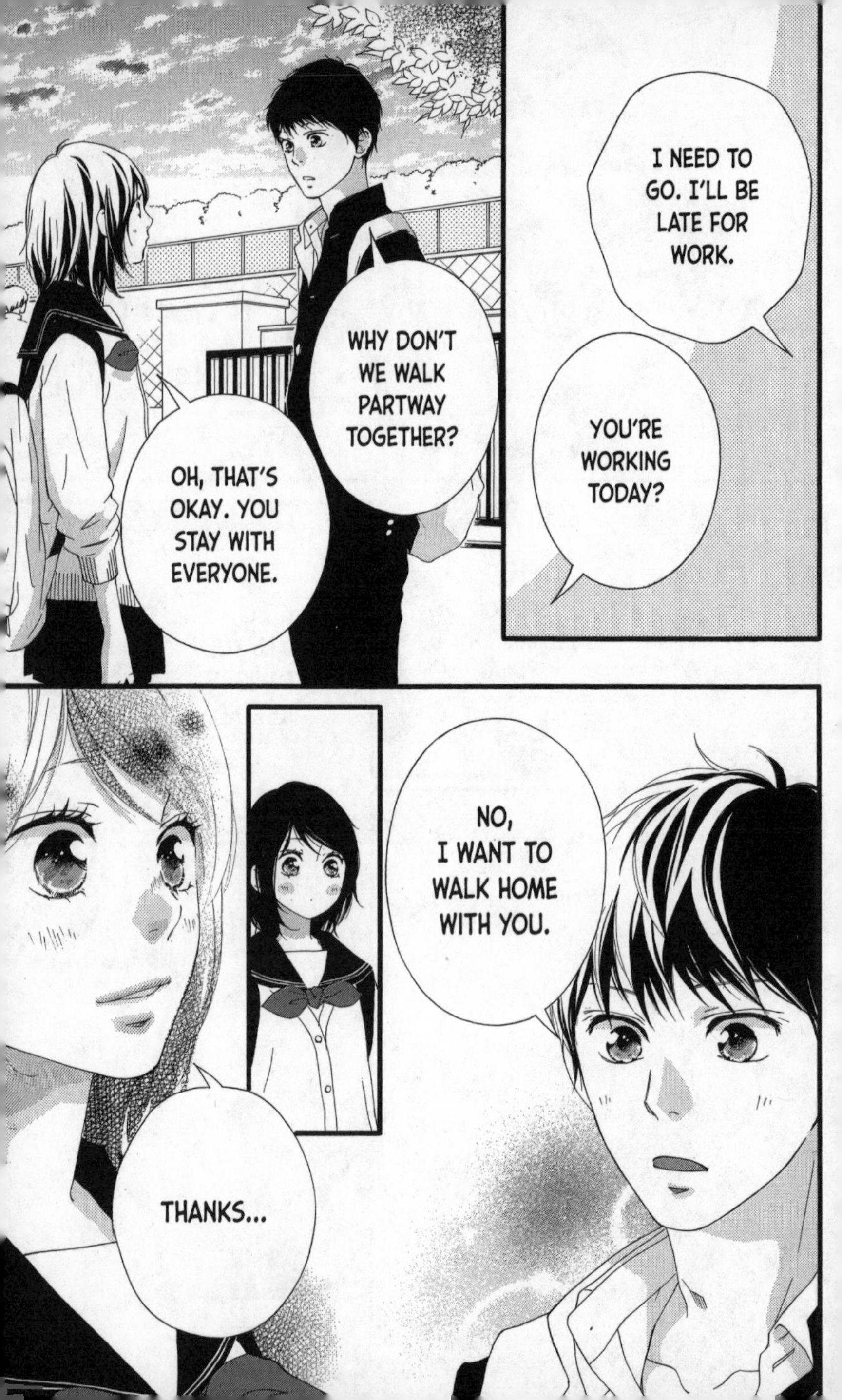
I NEED TO GO. I'LL BE LATE FOR WORK.
YOU'RE WORKING TODAY?
WHY DON'T WE WALK PARTWAY TOGETHER?
OH, THAT'S OKAY. YOU STAY WITH EVERYONE.
NO, I WANT TO WALK HOME WITH YOU.
THANKS...

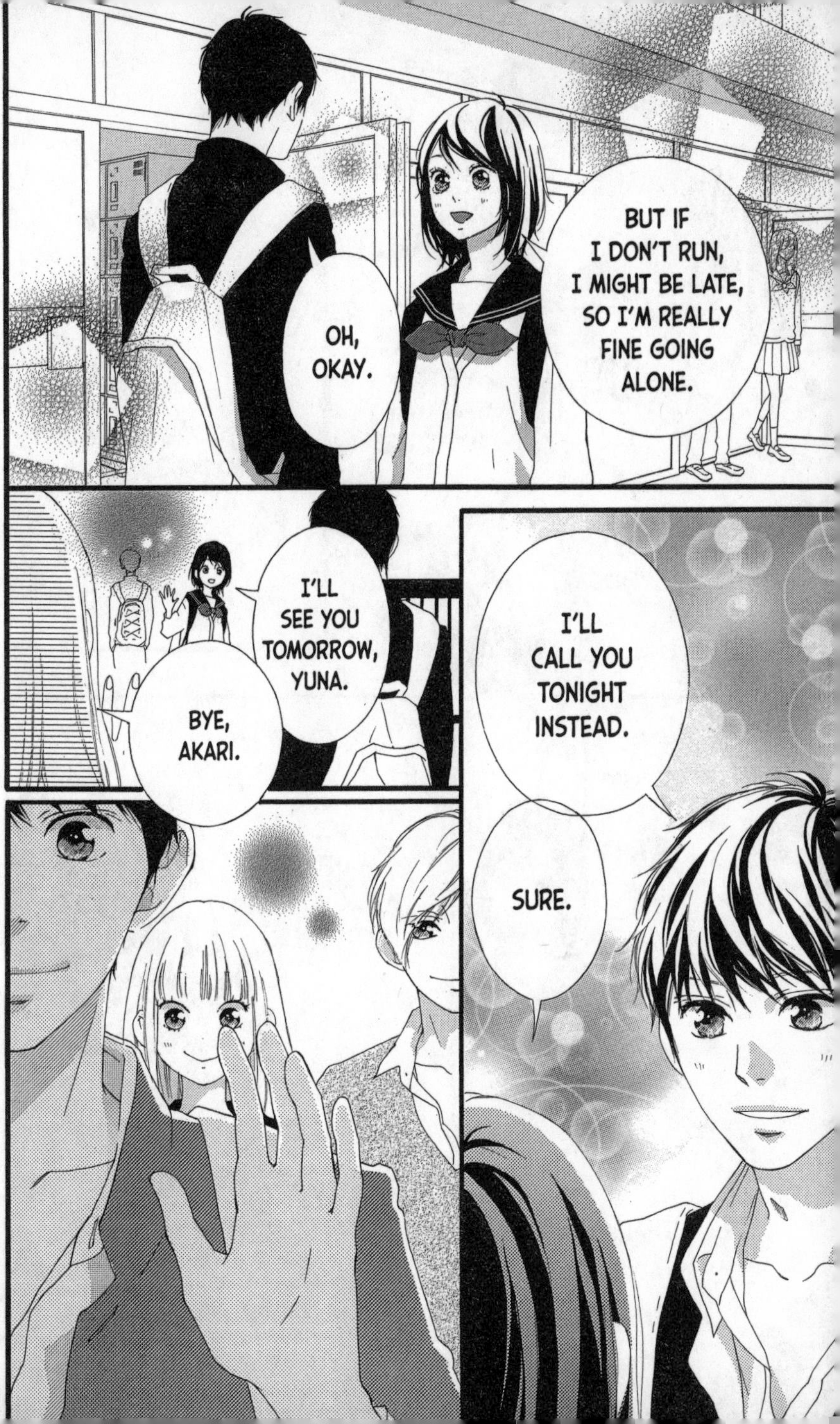
BUT IF I DON'T RUN, I MIGHT BE LATE, SO I'M REALLY FINE GOING ALONE.
OH, OKAY.
I'LL CALL YOU TONIGHT INSTEAD.
SURE.
I'LL SEE YOU TOMORROW, YUNA.
BYE, AKARI.

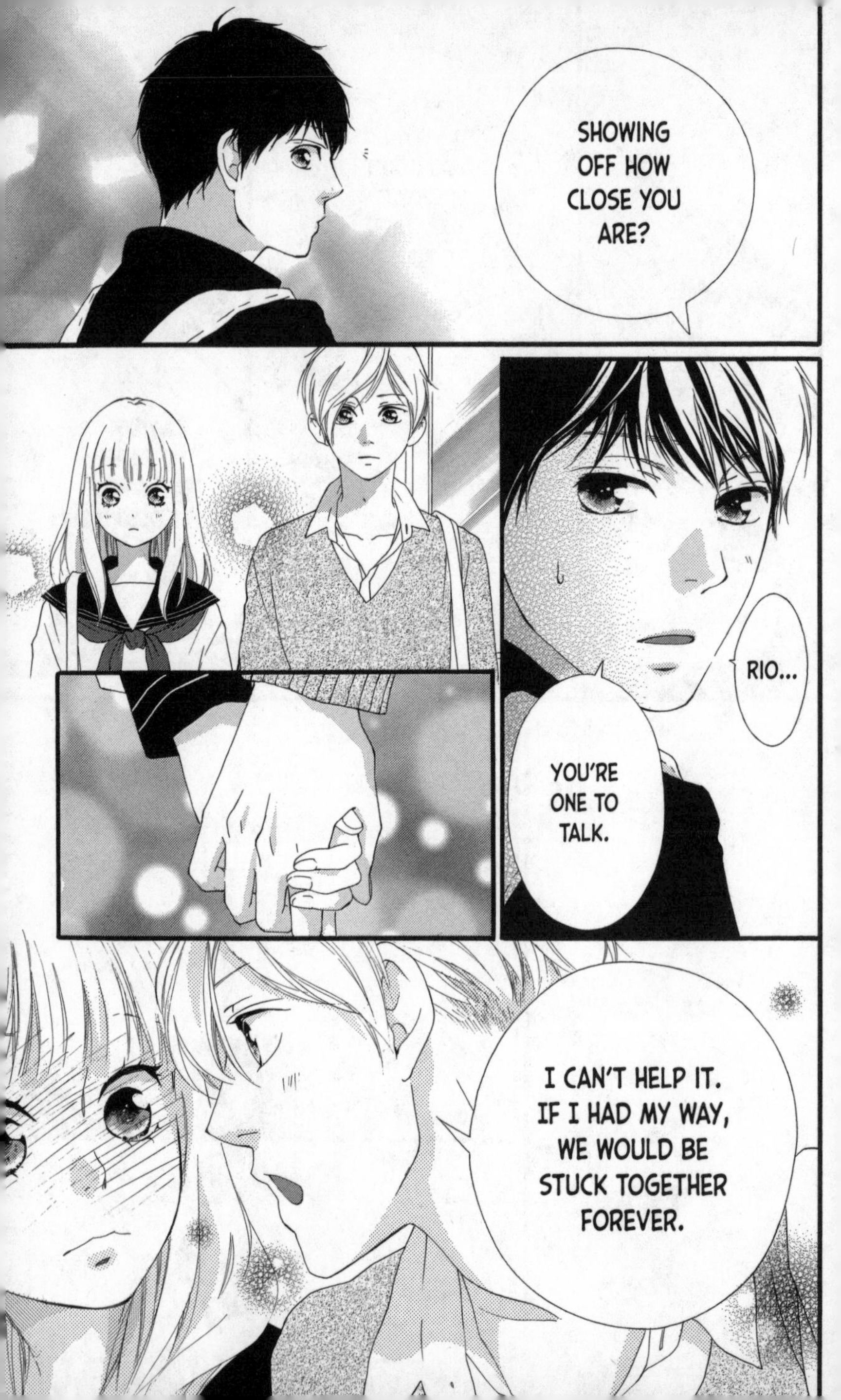
SHOWING OFF HOW CLOSE YOU ARE?
RIO...
YOU'RE ONE TO TALK.
I CAN'T HELP IT. IF I HAD MY WAY, WE WOULD BE STUCK TOGETHER FOREVER.

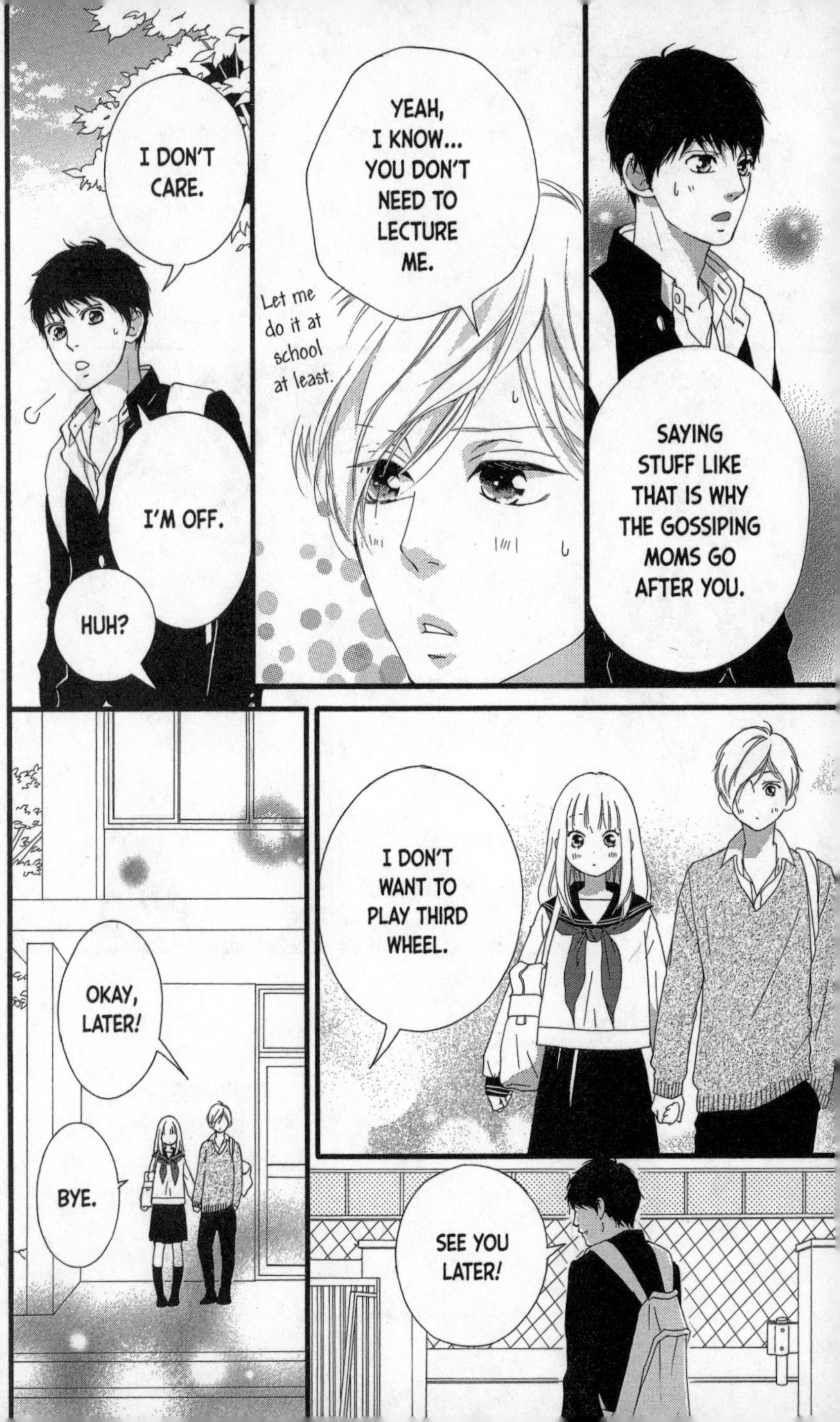
SAYING STUFF LIKE THAT IS WHY THE GOSSIPING MOMS GO AFTER YOU.
YEAH, I KNOW... YOU DON'T NEED TO LECTURE ME.
Let me do it at school at least.
I DON'T CARE.
I'M OFF.
HUH?
I DON'T WANT TO PLAY THIRD WHEEL.
SEE YOU LATER!
OKAY, LATER!
BYE.

The other day, my assistants planned a wrap party for the *Love Me, Love Me Not* series finale. I had planned to arrange it, but they said, "We'd like to take you out for a change!" (At this point, I was already very touched.) "Well, if you insist..." And that's how it happened. They picked a place pretty near my house, and we planned to meet up at the closest station. They were going to take me there, so the actual place was a secret. (So exciting!) They were considerate and picked a place that wasn't far away. I was touched by that too. It was actually very helpful because I had presents for everyone, and it turned out to be a lot to carry there. When I got to the nearest station, I met up with two assistants who were already waiting for me. A little bit later, another one came. I was told everyone else was already at the venue, so the four of us began walking. (Continues...)

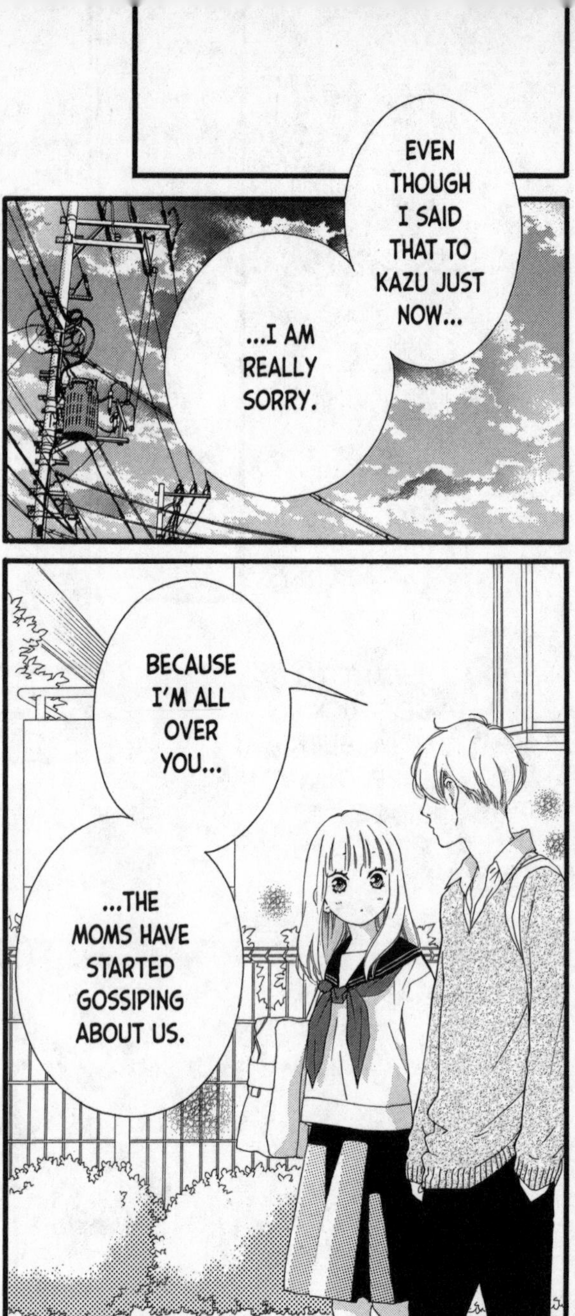

EVEN THOUGH I SAID THAT TO KAZU JUST NOW...
...I AM REALLY SORRY.
BECAUSE I'M ALL OVER YOU...
...THE MOMS HAVE STARTED GOSSIPING ABOUT US.

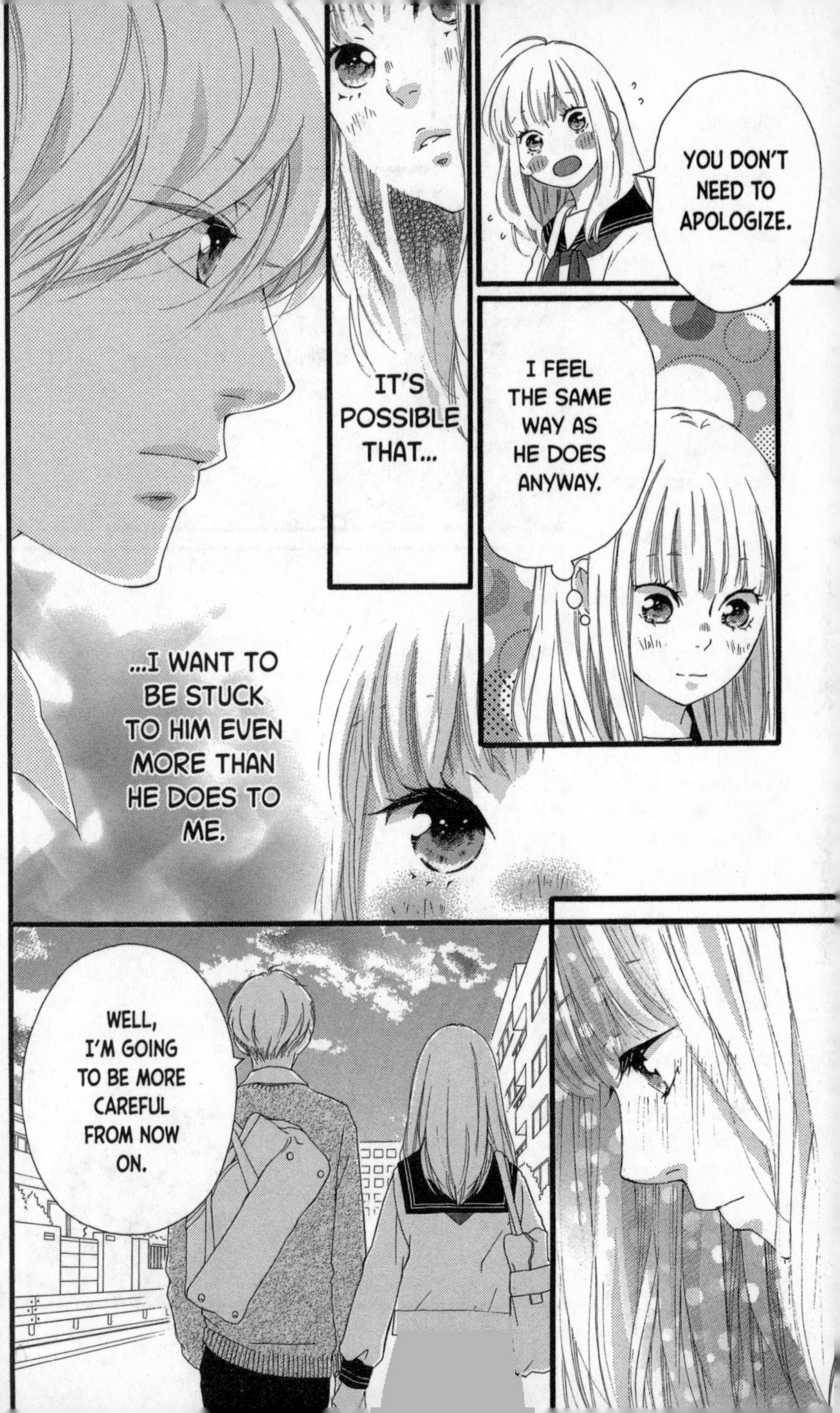
YOU DON'T NEED TO APOLOGIZE.
I FEEL THE SAME WAY AS HE DOES ANYWAY.
IT'S POSSIBLE THAT...
...I WANT TO BE STUCK TO HIM EVEN MORE THAN HE DOES TO ME.
WELL, I'M GOING TO BE MORE CAREFUL FROM NOW ON.

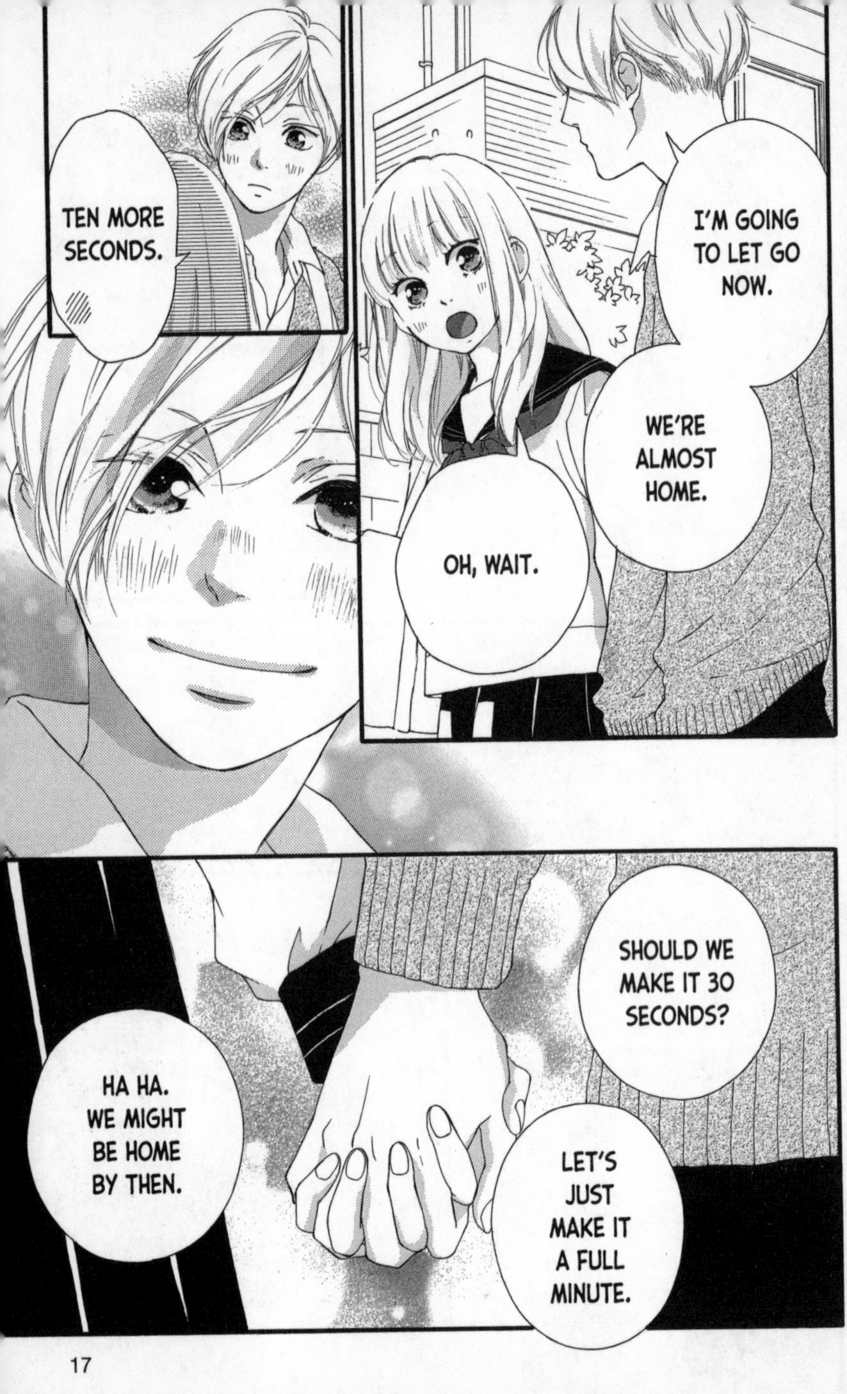
I'M GOING TO LET GO NOW.
WE'RE ALMOST HOME.
OH, WAIT.
TEN MORE SECONDS.
SHOULD WE MAKE IT 30 SECONDS?
LET'S JUST MAKE IT A FULL MINUTE.
HA HA. WE MIGHT BE HOME BY THEN.

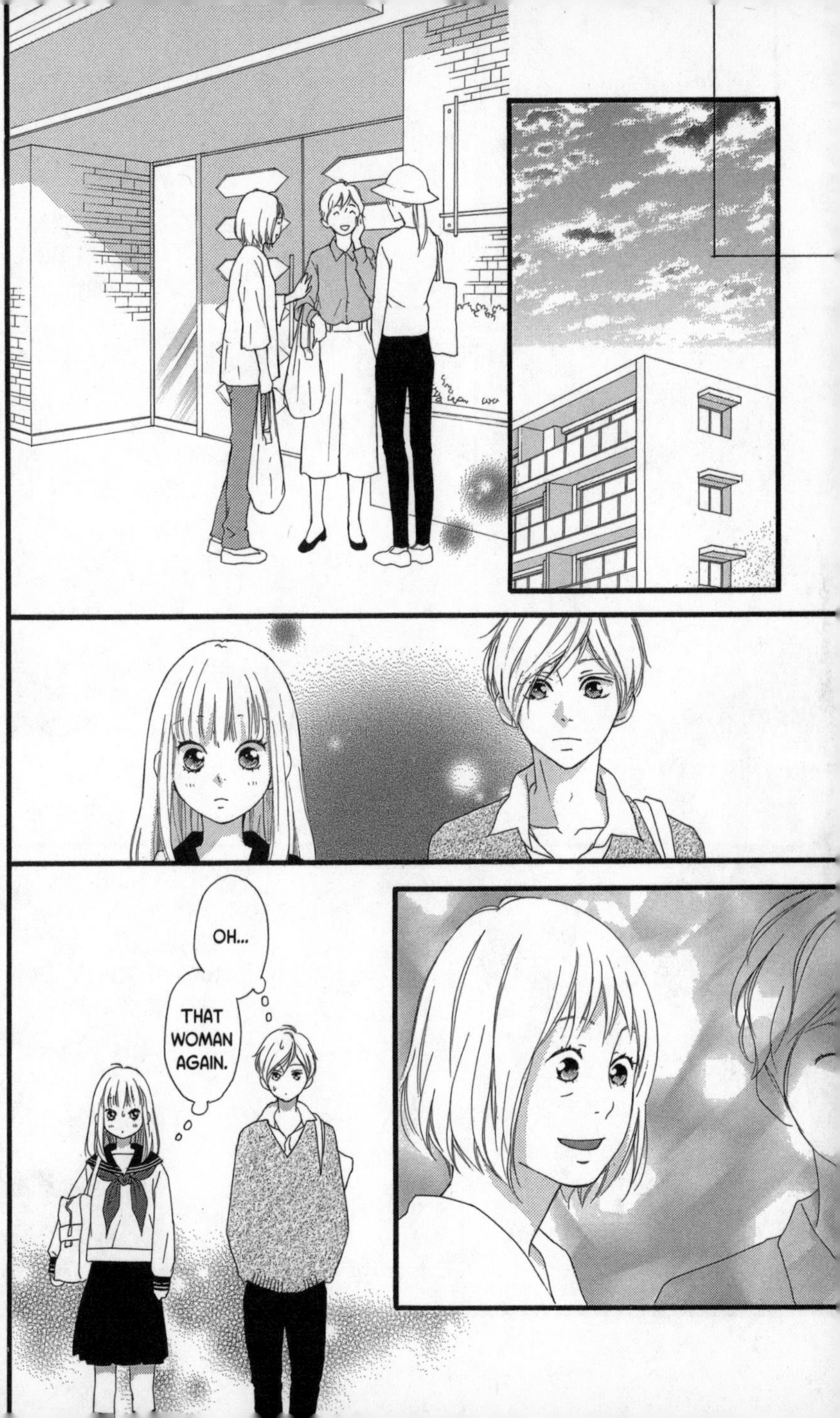
OH...
THAT WOMAN AGAIN.

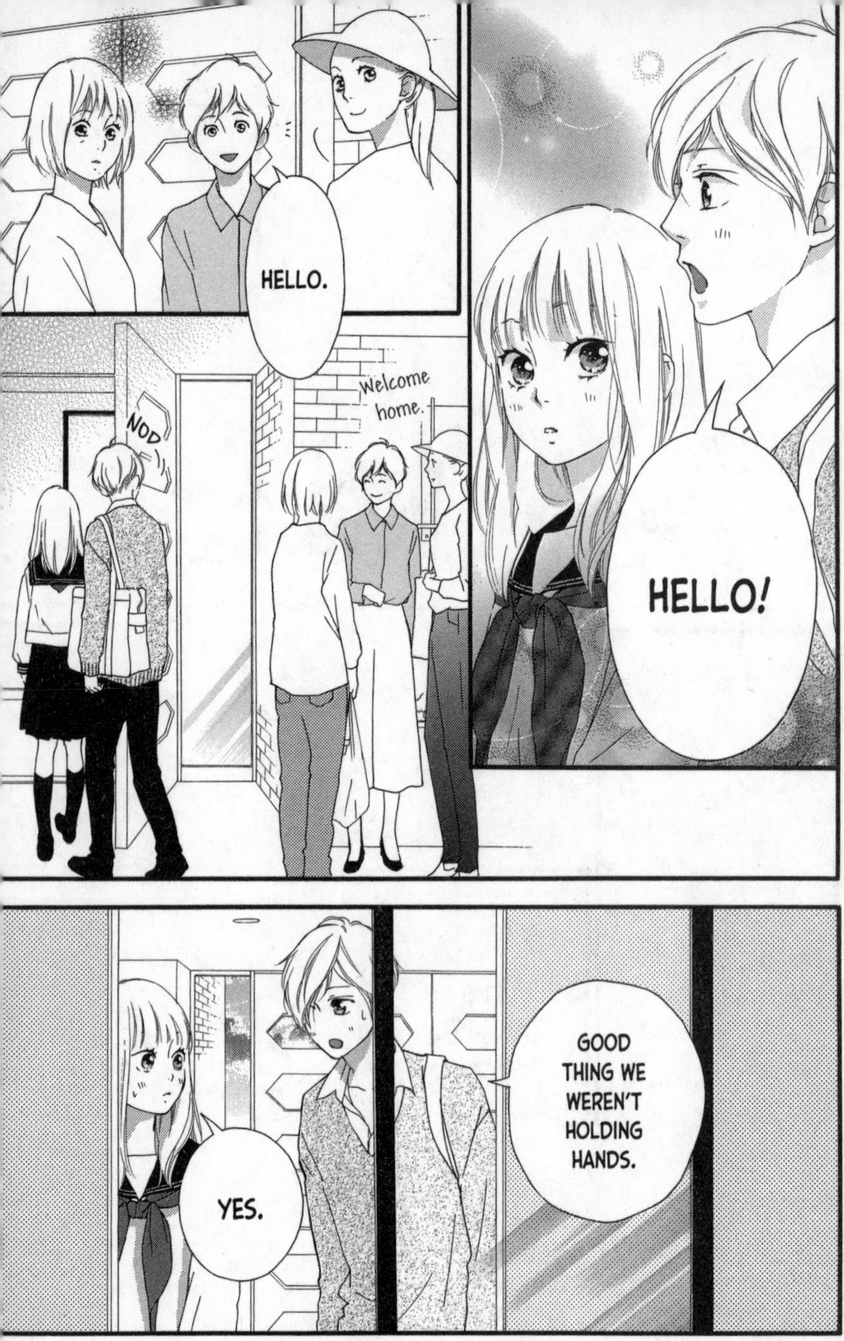
HELLO!
HELLO.
Welcome home.
NOD
GOOD THING WE WEREN'T HOLDING HANDS.
YES.

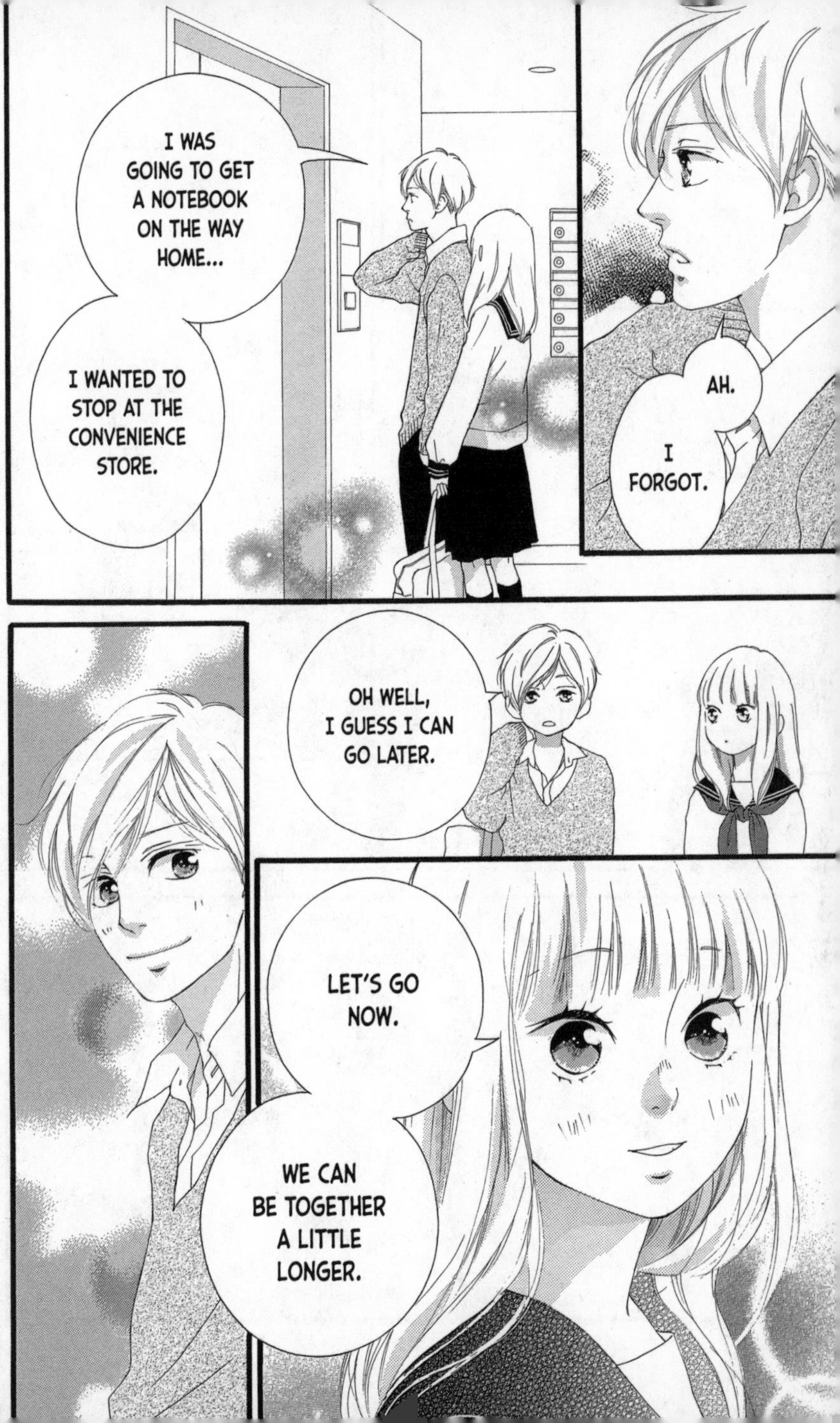
AH.
I FORGOT.
I WAS GOING TO GET A NOTEBOOK ON THE WAY HOME...
I WANTED TO STOP AT THE CONVENIENCE STORE.
OH WELL, I GUESS I CAN GO LATER.
LET'S GO NOW.
WE CAN BE TOGETHER A LITTLE LONGER.

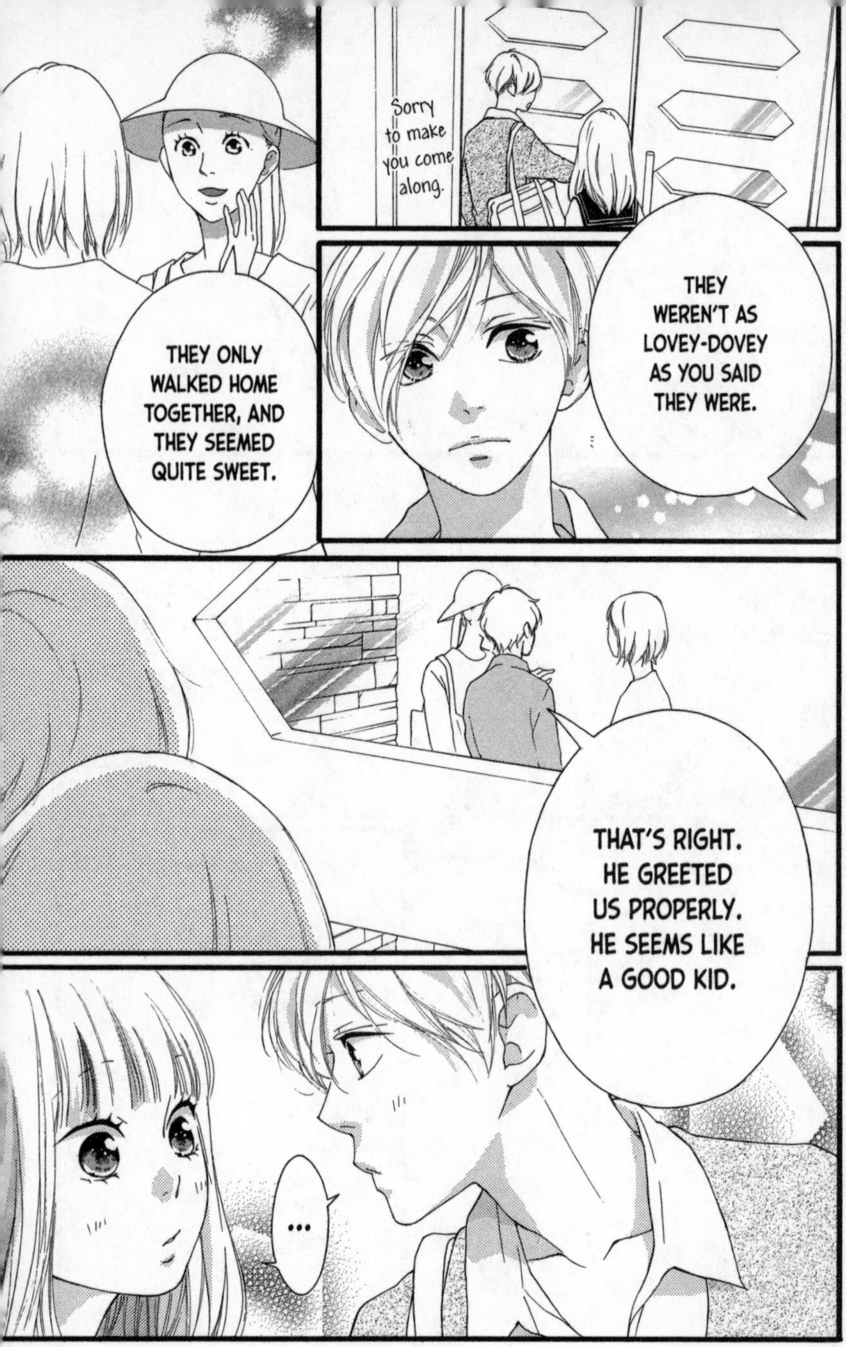
Sorry to make you come along.
THEY WEREN'T AS LOVEY-DOVEY AS YOU SAID THEY WERE.
THEY ONLY WALKED HOME TOGETHER, AND THEY SEEMED QUITE SWEET.
THAT'S RIGHT. HE GREETED US PROPERLY. HE SEEMS LIKE A GOOD KID.
...

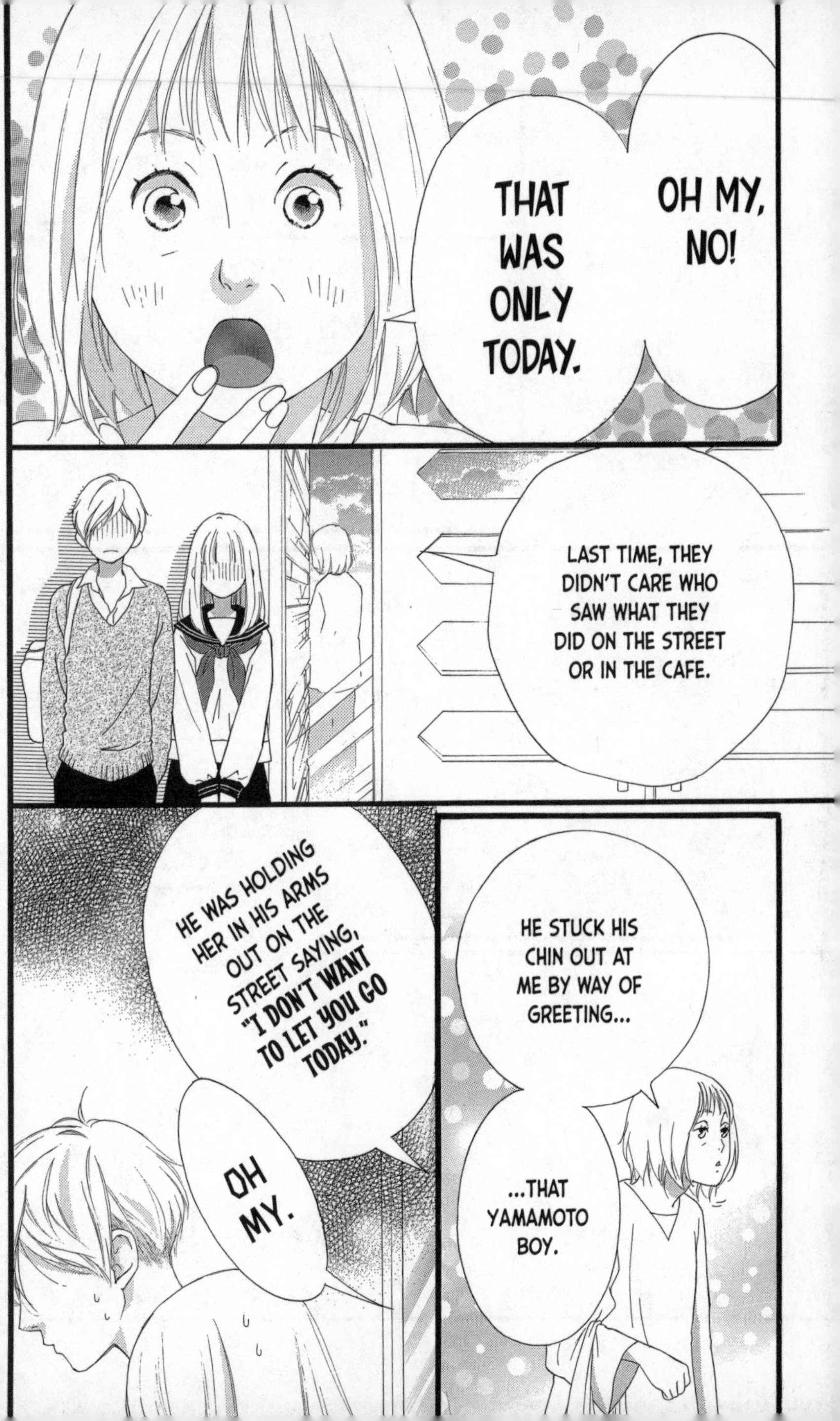
OH MY, NO!
THAT WAS ONLY TODAY.
LAST TIME, THEY DIDN'T CARE WHO SAW WHAT THEY DID ON THE STREET OR IN THE CAFE.
HE STUCK HIS CHIN OUT AT ME BY WAY OF GREETING...
...THAT YAMAMOTO BOY.
HE WAS HOLDING HER IN HIS ARMS OUT ON THE STREET SAYING, "I DON'T WANT TO LET YOU GO TODAY."
OH MY.

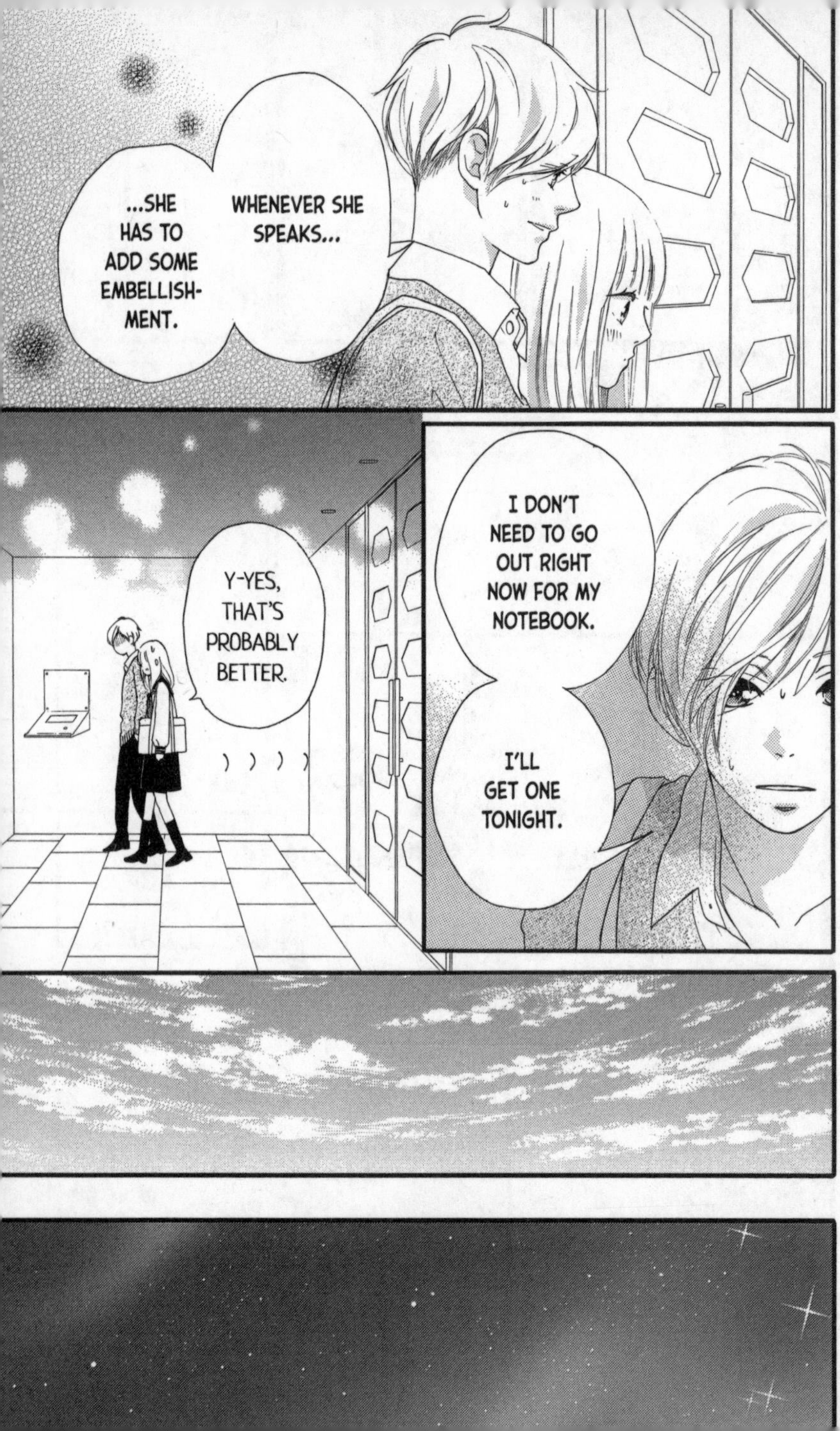
WHENEVER SHE SPEAKS...
...SHE HAS TO ADD SOME EMBELLISHMENT.
I DON'T NEED TO GO OUT RIGHT NOW FOR MY NOTEBOOK.
I'LL GET ONE TONIGHT.
Y-YES, THAT'S PROBABLY BETTER.

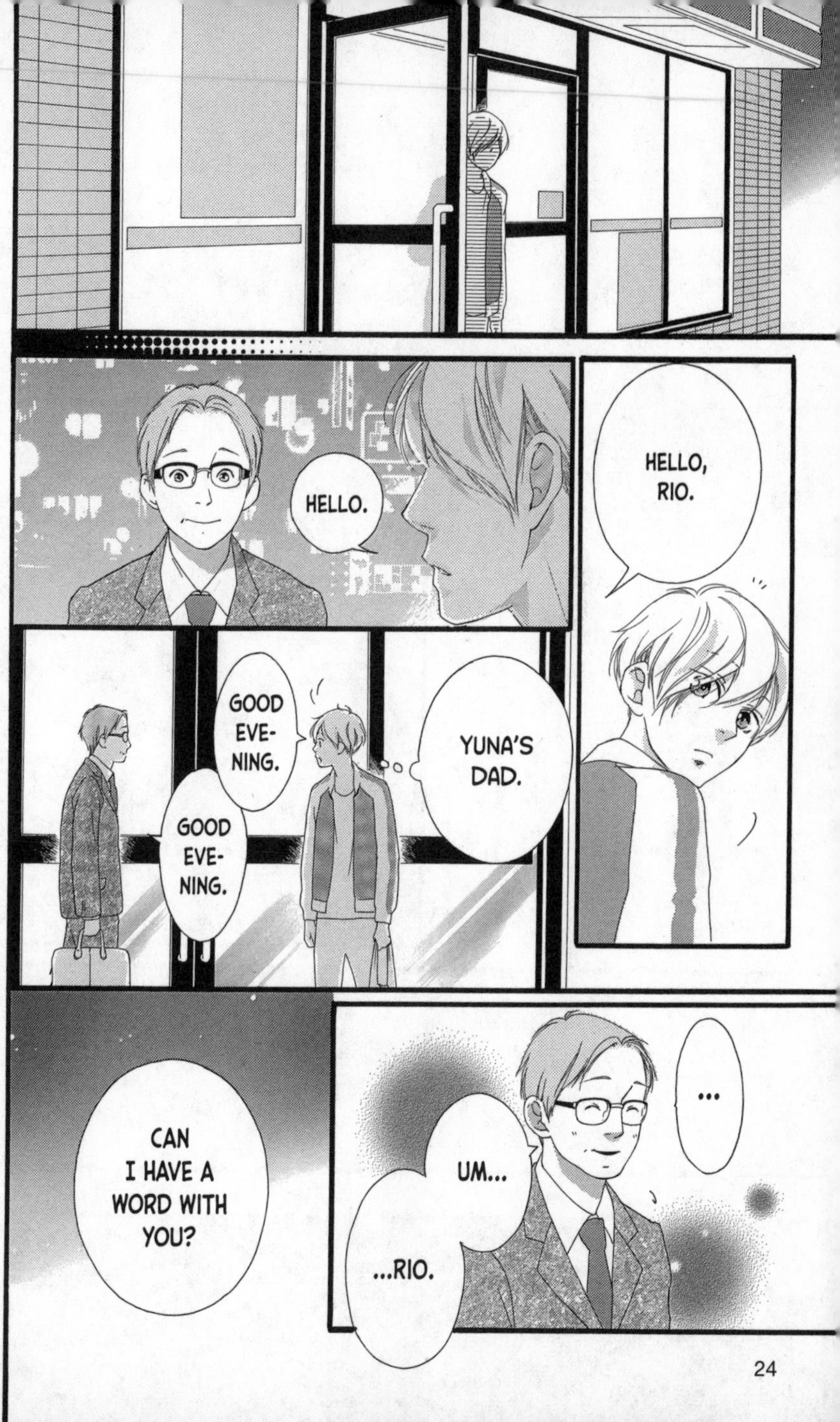
HELLO, RIO.
HELLO.
YUNA'S DAD.
GOOD EVE-NING.
GOOD EVE-NING.
...
UM...
...RIO.
CAN I HAVE A WORD WITH YOU?

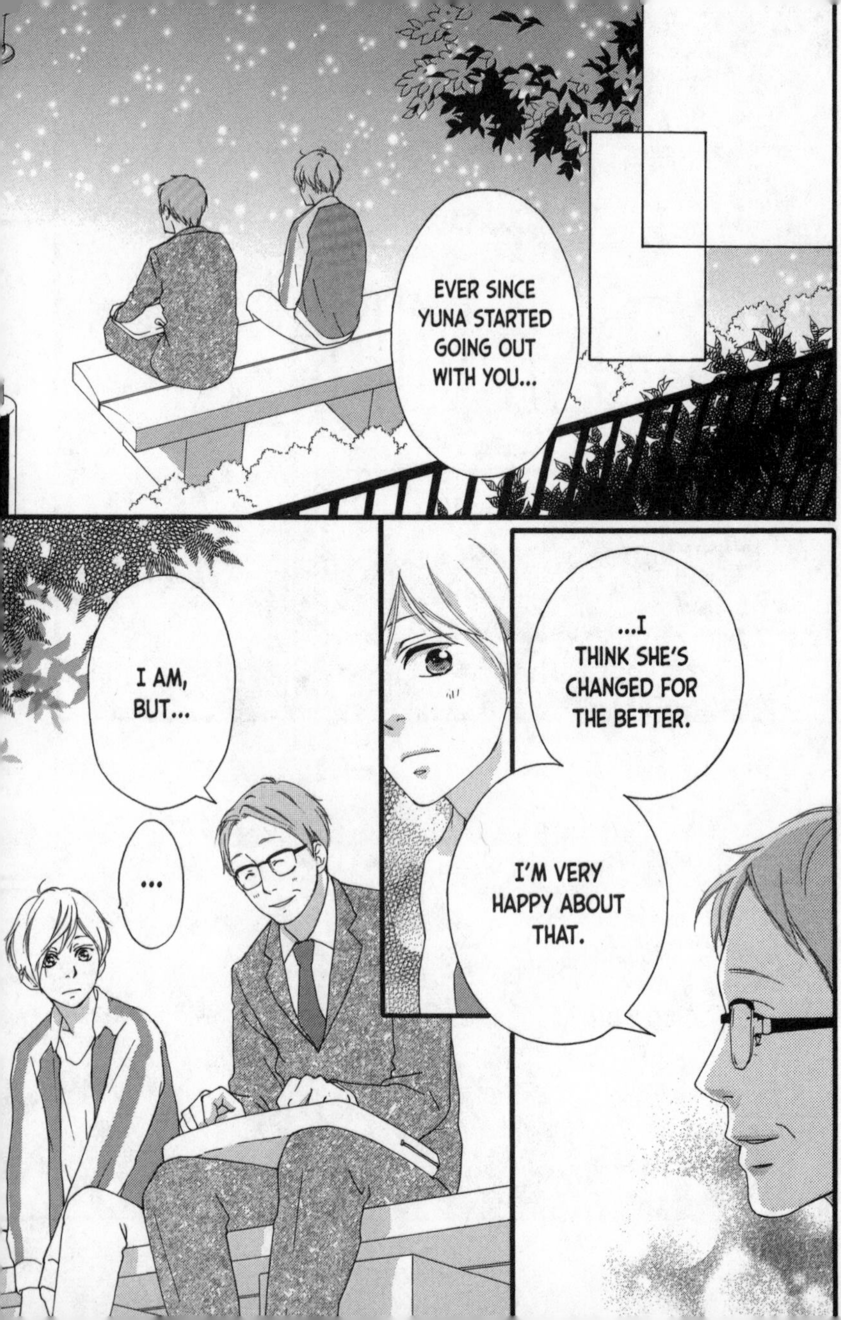
EVER SINCE YUNA STARTED GOING OUT WITH YOU...
...I THINK SHE'S CHANGED FOR THE BETTER.
I'M VERY HAPPY ABOUT THAT.
I AM, BUT...
...

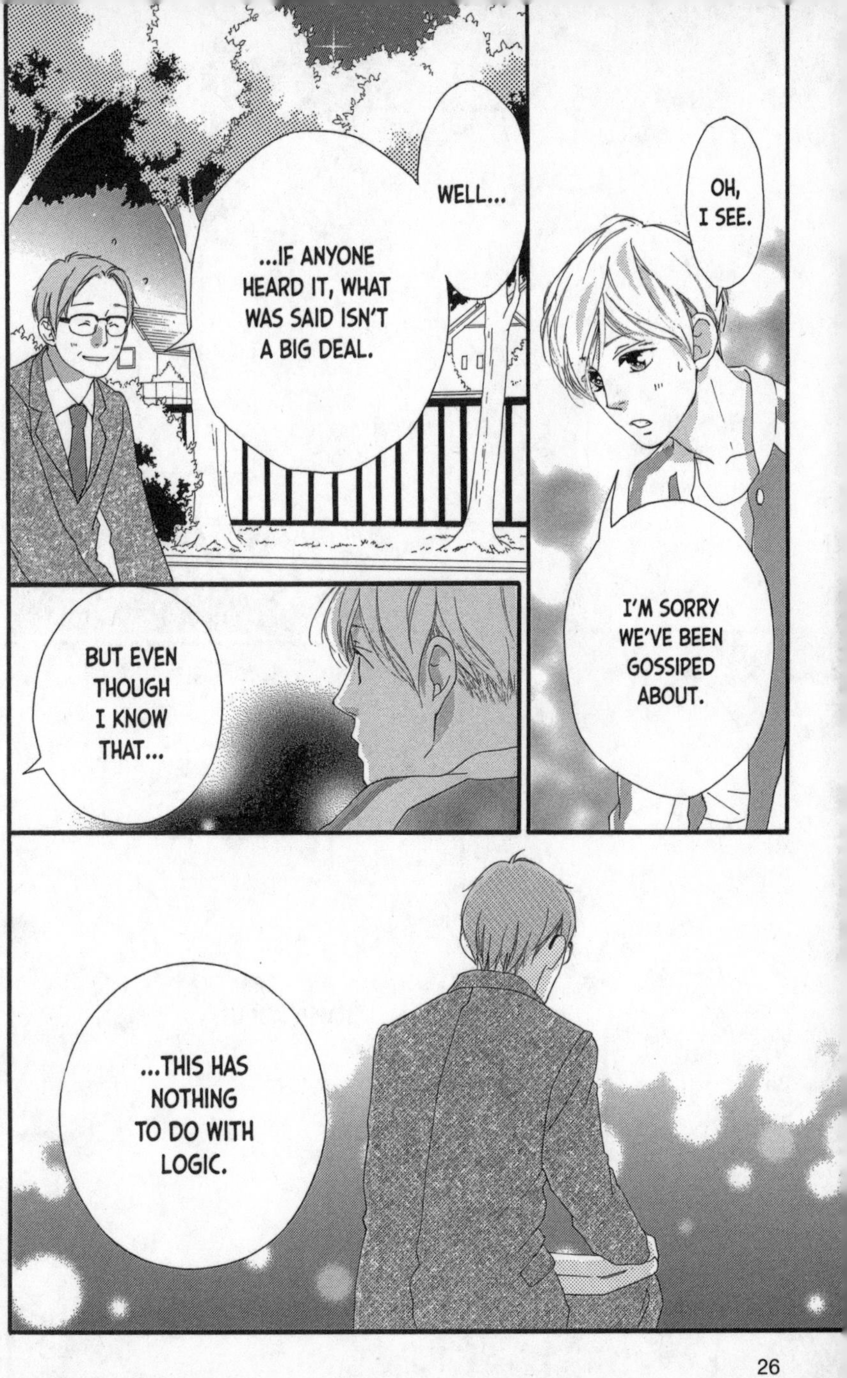
OH, I SEE.
I'M SORRY WE'VE BEEN GOSSIPED ABOUT.
WELL...
...IF ANYONE HEARD IT, WHAT WAS SAID ISN'T A BIG DEAL.
BUT EVEN THOUGH I KNOW THAT...
...THIS HAS NOTHING TO DO WITH LOGIC.

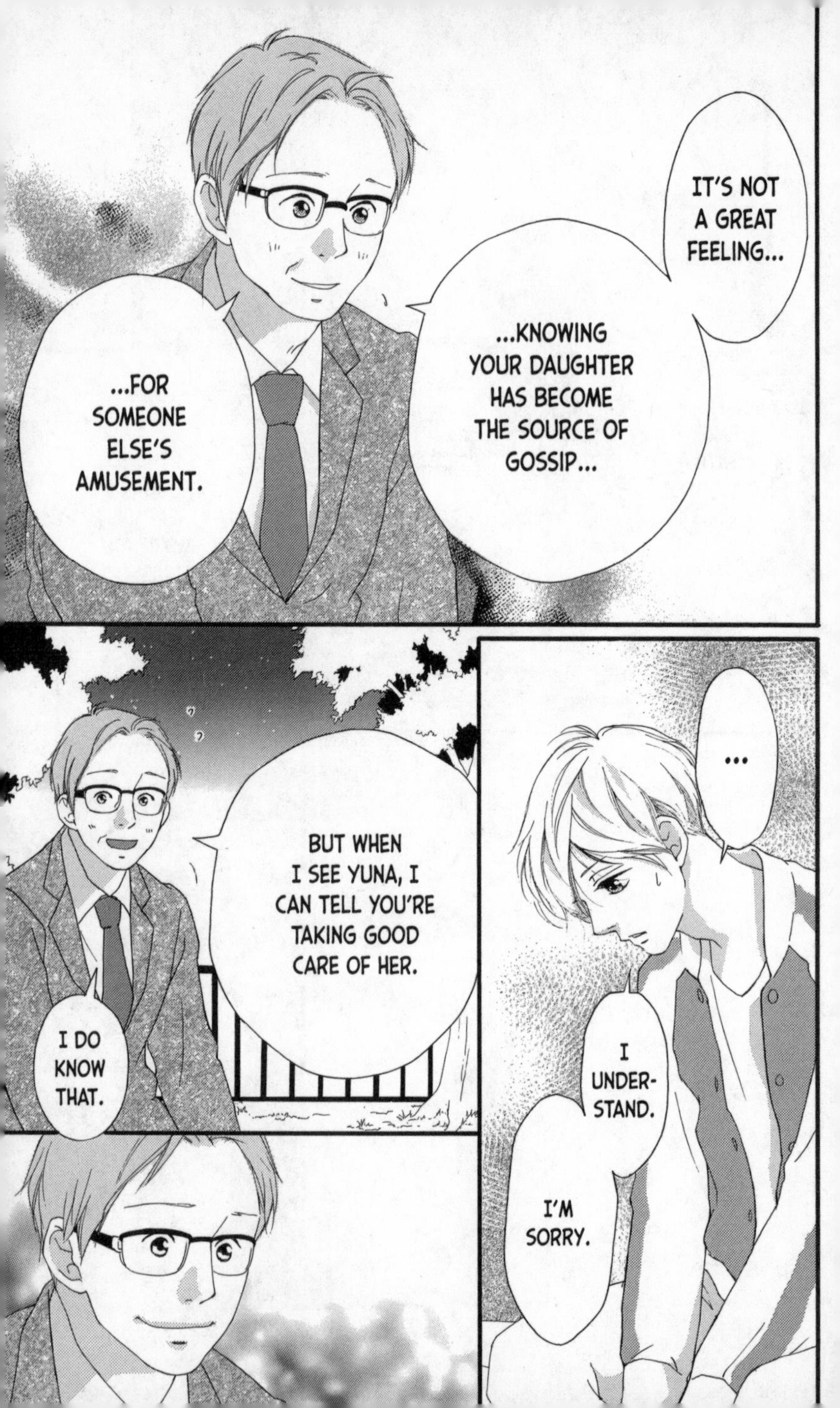
IT'S NOT A GREAT FEELING...
...KNOWING YOUR DAUGHTER HAS BECOME THE SOURCE OF GOSSIP...
...FOR SOMEONE ELSE'S AMUSEMENT.
...
I UNDER-STAND.
I'M SORRY.
BUT WHEN I SEE YUNA, I CAN TELL YOU'RE TAKING GOOD CARE OF HER.
I DO KNOW THAT.

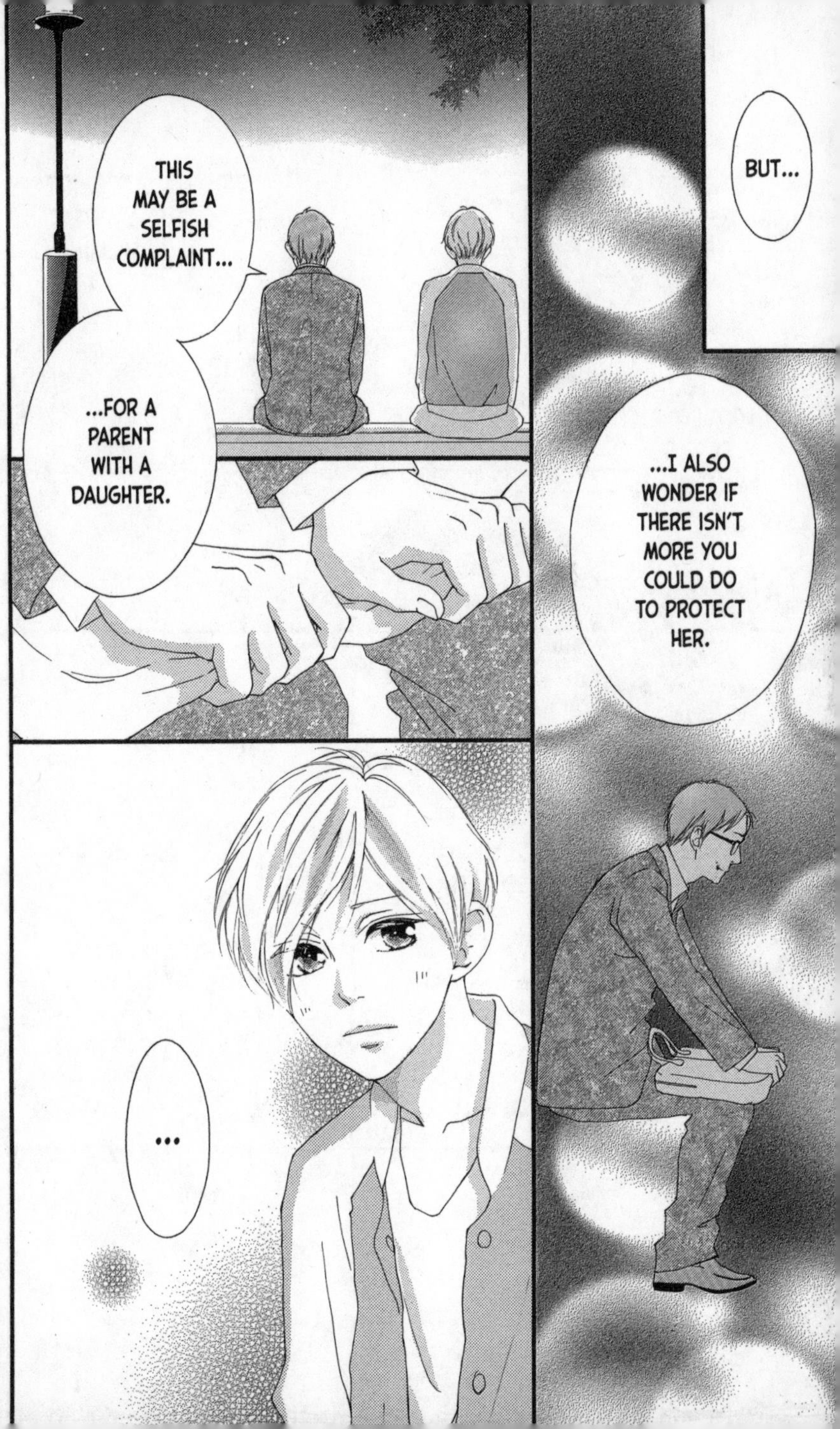

BUT...
...I ALSO WONDER IF THERE ISN'T MORE YOU COULD DO TO PROTECT HER.
THIS MAY BE A SELFISH COMPLAINT...
...FOR A PARENT WITH A DAUGHTER.
...

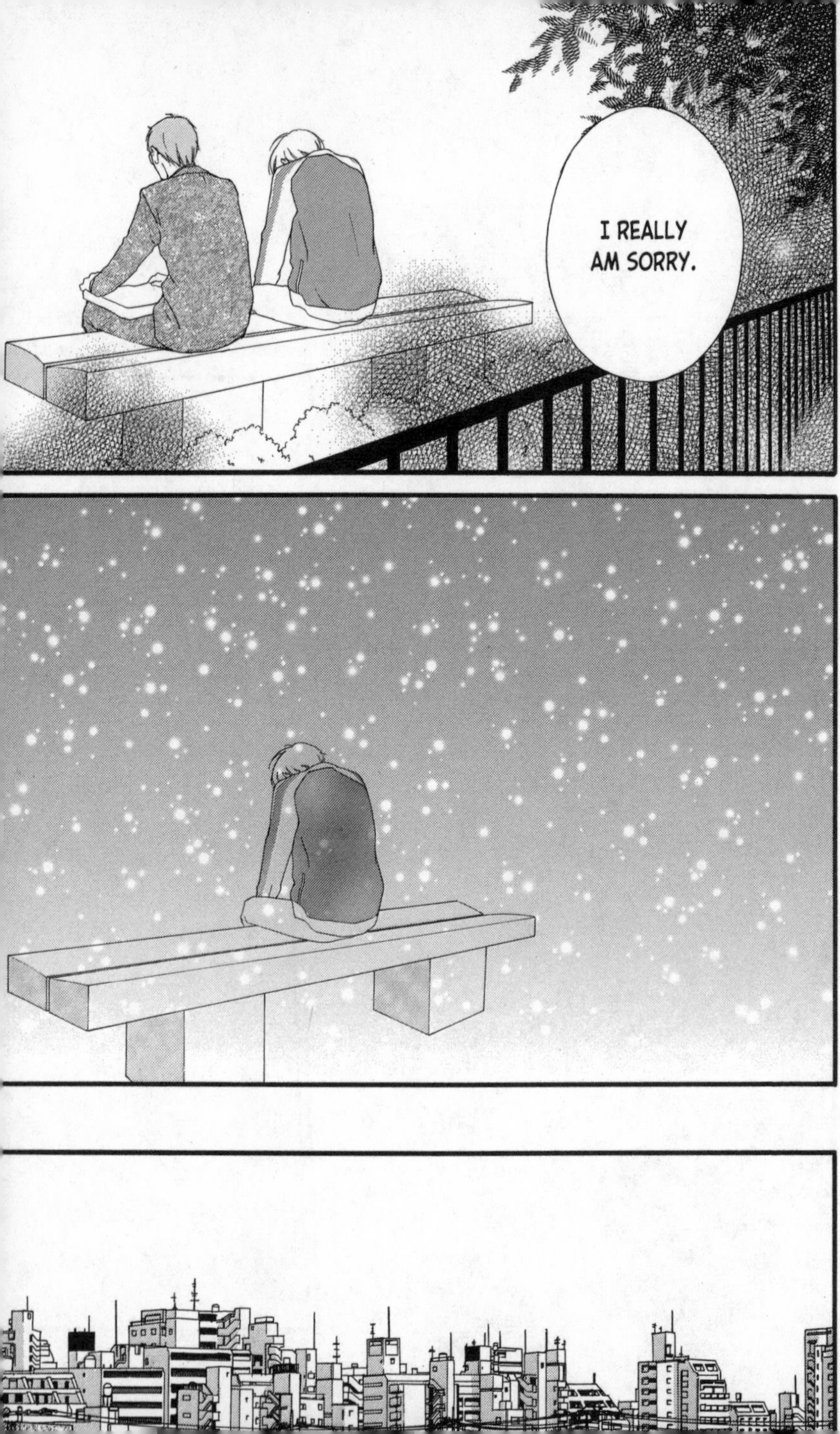
I REALLY AM SORRY.

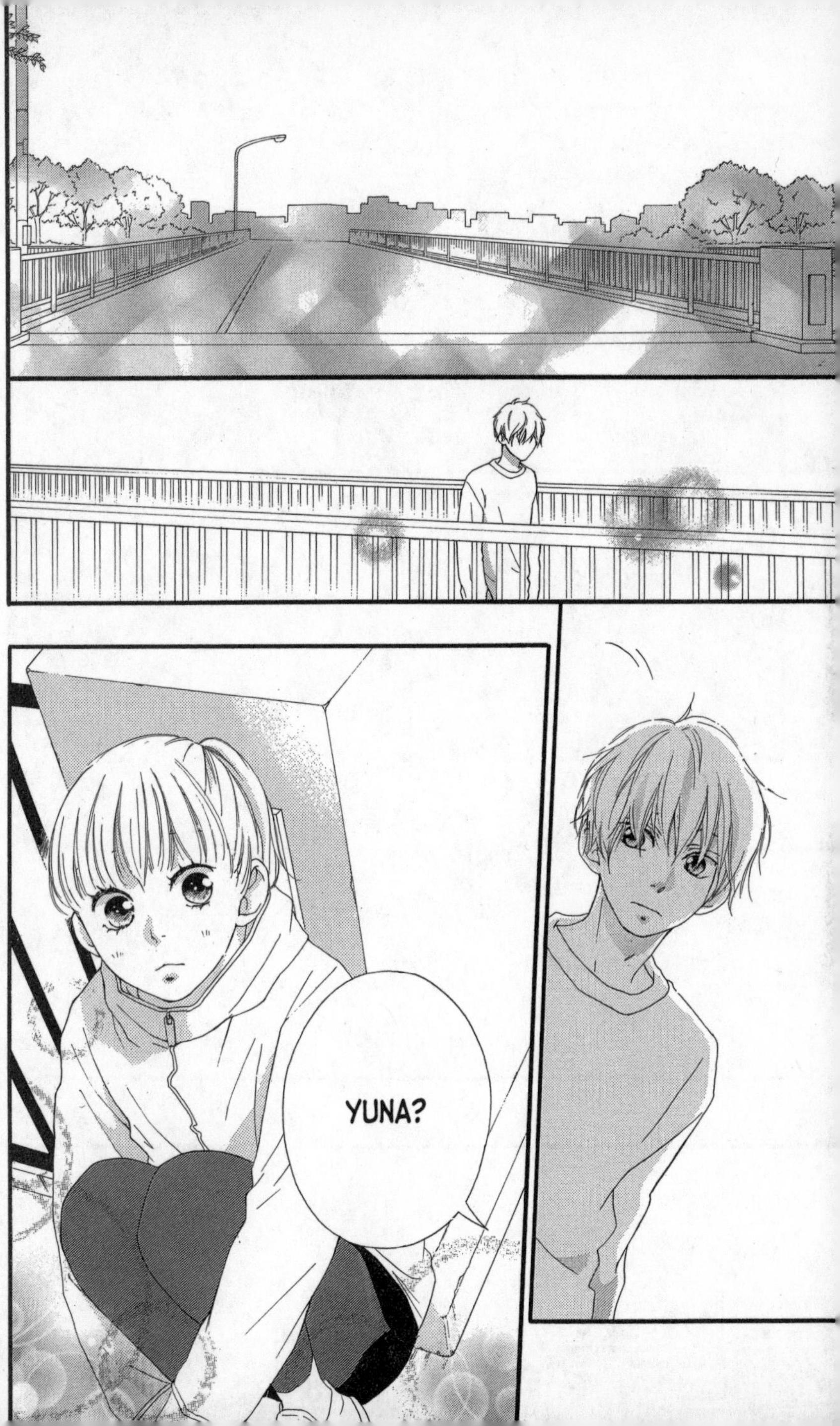
YUNA?

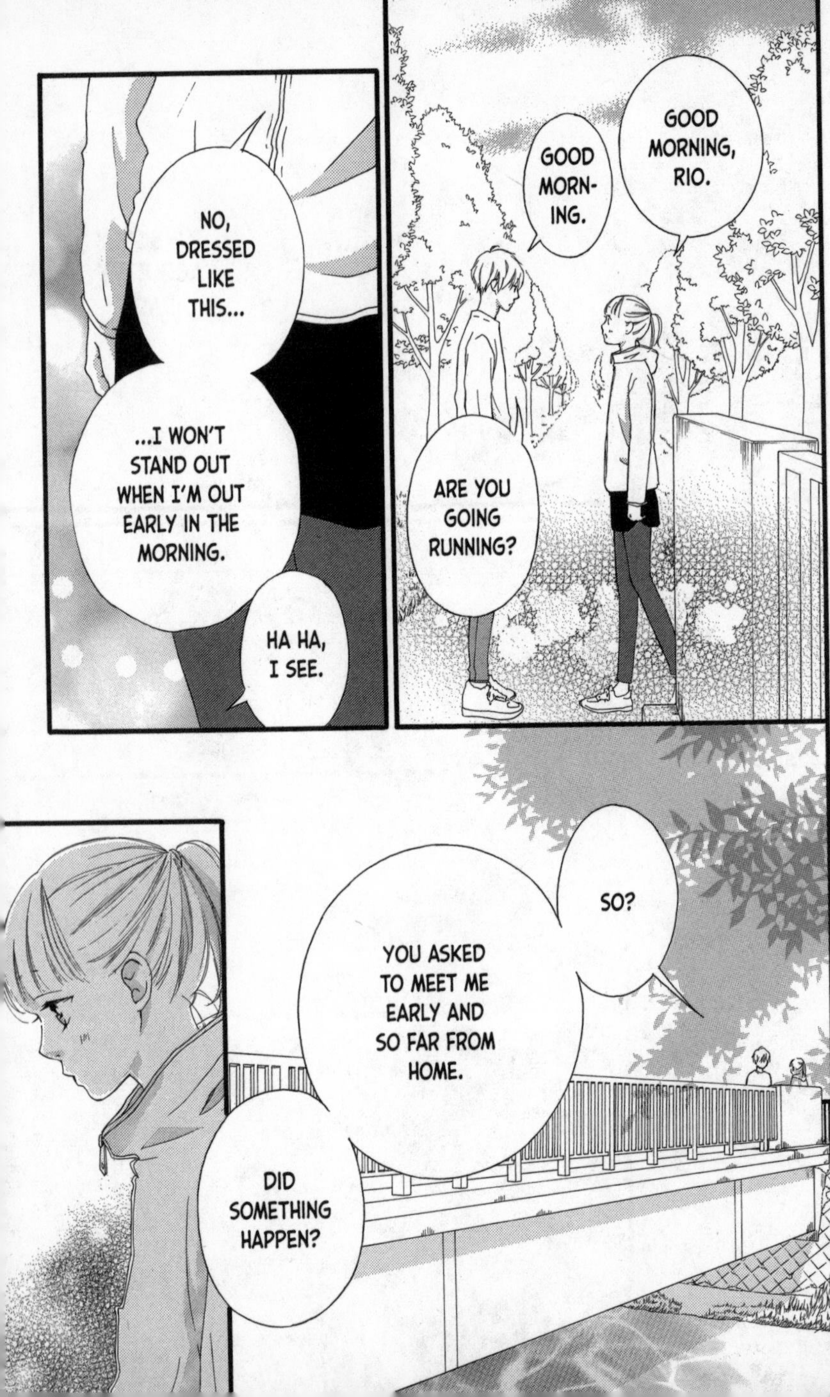
GOOD MORNING, RIO.
GOOD MORN-ING.
ARE YOU GOING RUNNING?
NO, DRESSED LIKE THIS...
...I WON'T STAND OUT WHEN I'M OUT EARLY IN THE MORNING.
HA HA, I SEE.
SO?
YOU ASKED TO MEET ME EARLY AND SO FAR FROM HOME.
DID SOMETHING HAPPEN?

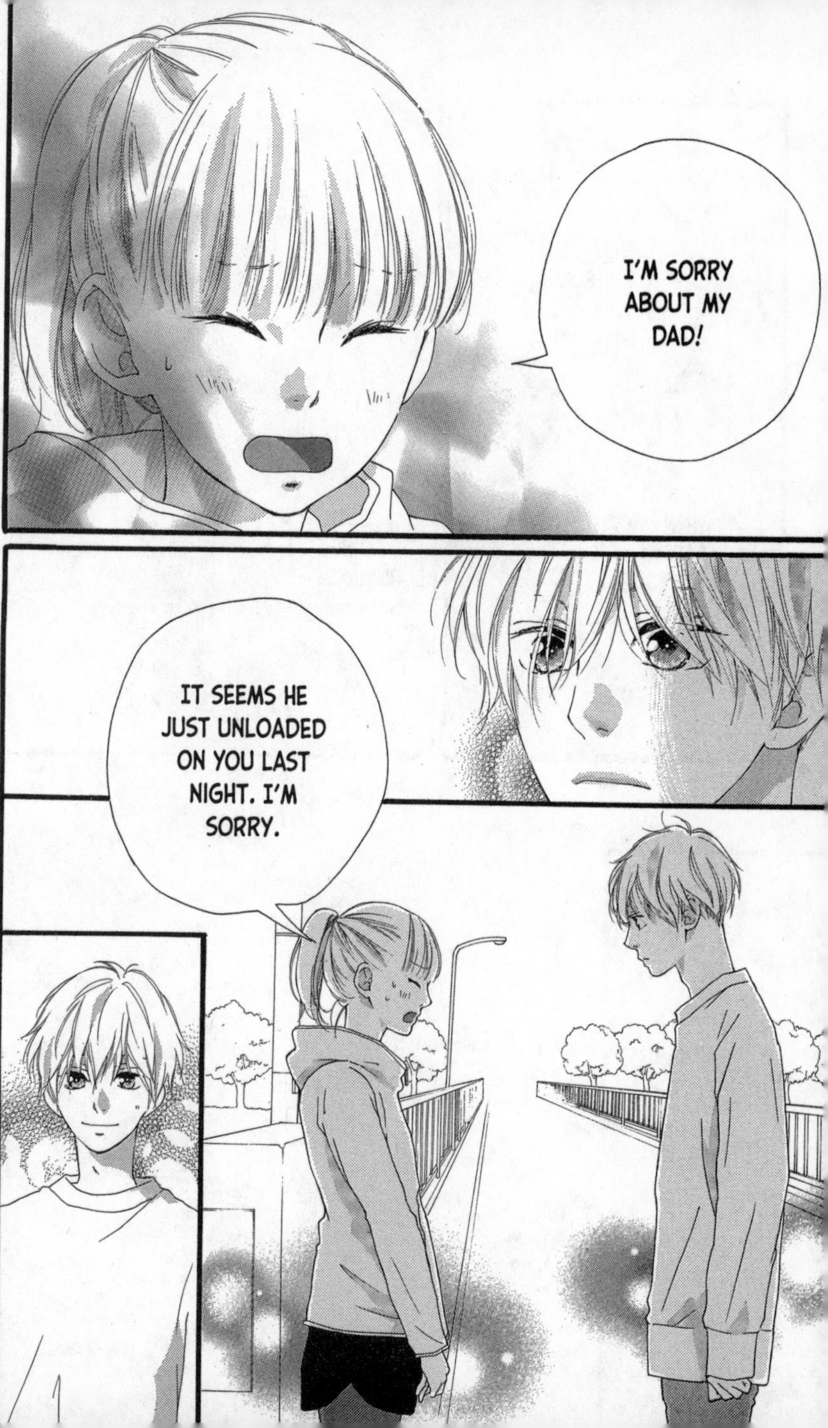
I'M SORRY ABOUT MY DAD!
IT SEEMS HE JUST UNLOADED ON YOU LAST NIGHT. I'M SORRY.

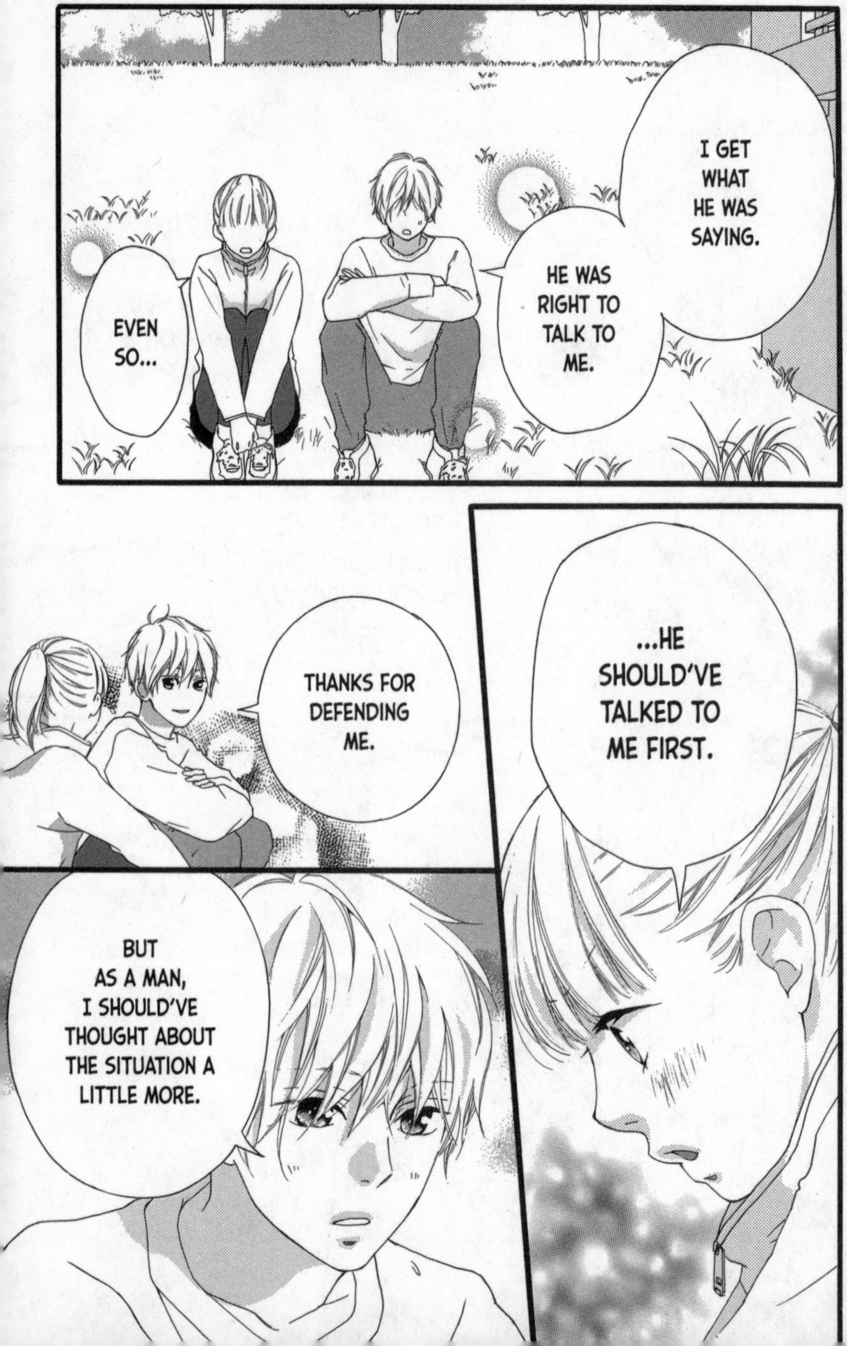
I GET WHAT HE WAS SAYING.
HE WAS RIGHT TO TALK TO ME.
EVEN SO...
...HE SHOULD'VE TALKED TO ME FIRST.
THANKS FOR DEFENDING ME.
BUT AS A MAN, I SHOULD'VE THOUGHT ABOUT THE SITUATION A LITTLE MORE.

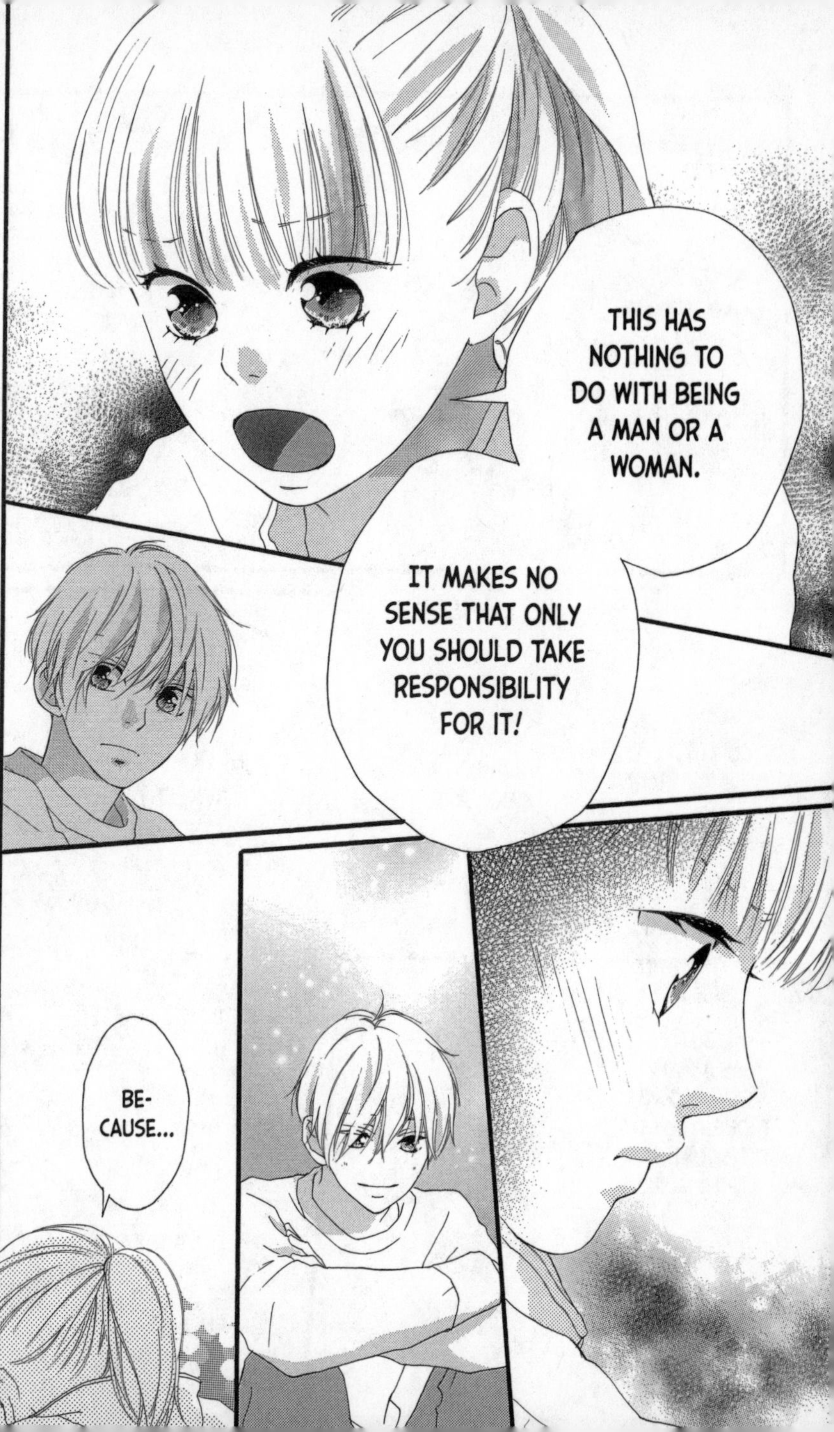
THIS HAS NOTHING TO DO WITH BEING A MAN OR A WOMAN.
IT MAKES NO SENSE THAT ONLY YOU SHOULD TAKE RESPONSIBILITY FOR IT!
BE-CAUSE...

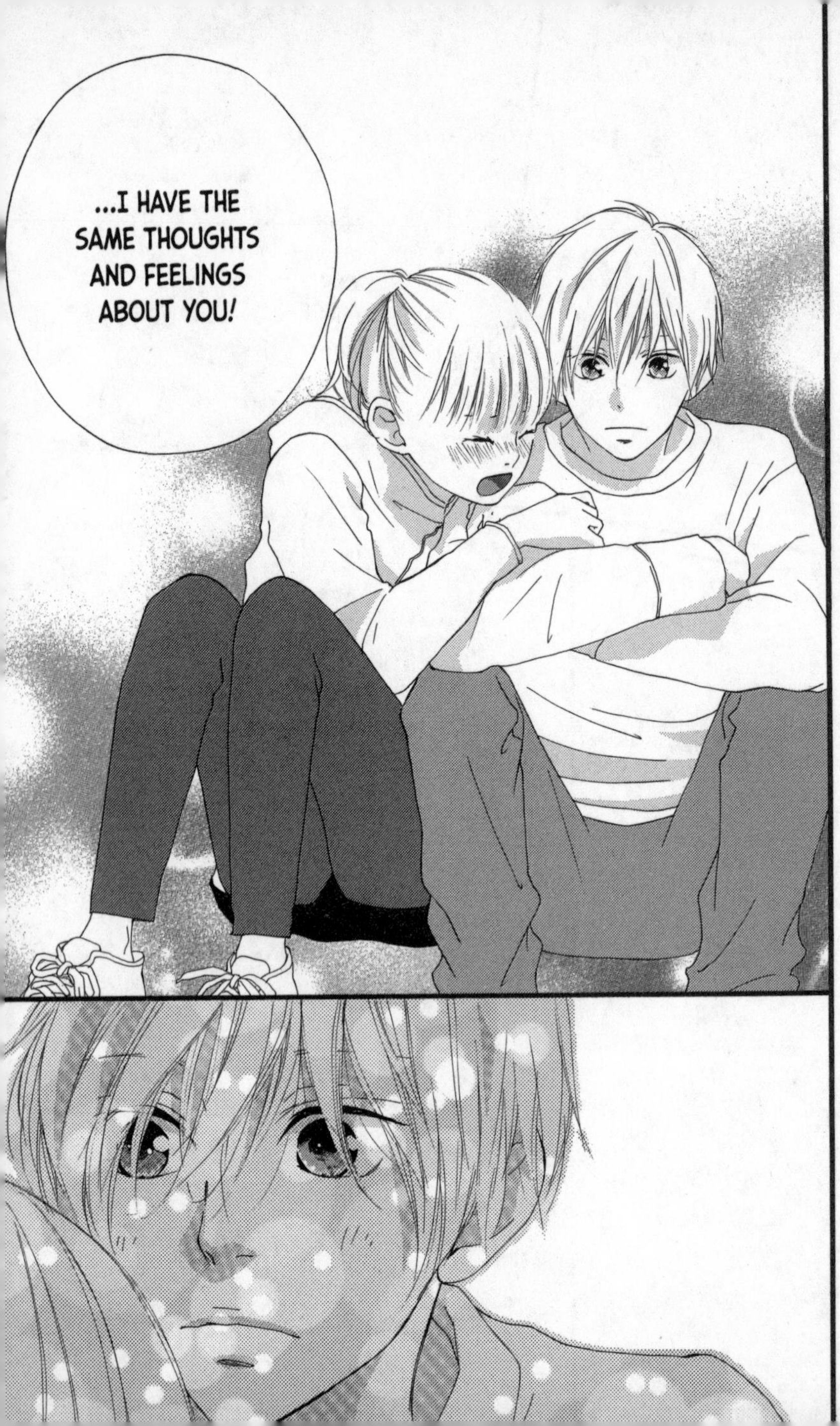
...I HAVE THE SAME THOUGHTS AND FEELINGS ABOUT YOU!

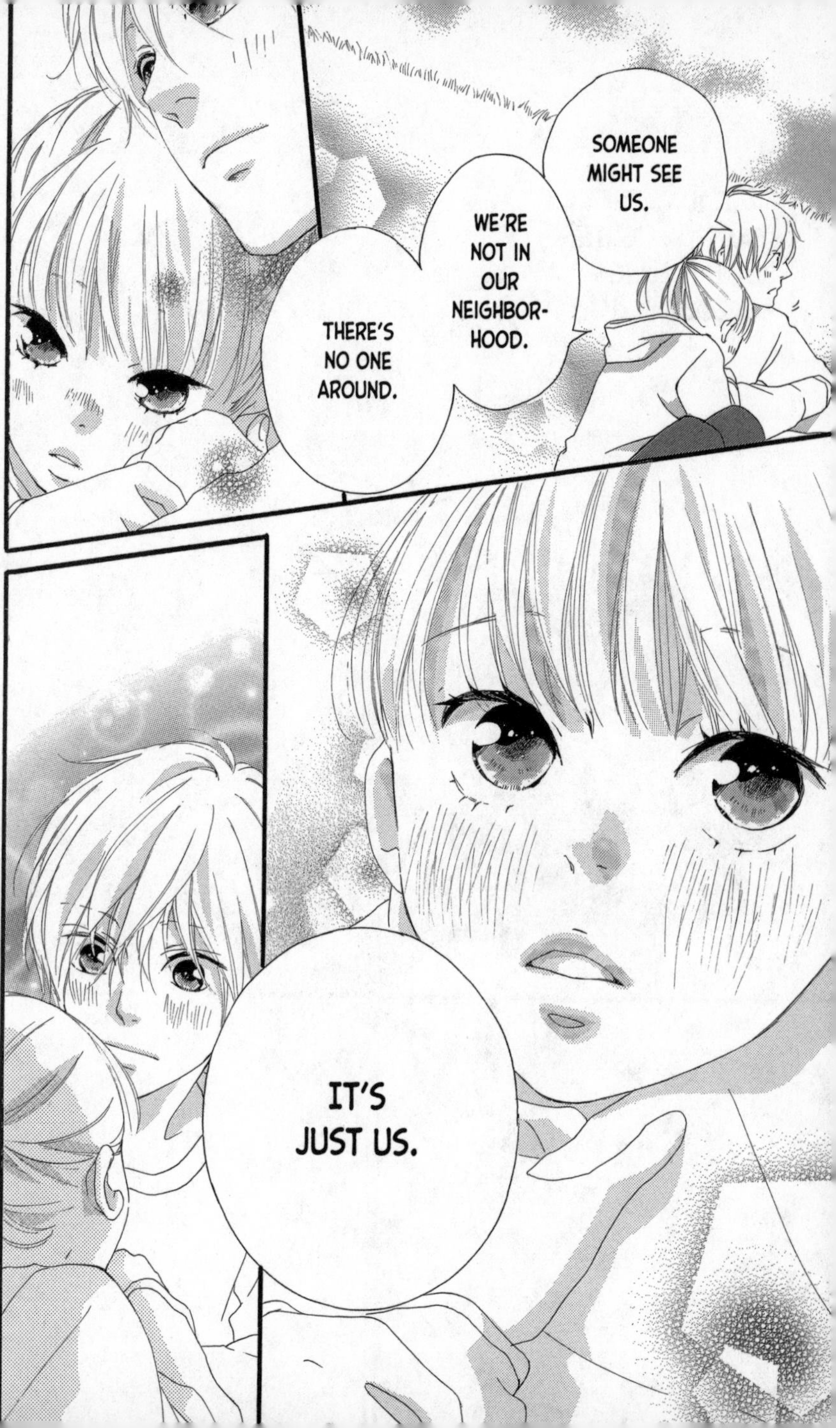
SOMEONE MIGHT SEE US.
WE'RE NOT IN OUR NEIGHBOR-HOOD.
THERE'S NO ONE AROUND.
IT'S JUST US.

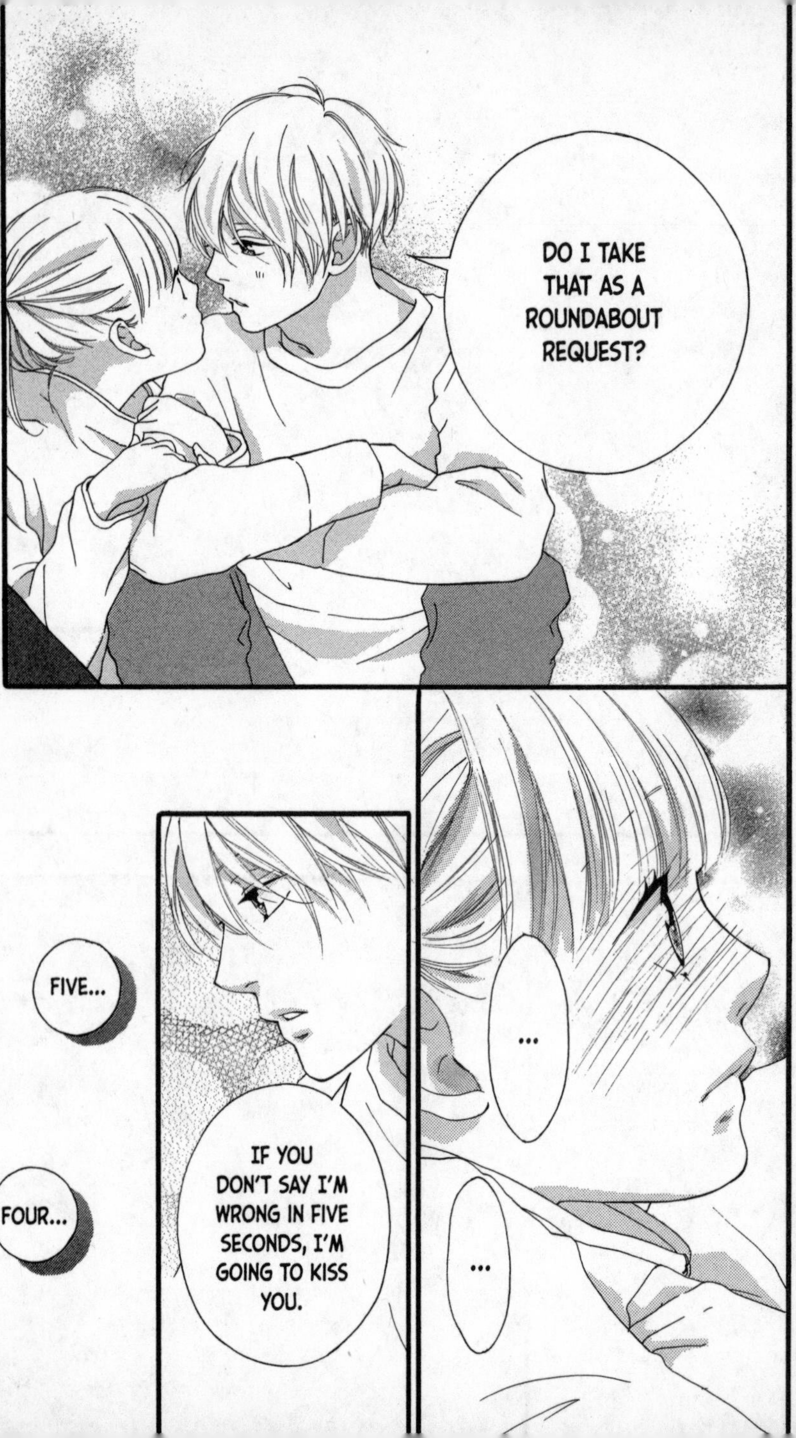
DO I TAKE THAT AS A ROUNDABOUT REQUEST?
...
...
IF YOU DON'T SAY I'M WRONG IN FIVE SECONDS, I'M GOING TO KISS YOU.
FIVE...
FOUR...

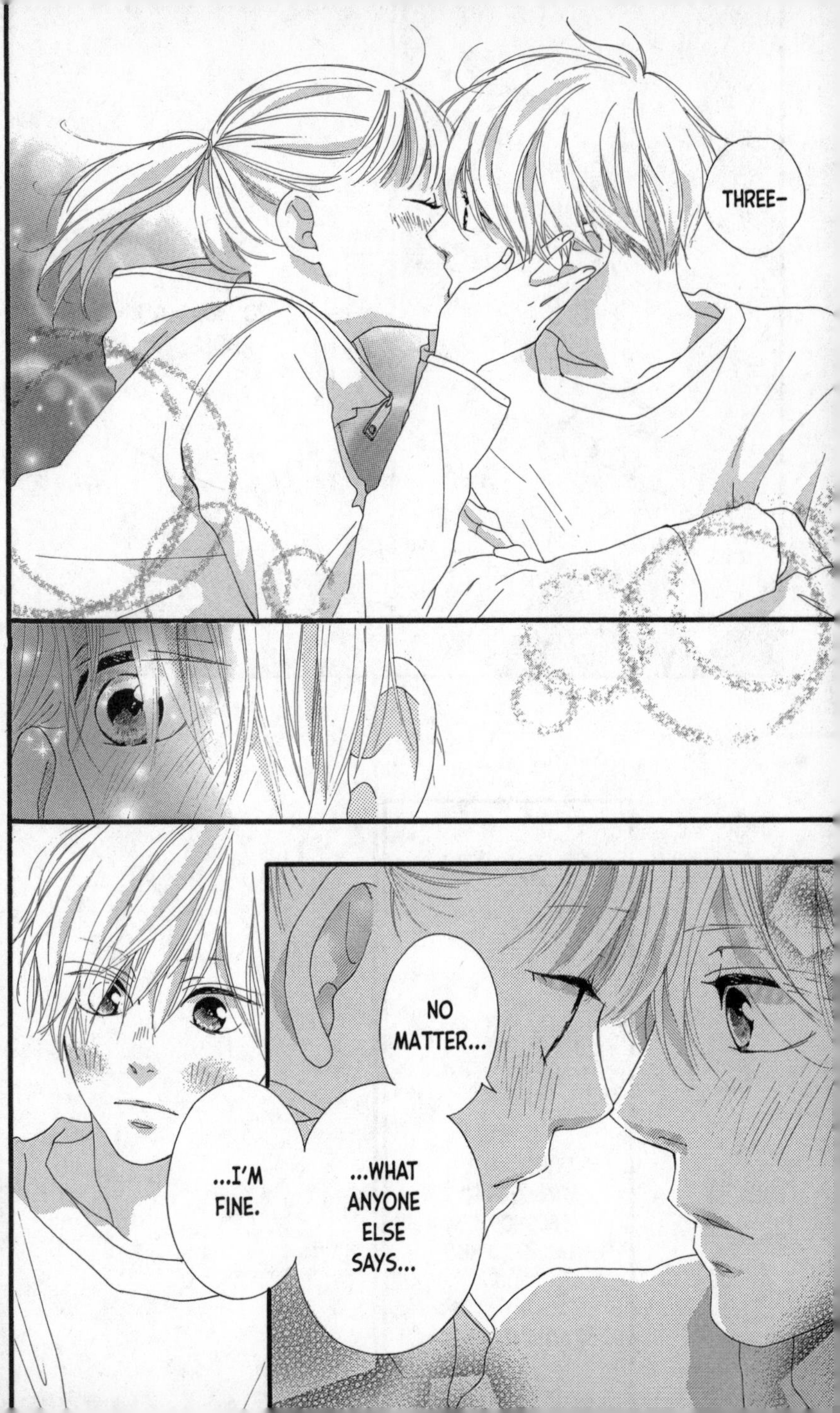
THREE-
NO MATTER...
...WHAT ANYONE ELSE SAYS...
...I'M FINE.

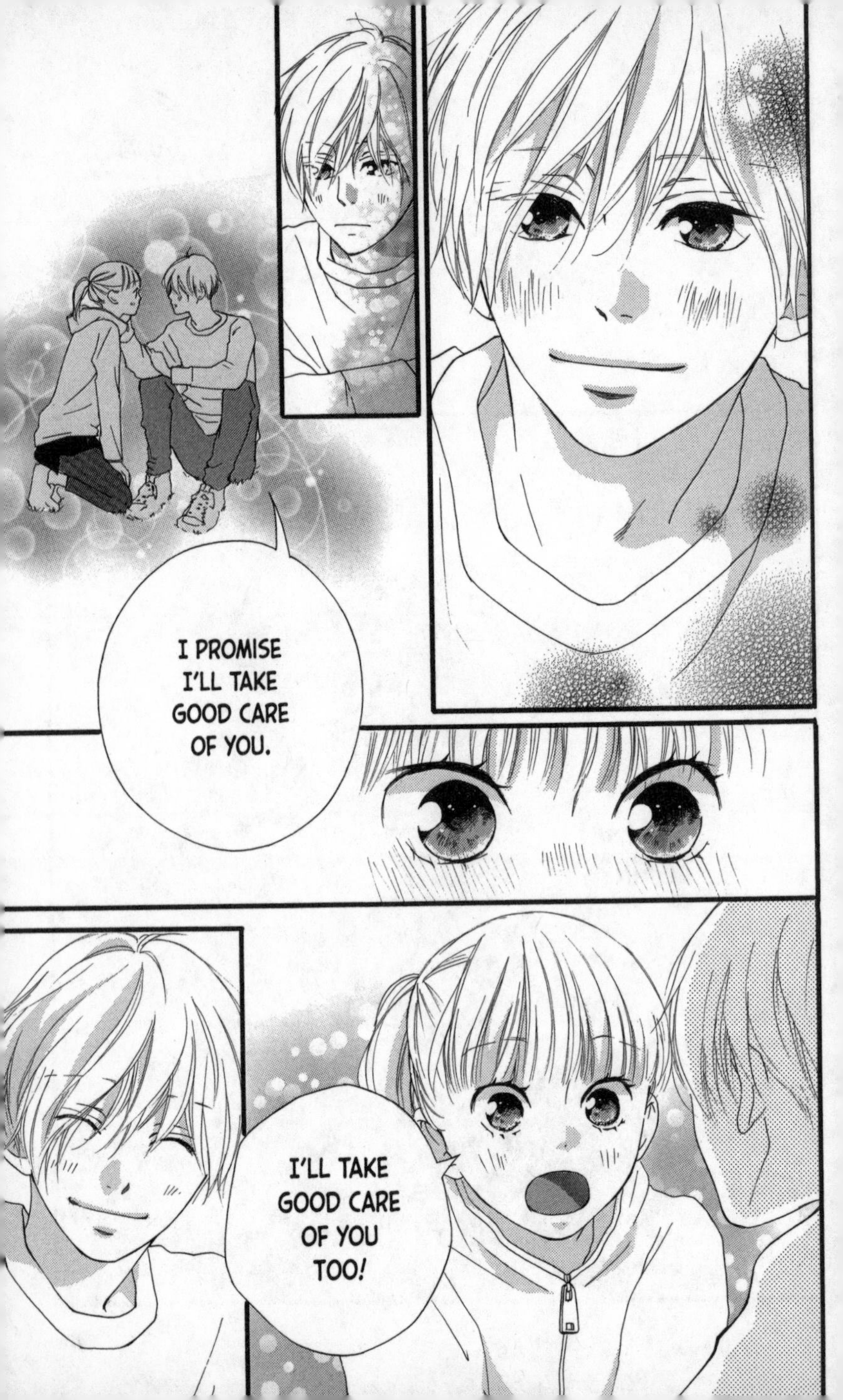
I PROMISE I'LL TAKE GOOD CARE OF YOU.
I'LL TAKE GOOD CARE OF YOU TOO!

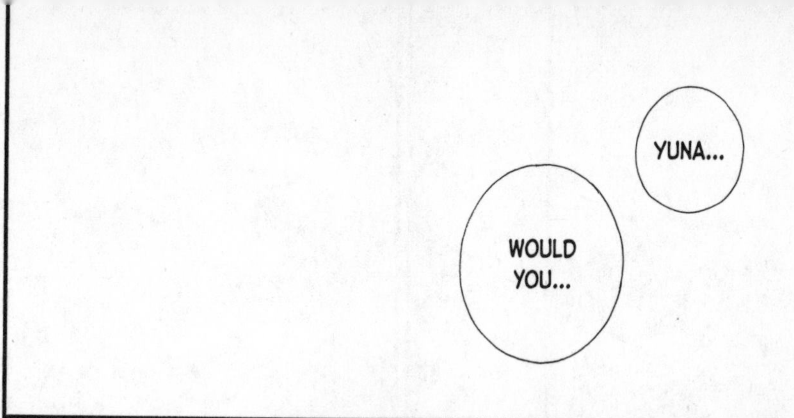
YUNA...
WOULD YOU...

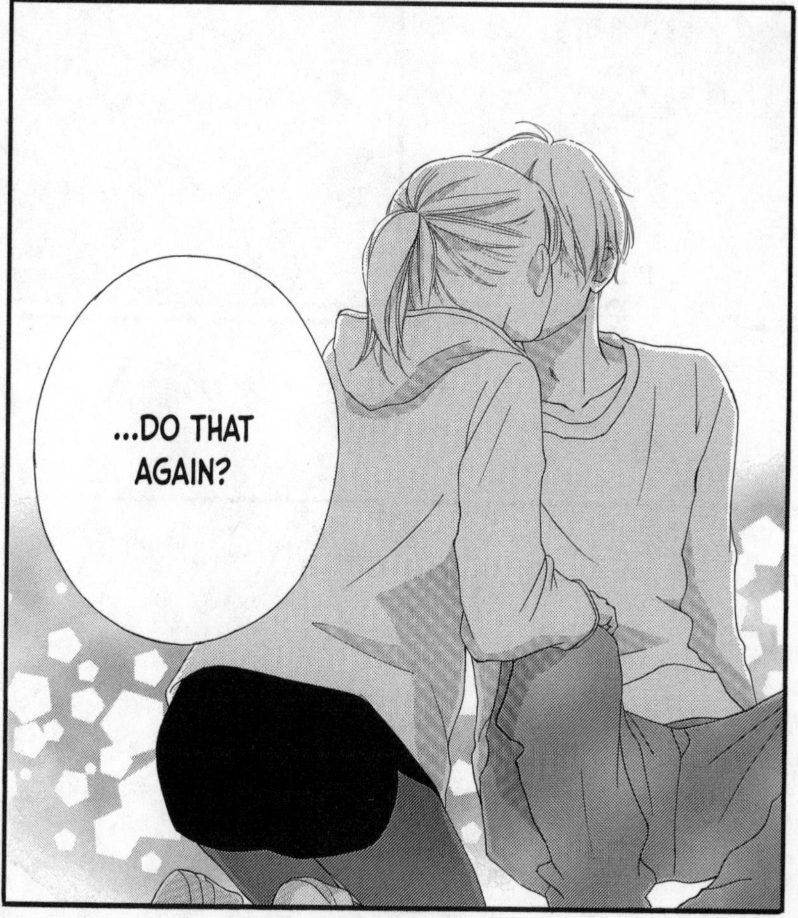
...DO THAT AGAIN?

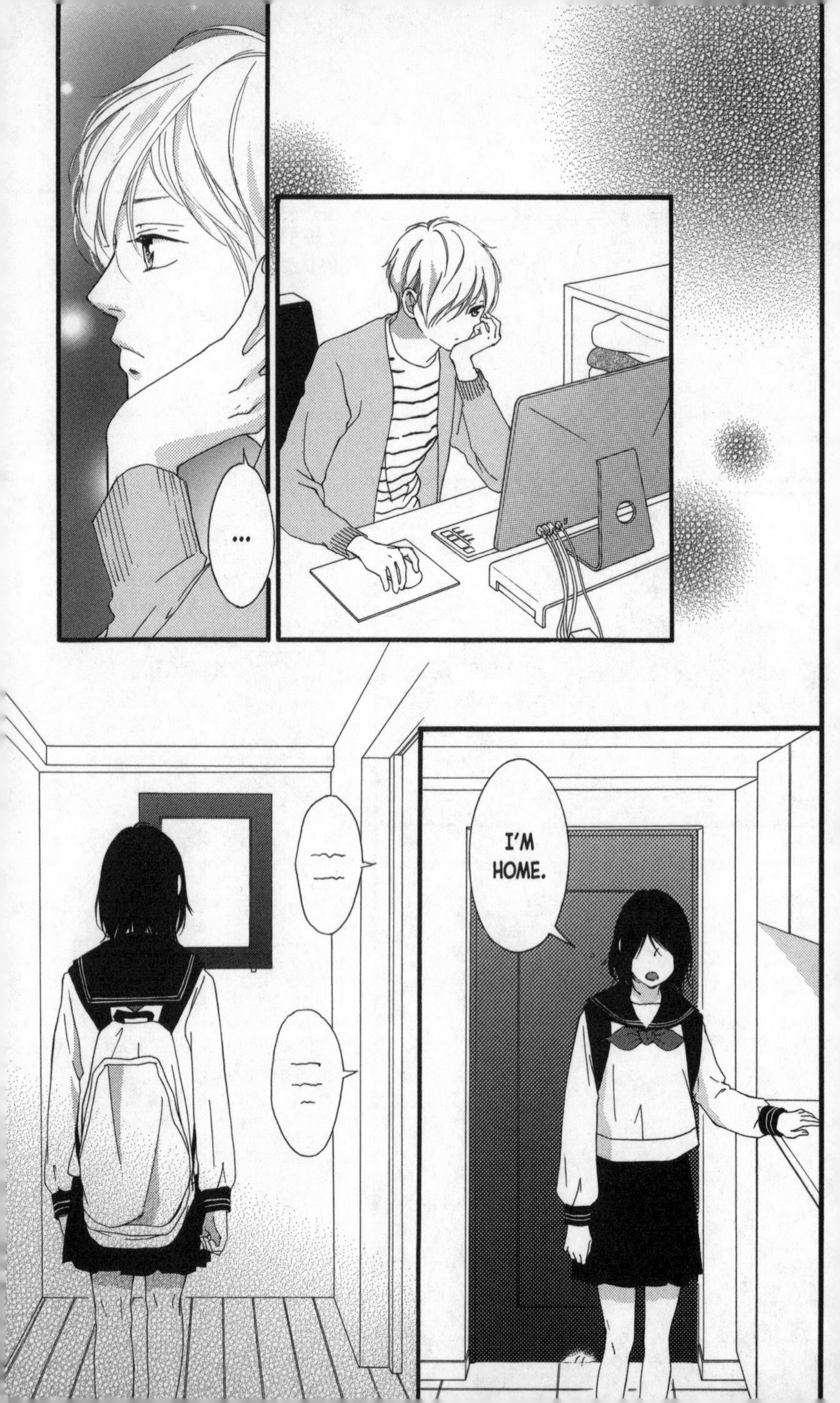
...
I'M HOME.

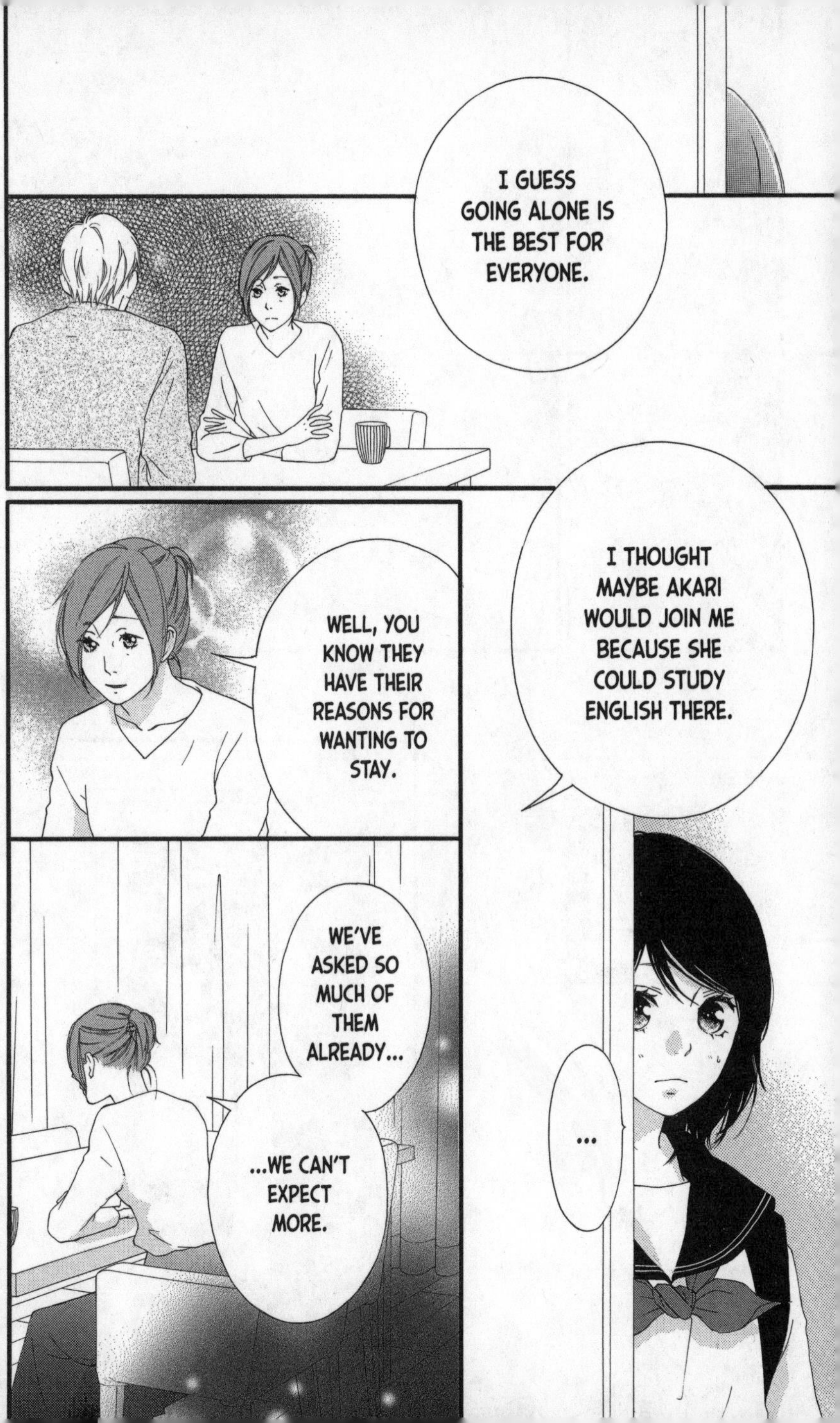
I GUESS GOING ALONE IS THE BEST FOR EVERYONE.
I THOUGHT MAYBE AKARI WOULD JOIN ME BECAUSE SHE COULD STUDY ENGLISH THERE.
...
WELL, YOU KNOW THEY HAVE THEIR REASONS FOR WANTING TO STAY.
WE'VE ASKED SO MUCH OF THEM ALREADY...
...WE CAN'T EXPECT MORE.

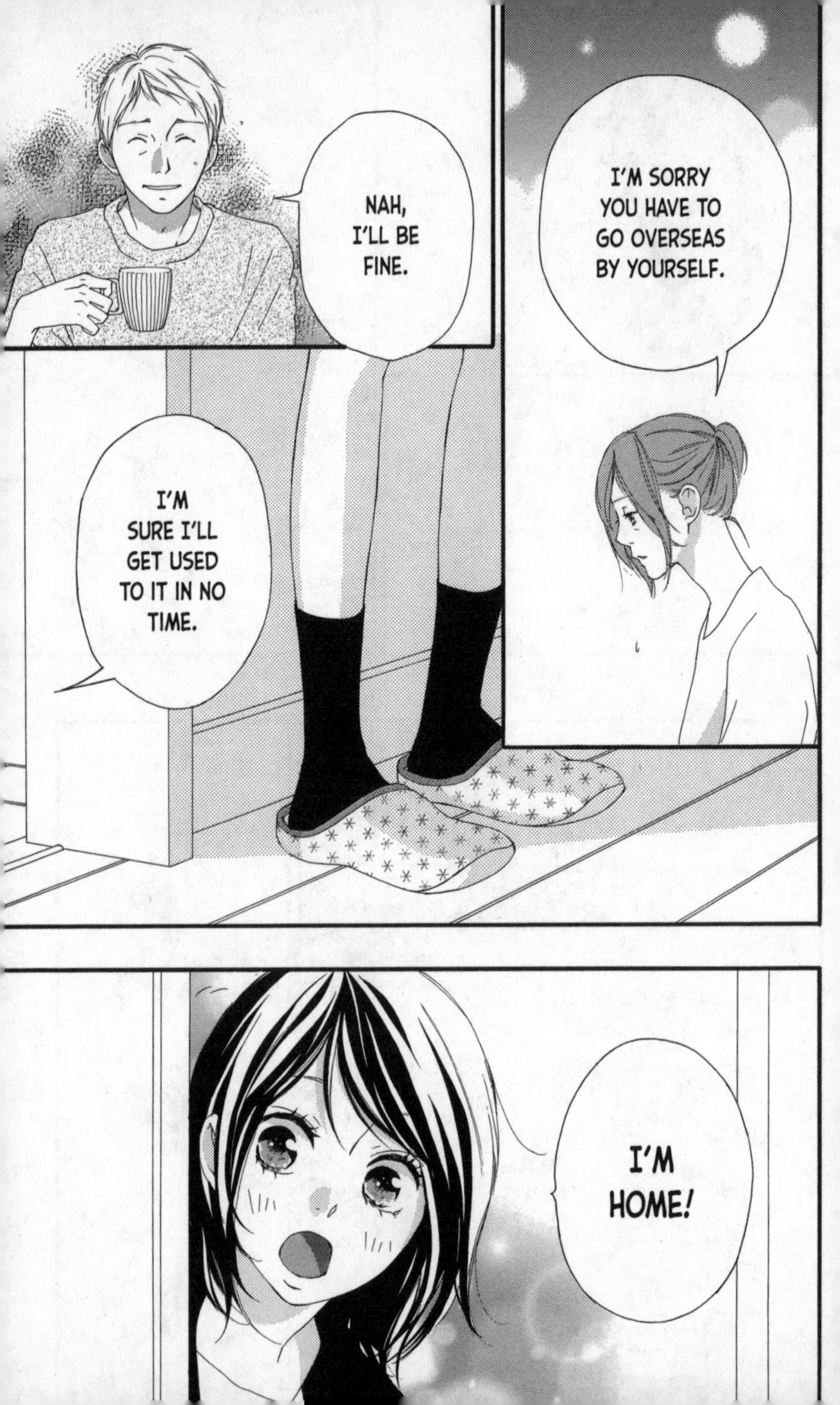
I'M SORRY YOU HAVE TO GO OVERSEAS BY YOURSELF.
NAH, I'LL BE FINE.
I'M SURE I'LL GET USED TO IT IN NO TIME.
I'M HOME!

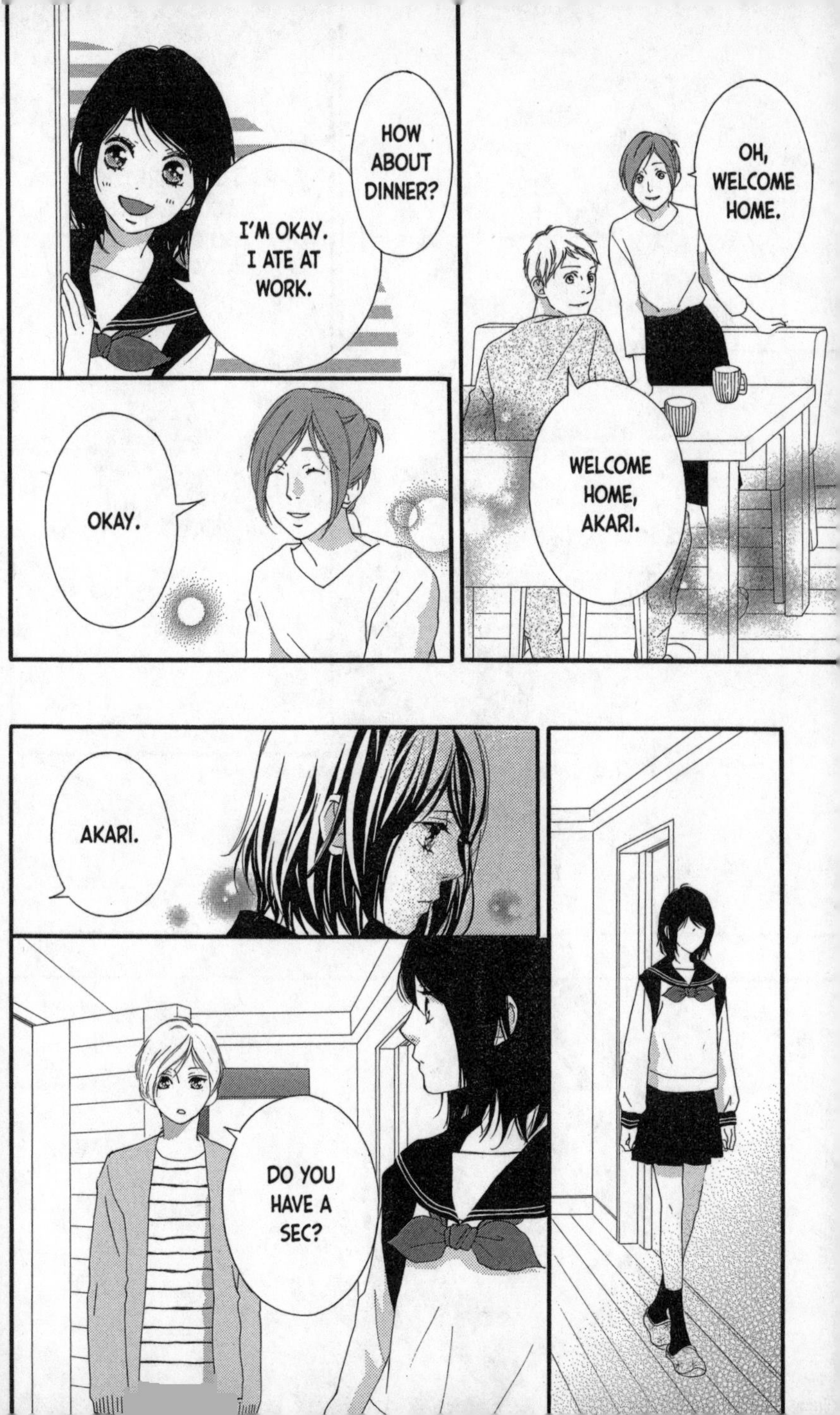
OH, WELCOME HOME.
WELCOME HOME, AKARI.
HOW ABOUT DINNER?
I'M OKAY. I ATE AT WORK.
OKAY.
AKARI.
DO YOU HAVE A SEC?

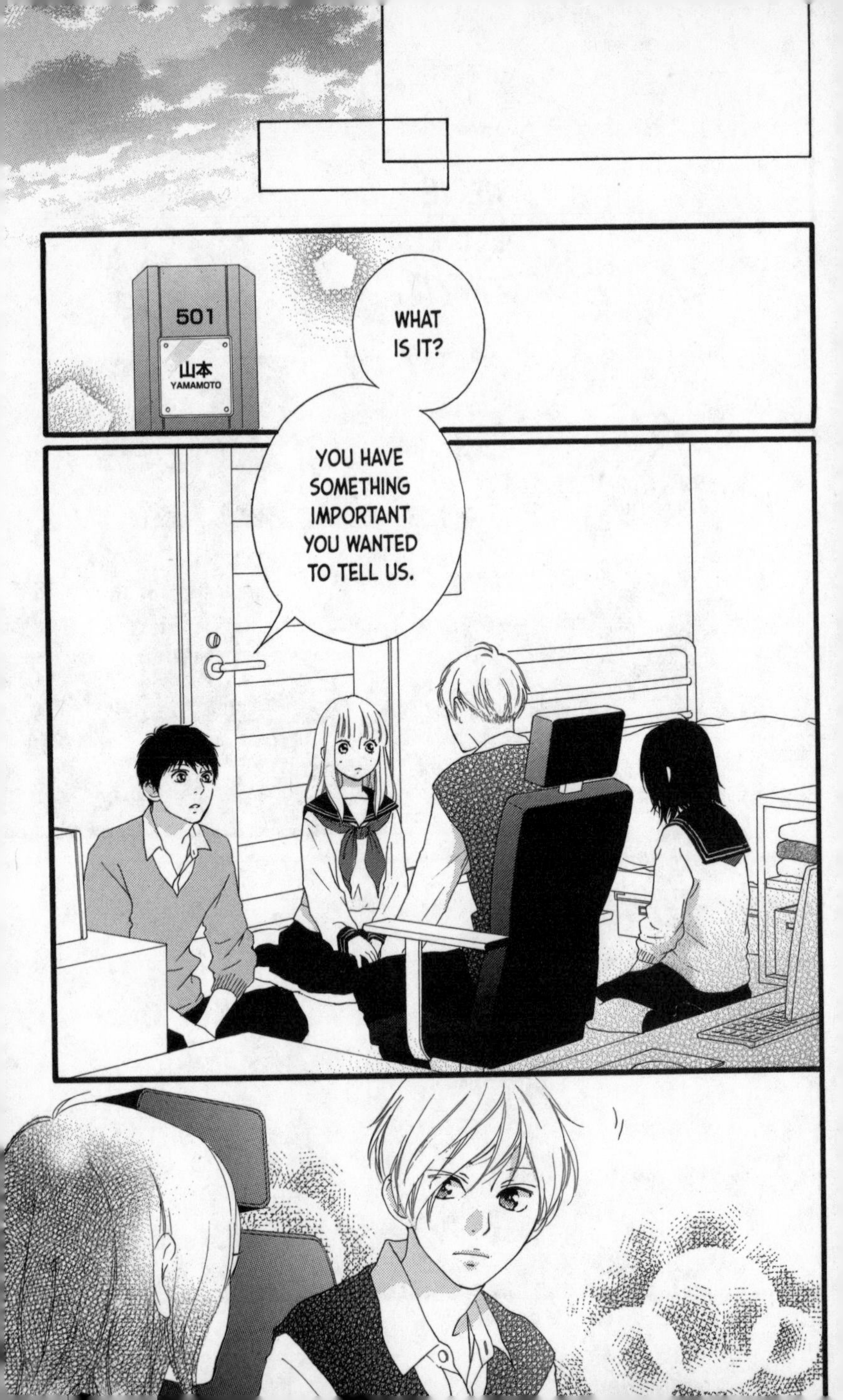
501
山本
YAMAMOTO
WHAT IS IT?
YOU HAVE SOMETHING IMPORTANT YOU WANTED TO TELL US.

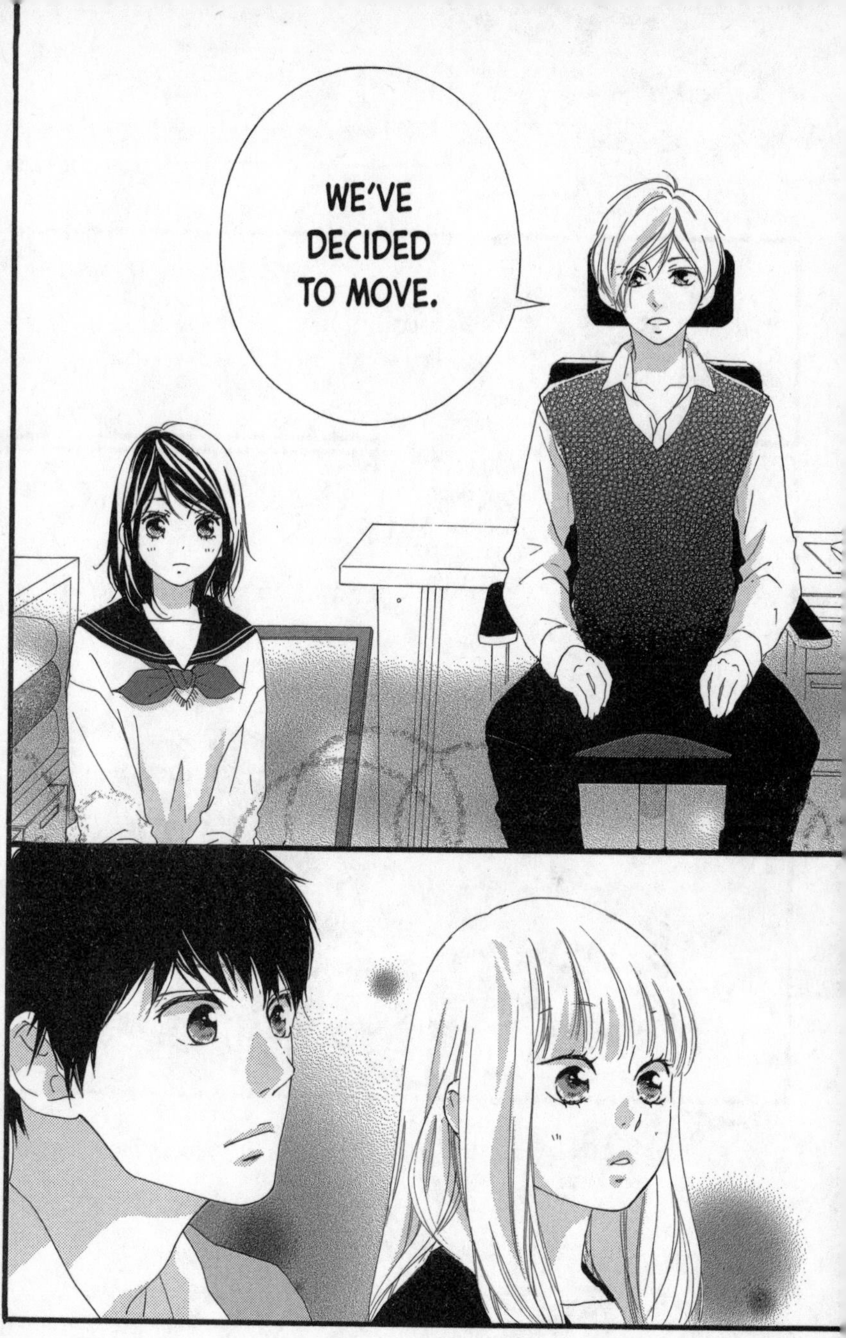
WE'VE DECIDED TO MOVE.

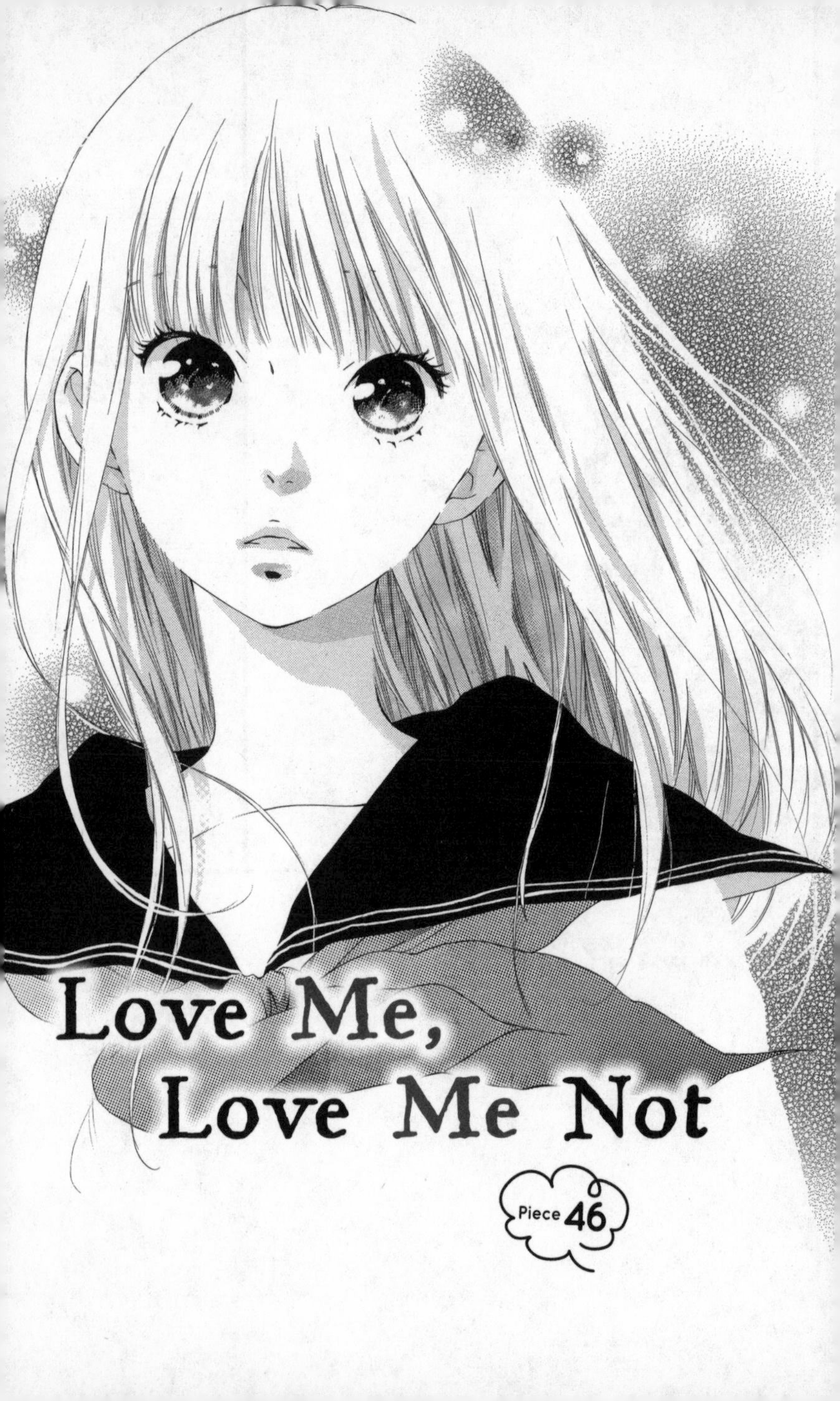
Love Me,
Love Me Not
Piece 46

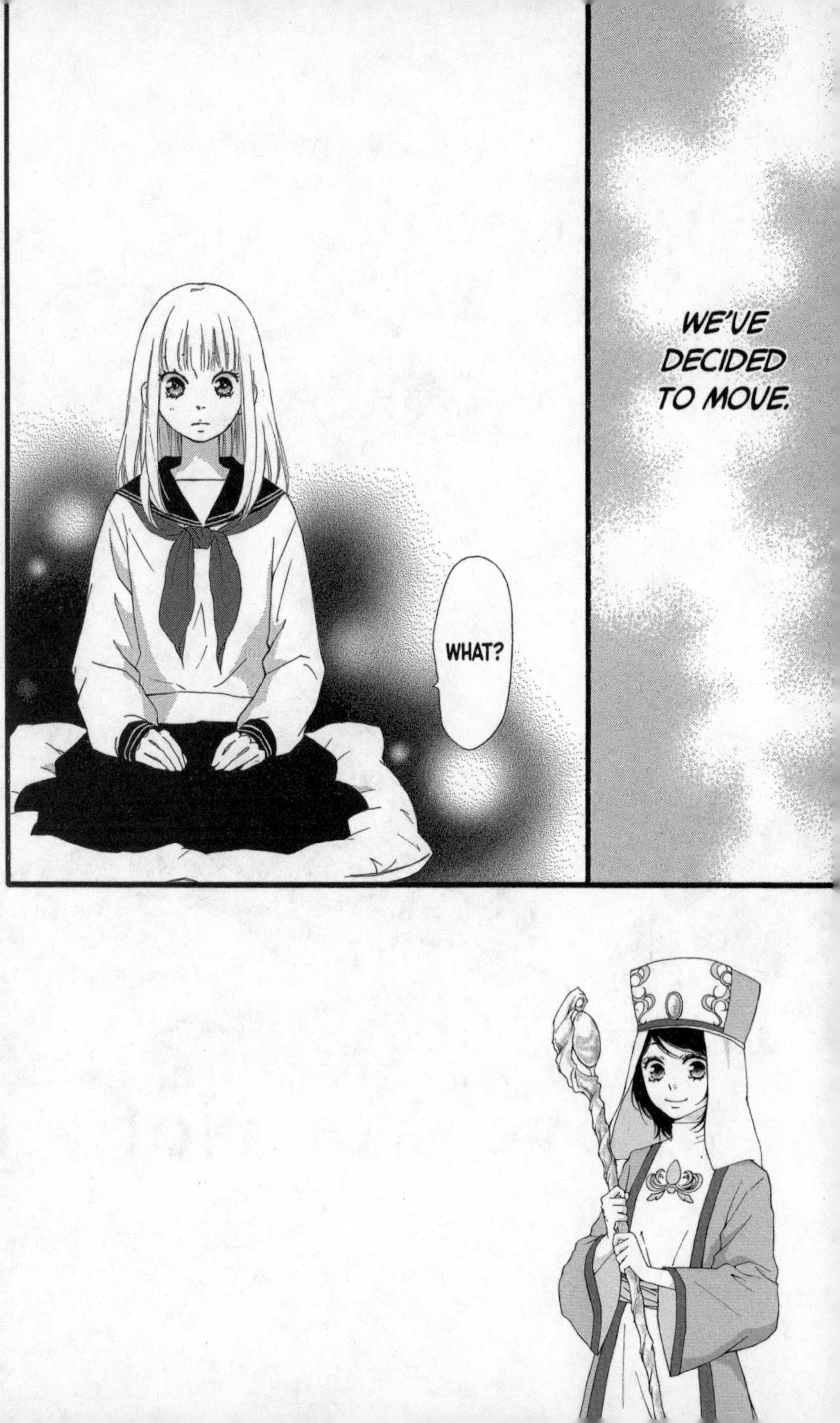
WE'VE DECIDED TO MOVE.
WHAT?

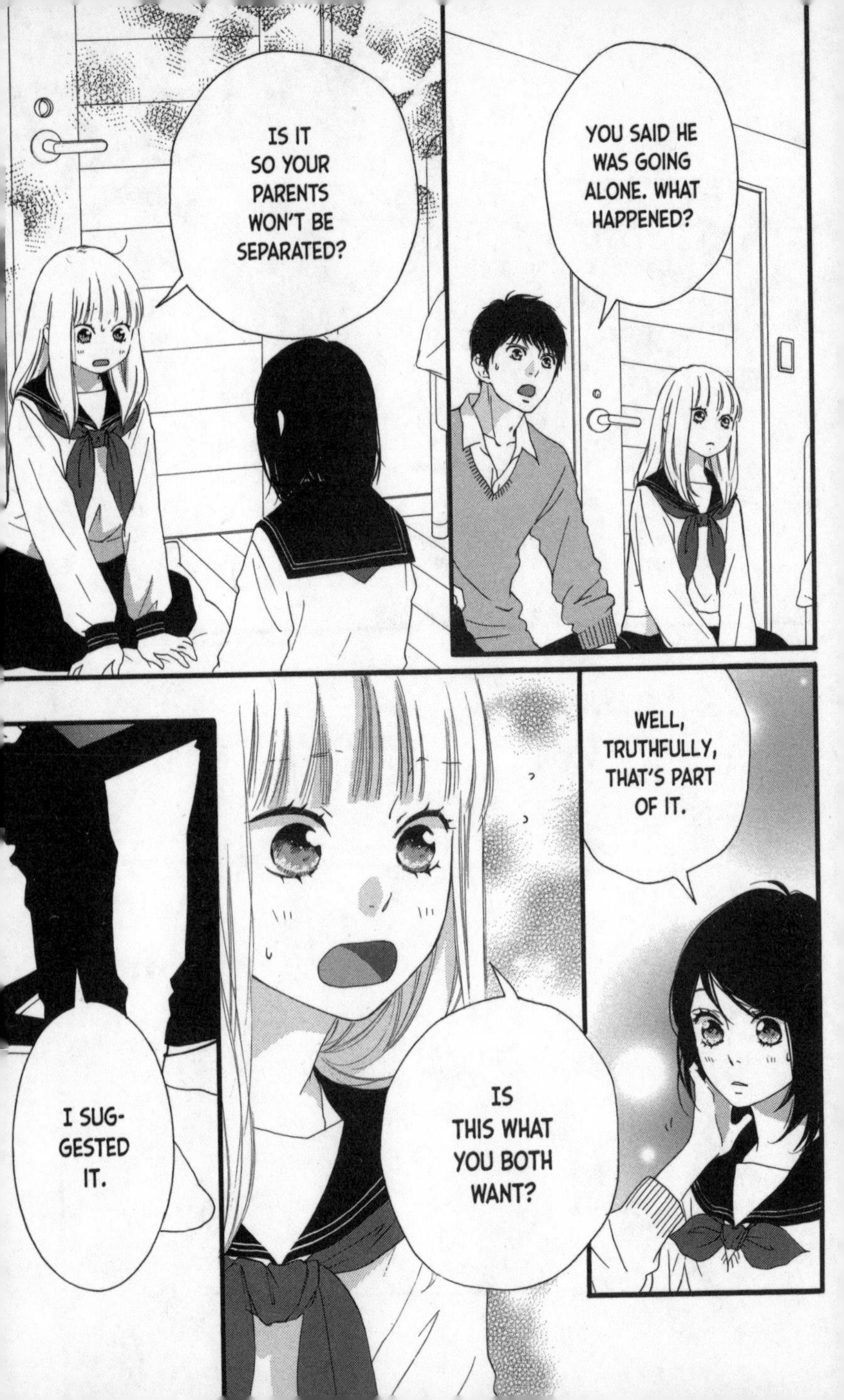
YOU SAID HE WAS GOING ALONE. WHAT HAPPENED?
IS IT SO YOUR PARENTS WON'T BE SEPARATED?
WELL, TRUTHFULLY, THAT'S PART OF IT.
IS THIS WHAT YOU BOTH WANT?
I SUG-GESTED IT.

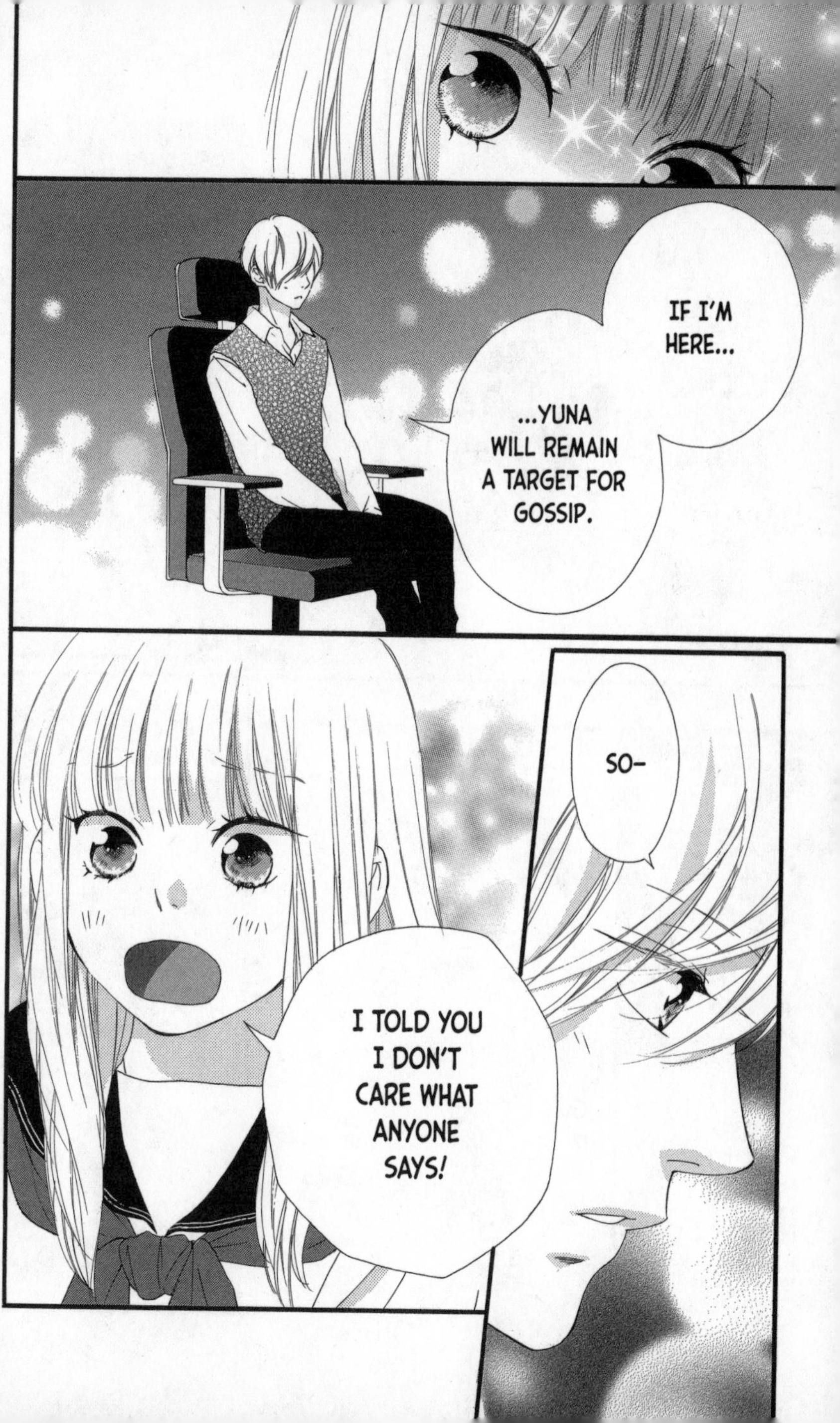
IF I'M HERE...
...YUNA WILL REMAIN A TARGET FOR GOSSIP.
SO-
I TOLD YOU I DON'T CARE WHAT ANYONE SAYS!

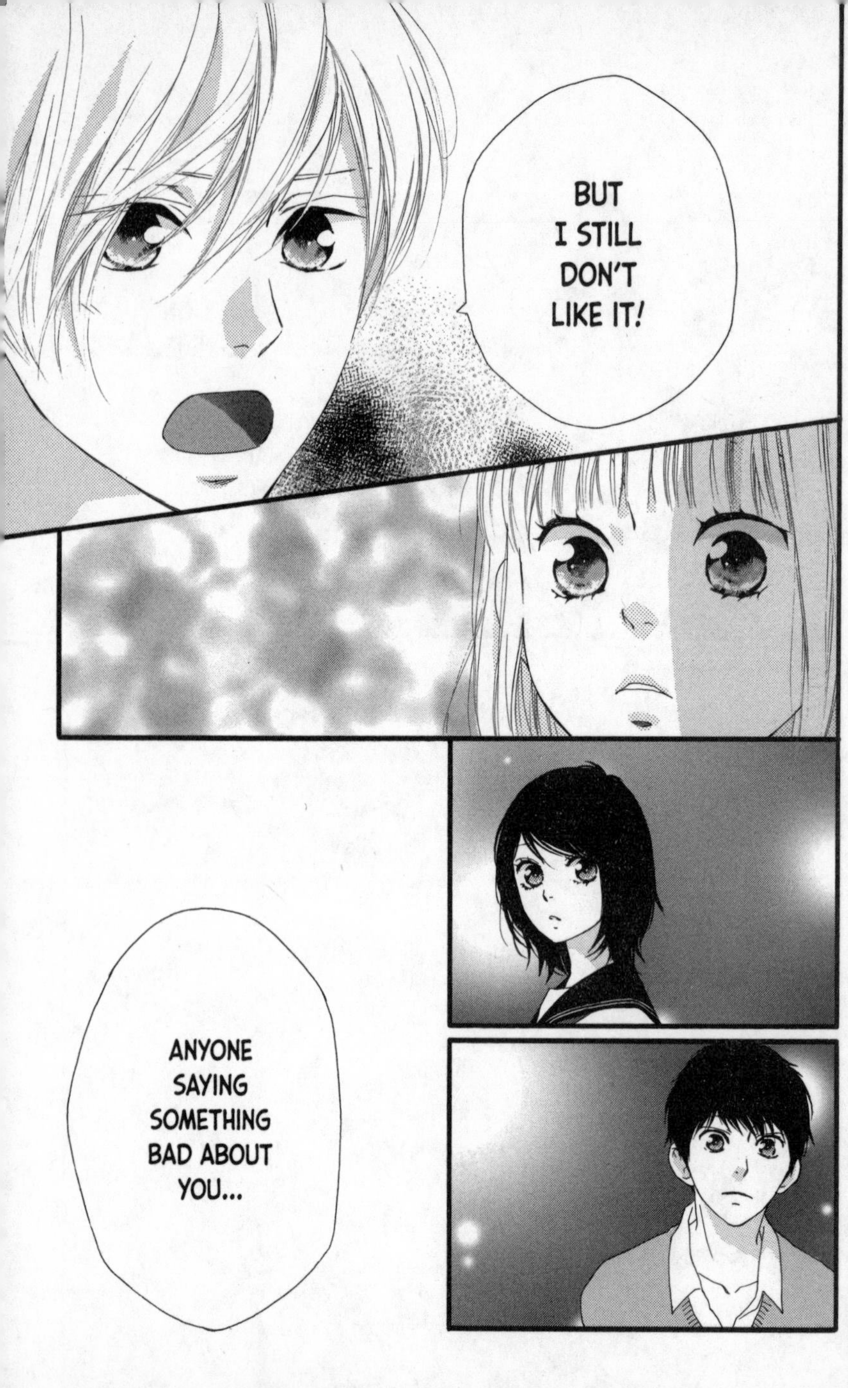
BUT I STILL DON'T LIKE IT!
ANYONE SAYING SOMETHING BAD ABOUT YOU...

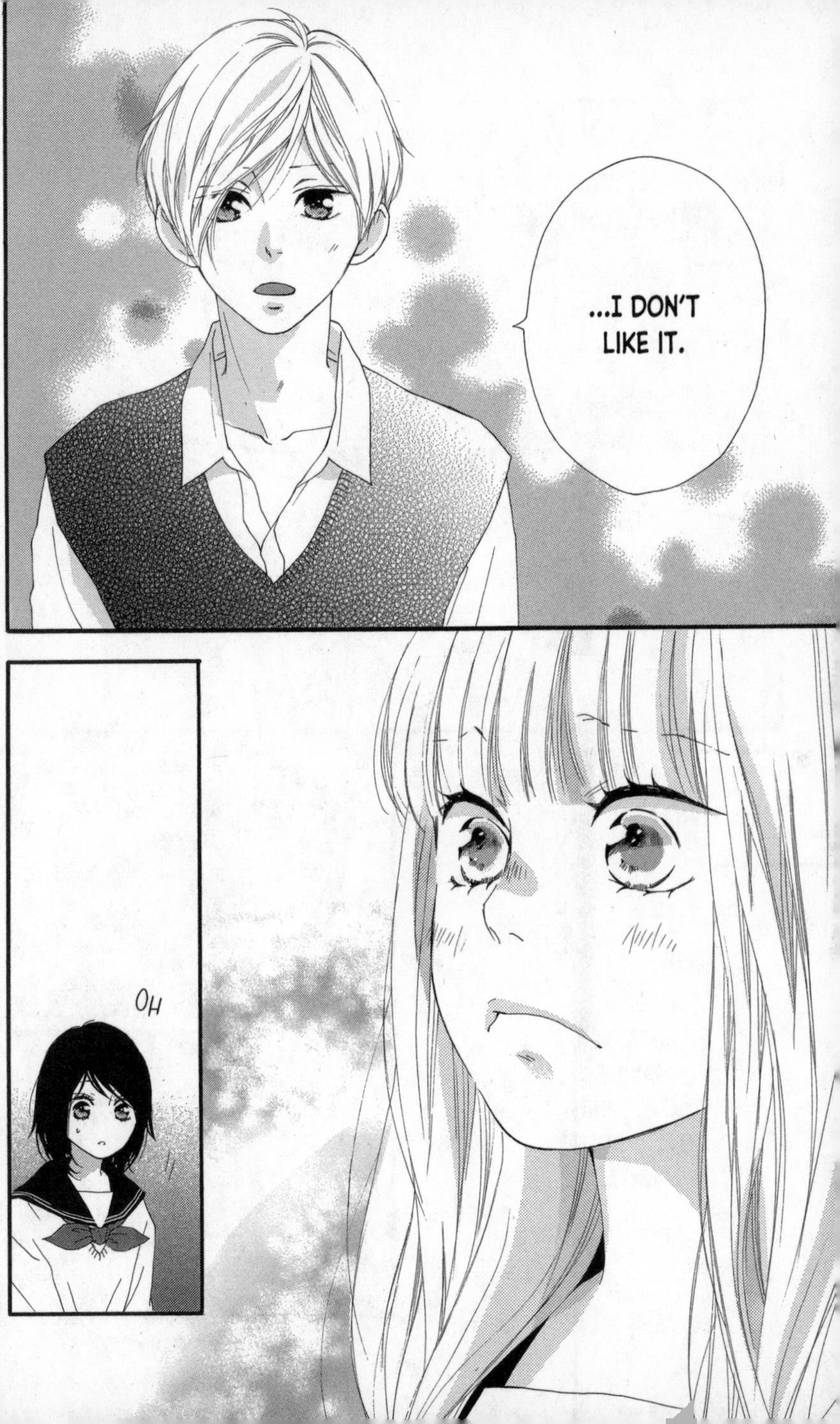
...I DON'T LIKE IT.
OH

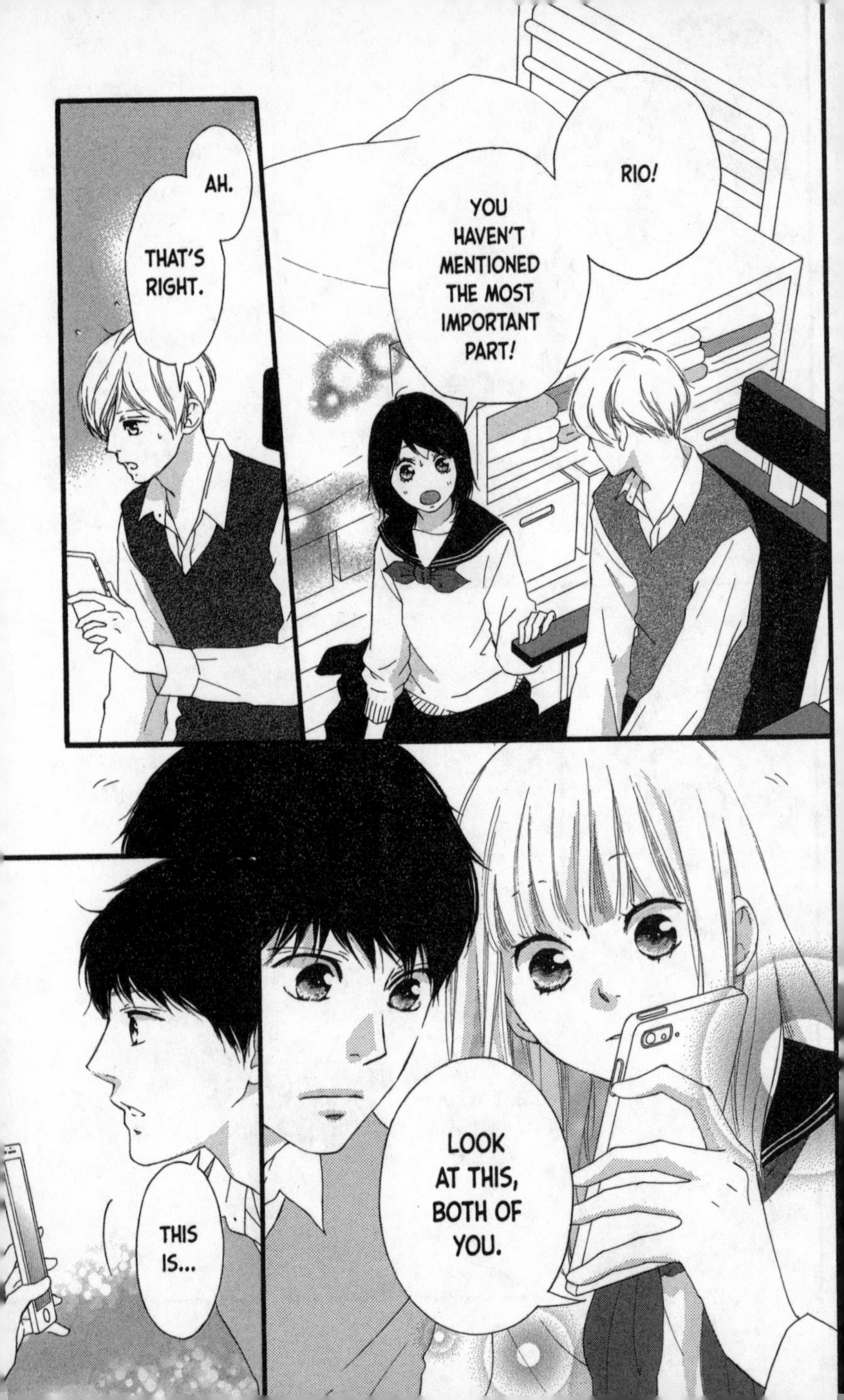
RIO!
YOU HAVEN'T MENTIONED THE MOST IMPORTANT PART!
AH.
THAT'S RIGHT.
LOOK AT THIS, BOTH OF YOU.
THIS IS...

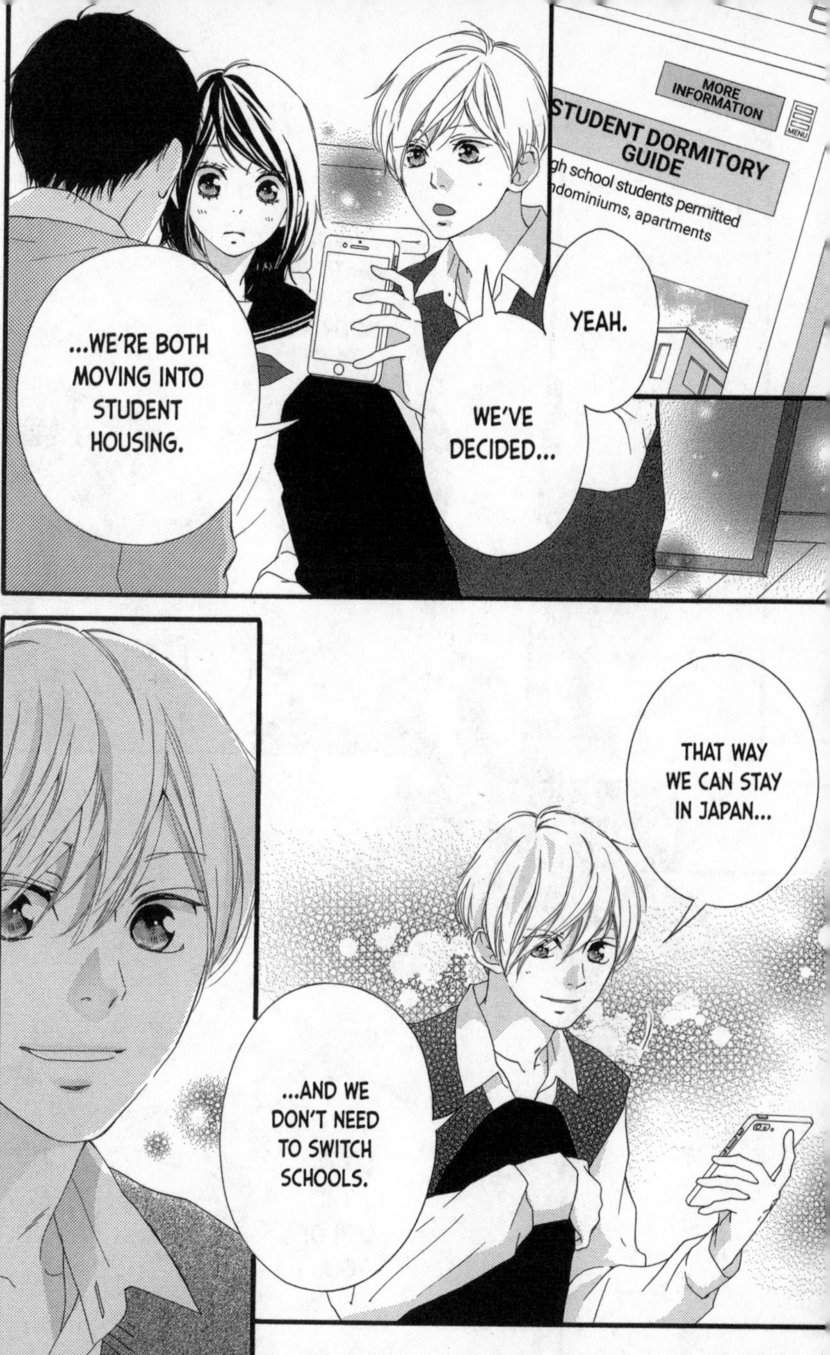
MORE INFORMATION
MENU
STUDENT DORMITORY GUIDE
gh school students permitted
ndominiums, apartments
YEAH.
WE'VE DECIDED...
...WE'RE BOTH MOVING INTO STUDENT HOUSING.
THAT WAY WE CAN STAY IN JAPAN...
...AND WE DON'T NEED TO SWITCH SCHOOLS.

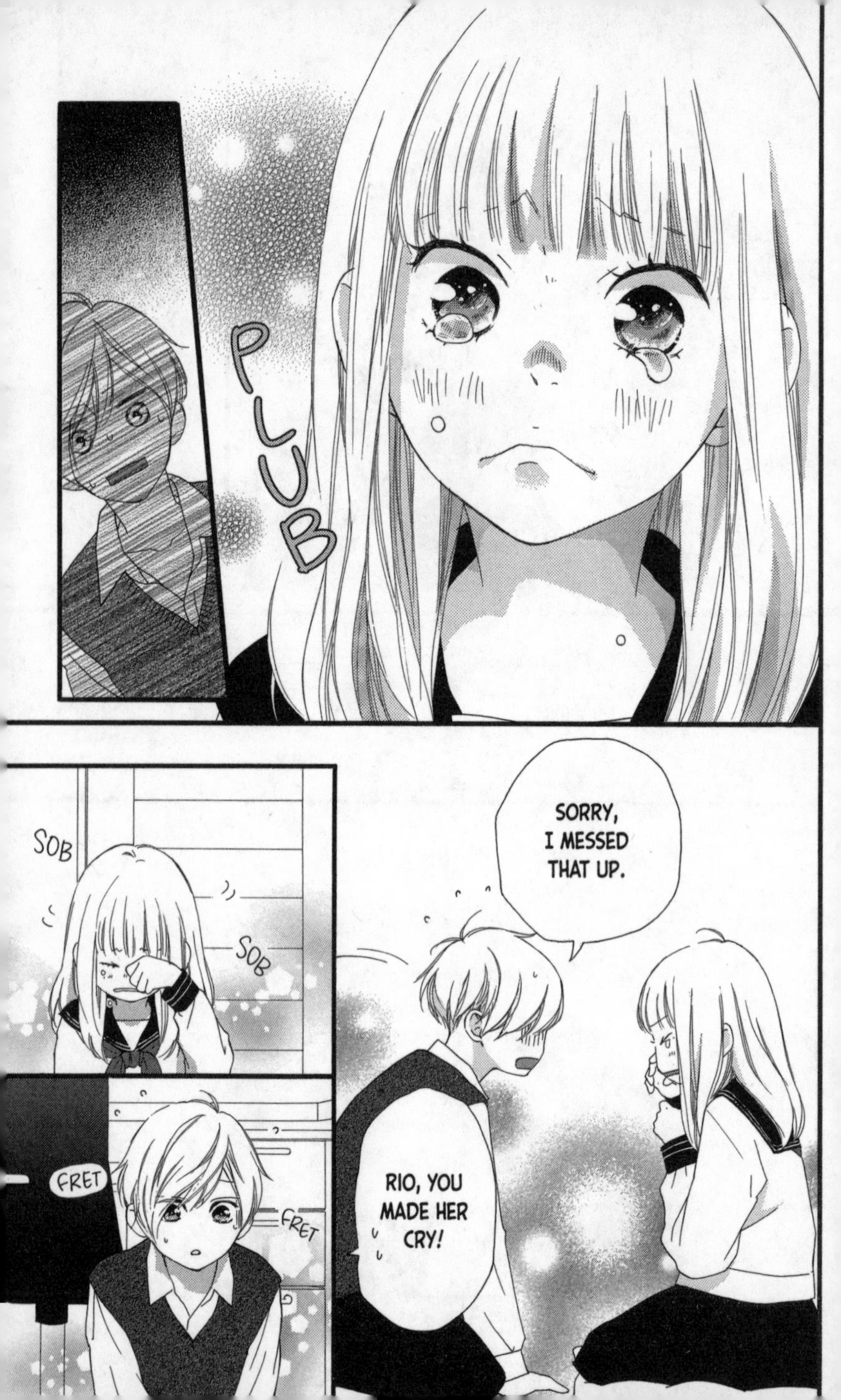
PLUB
SORRY, I MESSED THAT UP.
RIO, YOU MADE HER CRY!
SOB
SOB
FRET
FRET

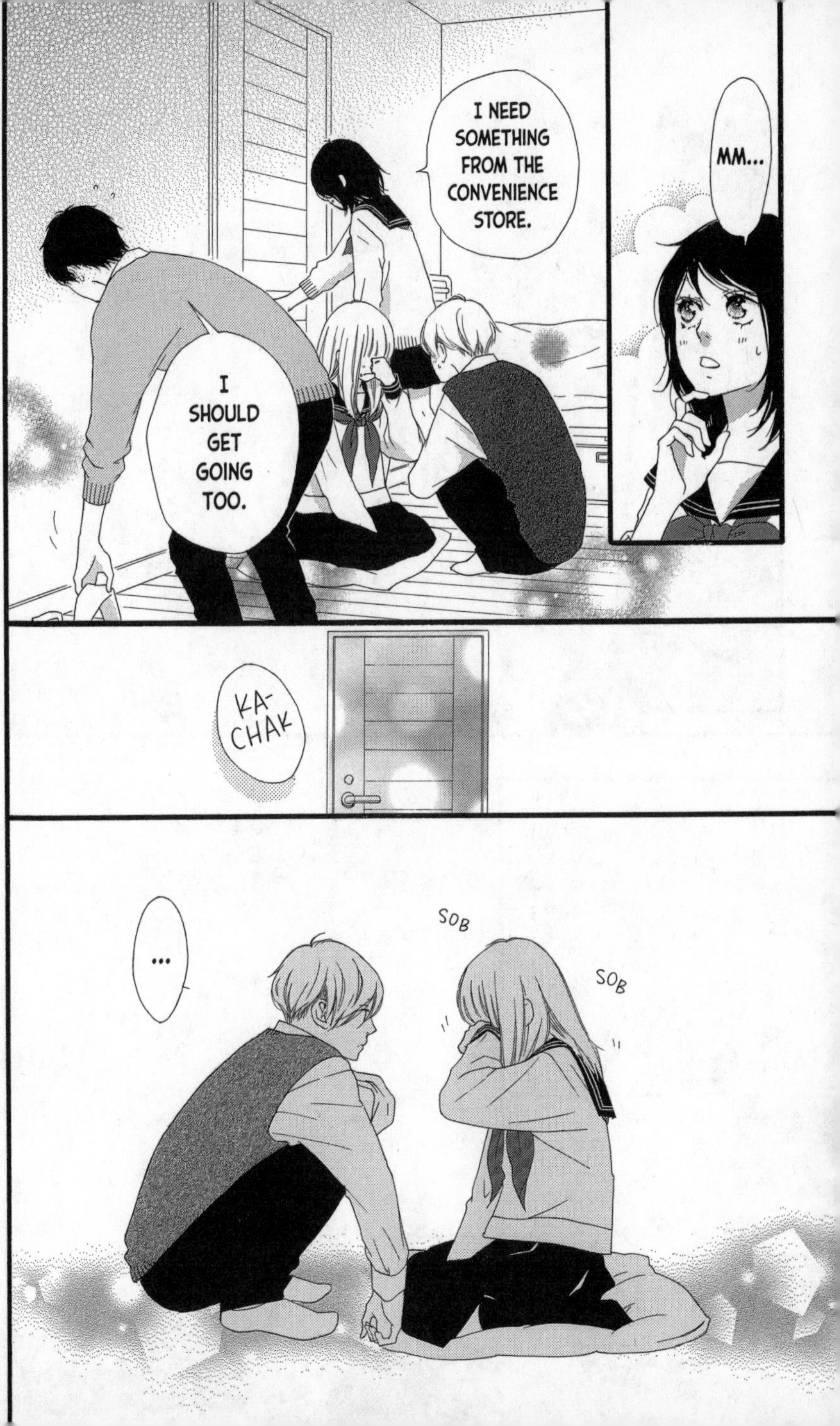
MM...
I NEED SOMETHING FROM THE CONVENIENCE STORE.
I SHOULD GET GOING TOO.
KA-CHAK
SOB
SOB
...

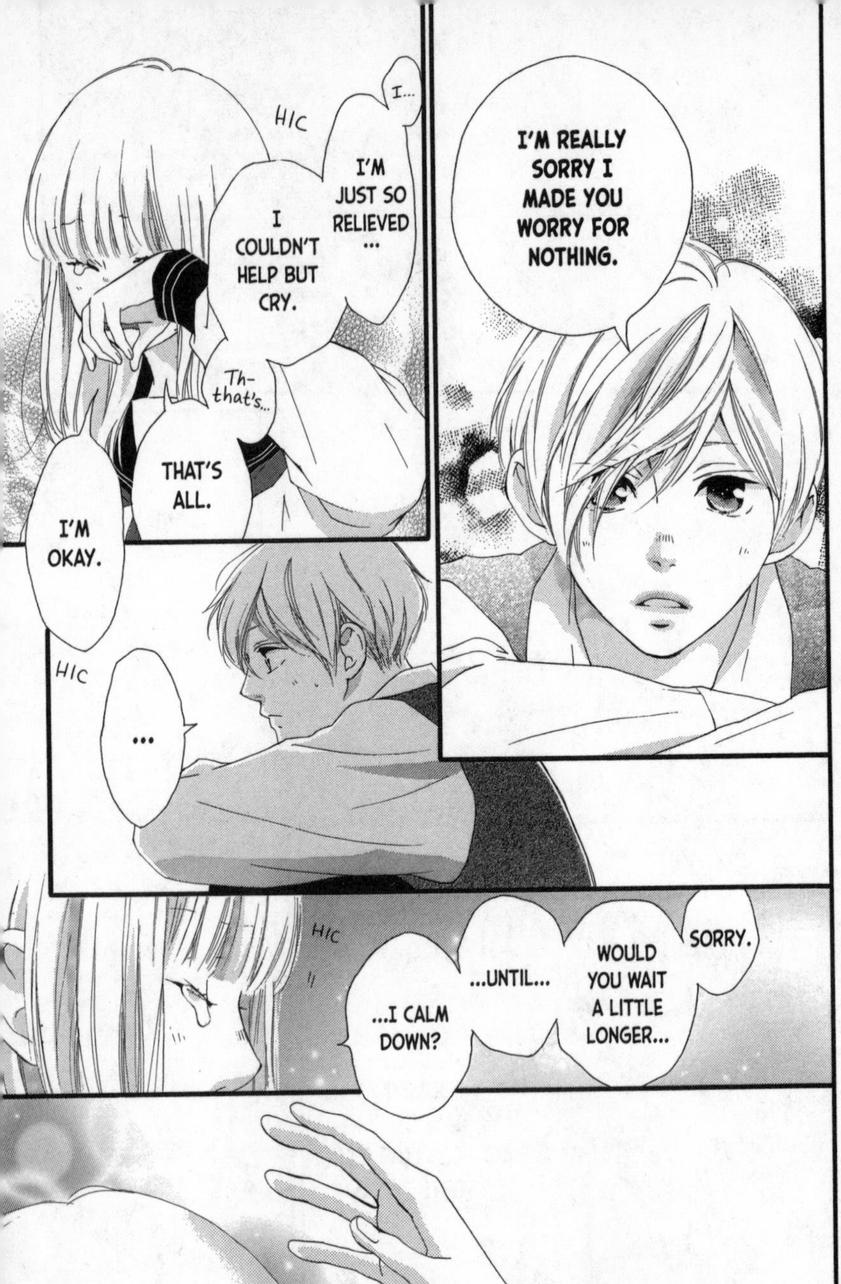
I'M REALLY SORRY I MADE YOU WORRY FOR NOTHING.
I...
HIC
I'M JUST SO RELIEVED...
I COULDN'T HELP BUT CRY.
Th-that's...
THAT'S ALL.
I'M OKAY.
HIC
...
SORRY.
WOULD YOU WAIT A LITTLE LONGER...
...UNTIL...
HIC
...I CALM DOWN?

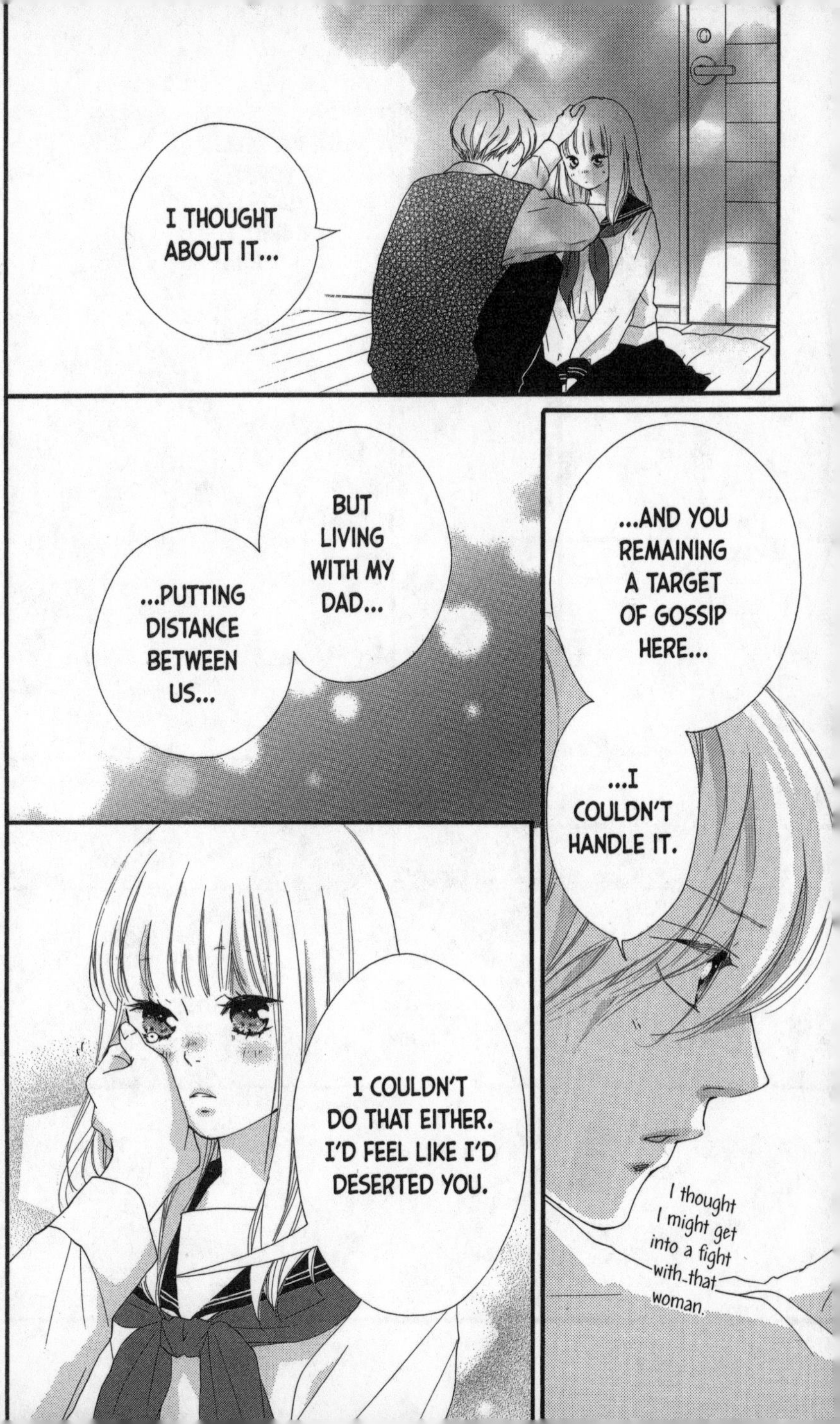
I THOUGHT ABOUT IT...
...AND YOU REMAINING A TARGET OF GOSSIP HERE...
...I COULDN'T HANDLE IT.
I thought I might get into a fight with that woman.
BUT LIVING WITH MY DAD...
...PUTTING DISTANCE BETWEEN US...
I COULDN'T DO THAT EITHER. I'D FEEL LIKE I'D DESERTED YOU.

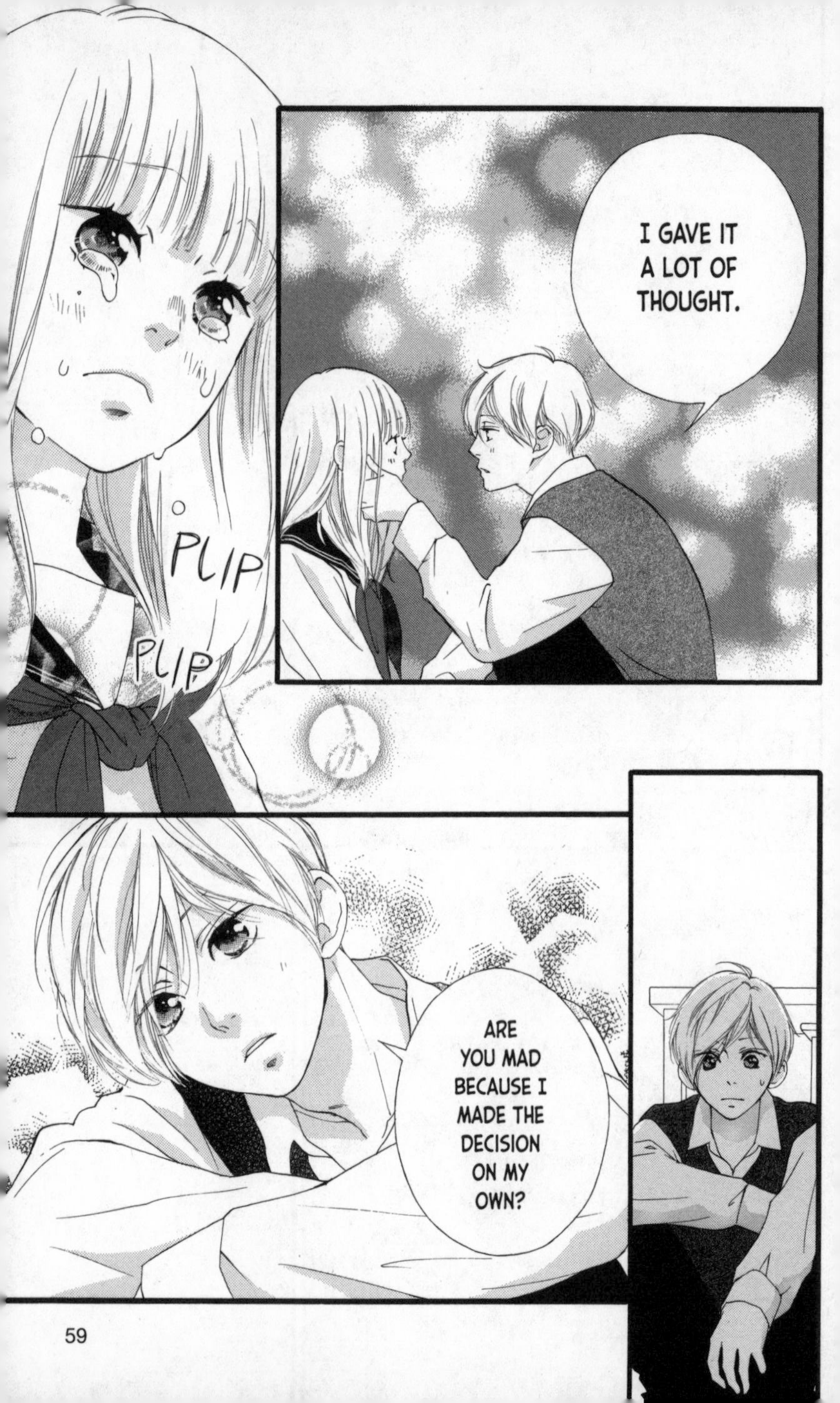
I GAVE IT A LOT OF THOUGHT.
PLIP
PLIP
ARE YOU MAD BECAUSE I MADE THE DECISION ON MY OWN?

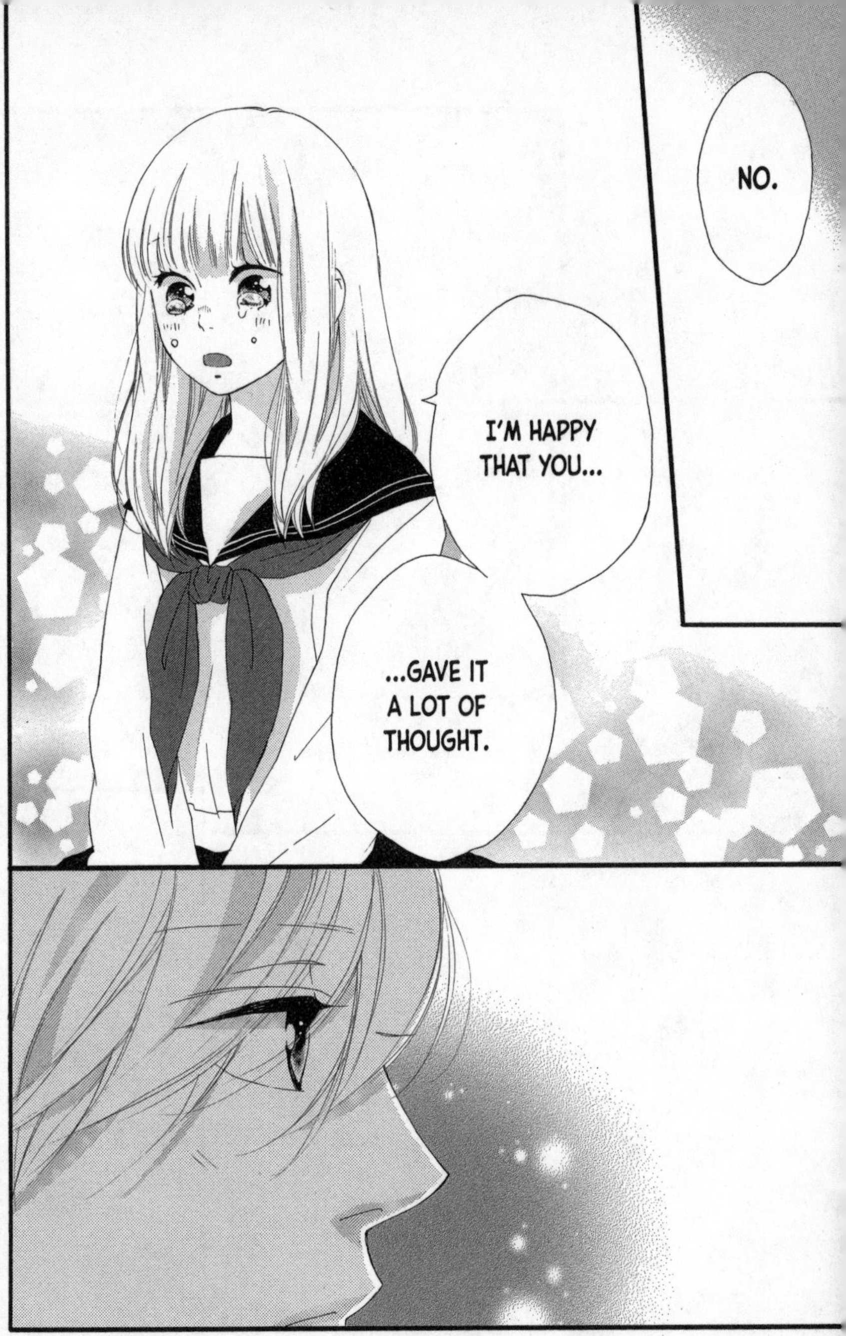
NO.
I'M HAPPY THAT YOU...
...GAVE IT A LOT OF THOUGHT.

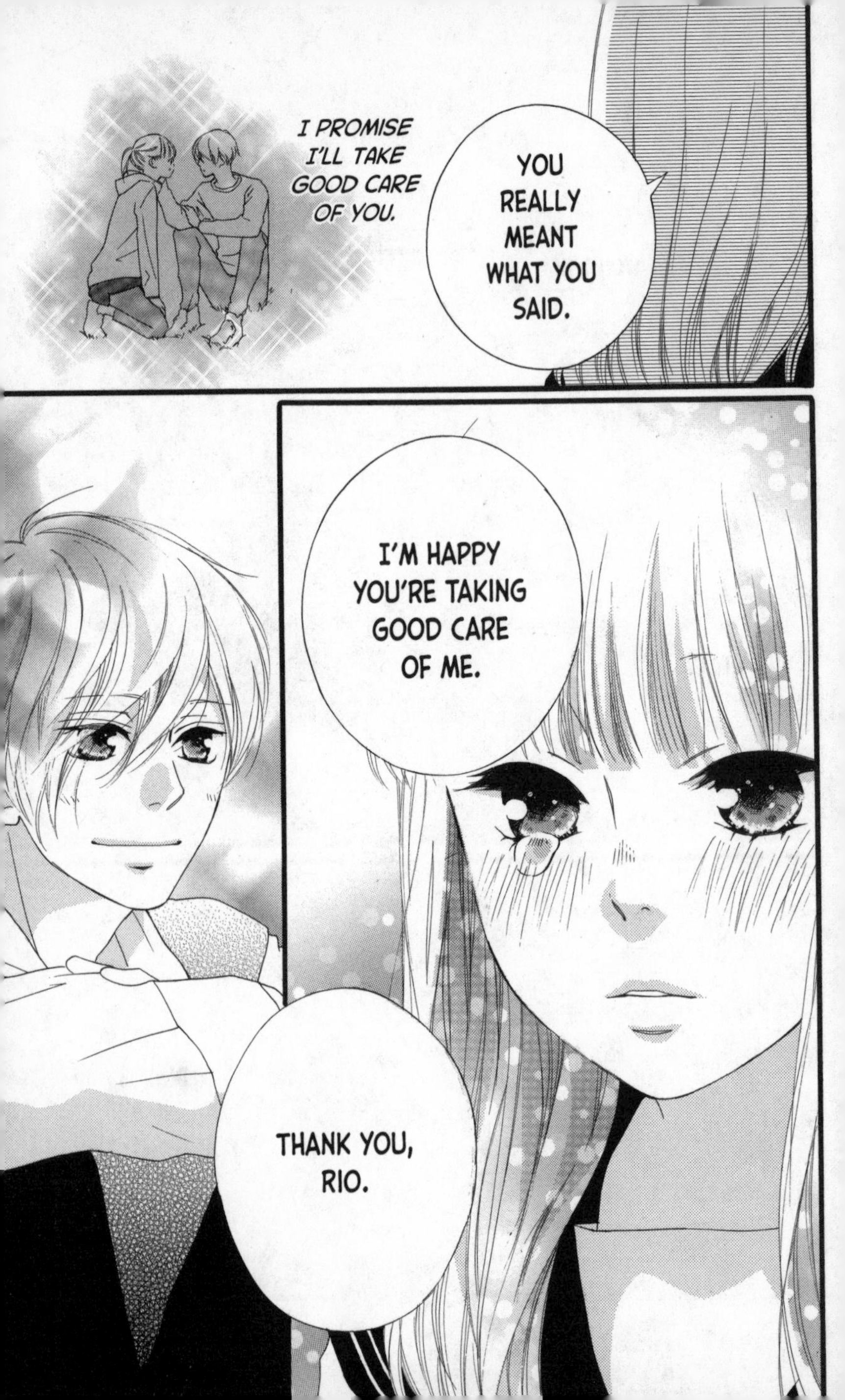
YOU REALLY MEANT WHAT YOU SAID.
I PROMISE I'LL TAKE GOOD CARE OF YOU.
I'M HAPPY YOU'RE TAKING GOOD CARE OF ME.
THANK YOU, RIO.

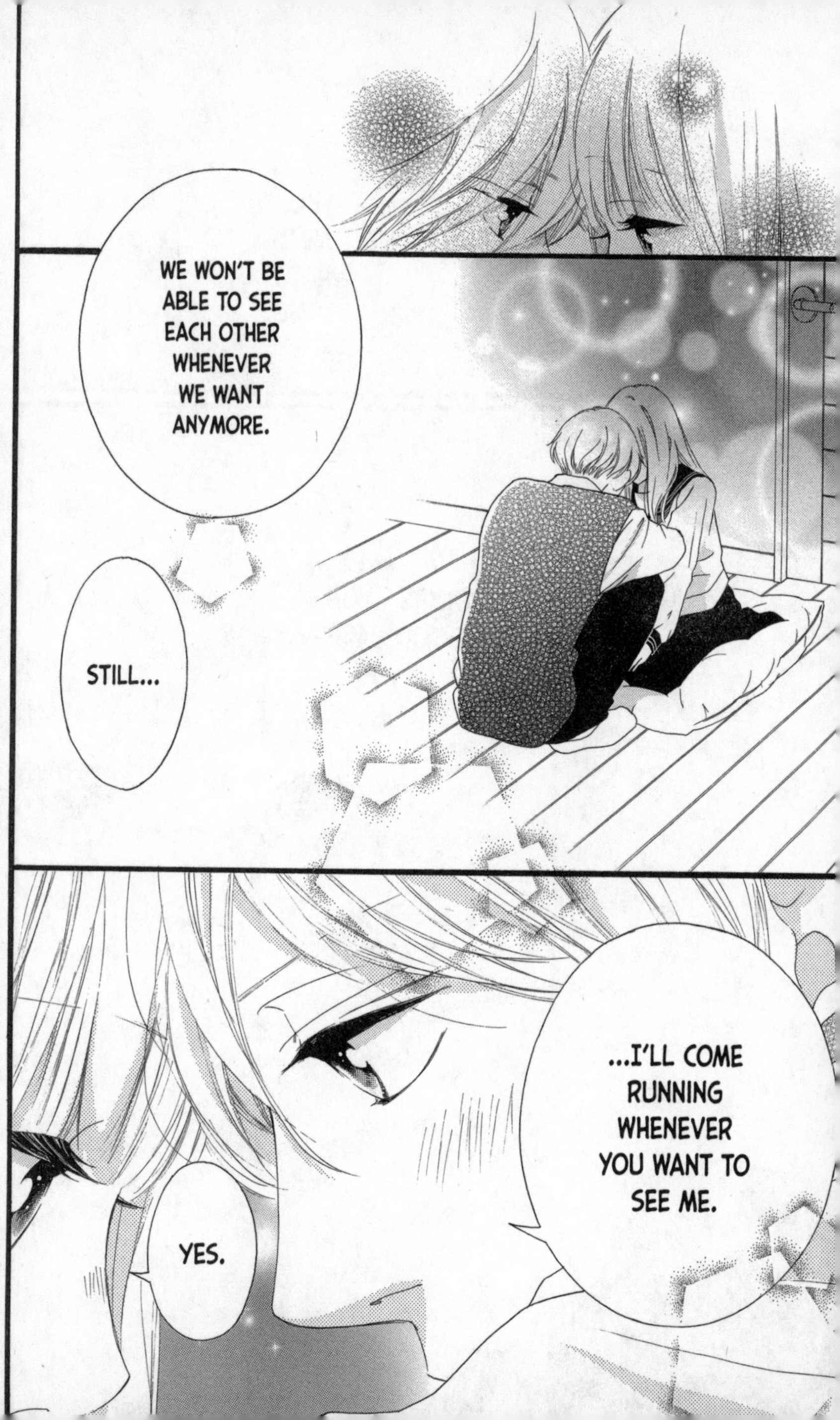
WE WON'T BE ABLE TO SEE EACH OTHER WHENEVER WE WANT ANYMORE.
STILL...
...I'LL COME RUNNING WHENEVER YOU WANT TO SEE ME.
YES.

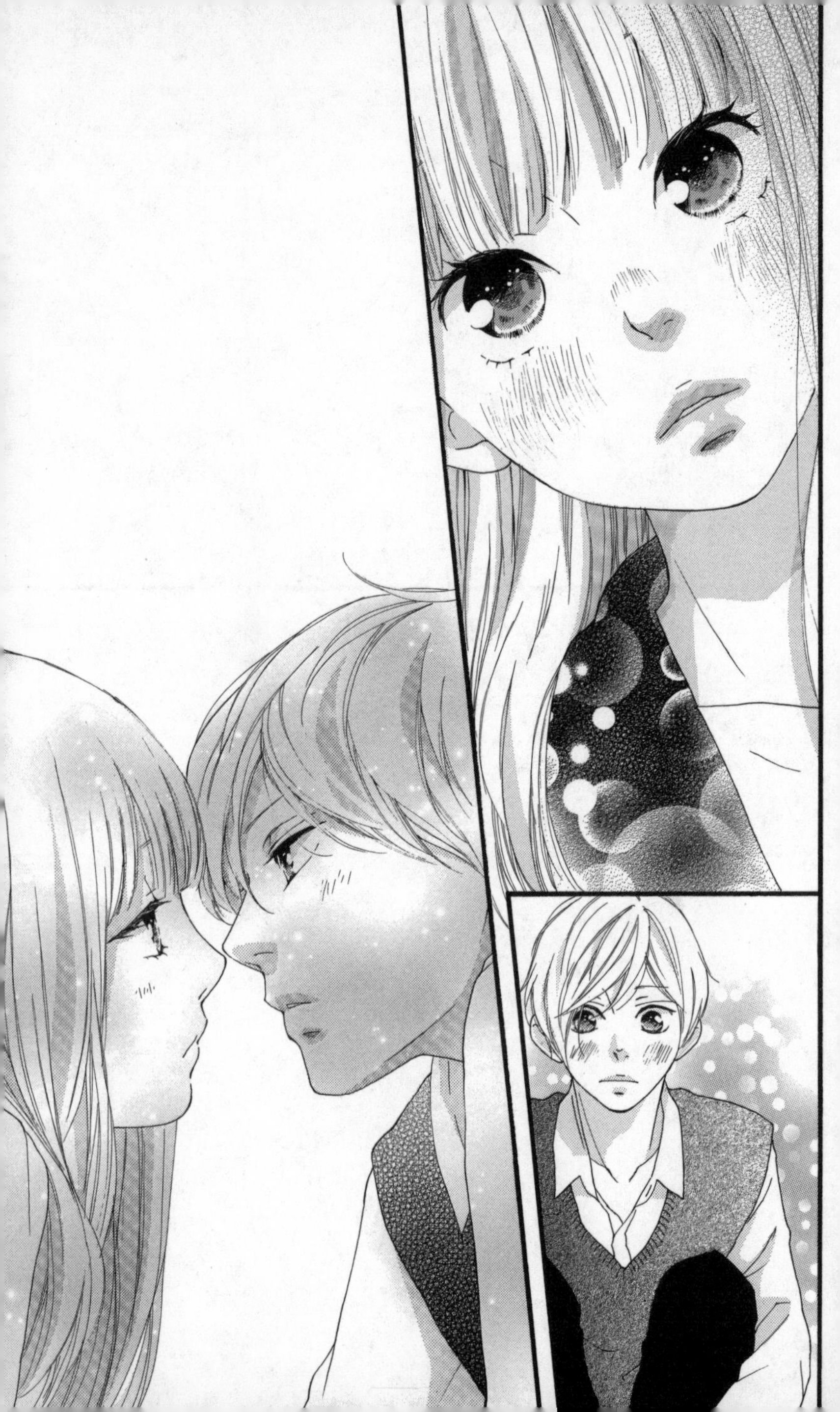

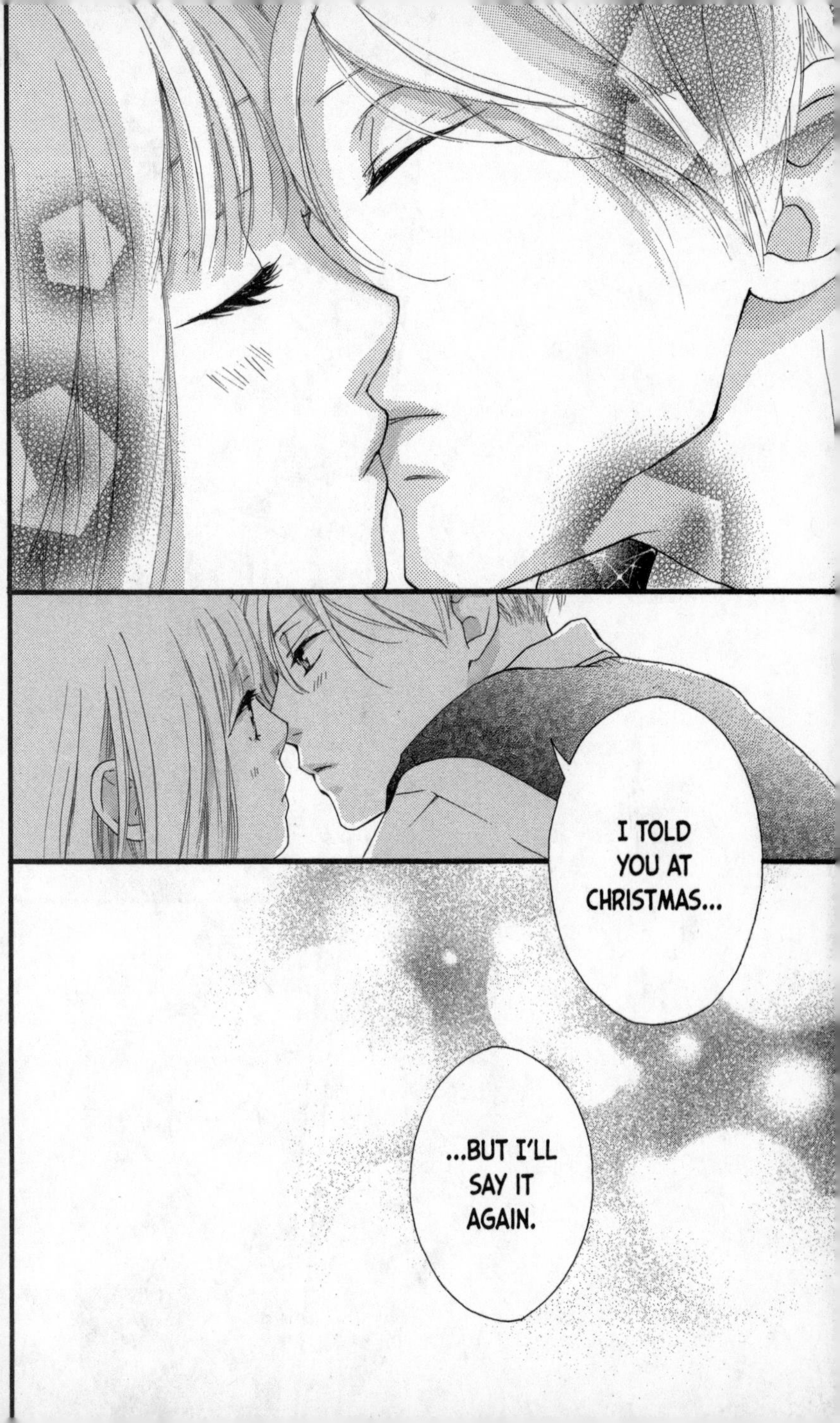
I TOLD YOU AT CHRISTMAS...
...BUT I'LL SAY IT AGAIN.

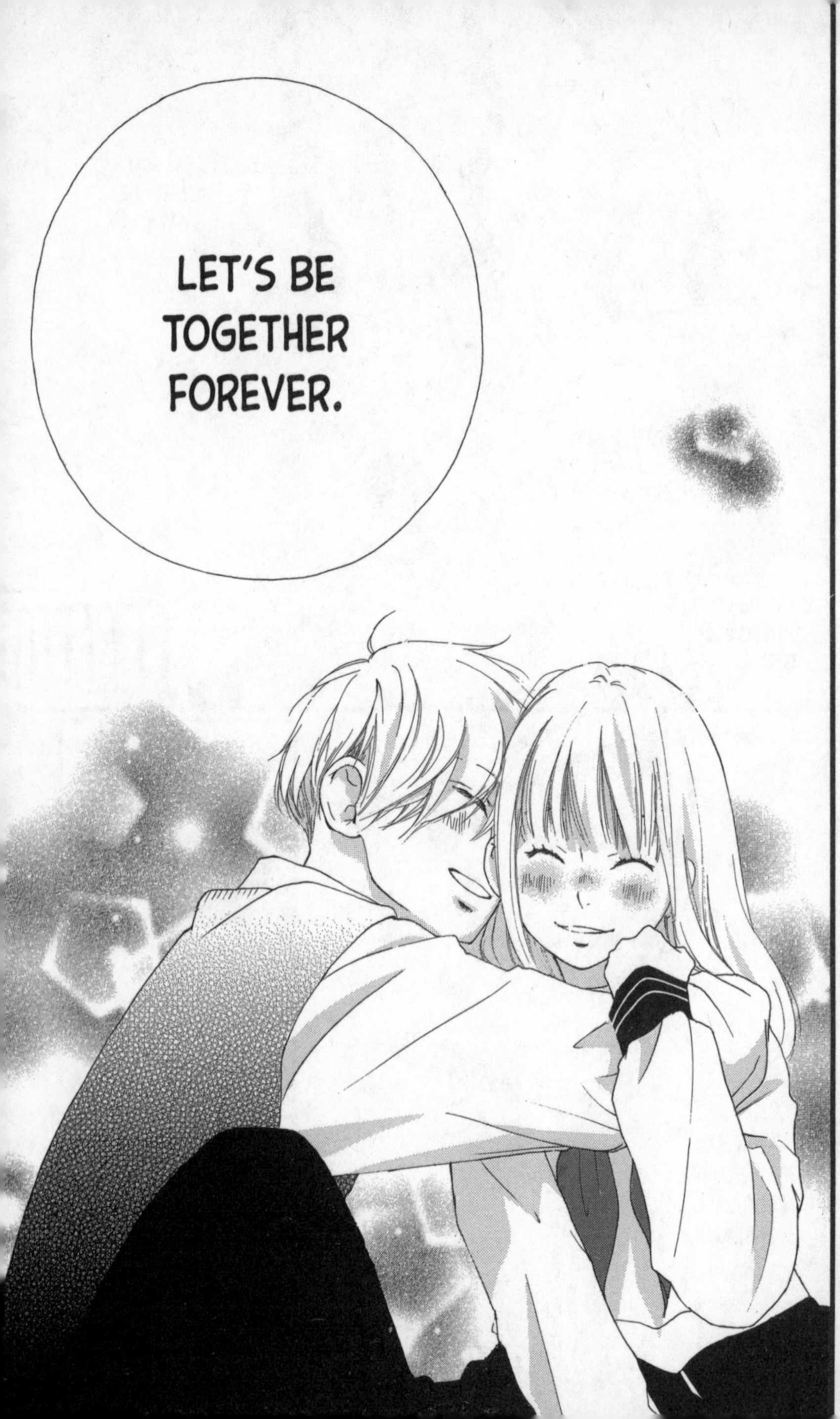
LET'S BE TOGETHER FOREVER.

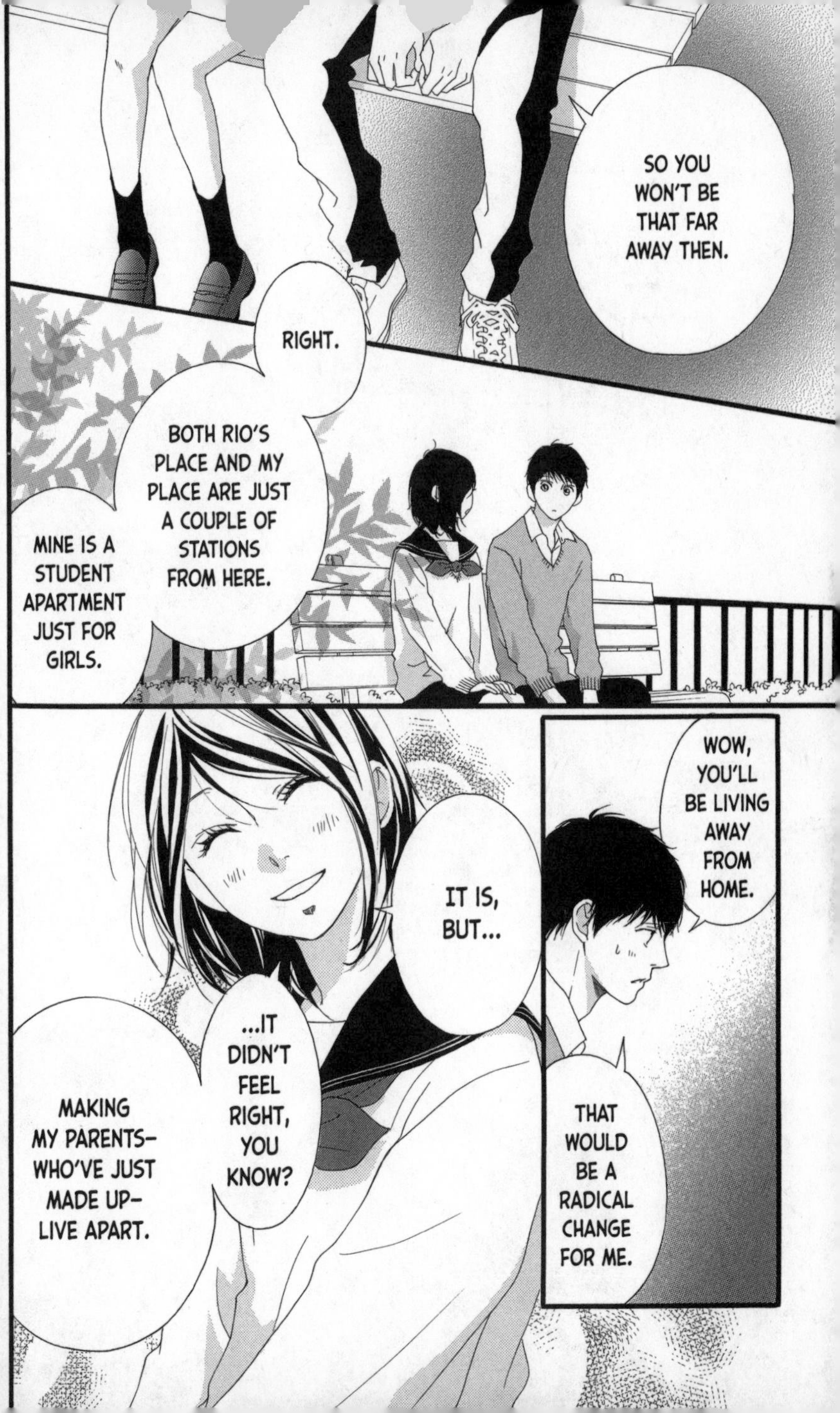
SO YOU WON'T BE THAT FAR AWAY THEN.
RIGHT.
BOTH RIO'S PLACE AND MY PLACE ARE JUST A COUPLE OF STATIONS FROM HERE.
MINE IS A STUDENT APARTMENT JUST FOR GIRLS.
WOW, YOU'LL BE LIVING AWAY FROM HOME.
THAT WOULD BE A RADICAL CHANGE FOR ME.
IT IS, BUT...
...IT DIDN'T FEEL RIGHT, YOU KNOW?
MAKING MY PARENTS—WHO'VE JUST MADE UP—LIVE APART.

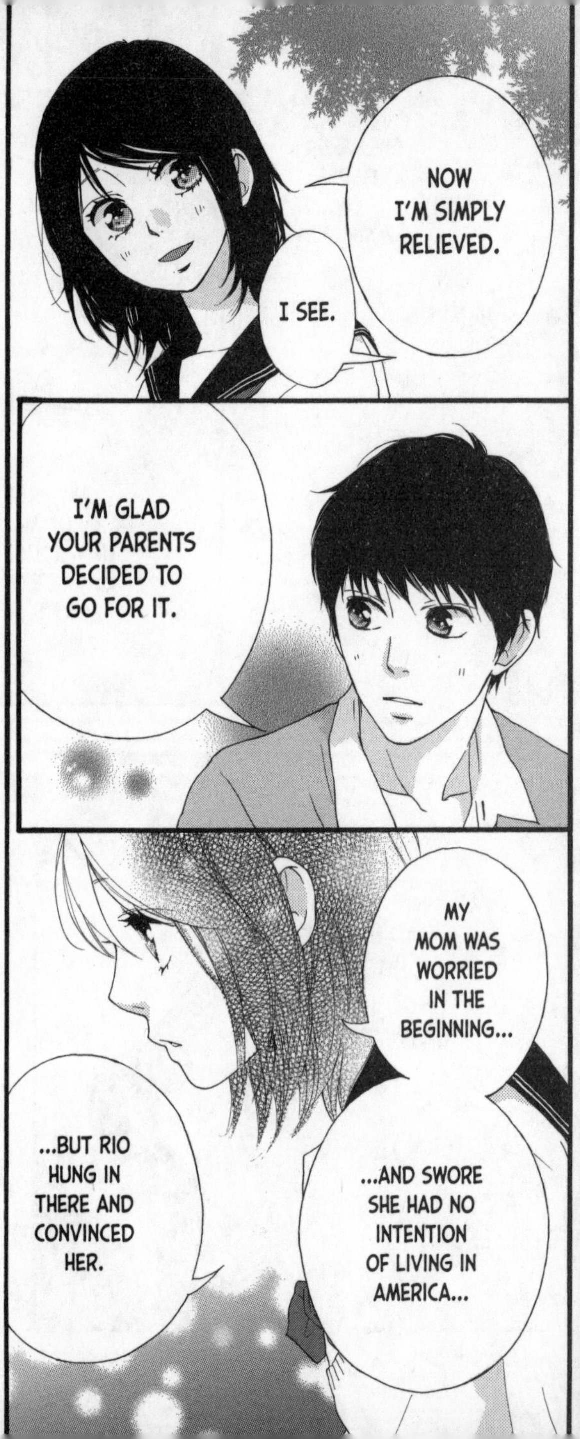
NOW I'M SIMPLY RELIEVED.
I SEE.
I'M GLAD YOUR PARENTS DECIDED TO GO FOR IT.
MY MOM WAS WORRIED IN THE BEGINNING...
...AND SWORE SHE HAD NO INTENTION OF LIVING IN AMERICA...
...BUT RIO HUNG IN THERE AND CONVINCED HER.

(Continued...) F took the lead and guided us using a map app. On the way, YR started worrying and asked, "We've managed to keep the place a secret, but what if she's already been there?" But I'm a world-class shut-in who doesn't know anything about my neighborhood. I swore that it wasn't possible. While we were walking along chatting excitedly, a large white object on a big street came into view. I was thinking, "That's unusual. I wonder if there's something special going on today." As I was looking at it, the door suddenly opened. The white object was a limousine. Why had the door opened? No way... I was completely confused, but F said something, and the driver urged me to get in. All the people who were supposed to have gone ahead were sitting in the limo... (Continues...)

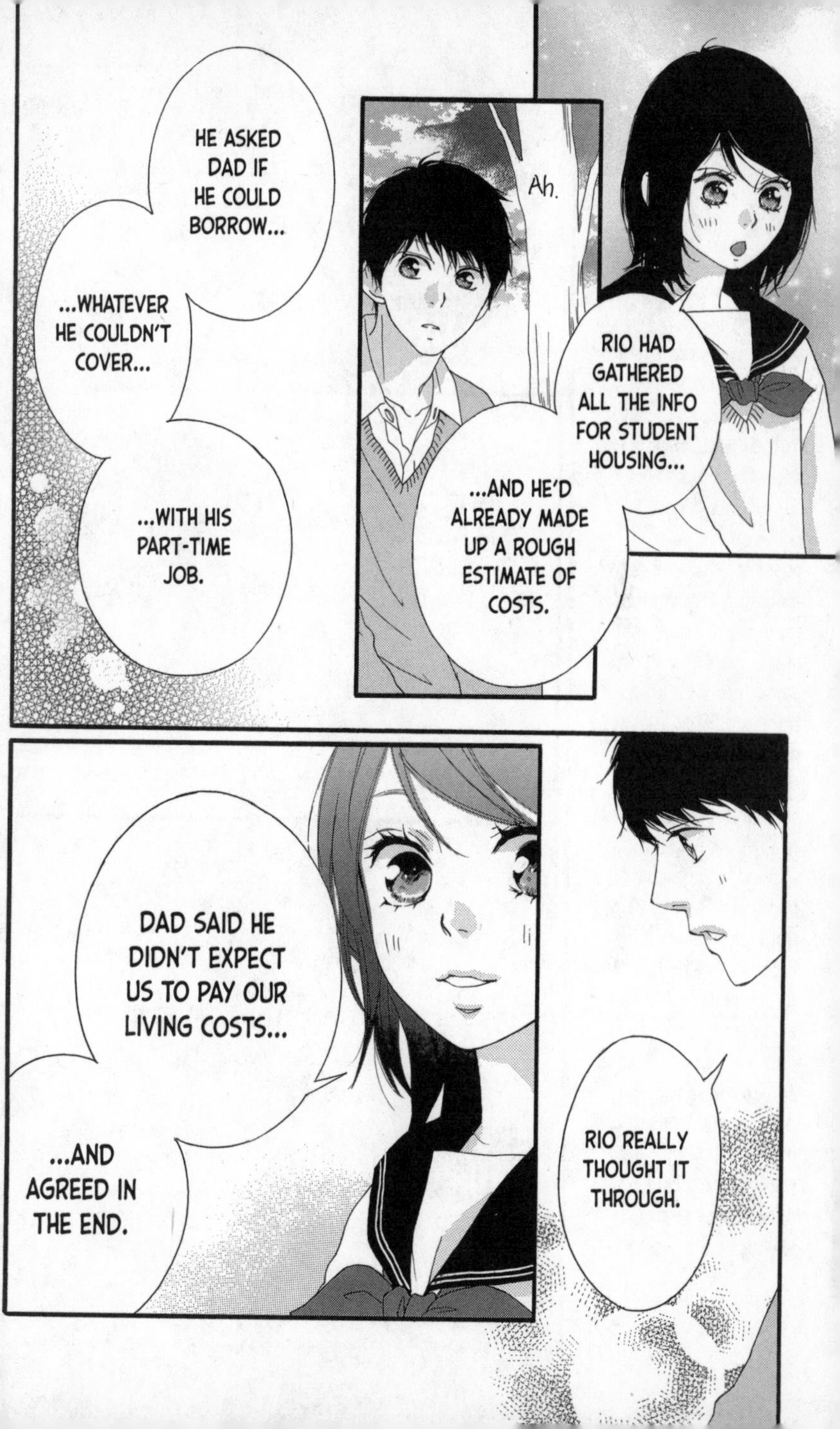
Ah.
RIO HAD GATHERED ALL THE INFO FOR STUDENT HOUSING...
...AND HE'D ALREADY MADE UP A ROUGH ESTIMATE OF COSTS.
HE ASKED DAD IF HE COULD BORROW...
...WHATEVER HE COULDN'T COVER...
...WITH HIS PART-TIME JOB.
RIO REALLY THOUGHT IT THROUGH.
DAD SAID HE DIDN'T EXPECT US TO PAY OUR LIVING COSTS...
...AND AGREED IN THE END.

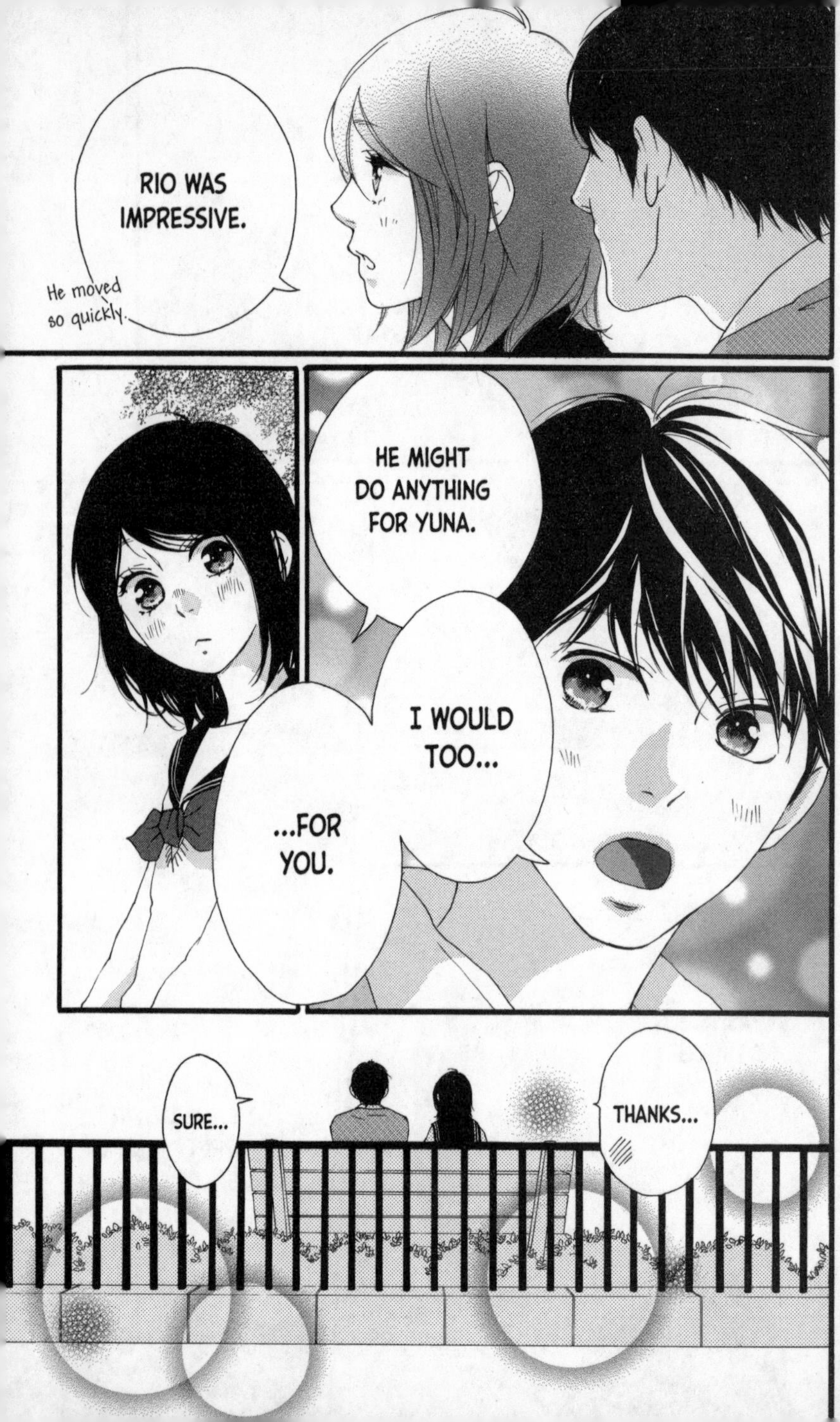
RIO WAS IMPRESSIVE.
He moved so quickly.
HE MIGHT DO ANYTHING FOR YUNA.
I WOULD TOO...
...FOR YOU.
THANKS...
SURE...

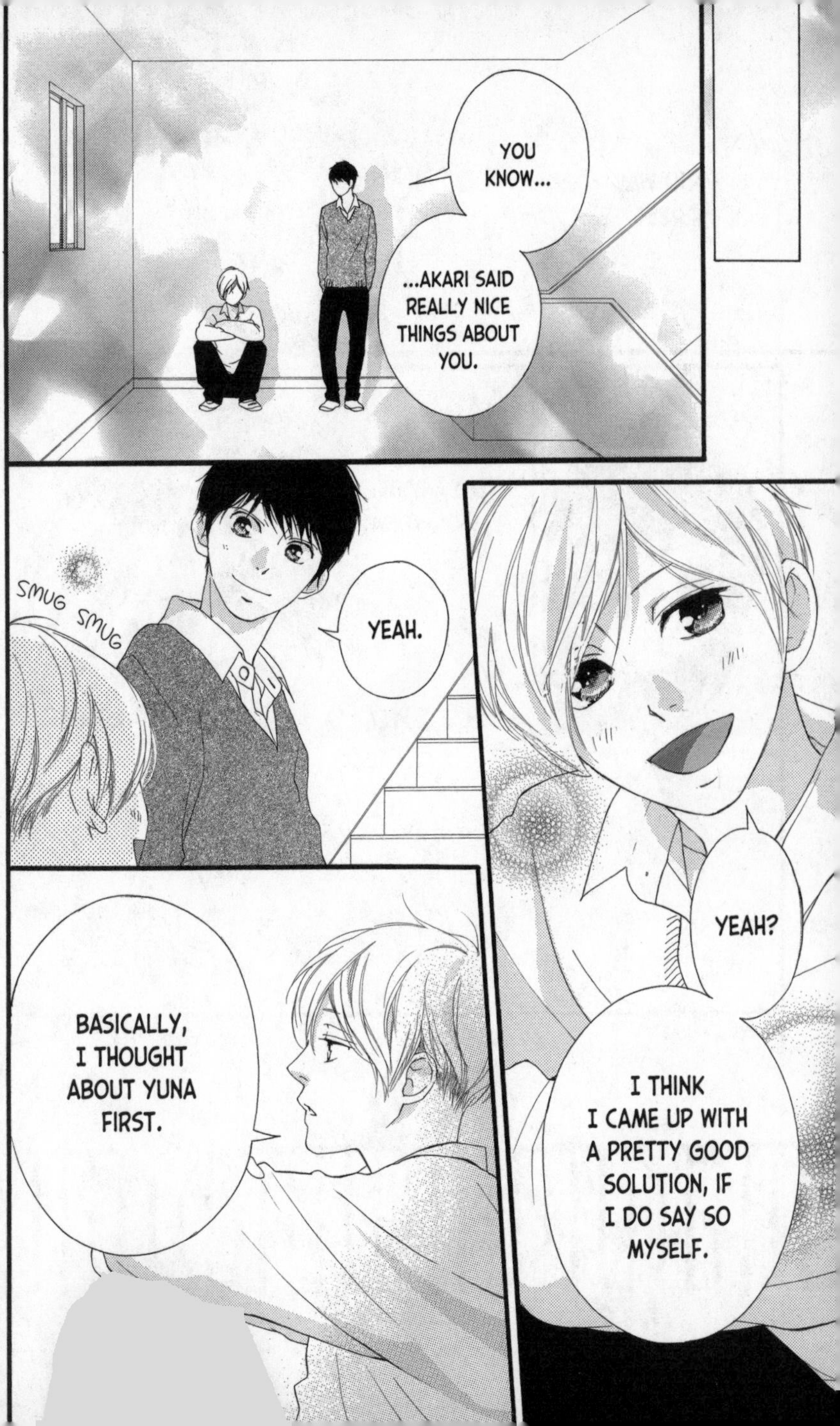
YOU KNOW...
...AKARI SAID REALLY NICE THINGS ABOUT YOU.
YEAH?
I THINK I CAME UP WITH A PRETTY GOOD SOLUTION, IF I DO SAY SO MYSELF.
YEAH.
SMUG SMUG
BASICALLY, I THOUGHT ABOUT YUNA FIRST.

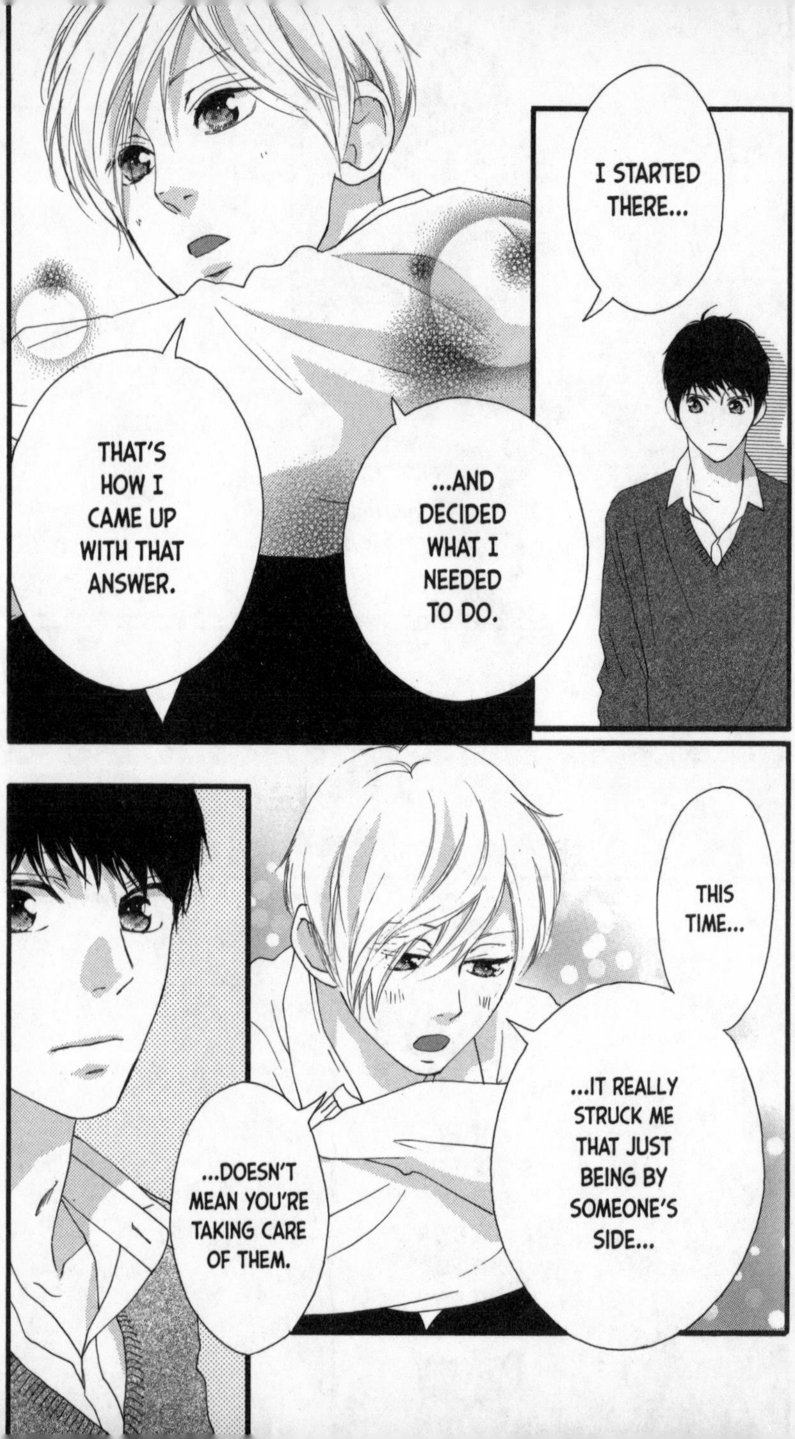
I STARTED THERE...
...AND DECIDED WHAT I NEEDED TO DO.
THAT'S HOW I CAME UP WITH THAT ANSWER.
THIS TIME...
...IT REALLY STRUCK ME THAT JUST BEING BY SOMEONE'S SIDE...
...DOESN'T MEAN YOU'RE TAKING CARE OF THEM.

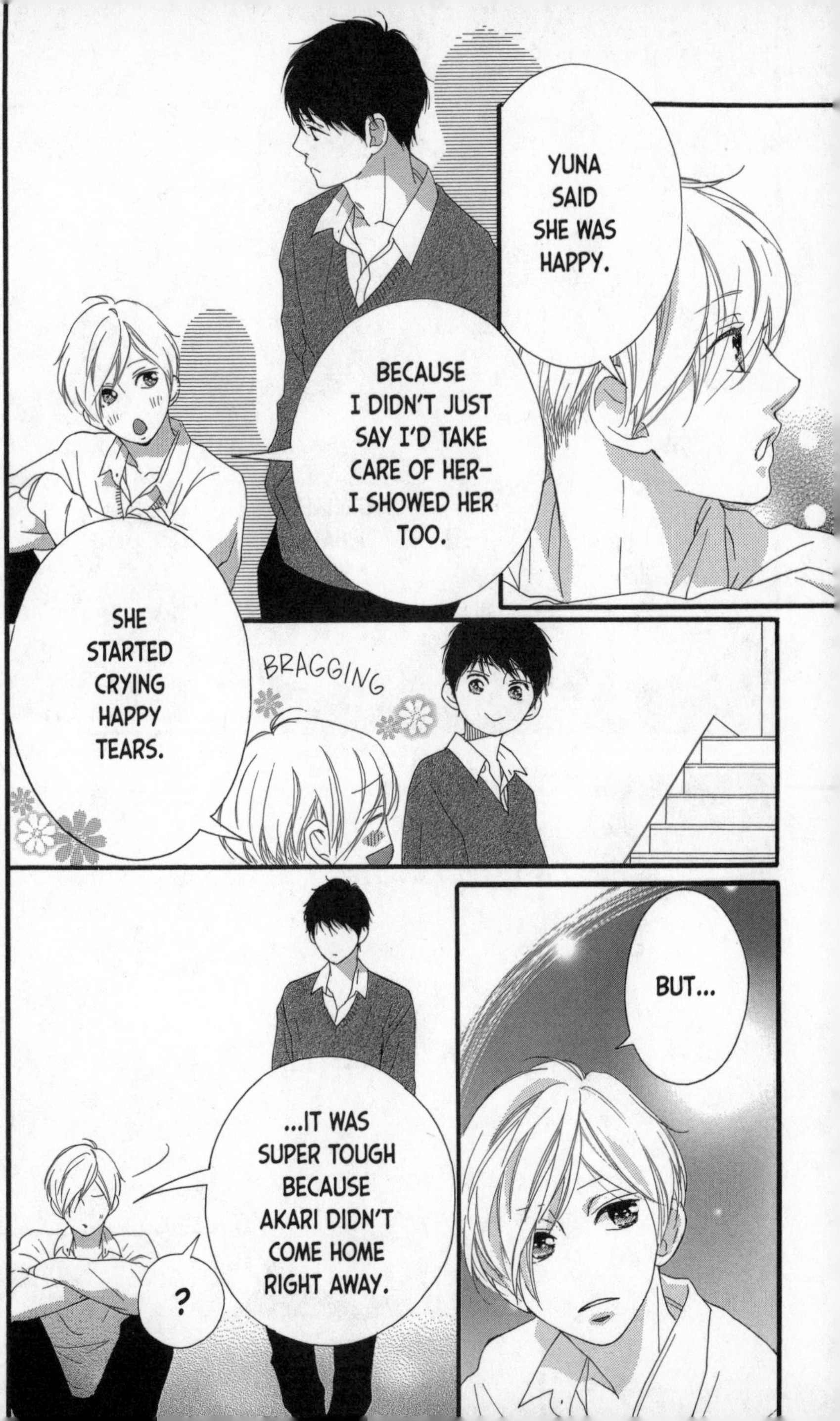
YUNA SAID SHE WAS HAPPY.
BECAUSE I DIDN'T JUST SAY I'D TAKE CARE OF HER— I SHOWED HER TOO.
SHE STARTED CRYING HAPPY TEARS.
BRAGGING
BUT...
...IT WAS SUPER TOUGH BECAUSE AKARI DIDN'T COME HOME RIGHT AWAY.
?

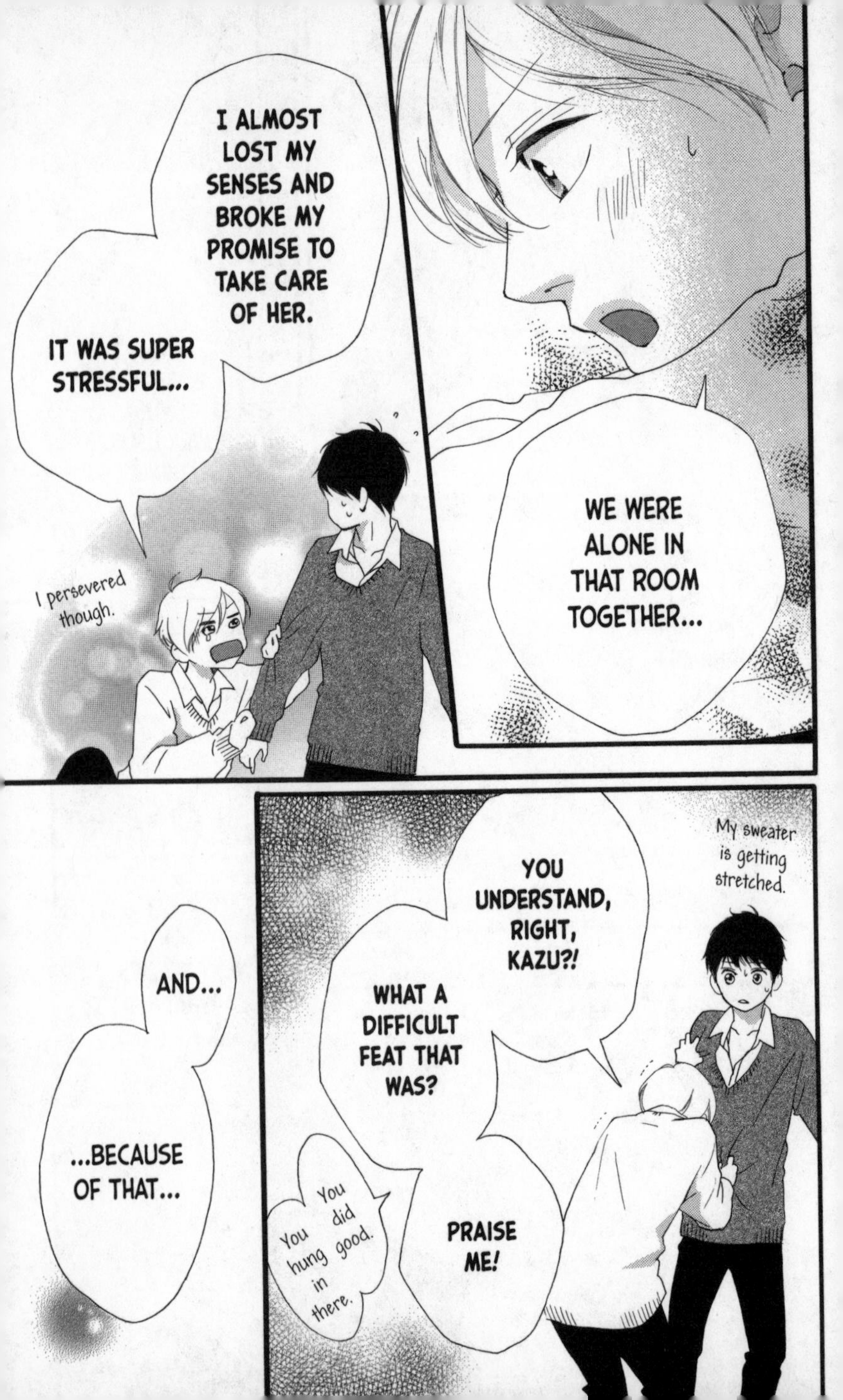
WE WERE ALONE IN THAT ROOM TOGETHER...
I ALMOST LOST MY SENSES AND BROKE MY PROMISE TO TAKE CARE OF HER.
IT WAS SUPER STRESSFUL...
I persevered though.
My sweater is getting stretched.
YOU UNDERSTAND, RIGHT, KAZU?!
WHAT A DIFFICULT FEAT THAT WAS?
PRAISE ME!
You did good. You hung in there.
AND...
...BECAUSE OF THAT...

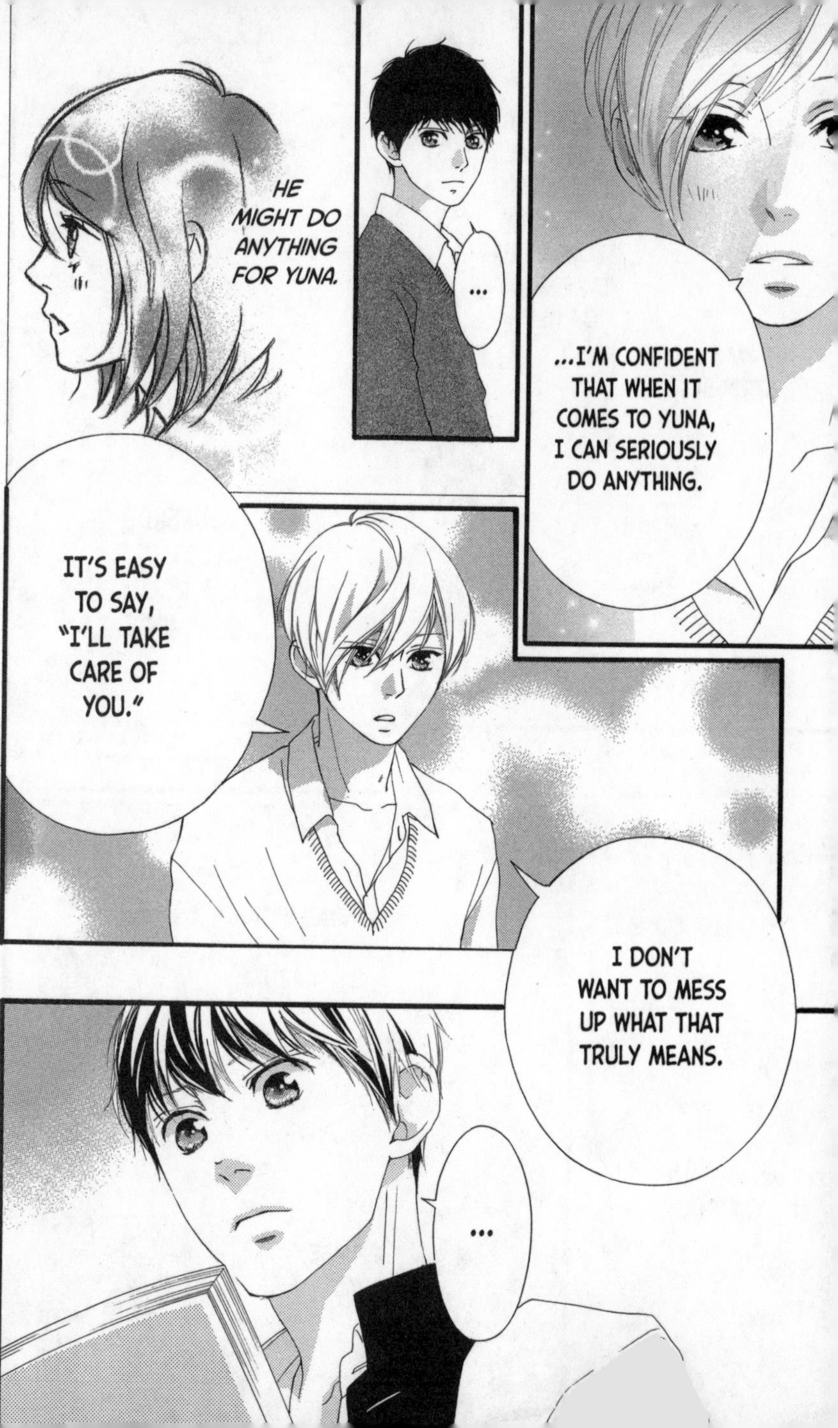
...I'M CONFIDENT THAT WHEN IT COMES TO YUNA, I CAN SERIOUSLY DO ANYTHING.
...
HE MIGHT DO ANYTHING FOR YUNA.
IT'S EASY TO SAY, "I'LL TAKE CARE OF YOU."
I DON'T WANT TO MESS UP WHAT THAT TRULY MEANS.
...

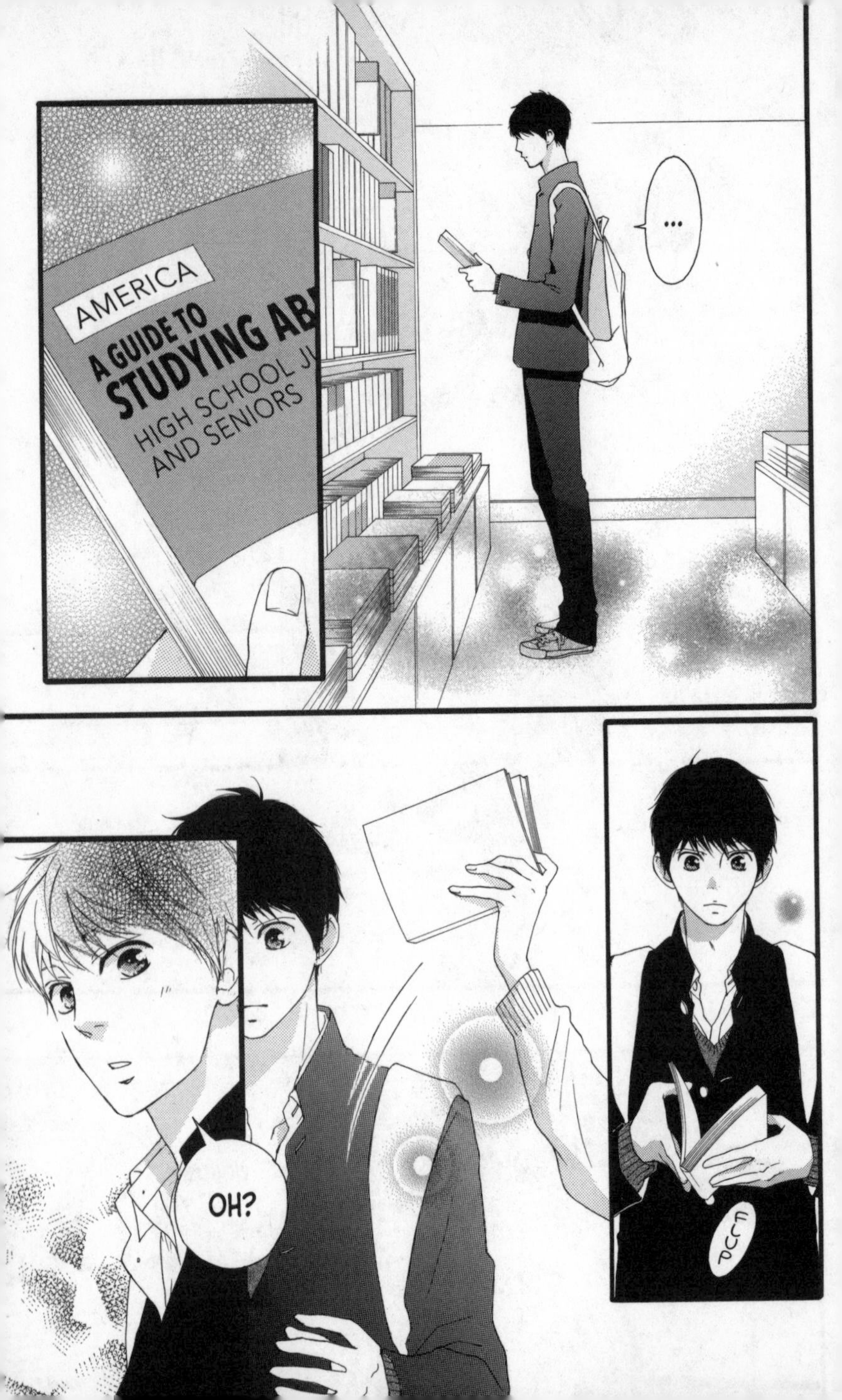
…
AMERICA
A GUIDE TO STUDYING AB
HIGH SCHOOL JU
AND SENIORS
FLIP
OH?

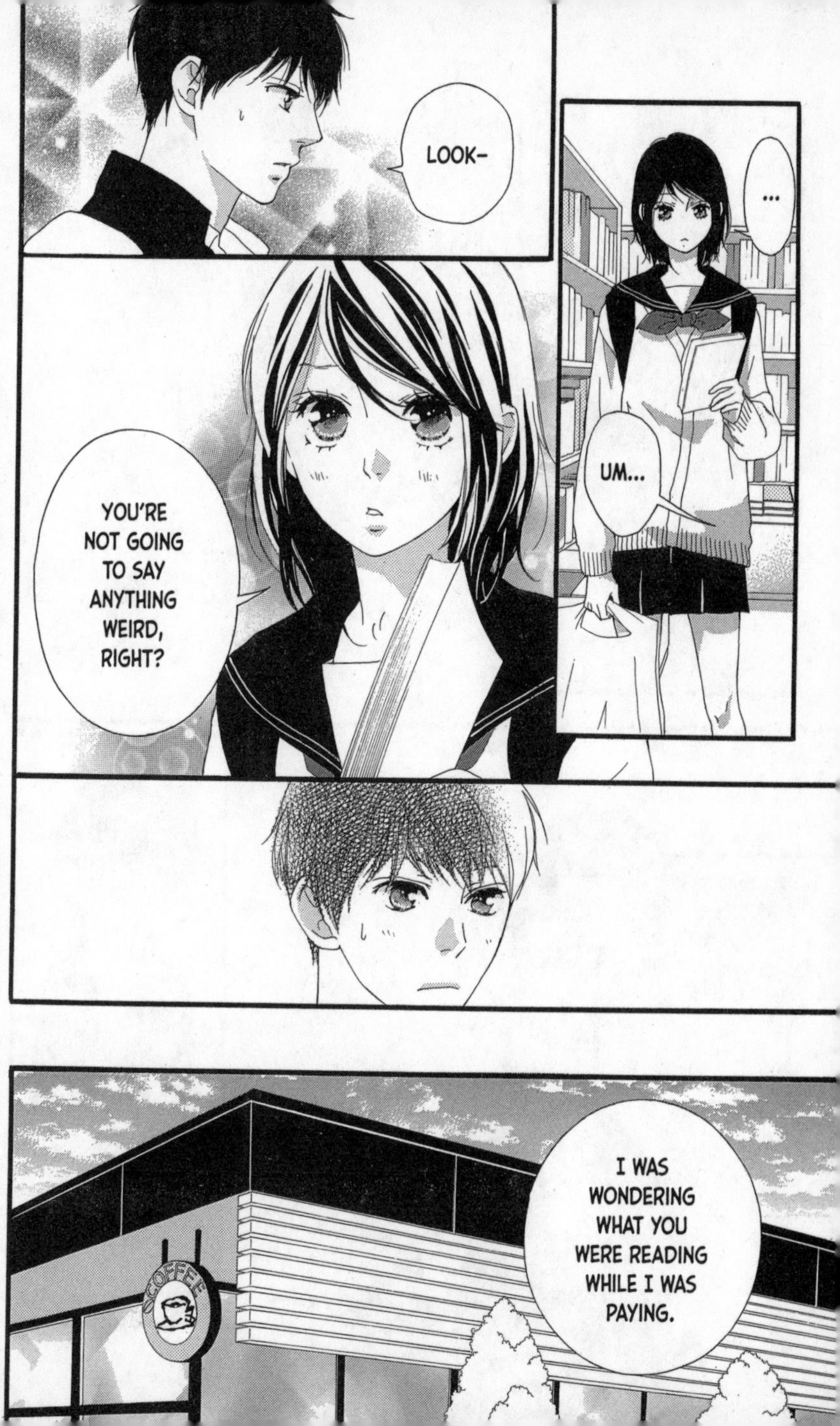
...
UM...
LOOK-
YOU'RE NOT GOING TO SAY ANYTHING WEIRD, RIGHT?
COFFEE
I WAS WONDERING WHAT YOU WERE READING WHILE I WAS PAYING.

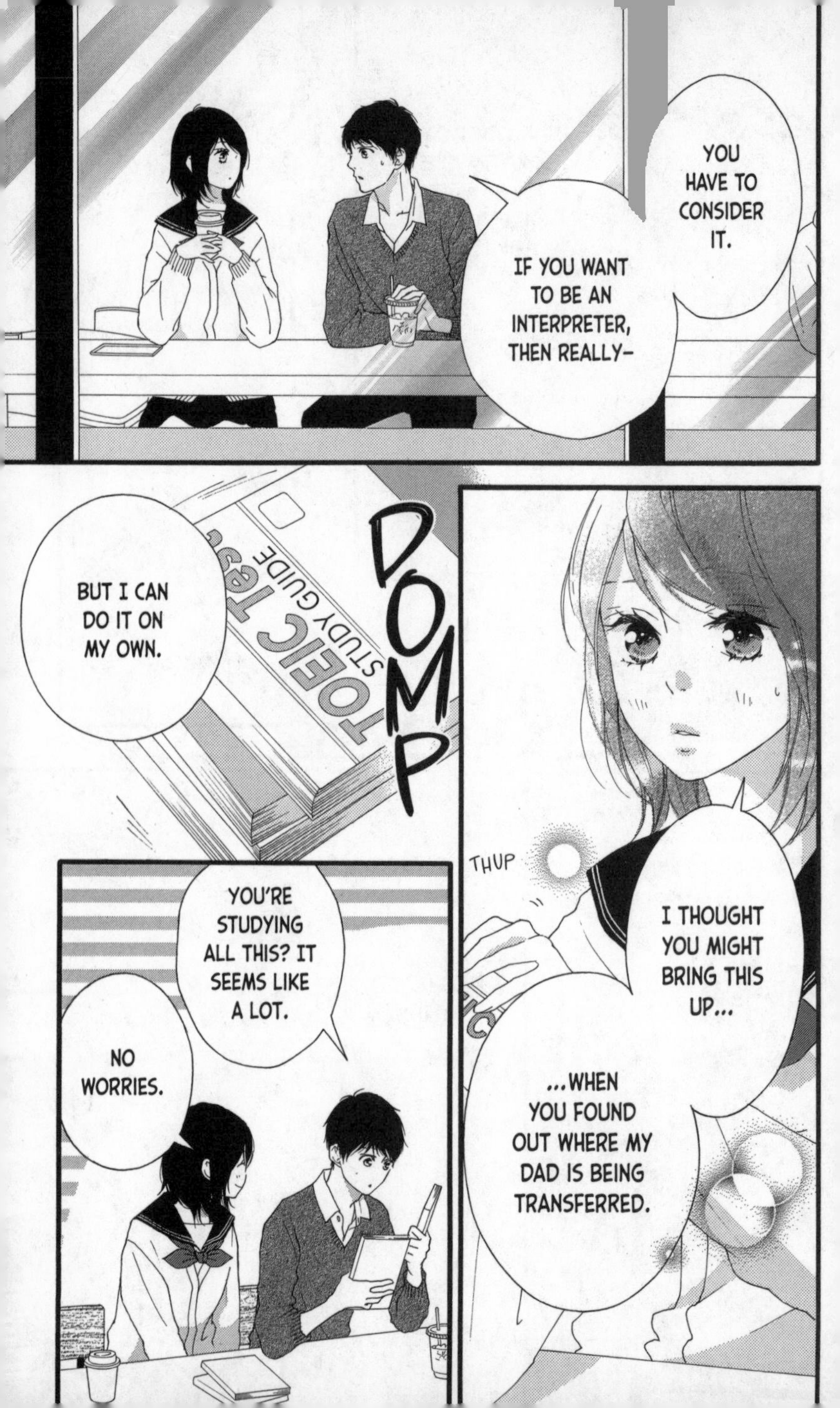
YOU HAVE TO CONSIDER IT.
IF YOU WANT TO BE AN INTERPRETER, THEN REALLY—
THUP
I THOUGHT YOU MIGHT BRING THIS UP...
...WHEN YOU FOUND OUT WHERE MY DAD IS BEING TRANSFERRED.
DOMP
TOEIC
STUDY GUIDE
BUT I CAN DO IT ON MY OWN.
YOU'RE STUDYING ALL THIS? IT SEEMS LIKE A LOT.
NO WORRIES.

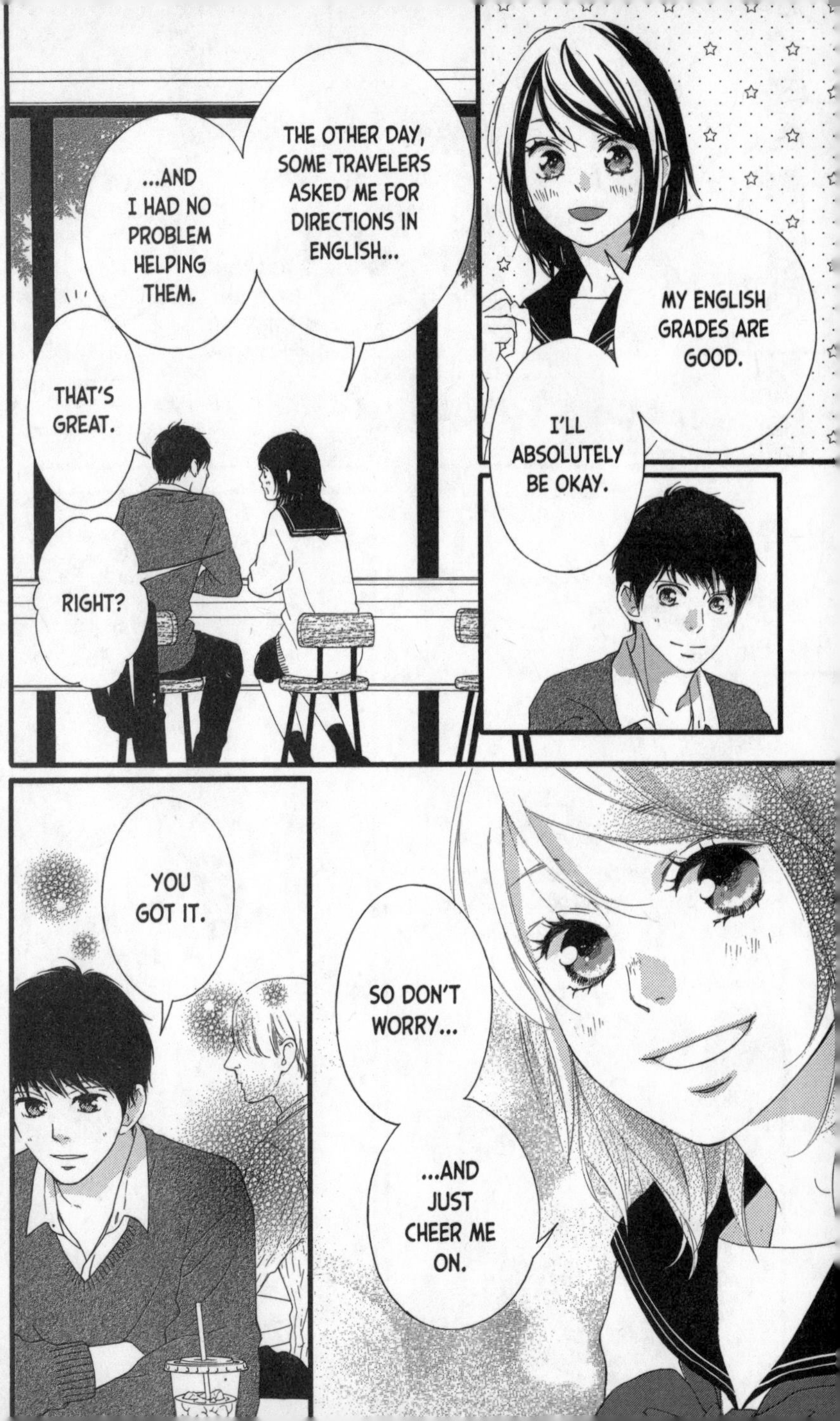
MY ENGLISH GRADES ARE GOOD.
I'LL ABSOLUTELY BE OKAY.
THE OTHER DAY, SOME TRAVELERS ASKED ME FOR DIRECTIONS IN ENGLISH...
...AND I HAD NO PROBLEM HELPING THEM.
THAT'S GREAT.
RIGHT?
SO DON'T WORRY...
...AND JUST CHEER ME ON.
YOU GOT IT.

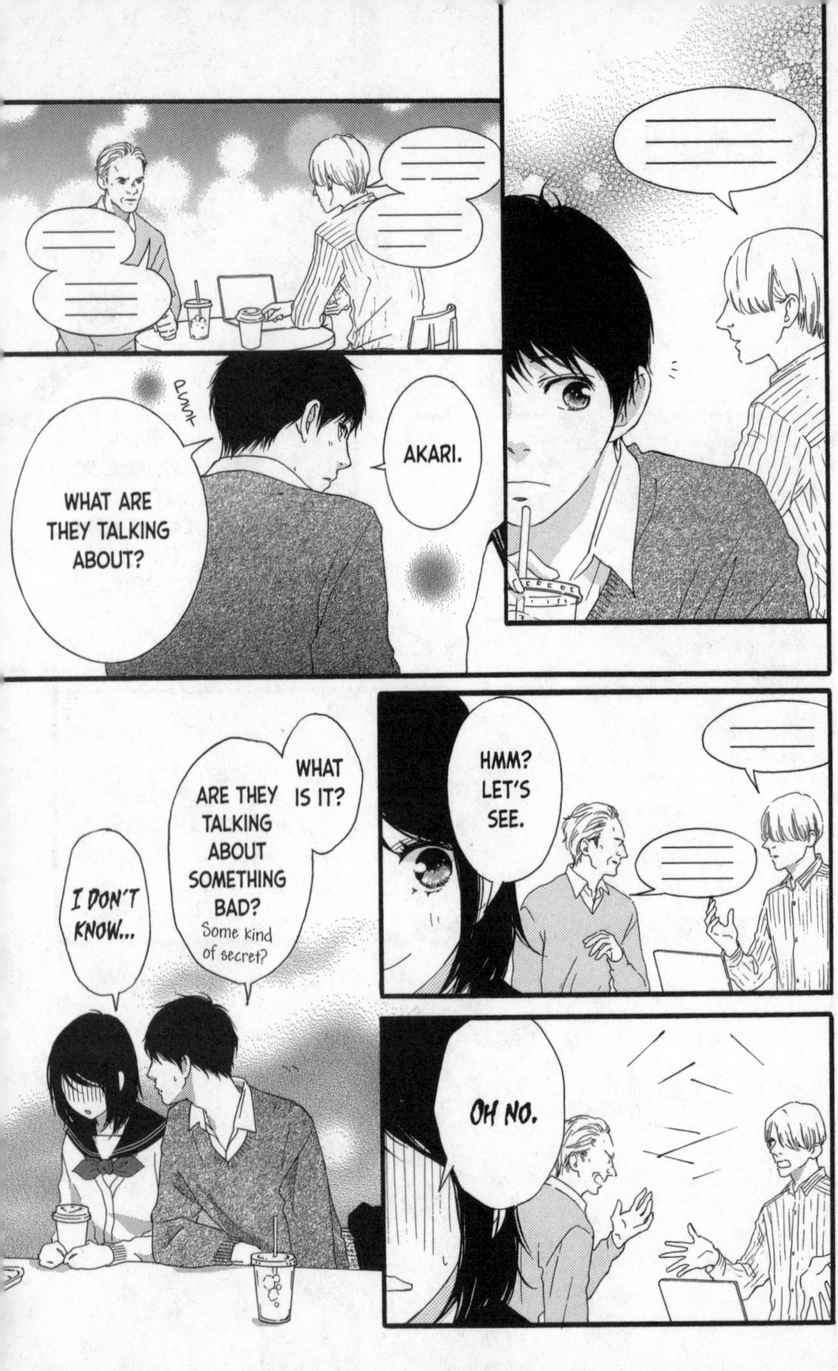
AKARI.
WHAT ARE THEY TALKING ABOUT?
HMM? LET'S SEE.
OH NO.
WHAT IS IT?
ARE THEY TALKING ABOUT SOMETHING BAD? Some kind of secret?
I DON'T KNOW...

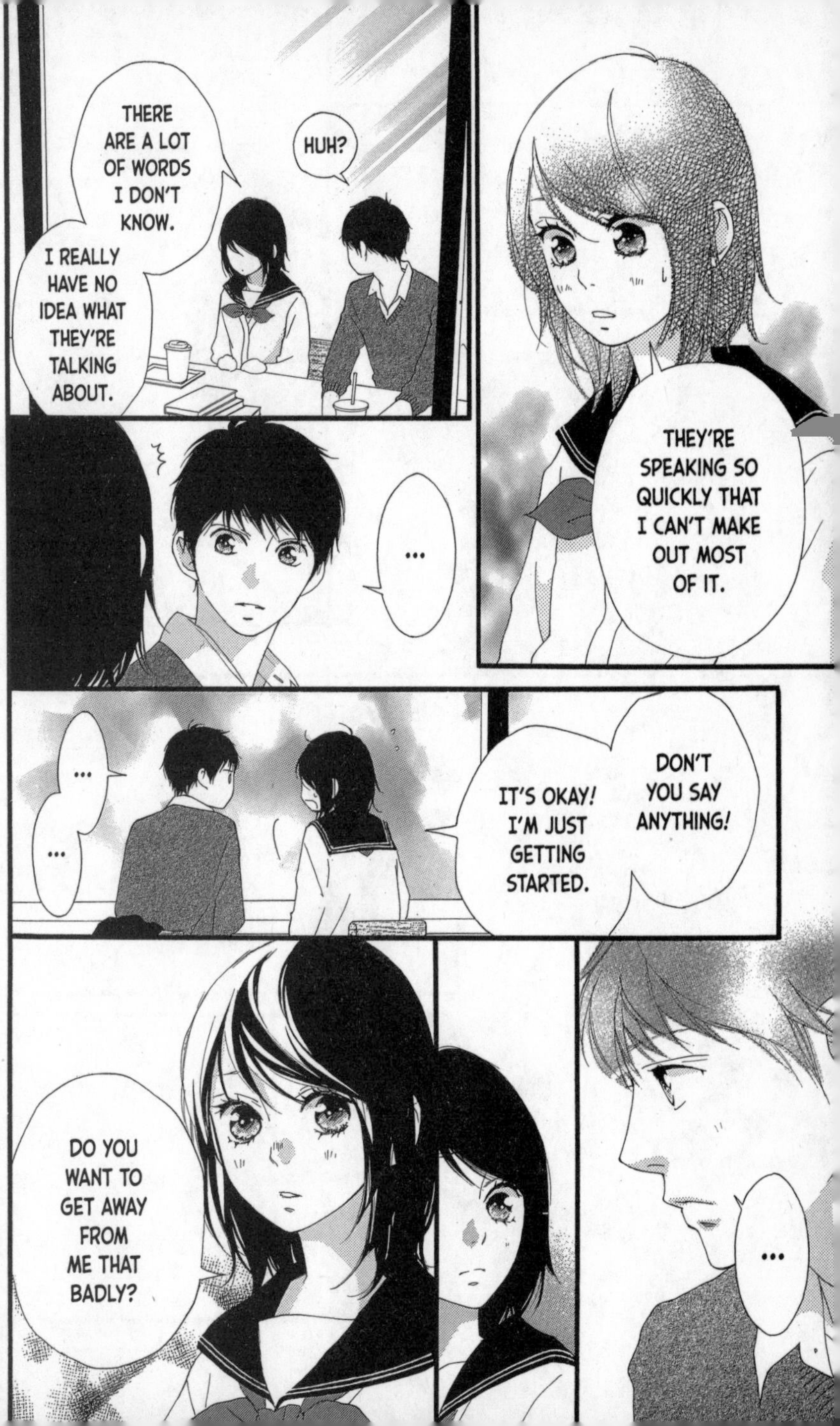
THEY'RE SPEAKING SO QUICKLY THAT I CAN'T MAKE OUT MOST OF IT.
THERE ARE A LOT OF WORDS I DON'T KNOW.
HUH?
I REALLY HAVE NO IDEA WHAT THEY'RE TALKING ABOUT.
...
DON'T YOU SAY ANYTHING!
IT'S OKAY! I'M JUST GETTING STARTED.
...
...
...
DO YOU WANT TO GET AWAY FROM ME THAT BADLY?

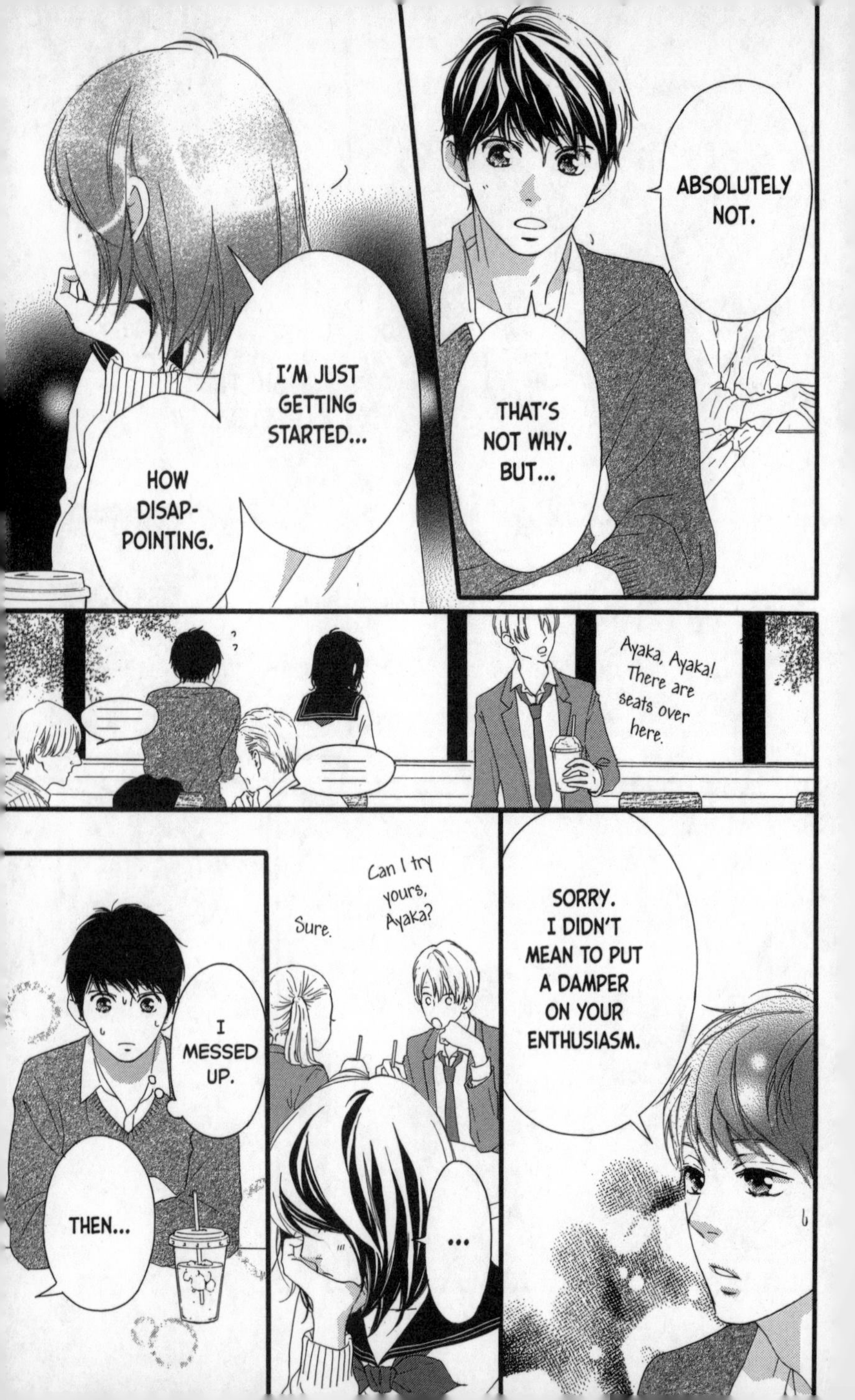
ABSOLUTELY NOT.
THAT'S NOT WHY. BUT...
I'M JUST GETTING STARTED...
HOW DISAP-POINTING.
Ayaka, Ayaka! There are seats over here.
SORRY. I DIDN'T MEAN TO PUT A DAMPER ON YOUR ENTHUSIASM.
Can I try yours, Ayaka?
Sure.
...
I MESSED UP.
THEN...

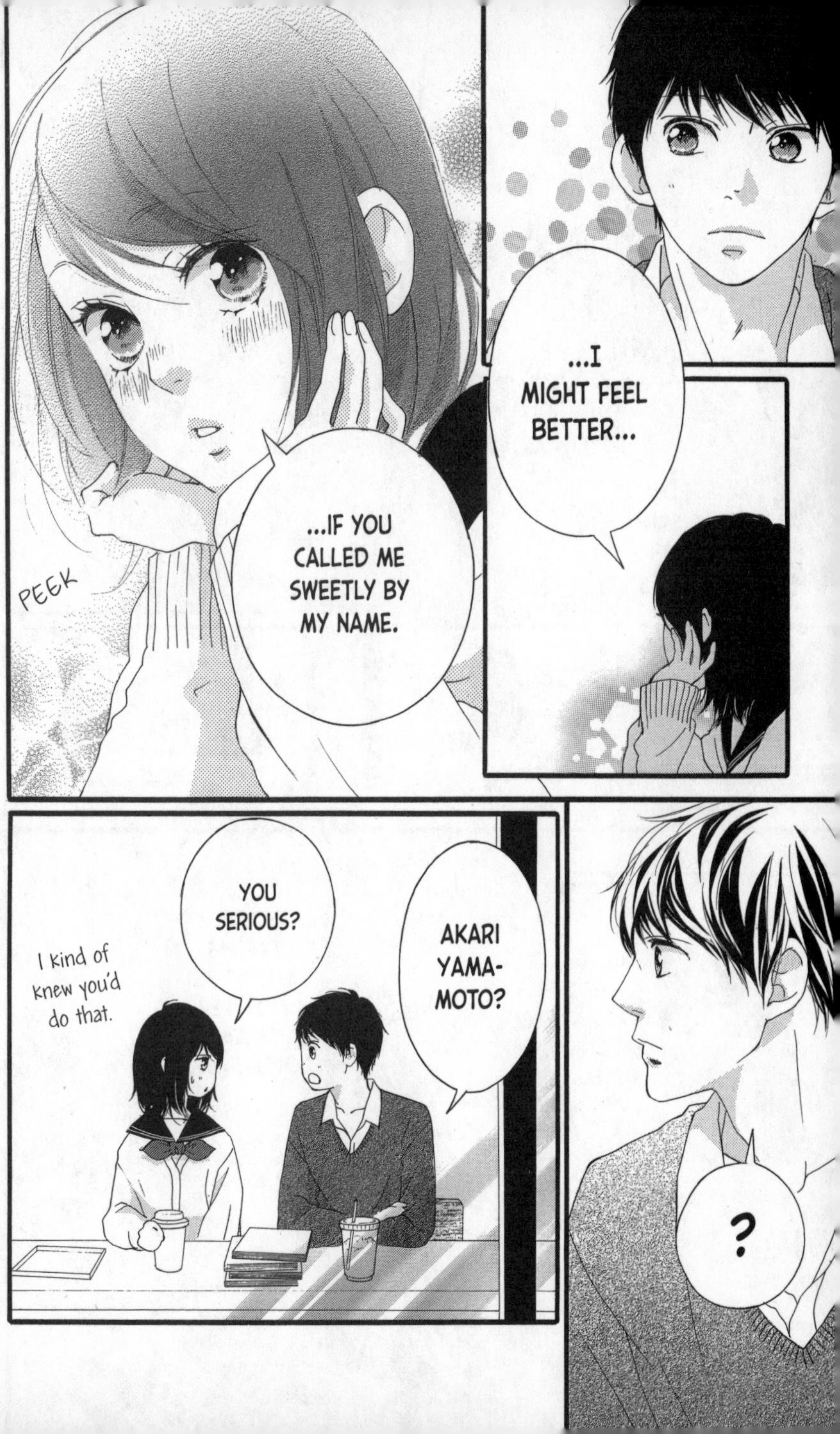
...I MIGHT FEEL BETTER...
...IF YOU CALLED ME SWEETLY BY MY NAME.
PEEK
?
AKARI YAMA-MOTO?
YOU SERIOUS?
I kind of knew you'd do that.

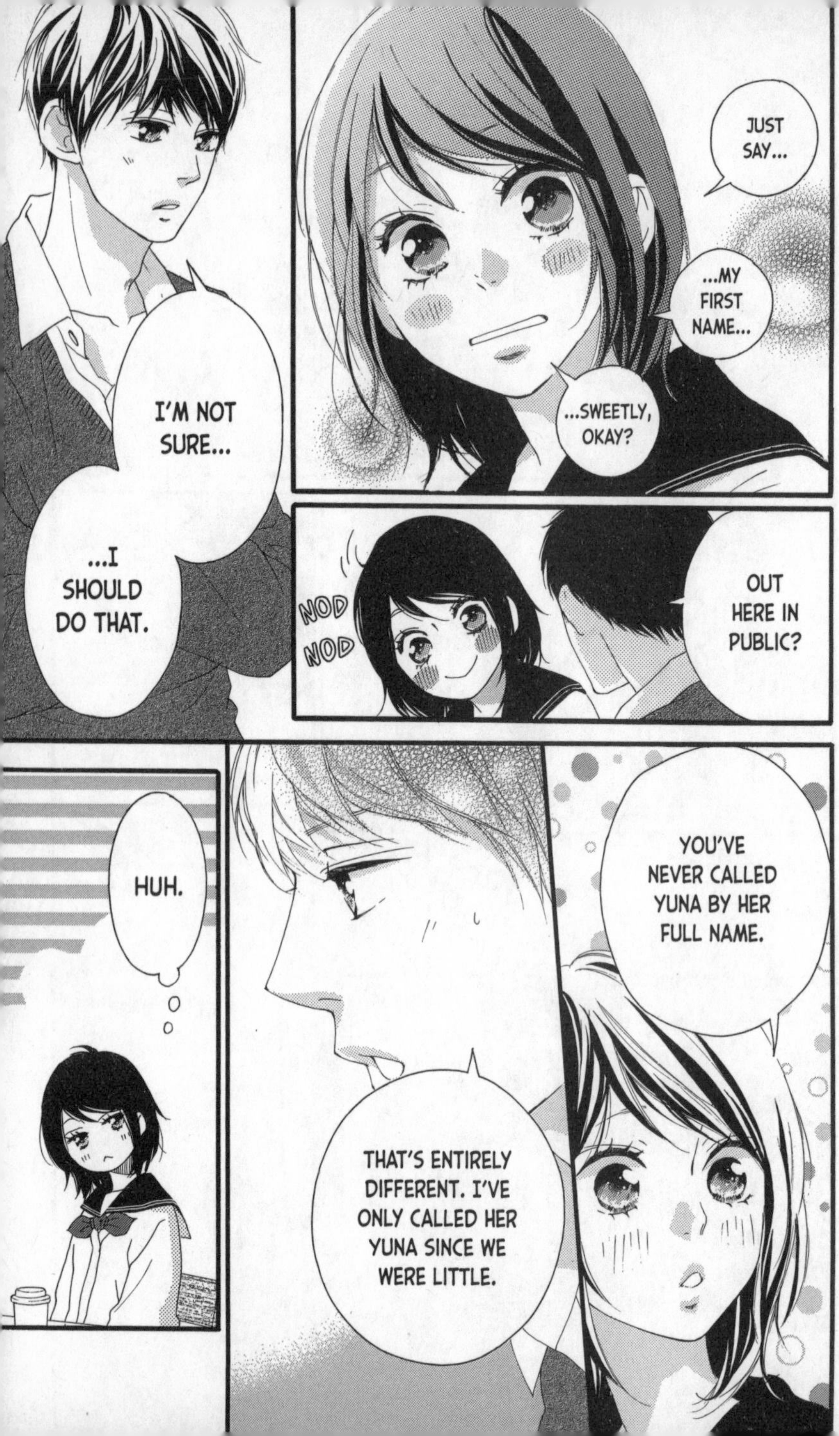
JUST SAY...
...MY FIRST NAME...
...SWEETLY, OKAY?
OUT HERE IN PUBLIC?
NOD NOD
I'M NOT SURE...
...I SHOULD DO THAT.
YOU'VE NEVER CALLED YUNA BY HER FULL NAME.
THAT'S ENTIRELY DIFFERENT. I'VE ONLY CALLED HER YUNA SINCE WE WERE LITTLE.
HUH.

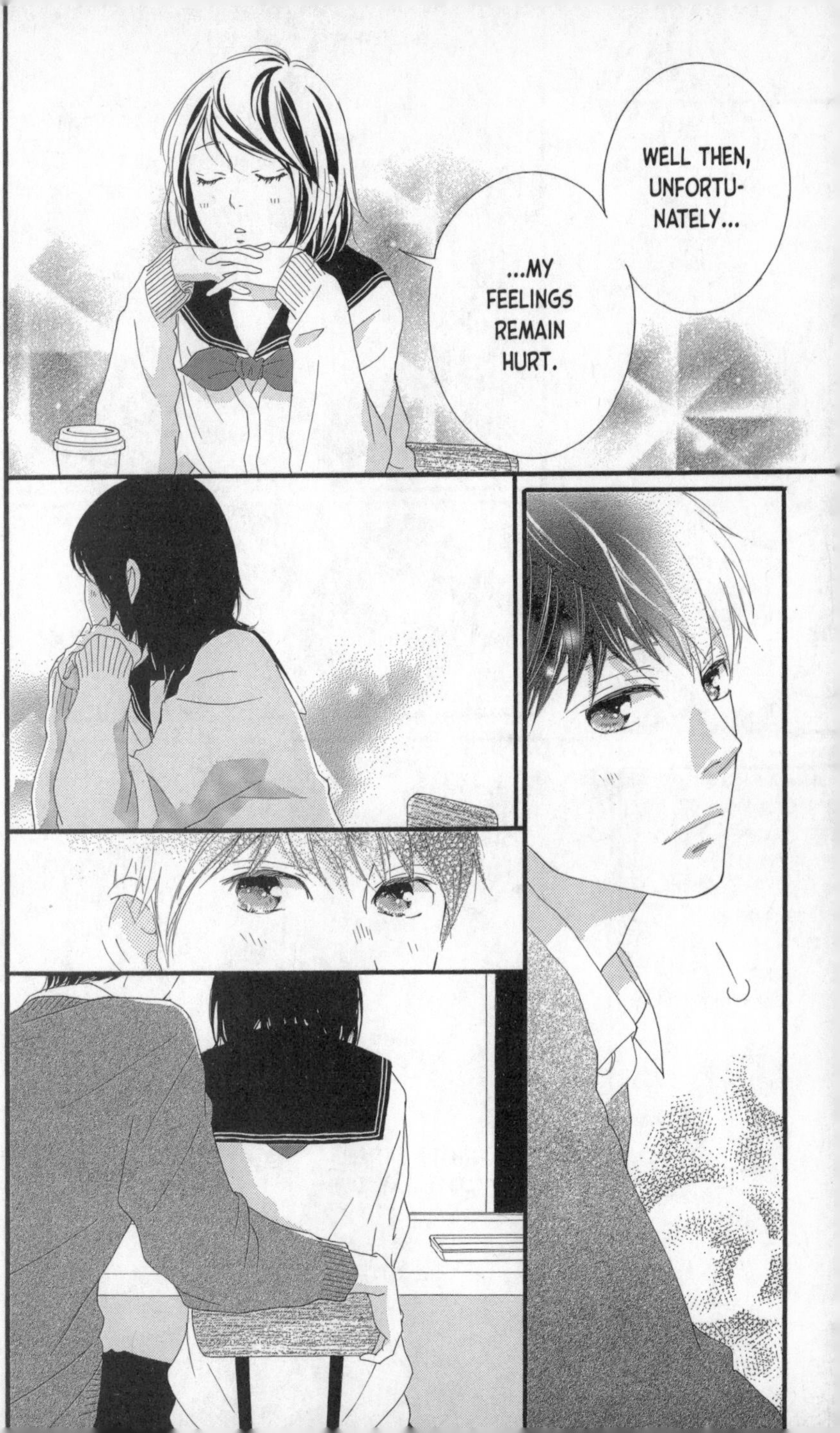
WELL THEN, UNFORTU- NATELY...
...MY FEELINGS REMAIN HURT.

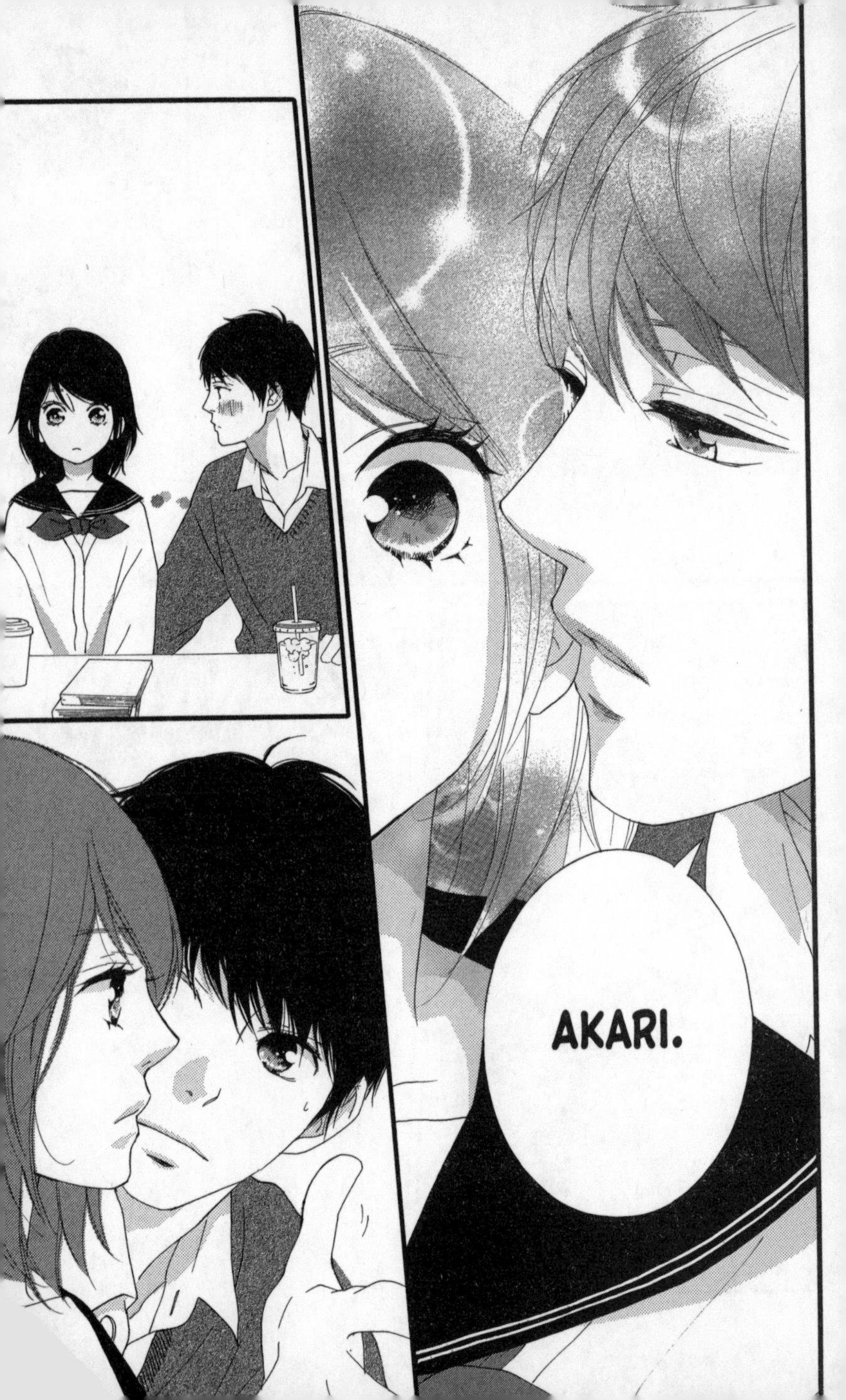
AKARI.

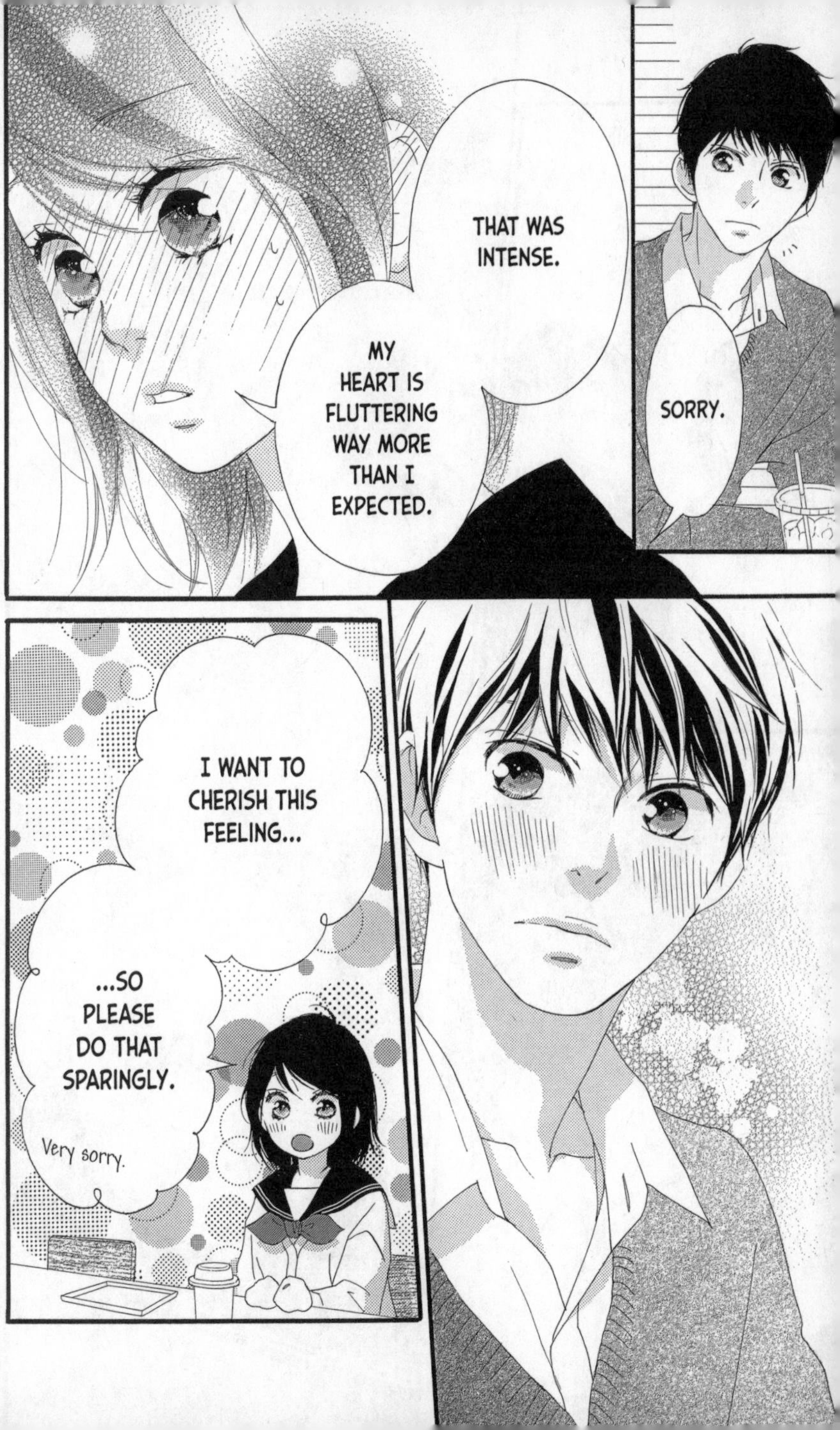
SORRY.
THAT WAS INTENSE.
MY HEART IS FLUTTERING WAY MORE THAN I EXPECTED.
I WANT TO CHERISH THIS FEELING...
...SO PLEASE DO THAT SPARINGLY.
Very sorry.

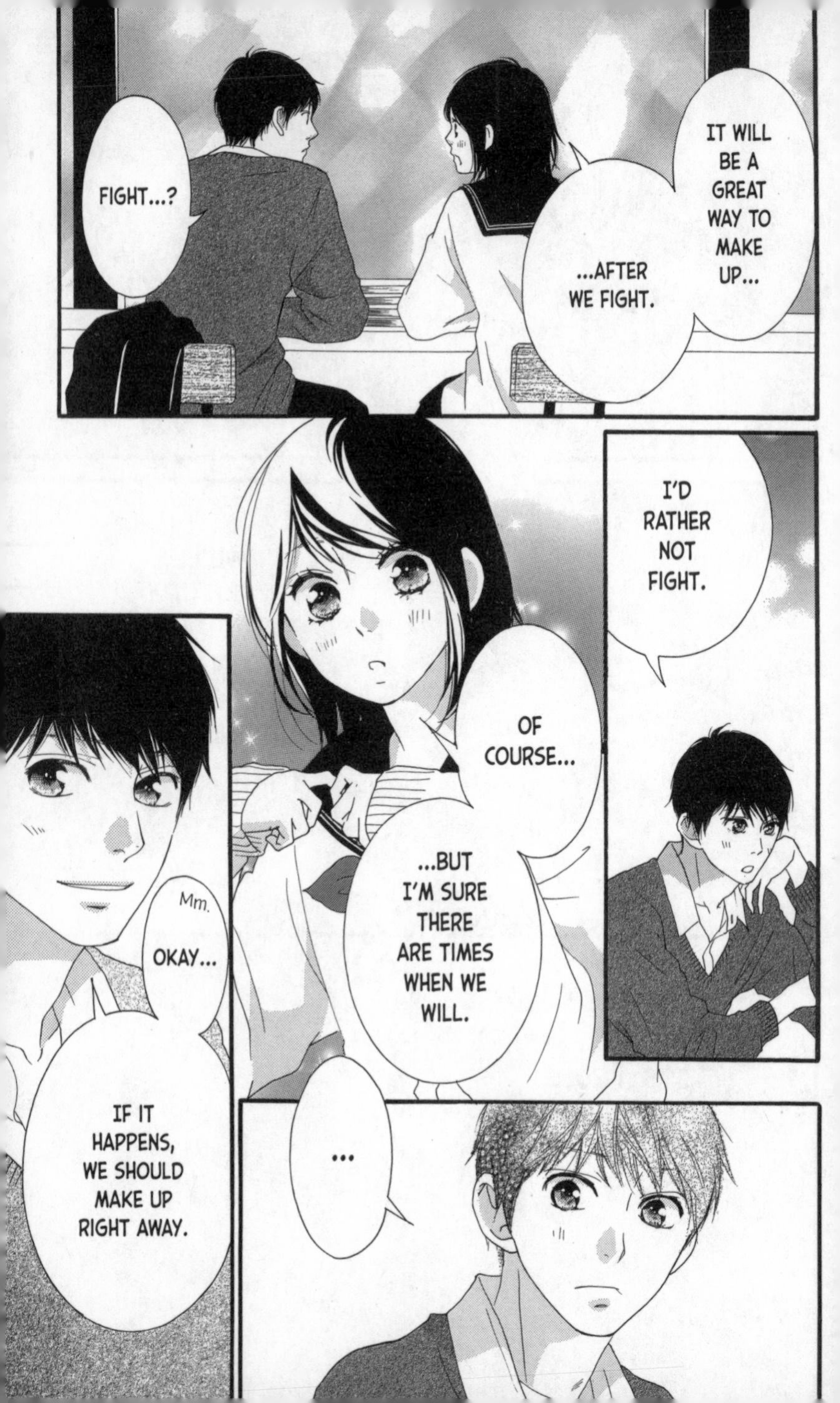
IT WILL BE A GREAT WAY TO MAKE UP...
...AFTER WE FIGHT.
FIGHT...?
I'D RATHER NOT FIGHT.
OF COURSE...
...BUT I'M SURE THERE ARE TIMES WHEN WE WILL.
Mm.
OKAY...
IF IT HAPPENS, WE SHOULD MAKE UP RIGHT AWAY.
...

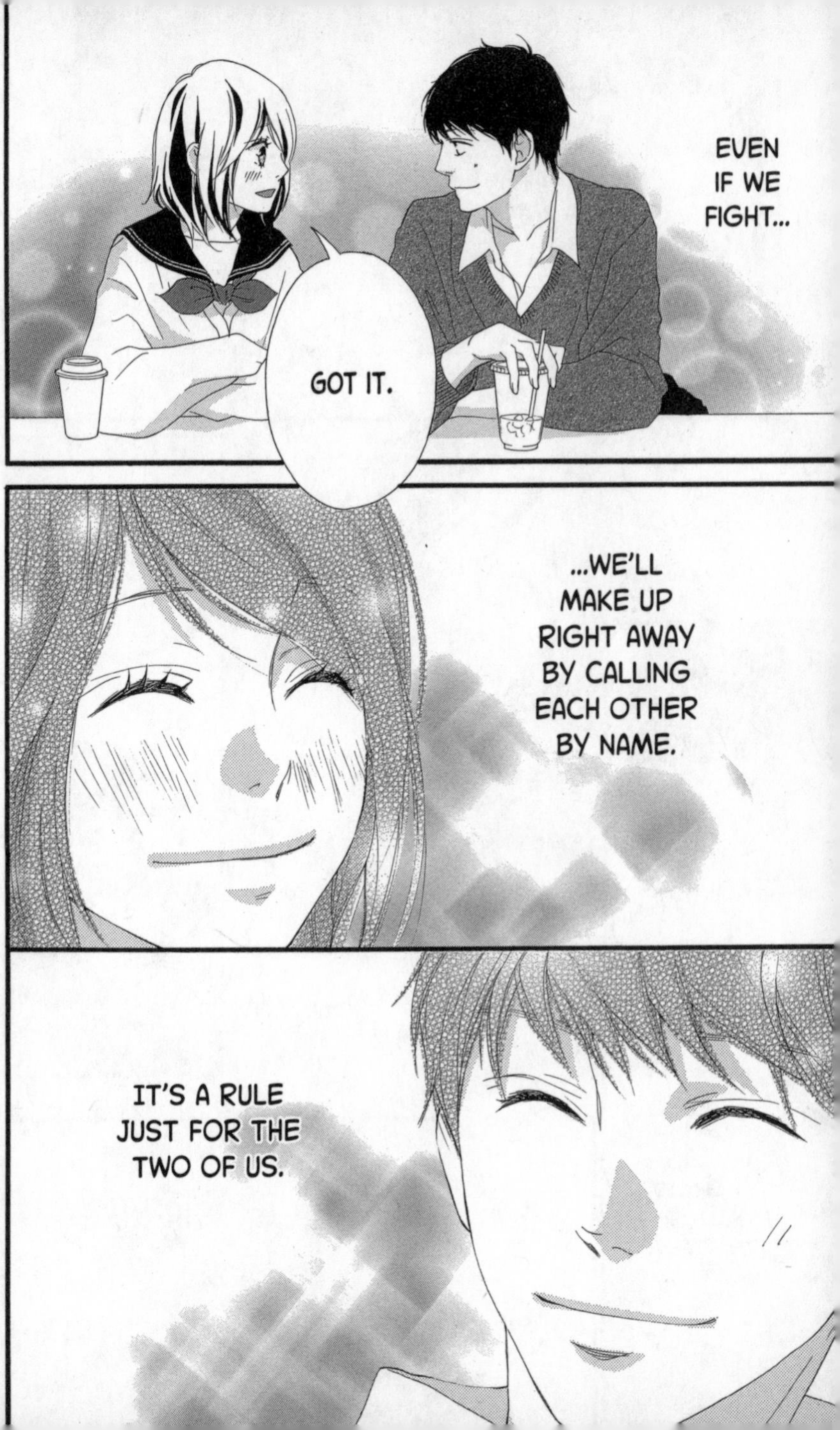
EVEN IF WE FIGHT...
GOT IT.
...WE'LL MAKE UP RIGHT AWAY BY CALLING EACH OTHER BY NAME.
IT'S A RULE JUST FOR THE TWO OF US.

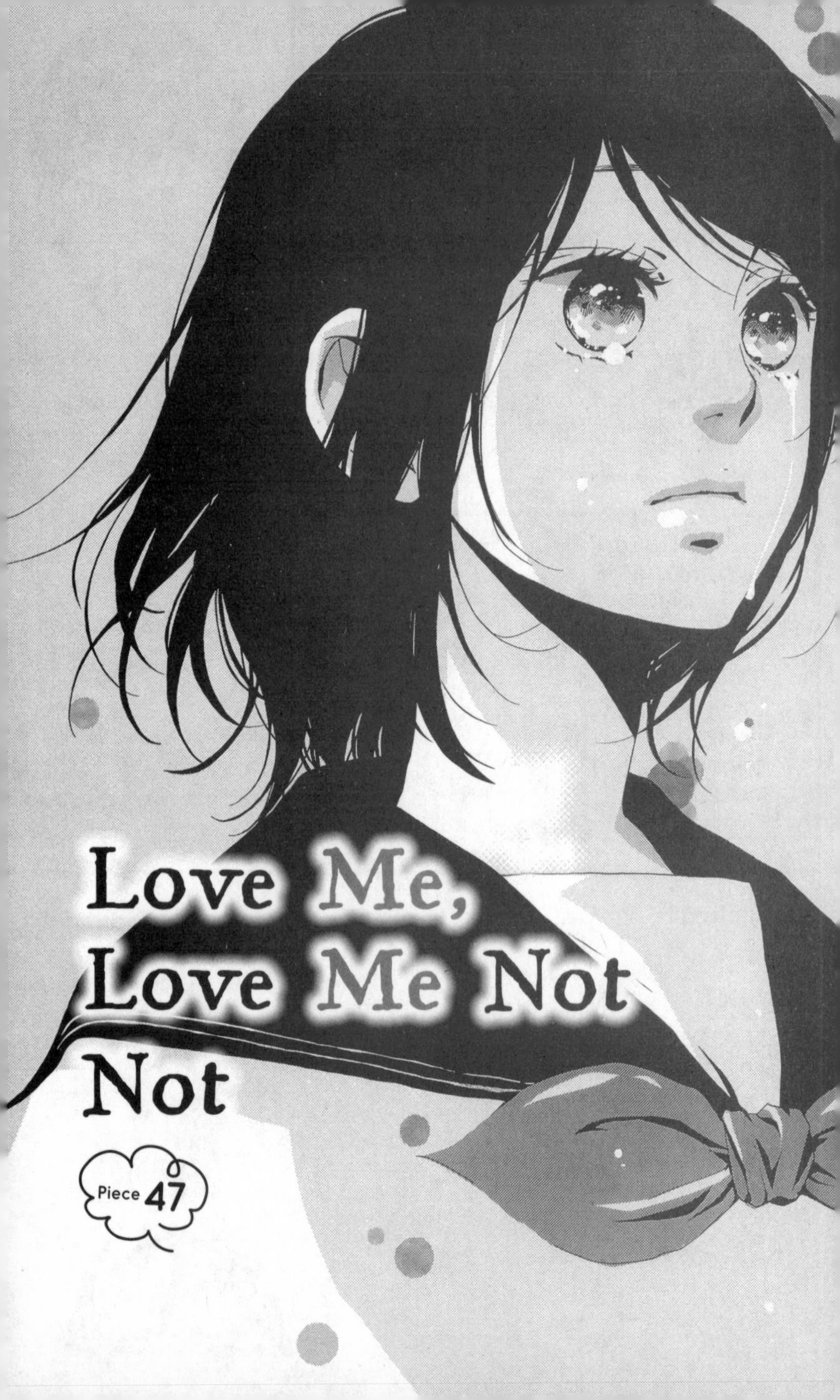
Love Me,
Love Me Not
Not
Piece 47

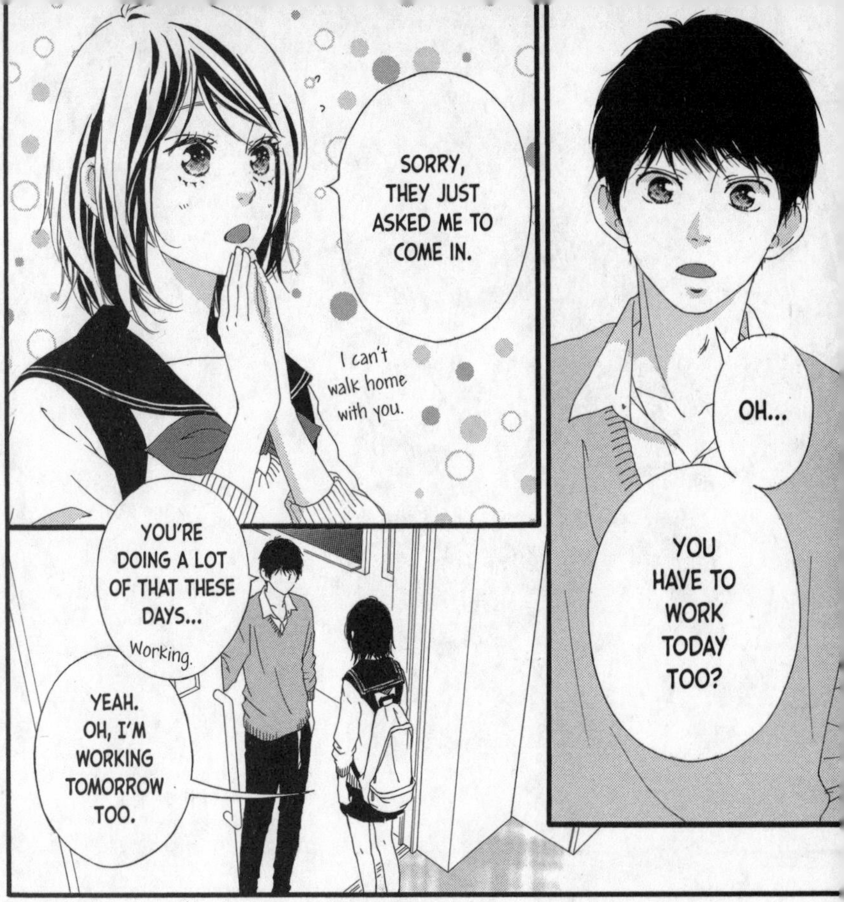
OH...
YOU HAVE TO WORK TODAY TOO?
SORRY, THEY JUST ASKED ME TO COME IN.
I can't walk home with you.
YOU'RE DOING A LOT OF THAT THESE DAYS...
Working.
YEAH. OH, I'M WORKING TOMORROW TOO.

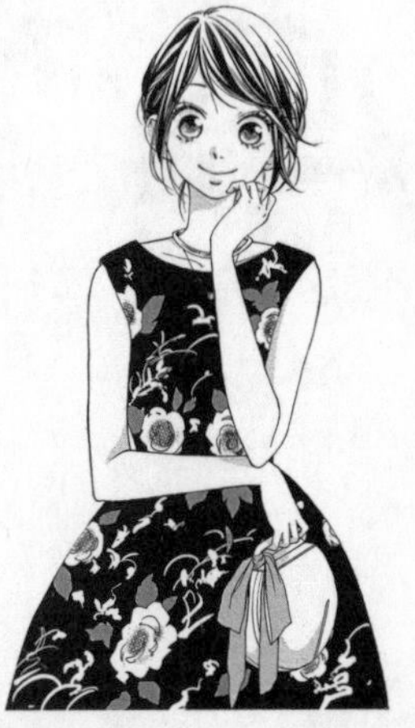

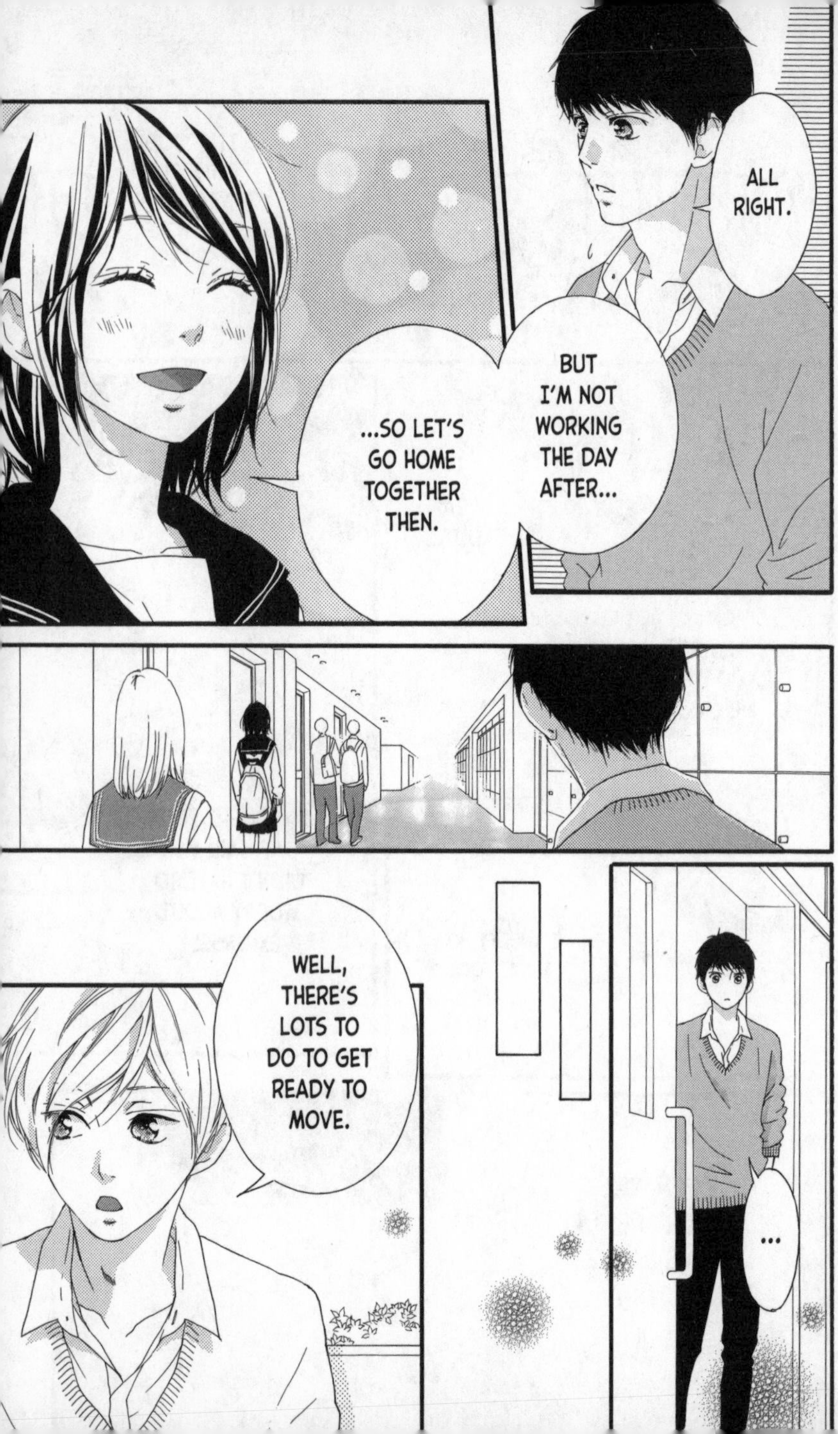
ALL RIGHT.
BUT I'M NOT WORKING THE DAY AFTER...
...SO LET'S GO HOME TOGETHER THEN.
...
WELL, THERE'S LOTS TO DO TO GET READY TO MOVE.

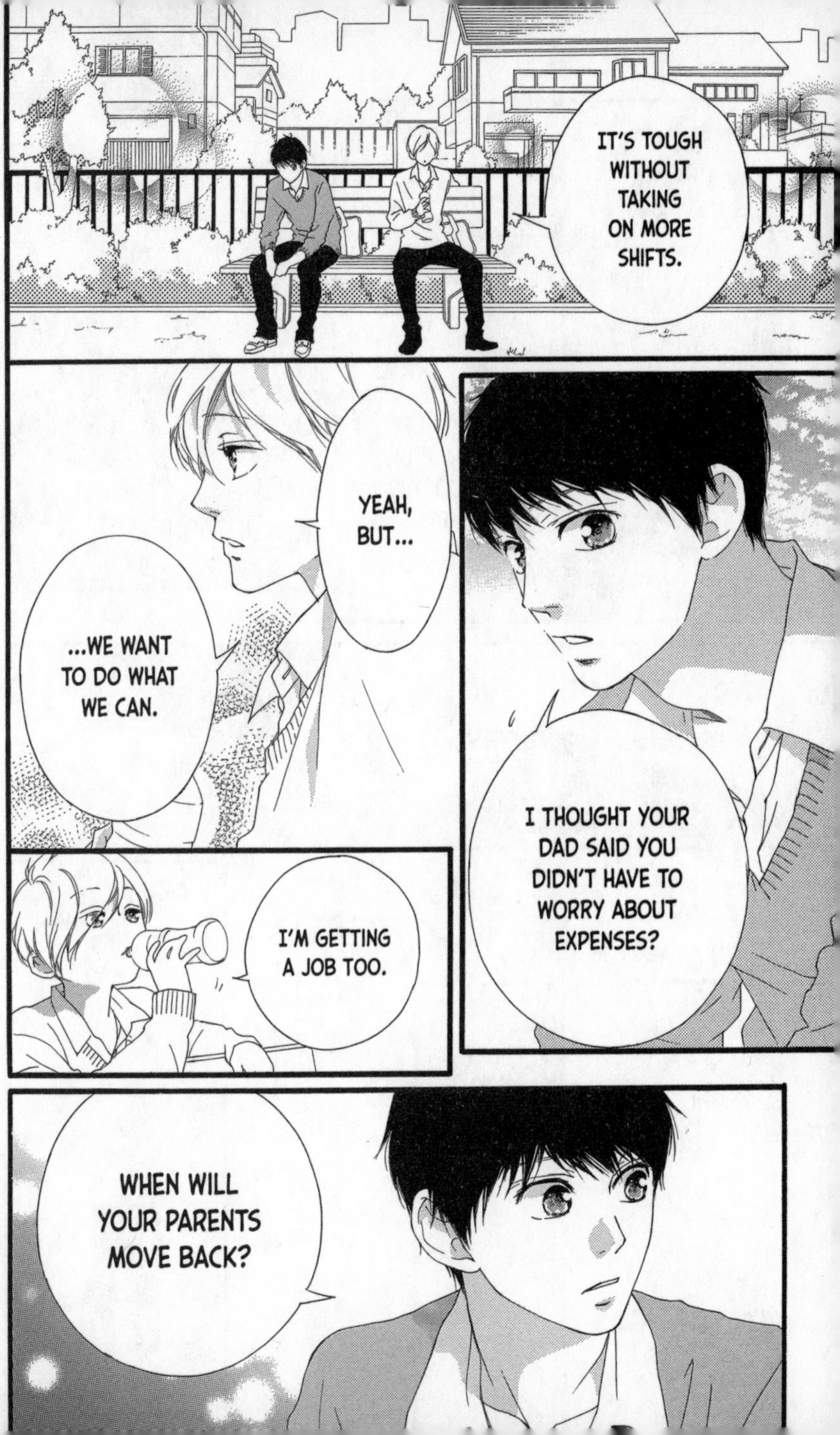

IT'S TOUGH WITHOUT TAKING ON MORE SHIFTS.
I THOUGHT YOUR DAD SAID YOU DIDN'T HAVE TO WORRY ABOUT EXPENSES?
YEAH, BUT...
...WE WANT TO DO WHAT WE CAN.
I'M GETTING A JOB TOO.
WHEN WILL YOUR PARENTS MOVE BACK?

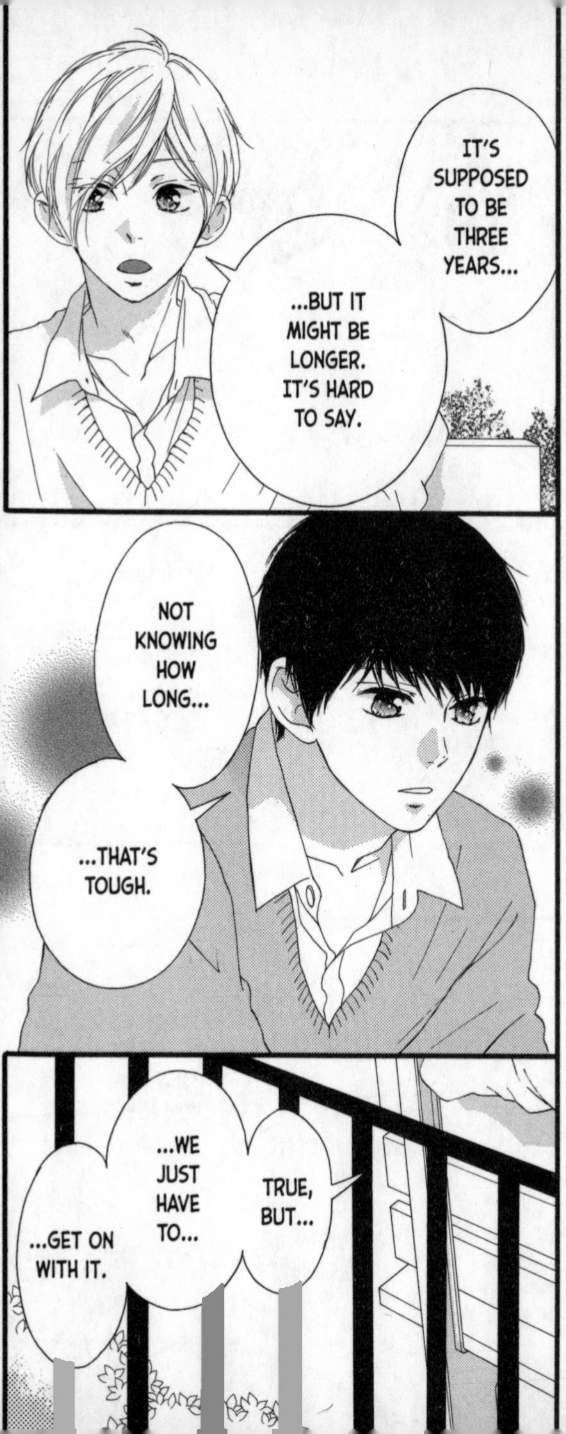
IT'S SUPPOSED TO BE THREE YEARS...
...BUT IT MIGHT BE LONGER. IT'S HARD TO SAY.
NOT KNOWING HOW LONG...
...THAT'S TOUGH.
TRUE, BUT...
...WE JUST HAVE TO...
...GET ON WITH IT.

(Continued...)
I finally realized that the whole thing was a surprise. When the limo door opened, apparently F said something like, "We have so much stuff, let's just hop in this limo since it's here." I was so lost that I really wasn't hearing much. (*laugh*) When I got in, everyone yelled "Good job!" and popped crackers. I felt like crying, but I thought it was way too early to start shedding tears. I worked hard on holding them in. So many fun things happened afterwards that I missed my chance to cry. The place being near my house was a lie. They just pretended to consult the app, and the one person turning up late was to make it seem authentic. In reality, everyone had been on standby for a while. (Continues...)

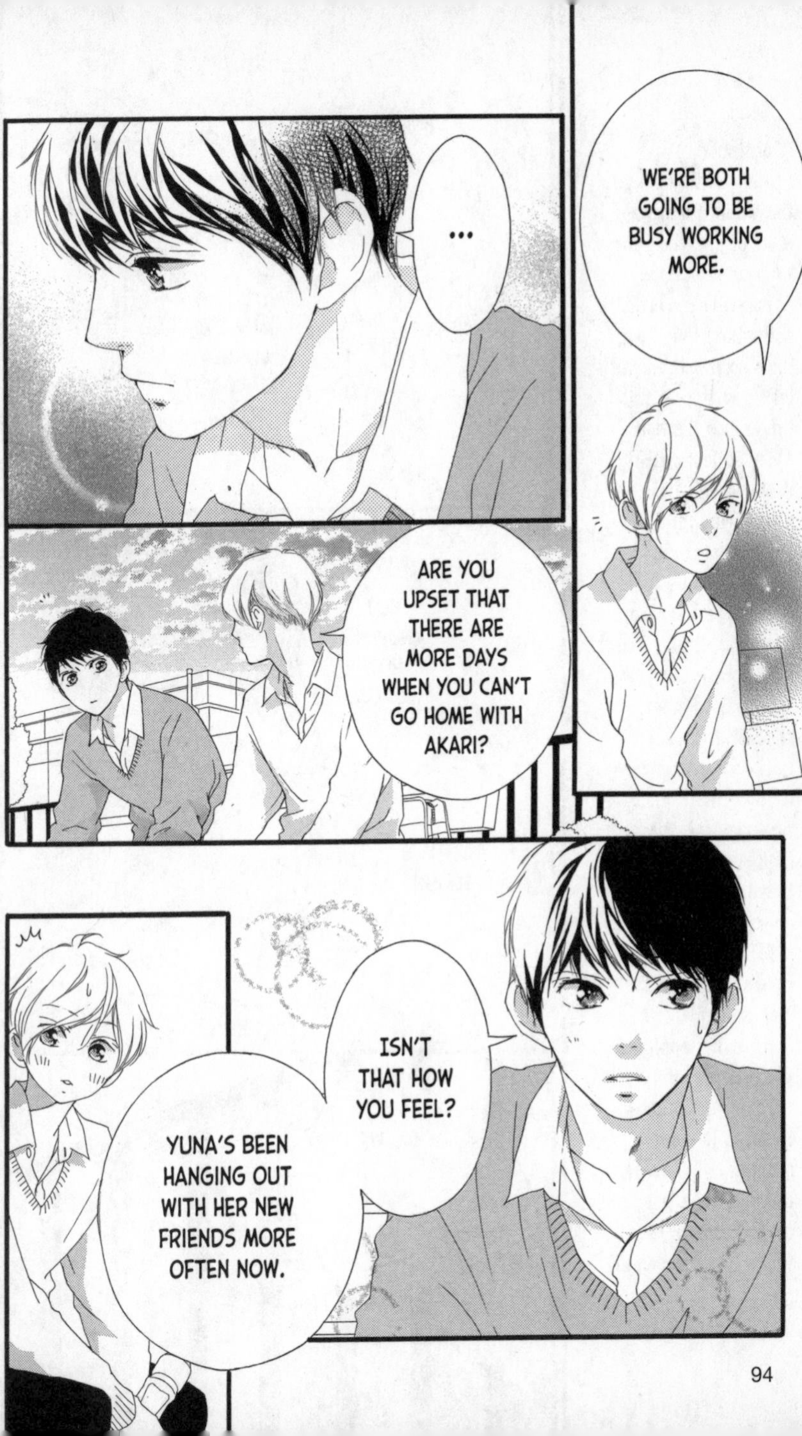
WE'RE BOTH GOING TO BE BUSY WORKING MORE.
...
ARE YOU UPSET THAT THERE ARE MORE DAYS WHEN YOU CAN'T GO HOME WITH AKARI?
ISN'T THAT HOW YOU FEEL?
YUNA'S BEEN HANGING OUT WITH HER NEW FRIENDS MORE OFTEN NOW.

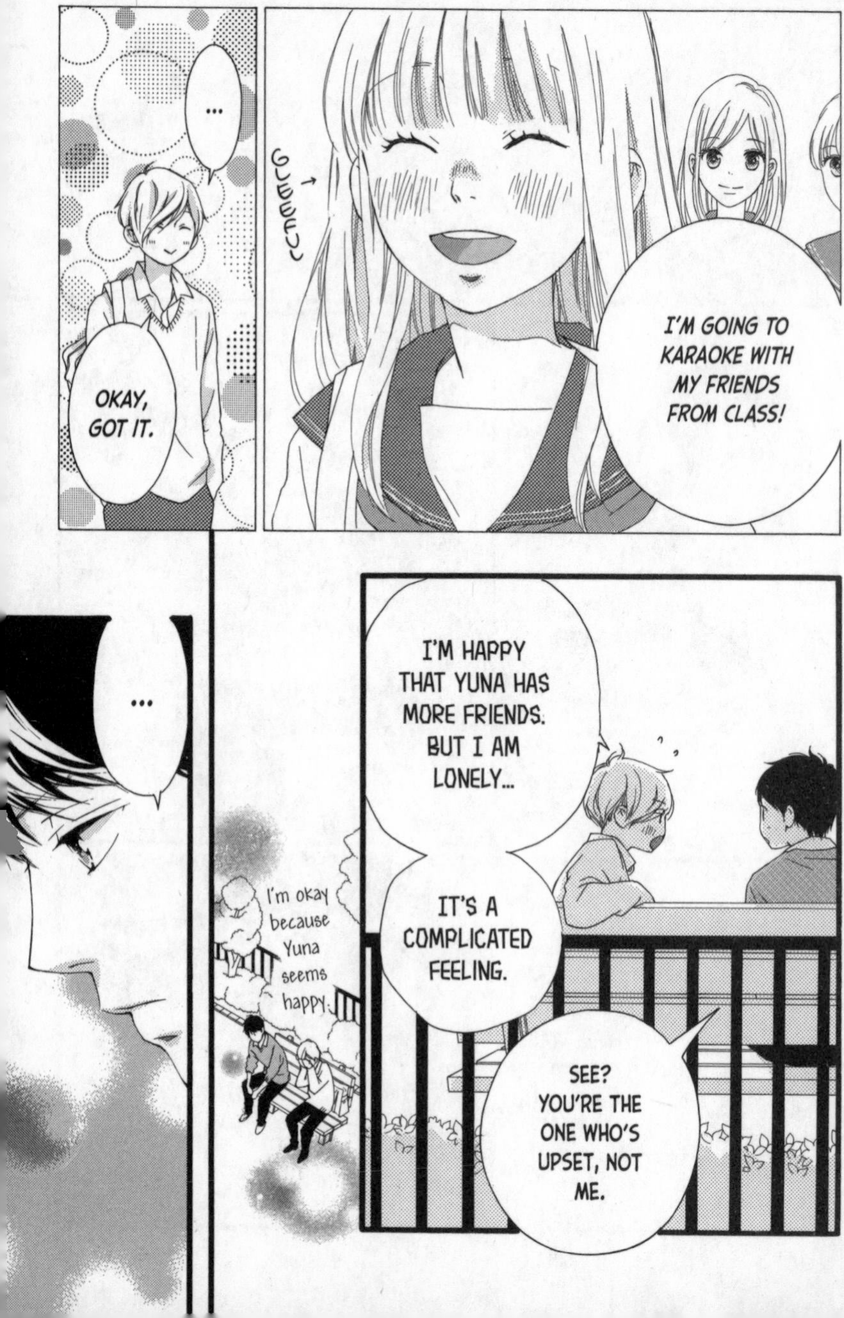
GLEEFUL
I'M GOING TO KARAOKE WITH MY FRIENDS FROM CLASS!
...
OKAY, GOT IT.
I'M HAPPY THAT YUNA HAS MORE FRIENDS. BUT I AM LONELY...
IT'S A COMPLICATED FEELING.
SEE? YOU'RE THE ONE WHO'S UPSET, NOT ME.
I'm okay because Yuna seems happy.
...

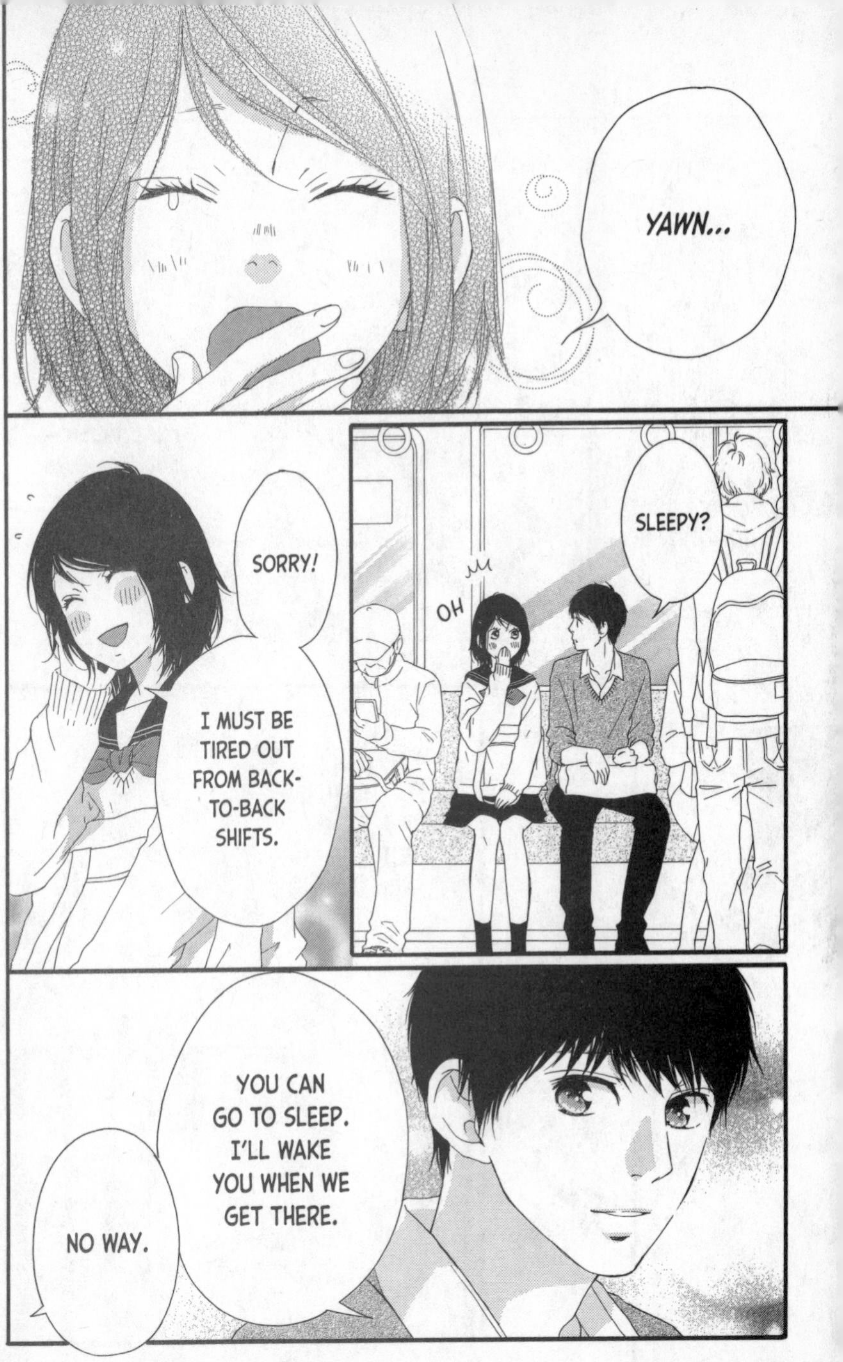
YAWN...
SLEEPY?
OH
SORRY!
I MUST BE TIRED OUT FROM BACK-TO-BACK SHIFTS.
YOU CAN GO TO SLEEP. I'LL WAKE YOU WHEN WE GET THERE.
NO WAY.

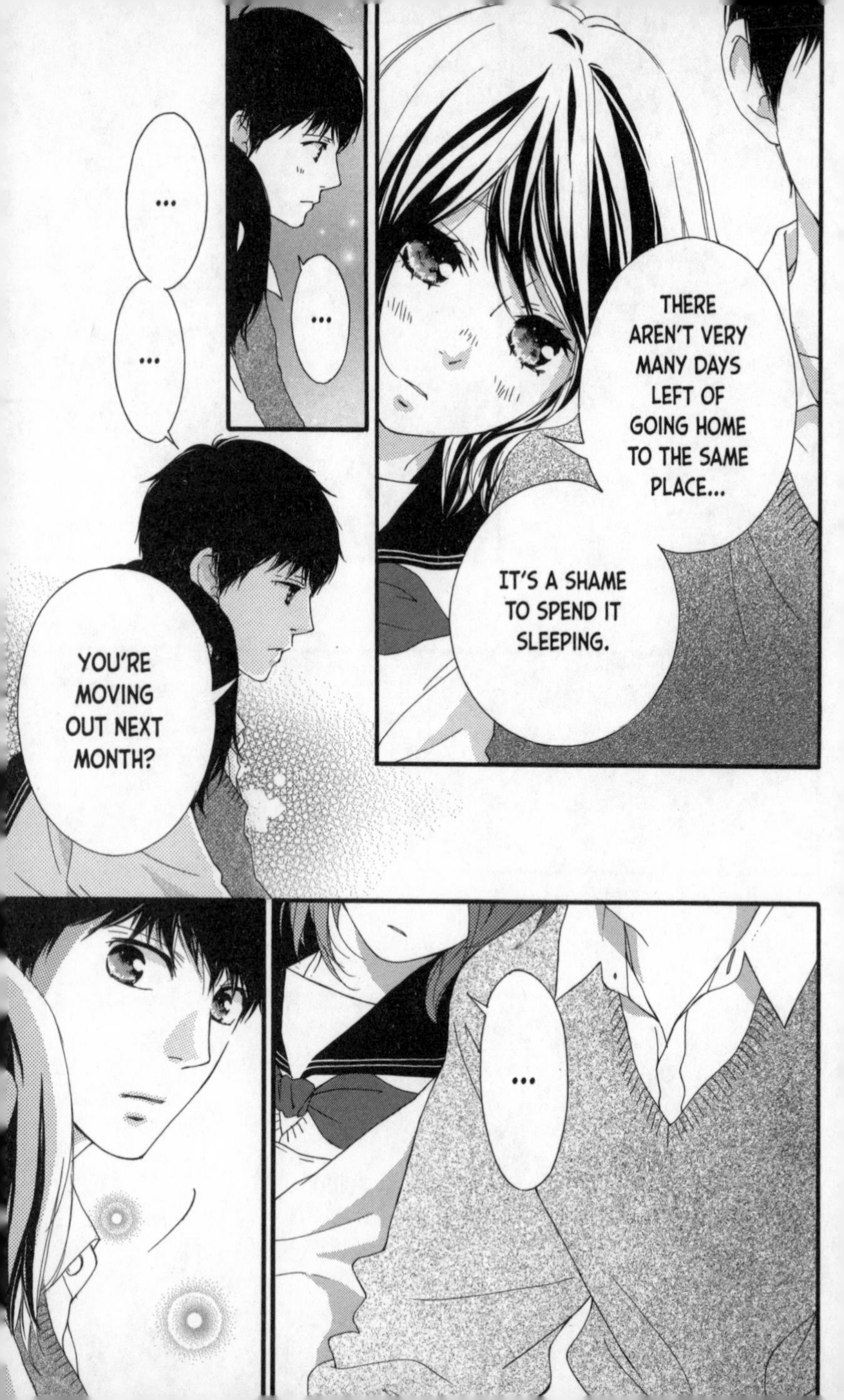
THERE AREN'T VERY MANY DAYS LEFT OF GOING HOME TO THE SAME PLACE...
IT'S A SHAME TO SPEND IT SLEEPING.
...
...
...
YOU'RE MOVING OUT NEXT MONTH?
...

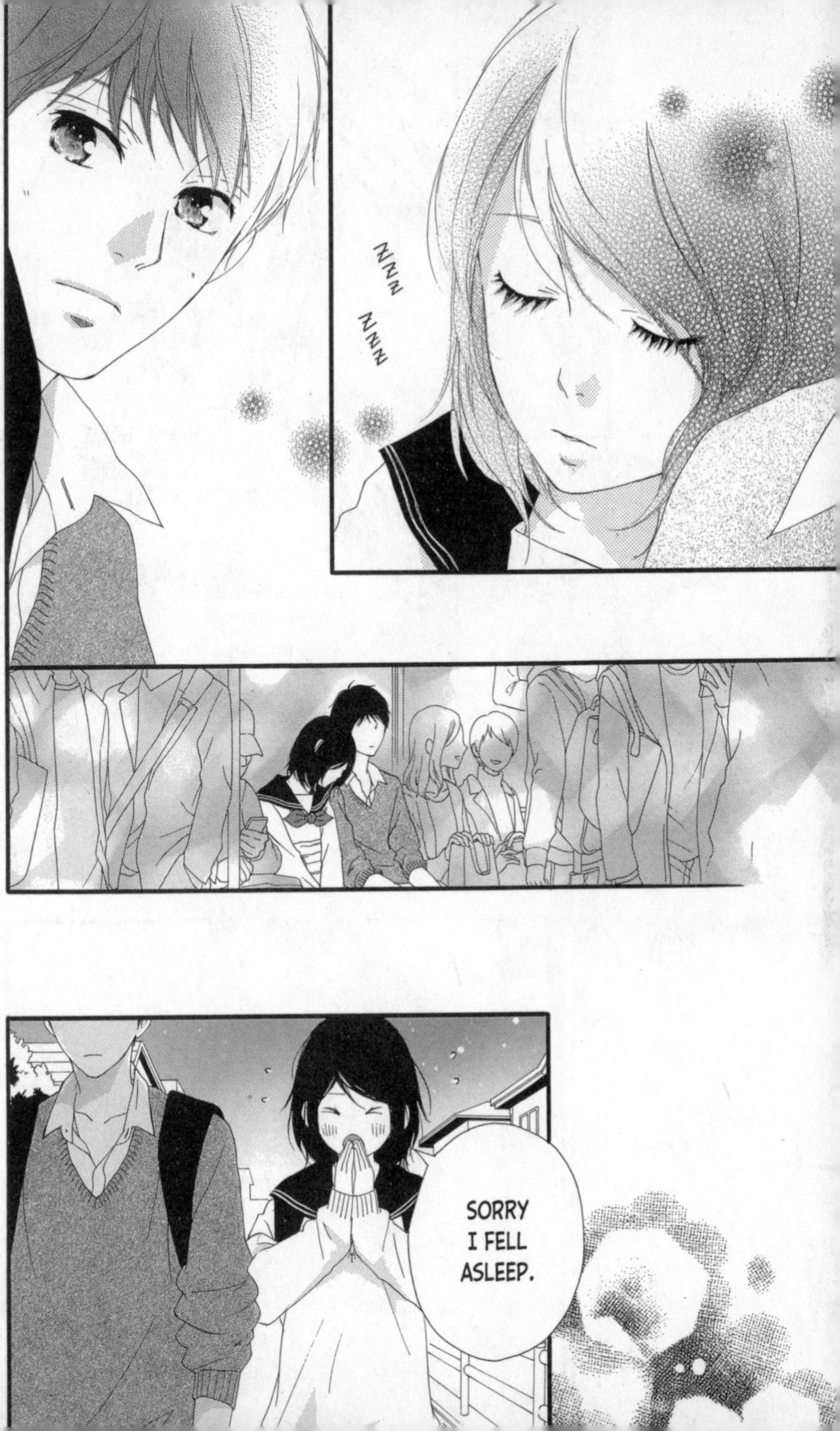
ZZZ
ZZZ
SORRY I FELL ASLEEP.

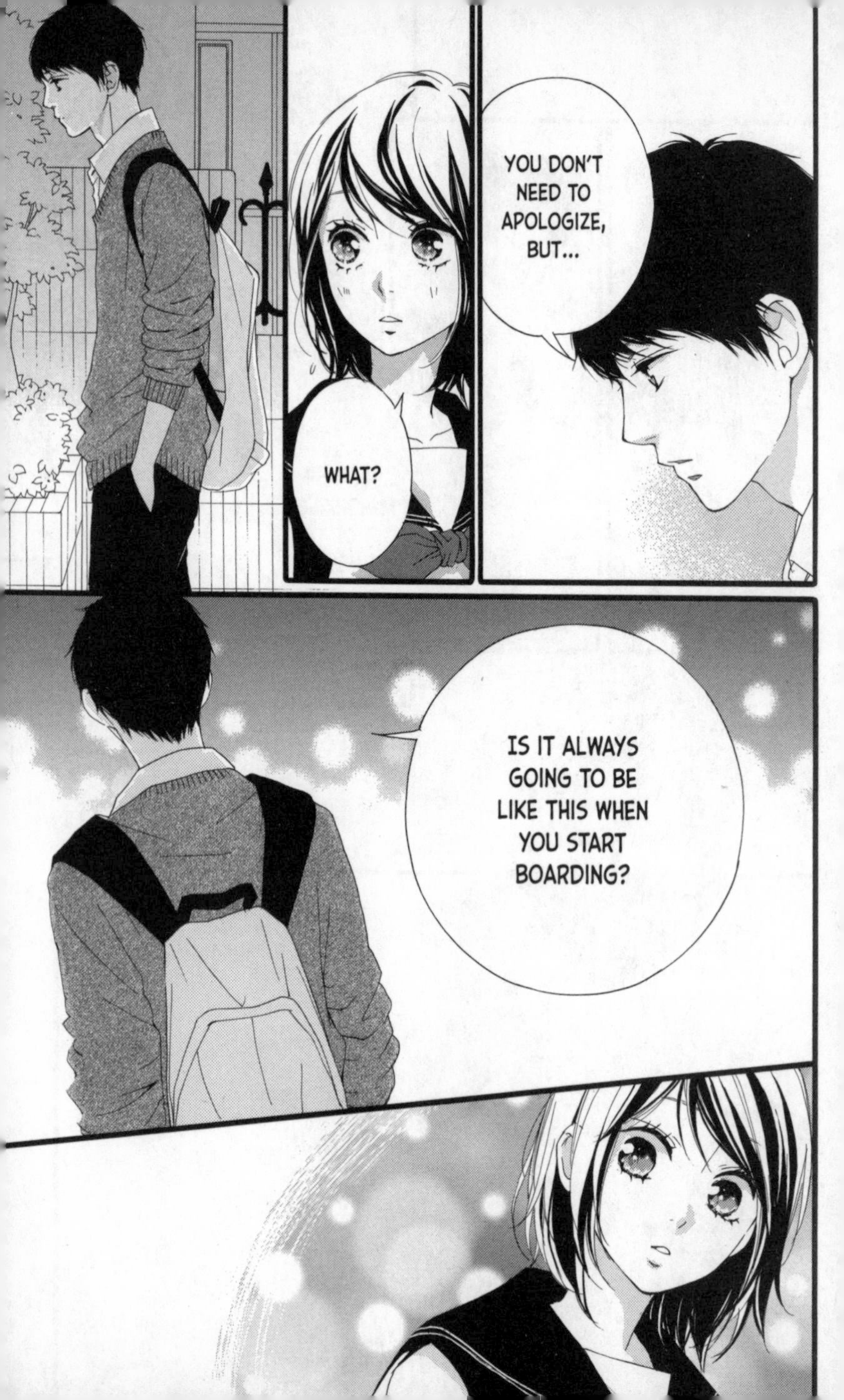
YOU DON'T NEED TO APOLOGIZE, BUT...
WHAT?
IS IT ALWAYS GOING TO BE LIKE THIS WHEN YOU START BOARDING?

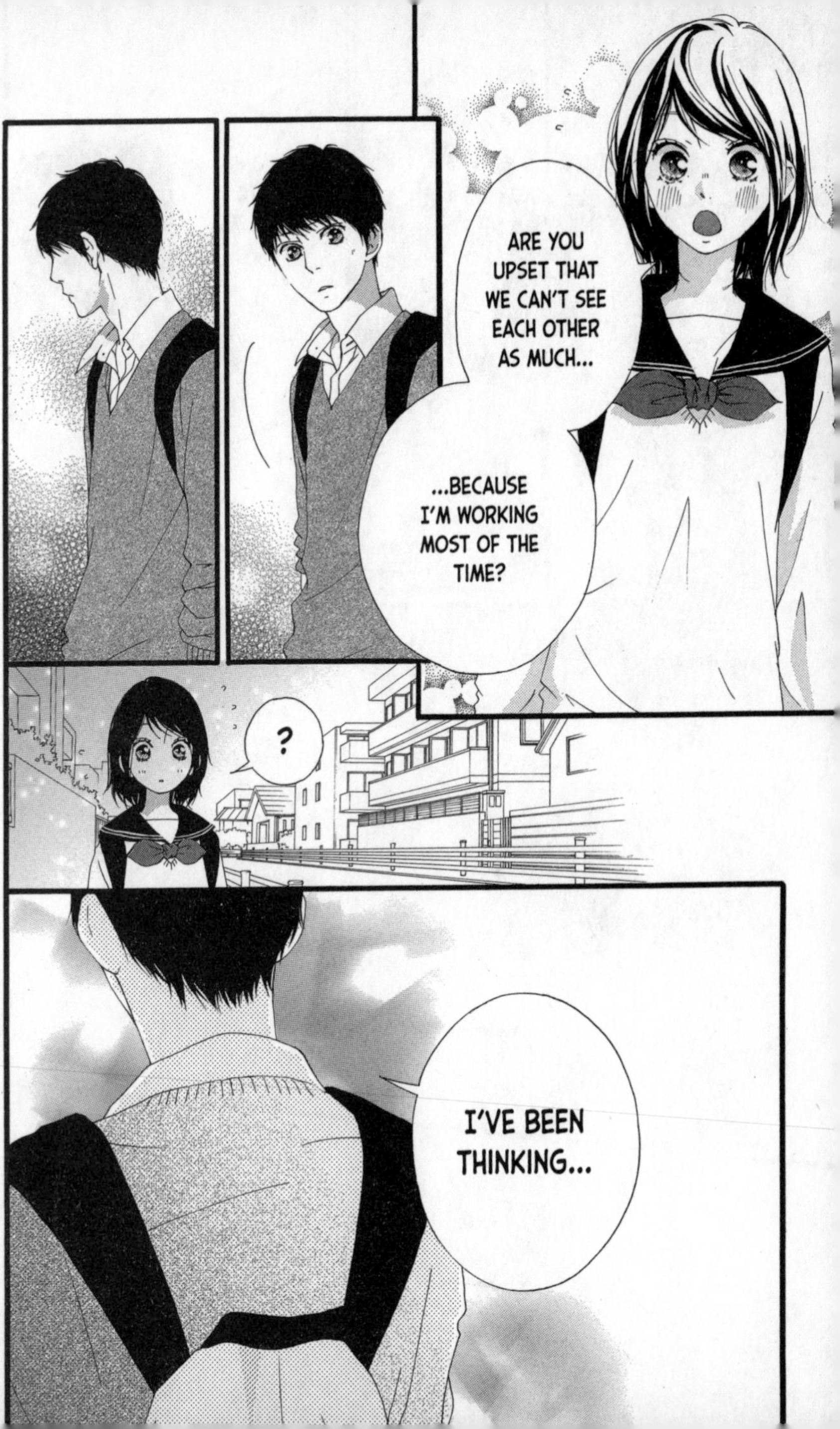
ARE YOU UPSET THAT WE CAN'T SEE EACH OTHER AS MUCH...
...BECAUSE I'M WORKING MOST OF THE TIME?
?
I'VE BEEN THINKING...

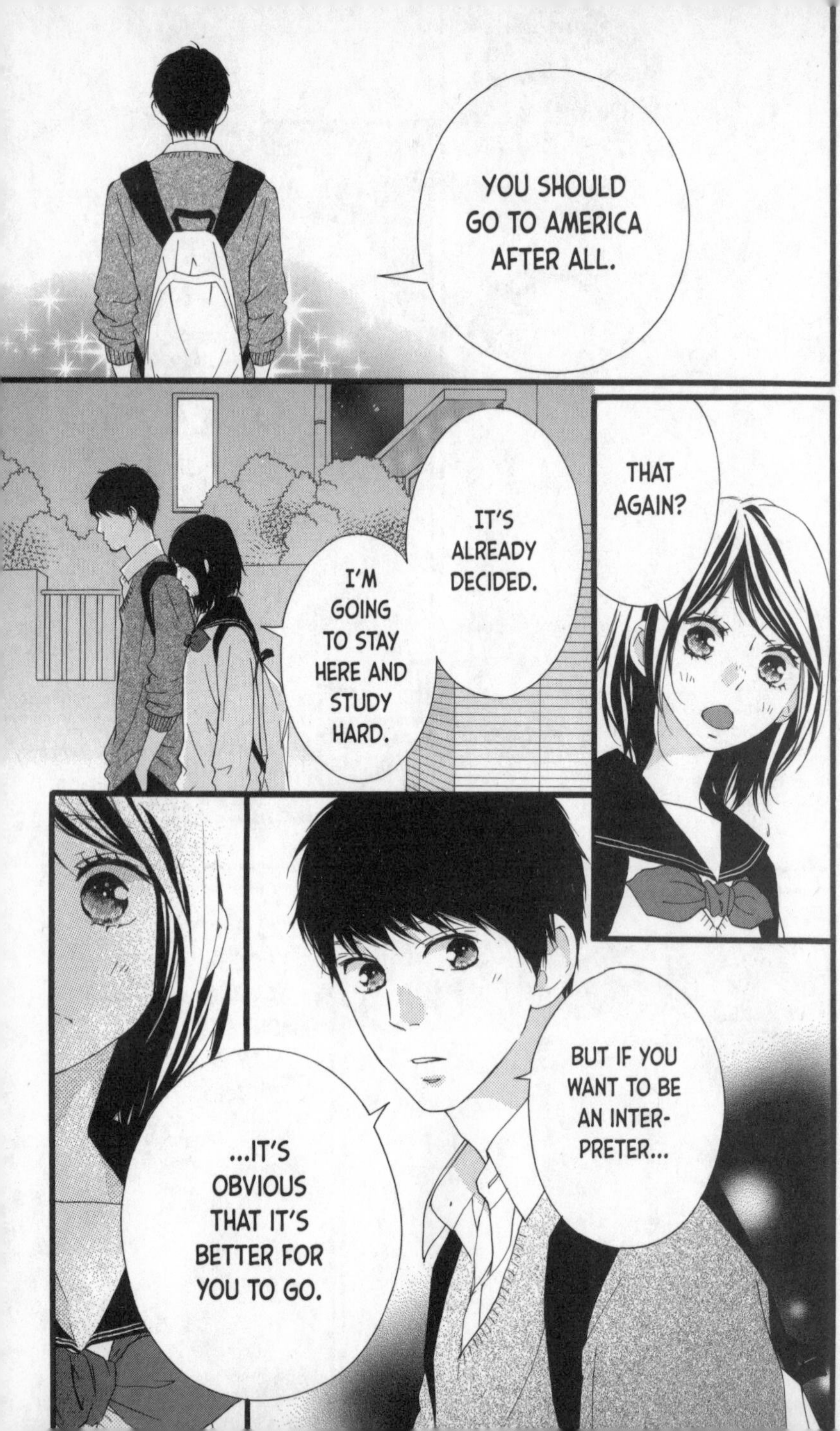
YOU SHOULD GO TO AMERICA AFTER ALL.
THAT AGAIN?
IT'S ALREADY DECIDED.
I'M GOING TO STAY HERE AND STUDY HARD.
BUT IF YOU WANT TO BE AN INTER-PRETER...
...IT'S OBVIOUS THAT IT'S BETTER FOR YOU TO GO.

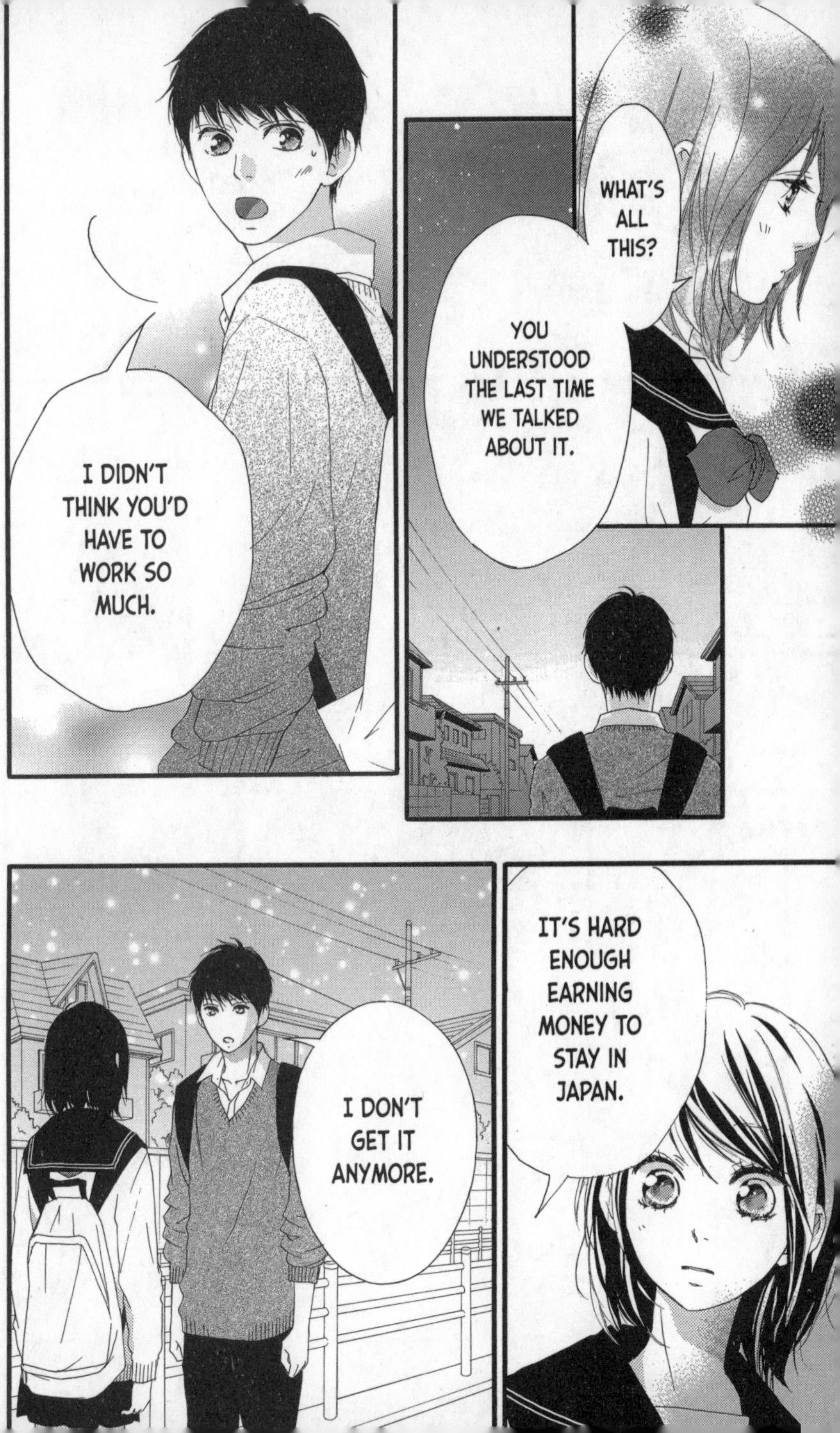
WHAT'S ALL THIS?
YOU UNDERSTOOD THE LAST TIME WE TALKED ABOUT IT.
I DIDN'T THINK YOU'D HAVE TO WORK SO MUCH.
IT'S HARD ENOUGH EARNING MONEY TO STAY IN JAPAN.
I DON'T GET IT ANYMORE.

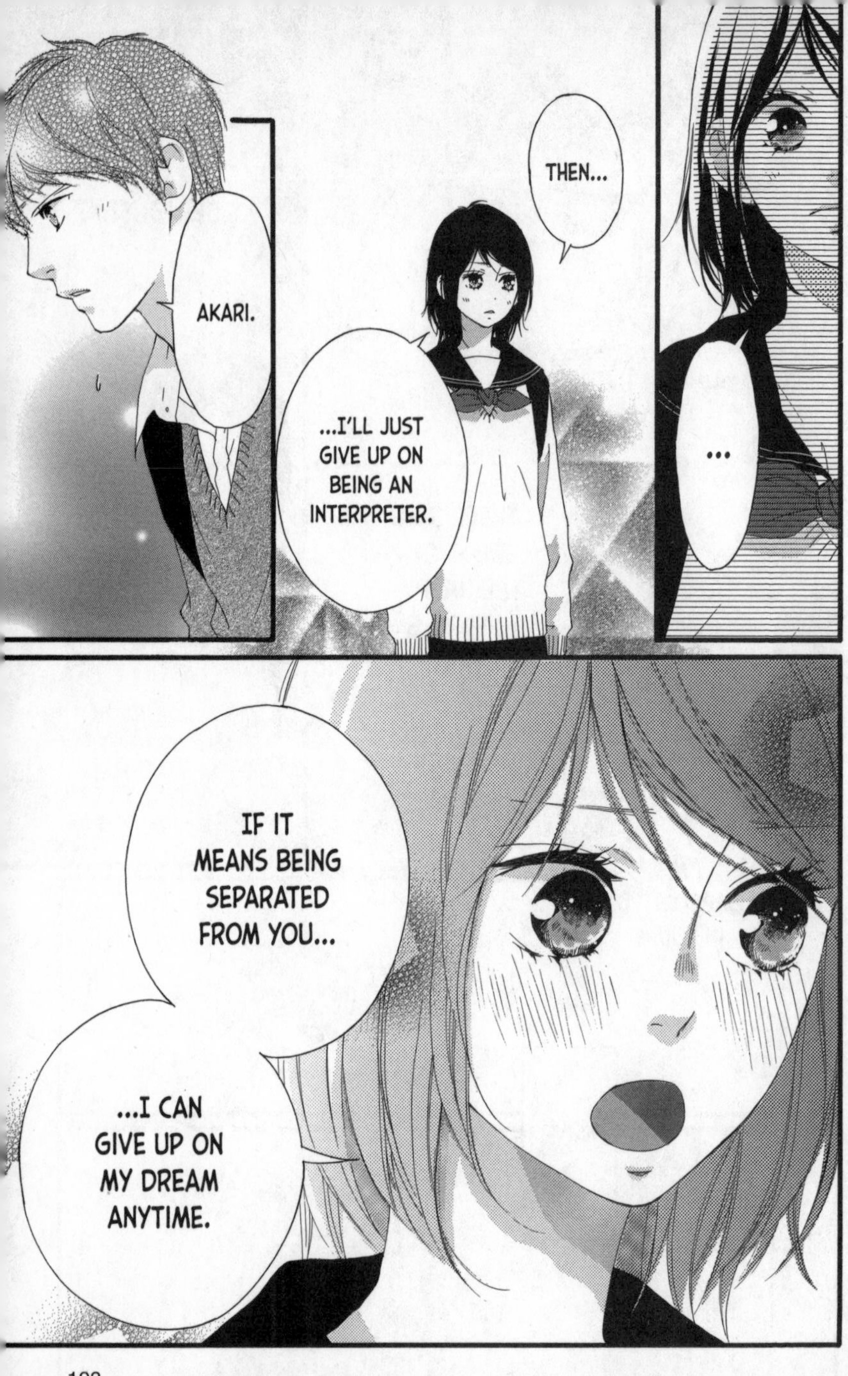
...
THEN...
...I'LL JUST GIVE UP ON BEING AN INTERPRETER.
AKARI.
IF IT MEANS BEING SEPARATED FROM YOU...
...I CAN GIVE UP ON MY DREAM ANYTIME.

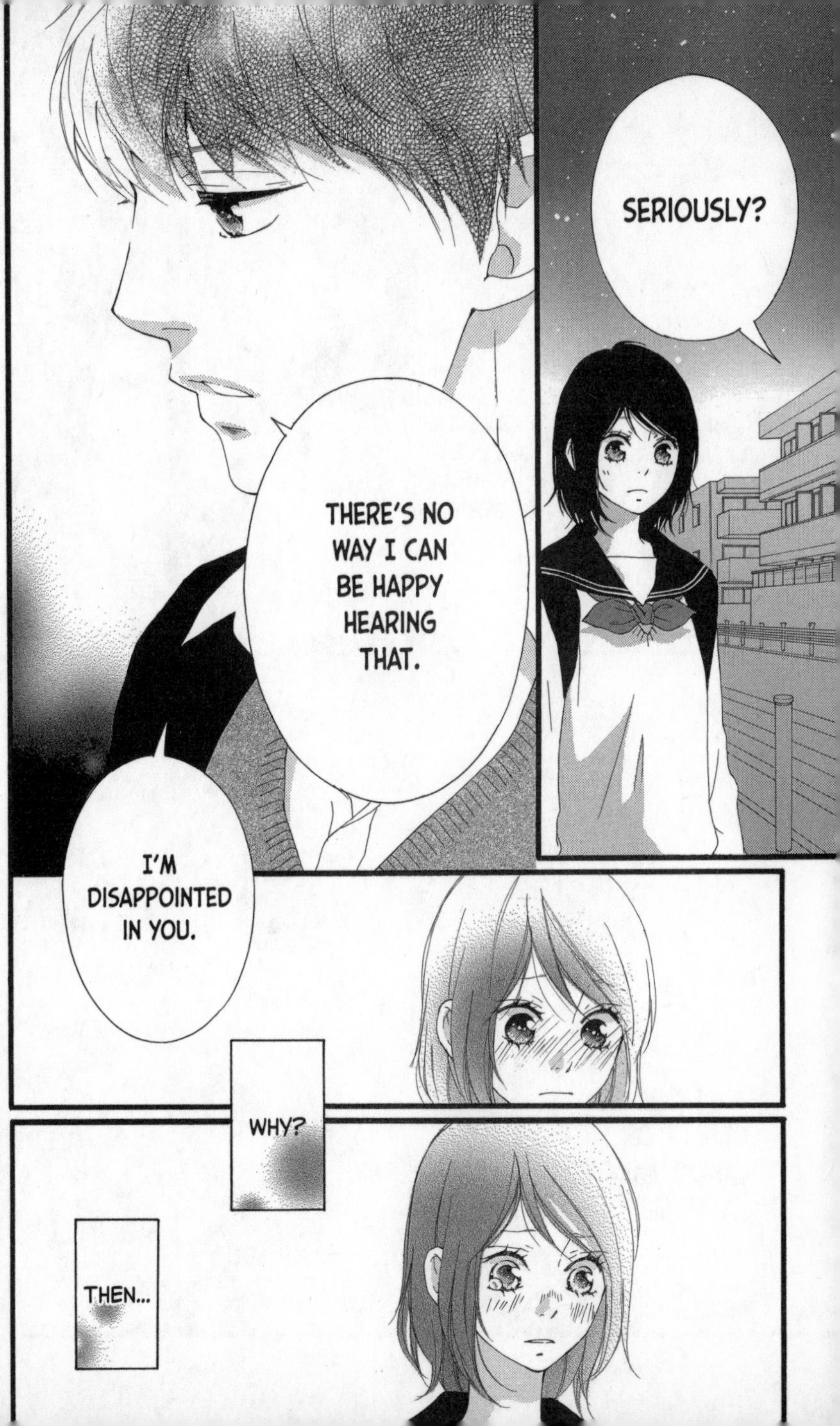
SERIOUSLY?
THERE'S NO WAY I CAN BE HAPPY HEARING THAT.
I'M DISAPPOINTED IN YOU.
WHY?
THEN...

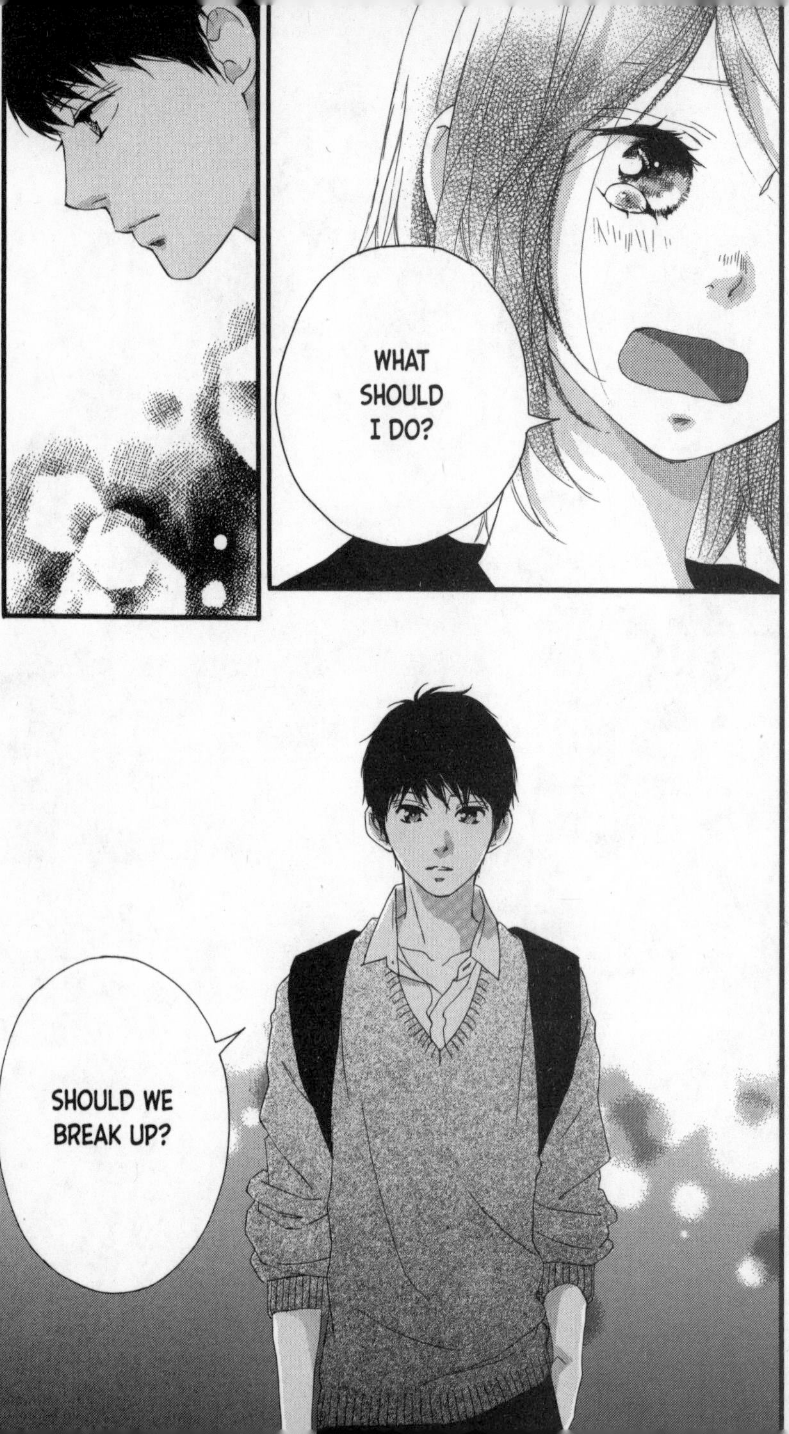
WHAT SHOULD I DO?
SHOULD WE BREAK UP?

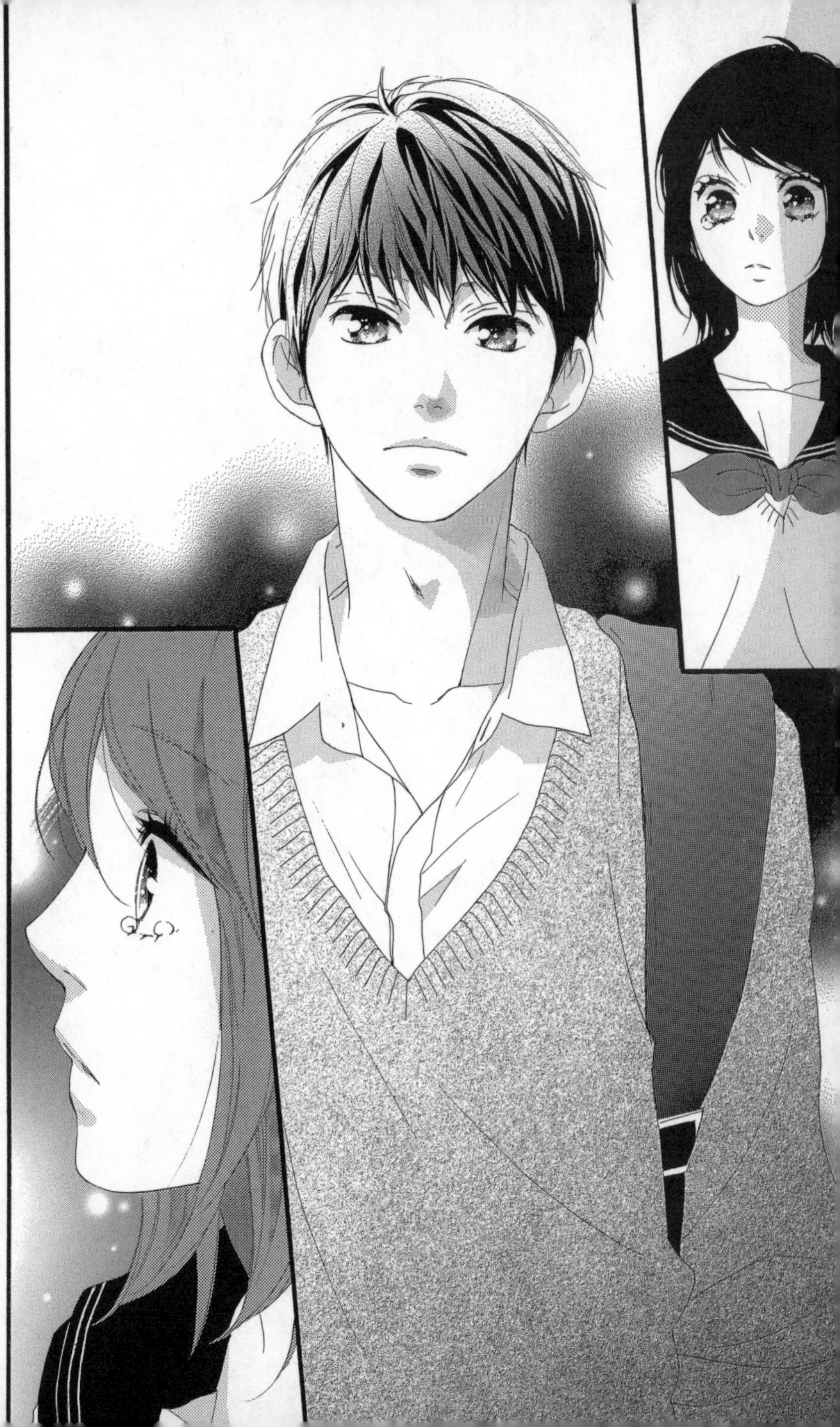

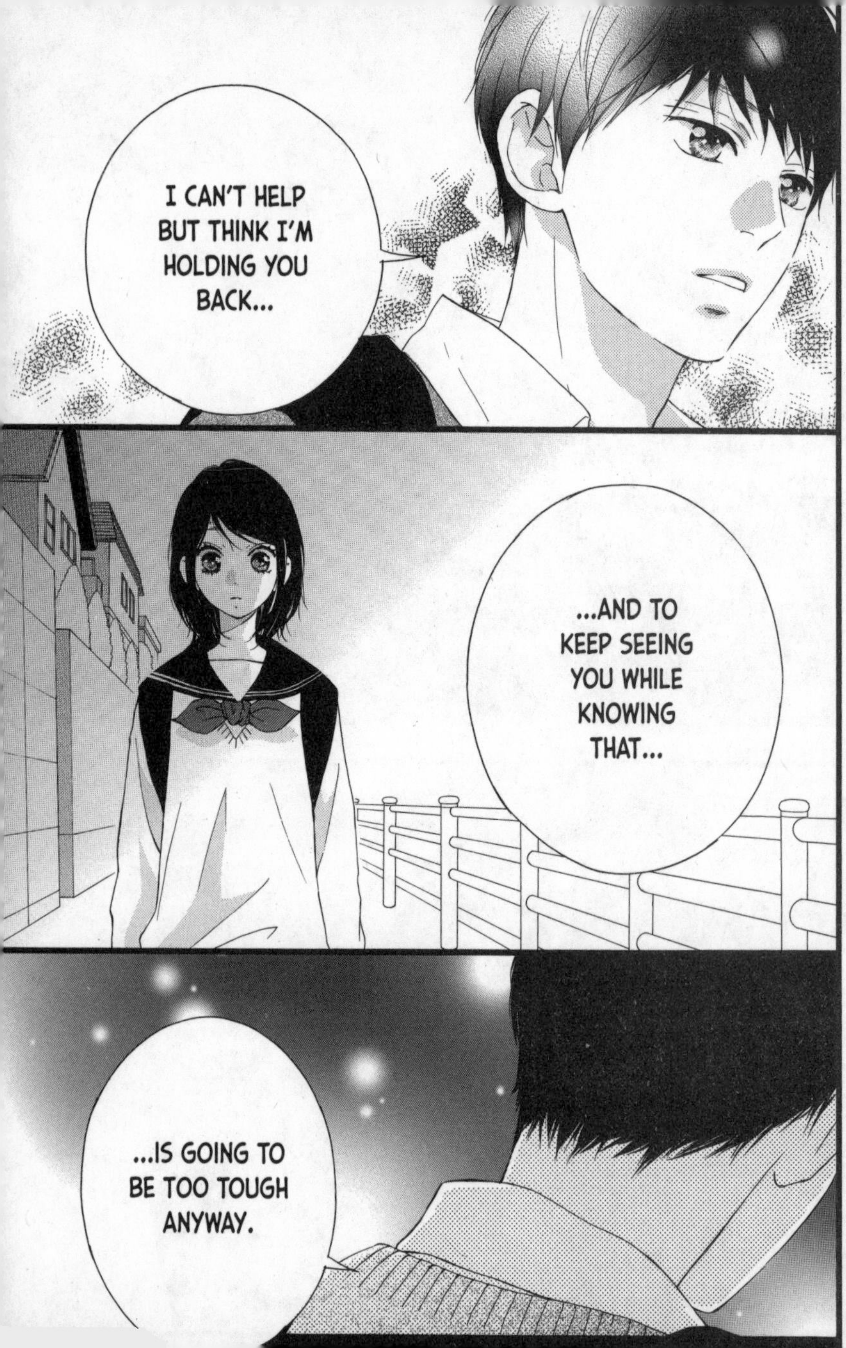
I CAN'T HELP BUT THINK I'M HOLDING YOU BACK...
...AND TO KEEP SEEING YOU WHILE KNOWING THAT...
...IS GOING TO BE TOO TOUGH ANYWAY.

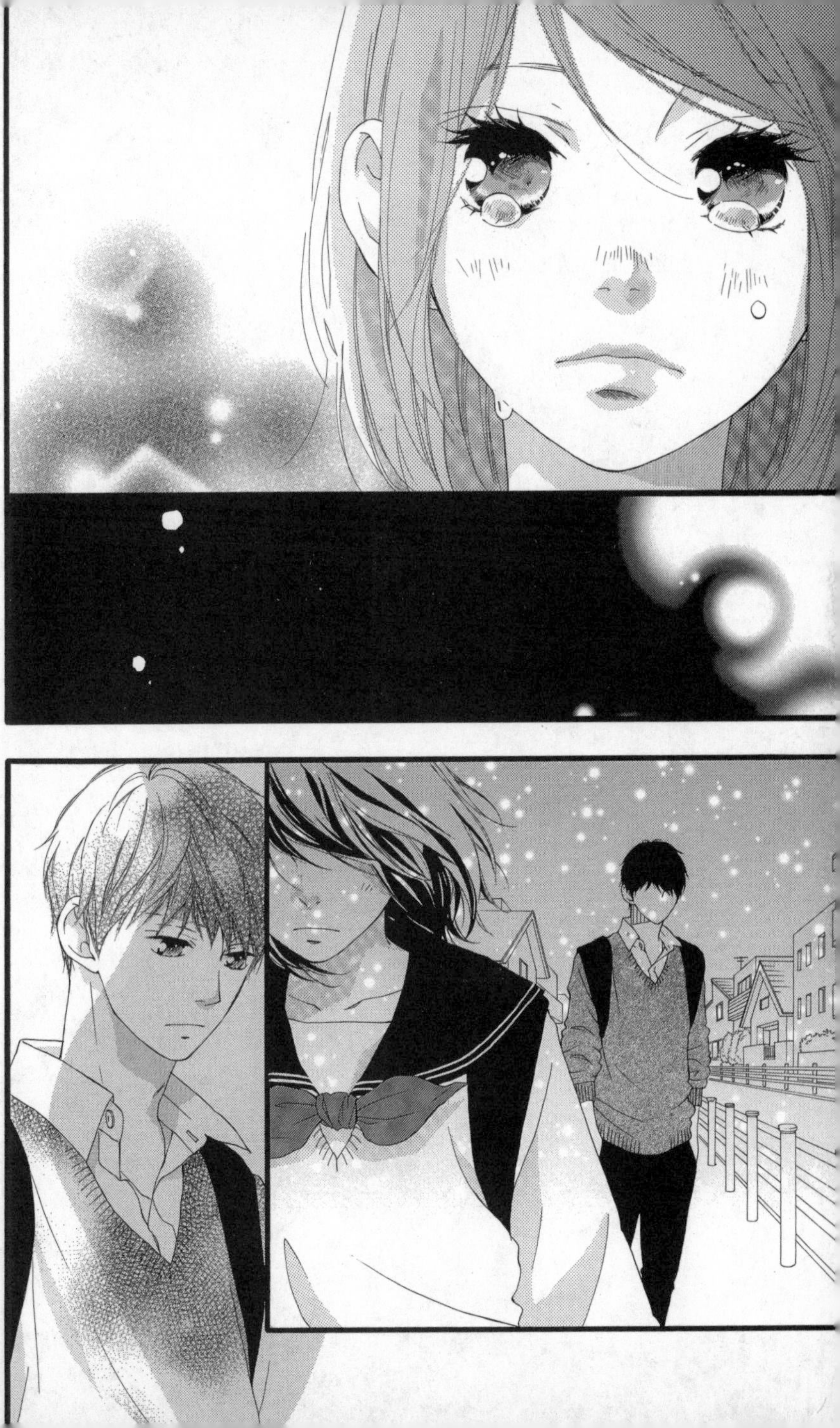

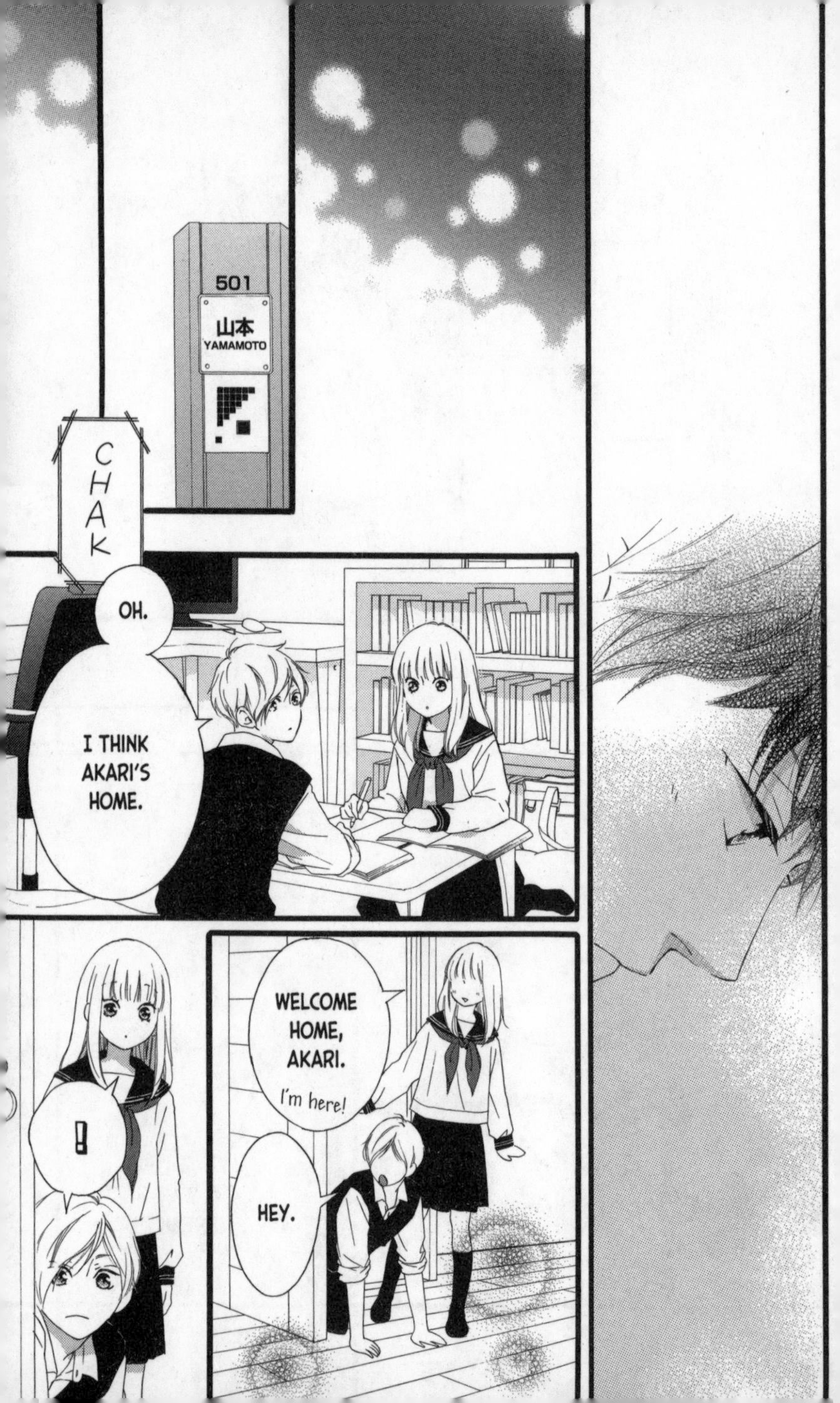
501
山本
YAMAMOTO
CHAK
OH.
I THINK AKARI'S HOME.
WELCOME HOME, AKARI.
I'm here!
HEY.
!

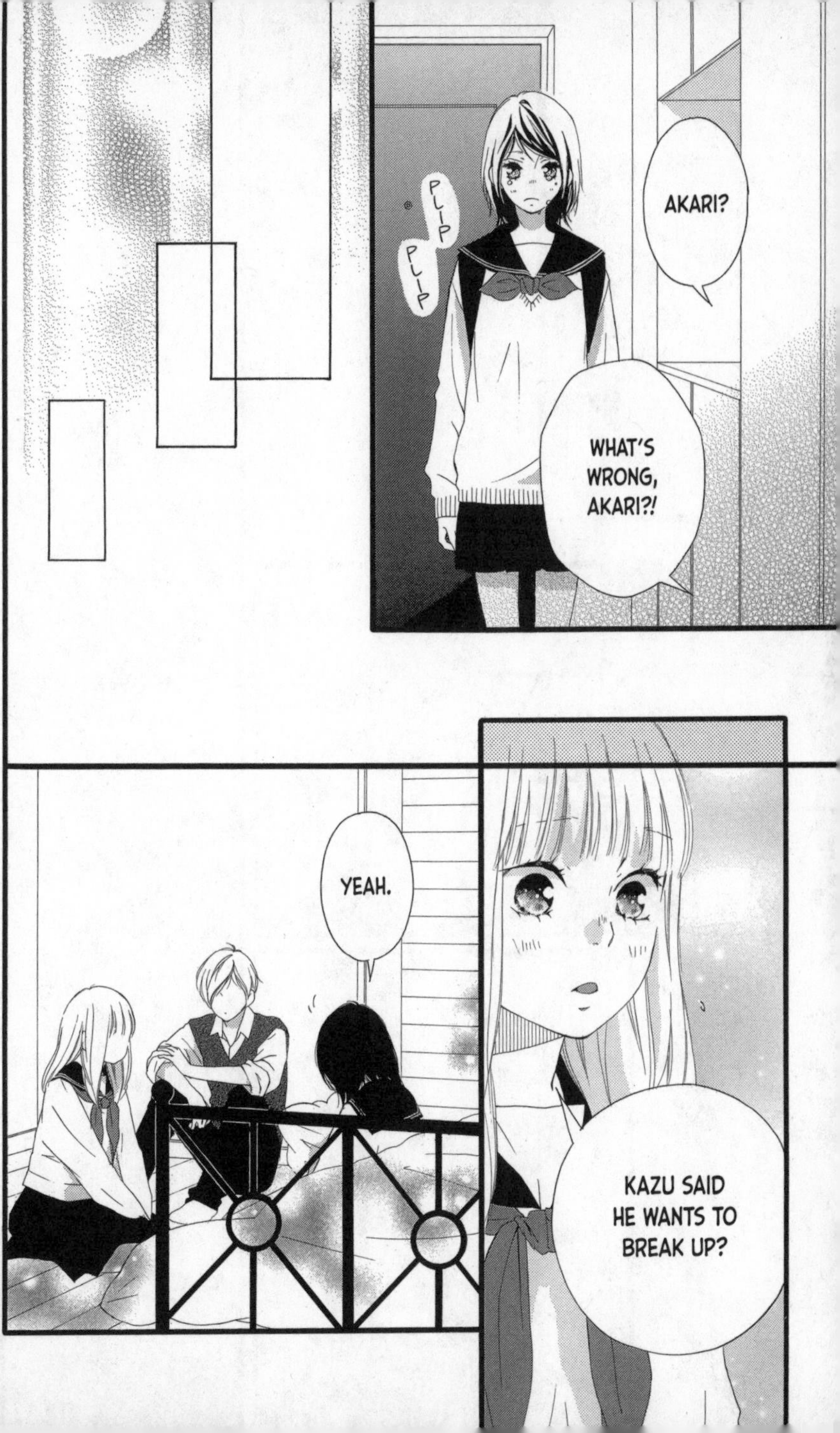
AKARI?
WHAT'S WRONG, AKARI?!
PLIP PLIP
KAZU SAID HE WANTS TO BREAK UP?
YEAH.

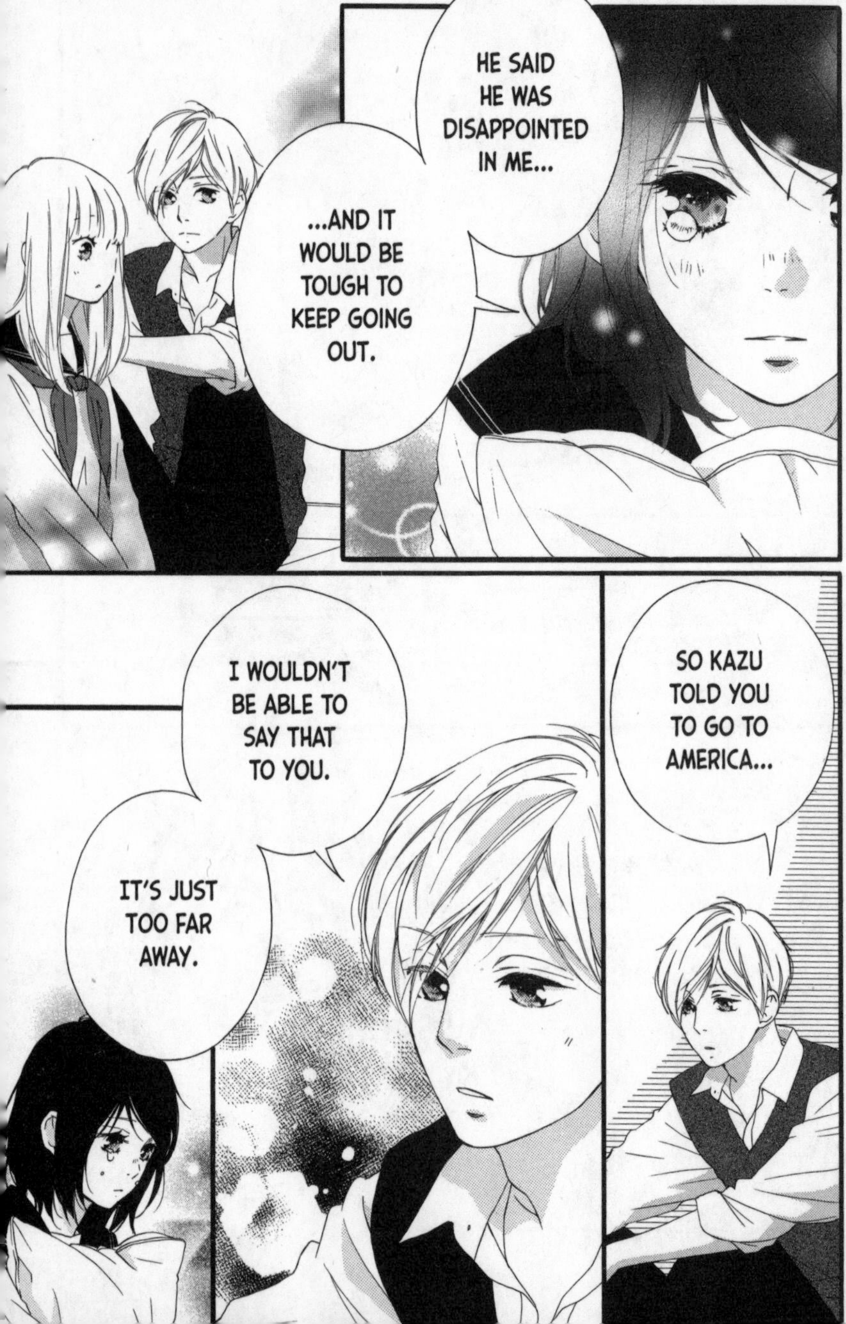
HE SAID HE WAS DISAPPOINTED IN ME...
...AND IT WOULD BE TOUGH TO KEEP GOING OUT.
SO KAZU TOLD YOU TO GO TO AMERICA...
I WOULDN'T BE ABLE TO SAY THAT TO YOU.
IT'S JUST TOO FAR AWAY.

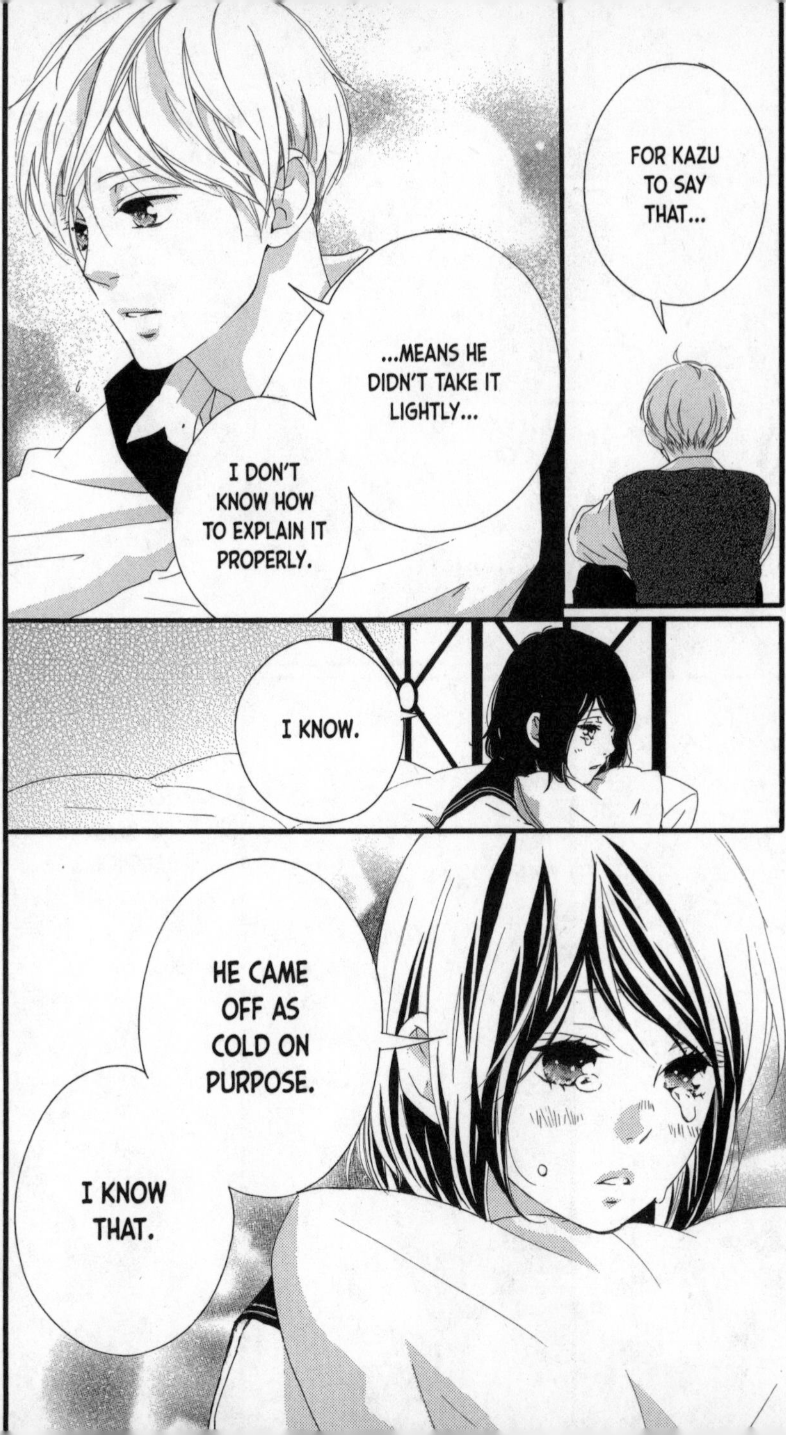
FOR KAZU TO SAY THAT...
...MEANS HE DIDN'T TAKE IT LIGHTLY...
I DON'T KNOW HOW TO EXPLAIN IT PROPERLY.
I KNOW.
HE CAME OFF AS COLD ON PURPOSE.
I KNOW THAT.

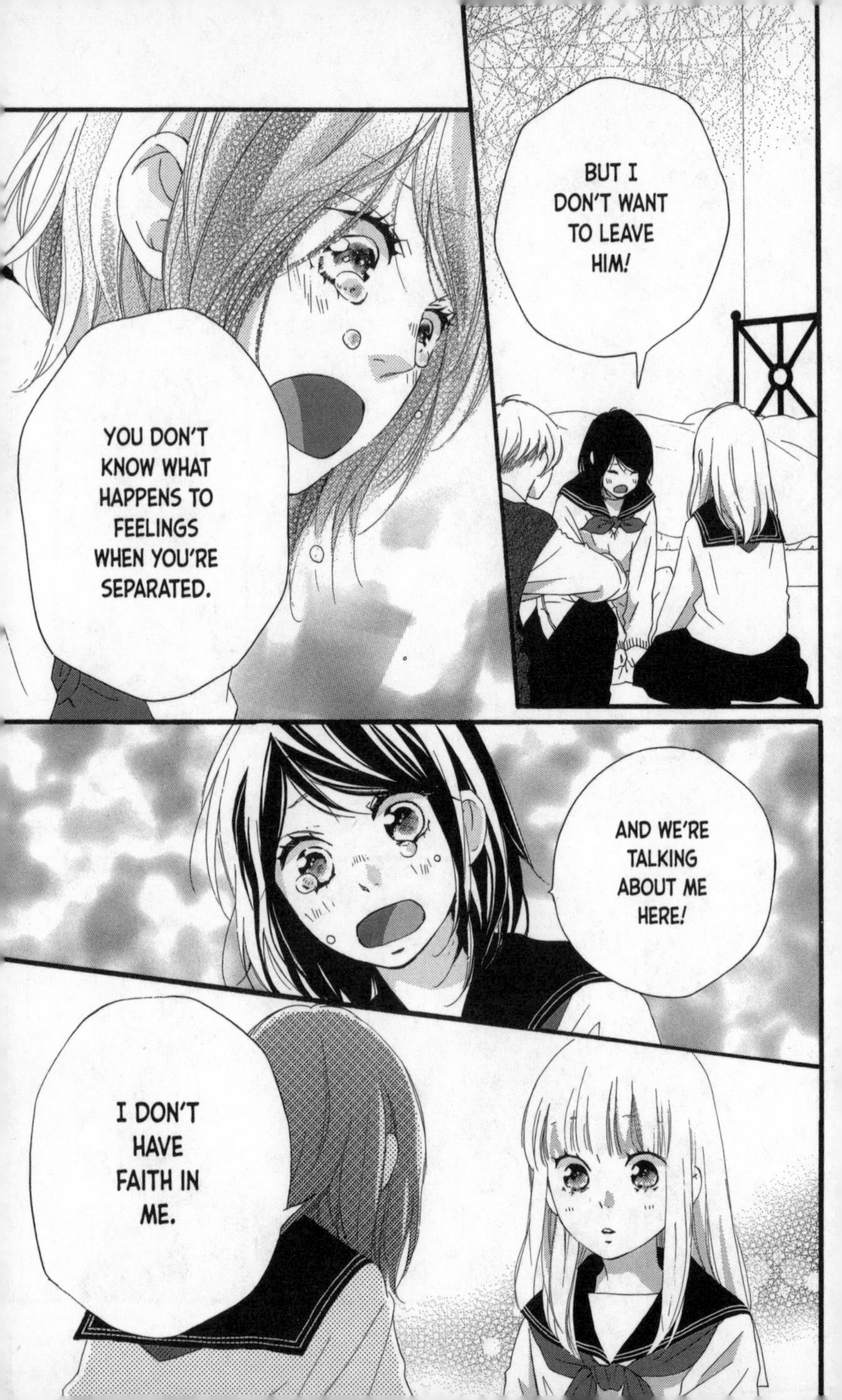
BUT I DON'T WANT TO LEAVE HIM!
YOU DON'T KNOW WHAT HAPPENS TO FEELINGS WHEN YOU'RE SEPARATED.
AND WE'RE TALKING ABOUT ME HERE!
I DON'T HAVE FAITH IN ME.

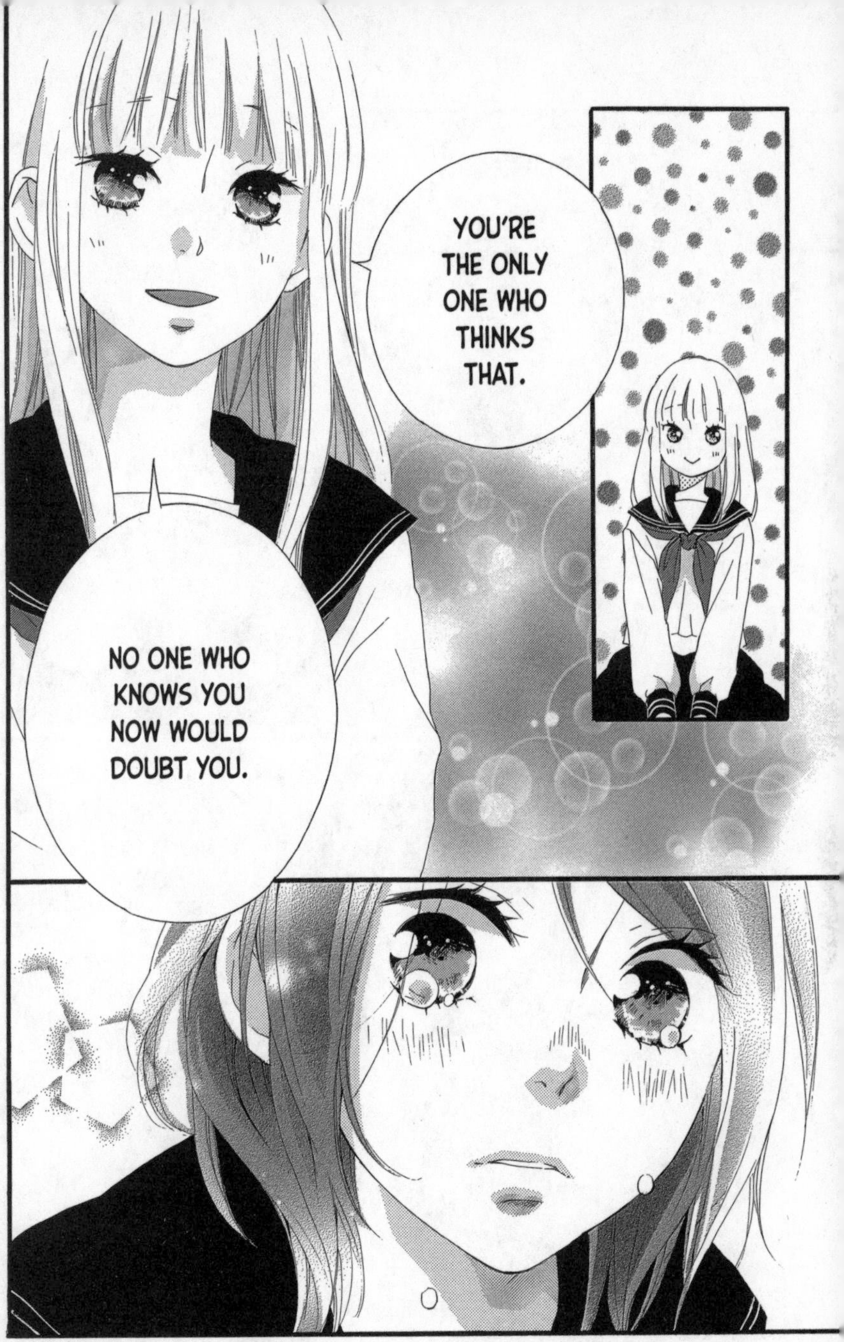
YOU'RE THE ONLY ONE WHO THINKS THAT.
NO ONE WHO KNOWS YOU NOW WOULD DOUBT YOU.

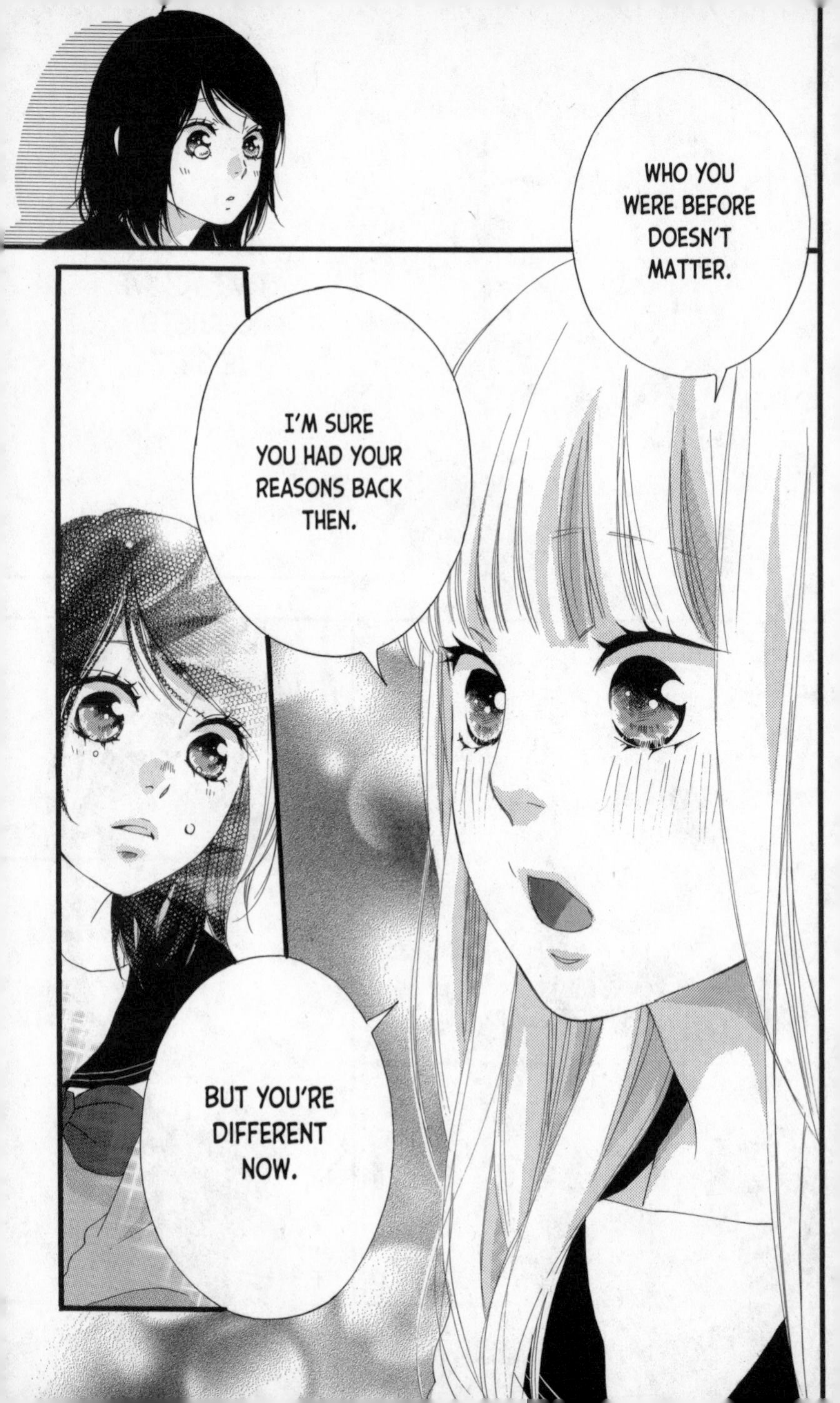
WHO YOU WERE BEFORE DOESN'T MATTER.
I'M SURE YOU HAD YOUR REASONS BACK THEN.
BUT YOU'RE DIFFERENT NOW.

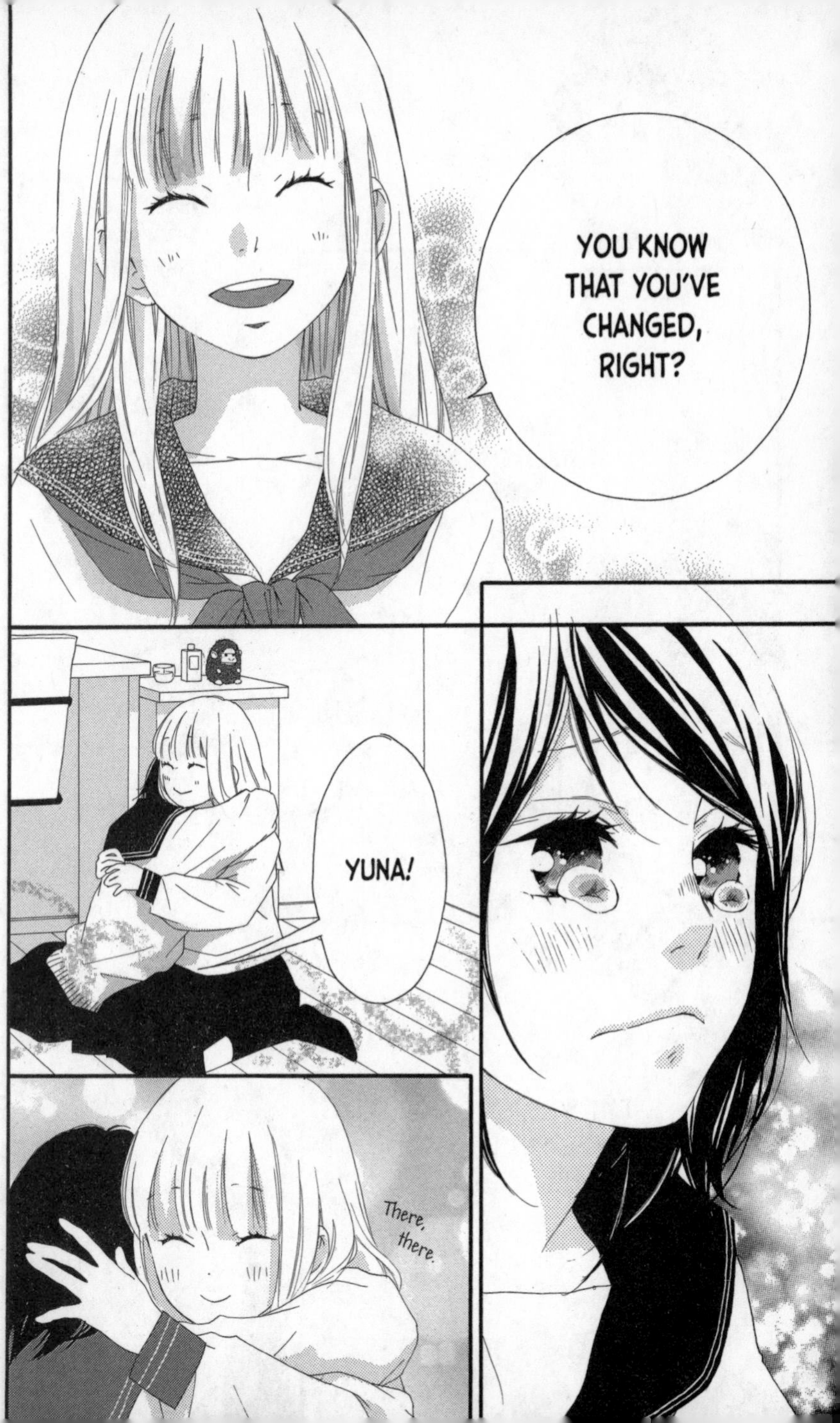
YOU KNOW THAT YOU'VE CHANGED, RIGHT?
YUNA!
There, there.

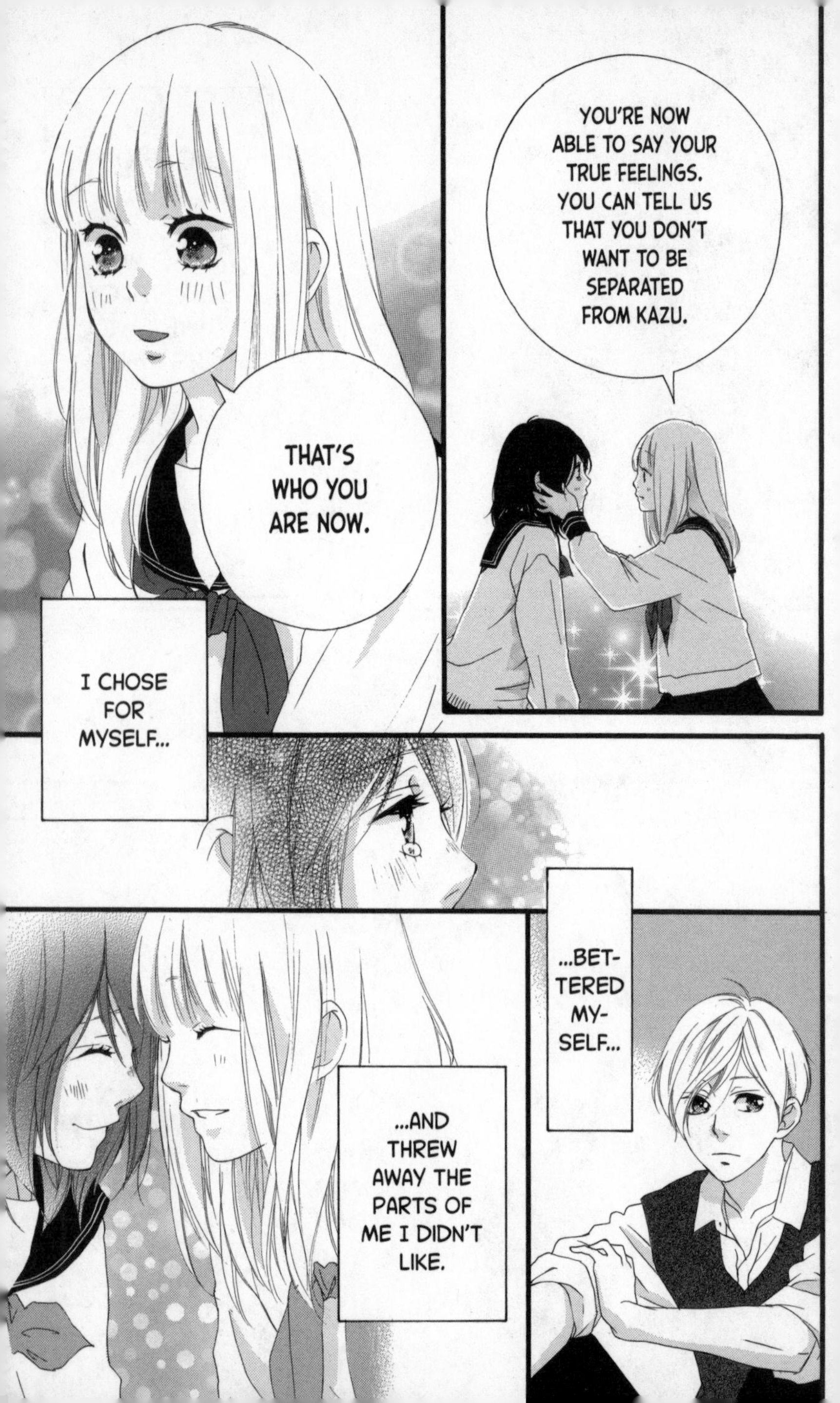
YOU'RE NOW ABLE TO SAY YOUR TRUE FEELINGS. YOU CAN TELL US THAT YOU DON'T WANT TO BE SEPARATED FROM KAZU.
THAT'S WHO YOU ARE NOW.
I CHOSE FOR MYSELF...
...BET-TERED MY-SELF...
...AND THREW AWAY THE PARTS OF ME I DIDN'T LIKE.

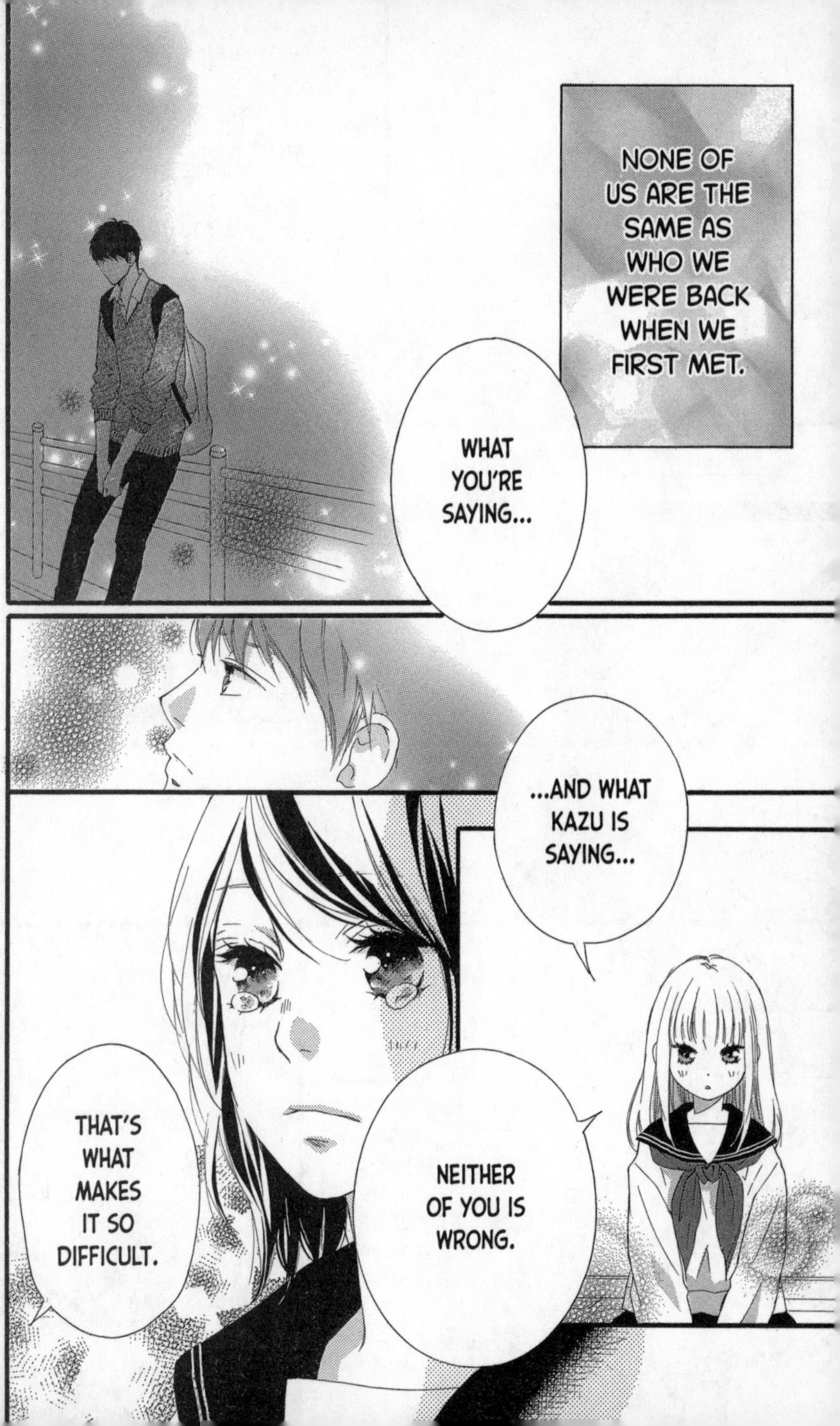
NONE OF US ARE THE SAME AS WHO WE WERE BACK WHEN WE FIRST MET.
WHAT YOU'RE SAYING...
...AND WHAT KAZU IS SAYING...
NEITHER OF YOU IS WRONG.
THAT'S WHAT MAKES IT SO DIFFICULT.

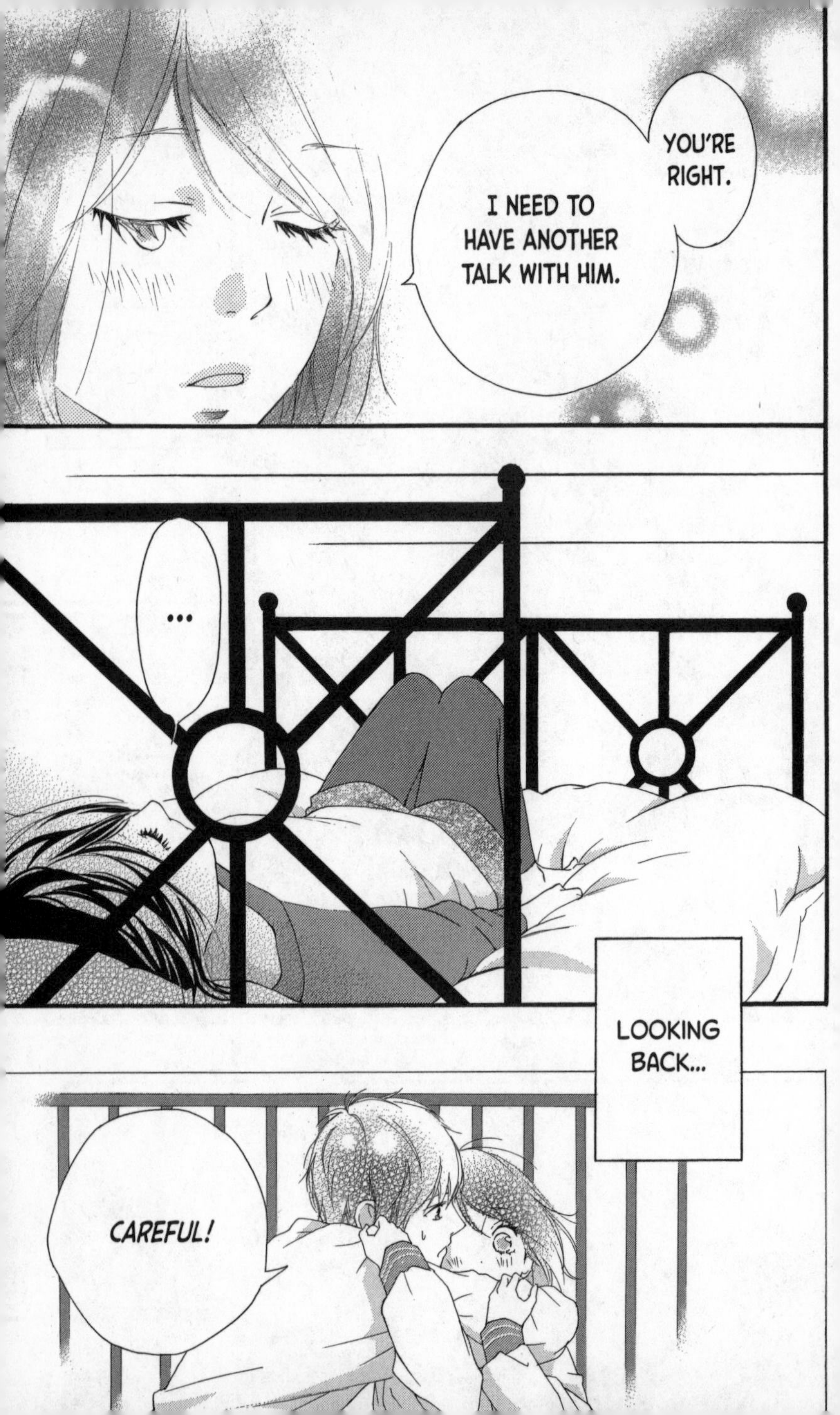
YOU'RE RIGHT.
I NEED TO HAVE ANOTHER TALK WITH HIM.
...
LOOKING BACK...
CAREFUL!

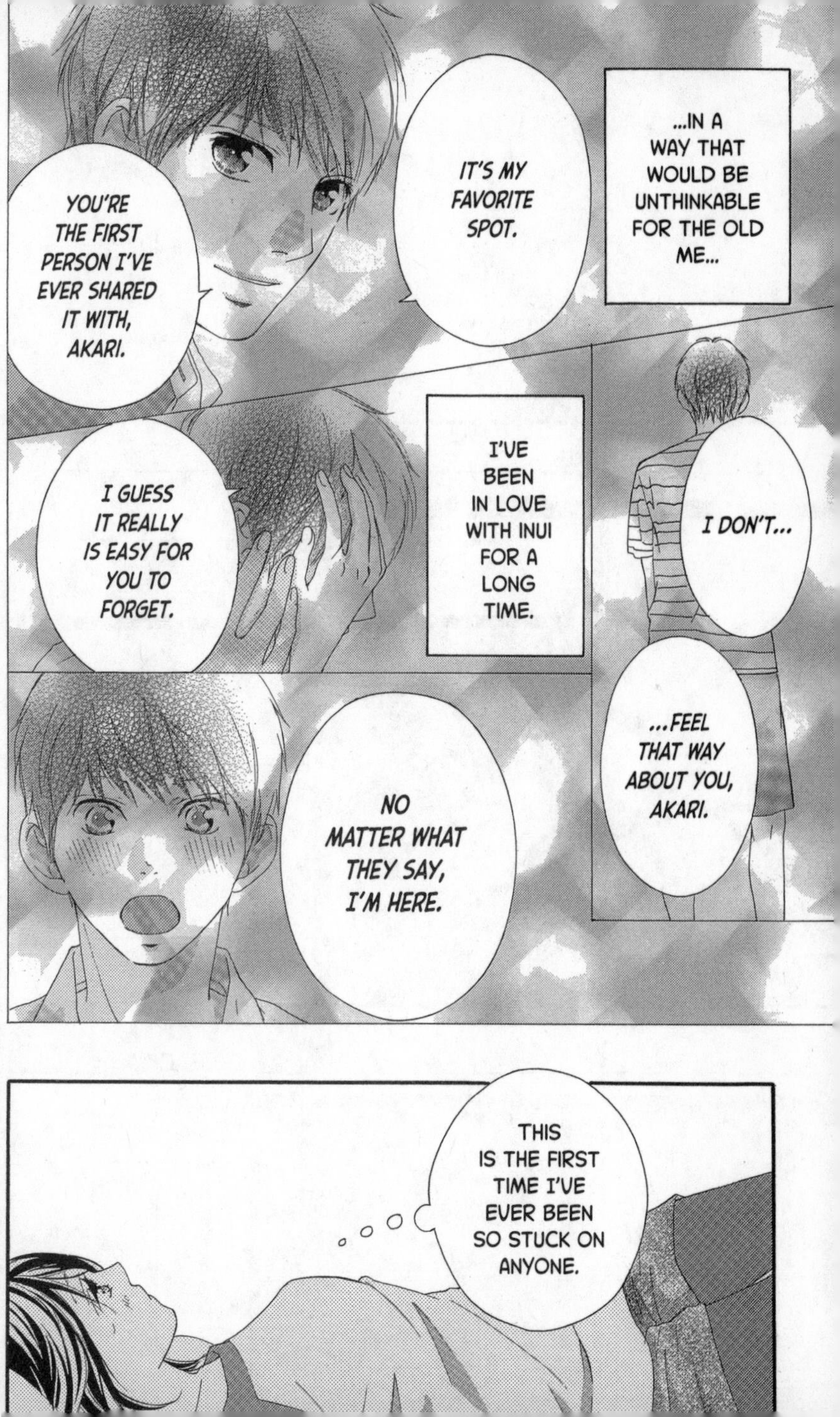
...IN A WAY THAT WOULD BE UNTHINKABLE FOR THE OLD ME...
IT'S MY FAVORITE SPOT.
YOU'RE THE FIRST PERSON I'VE EVER SHARED IT WITH, AKARI.
I DON'T...
...FEEL THAT WAY ABOUT YOU, AKARI.
I'VE BEEN IN LOVE WITH INUI FOR A LONG TIME.
I GUESS IT REALLY IS EASY FOR YOU TO FORGET.
NO MATTER WHAT THEY SAY, I'M HERE.
THIS IS THE FIRST TIME I'VE EVER BEEN SO STUCK ON ANYONE.

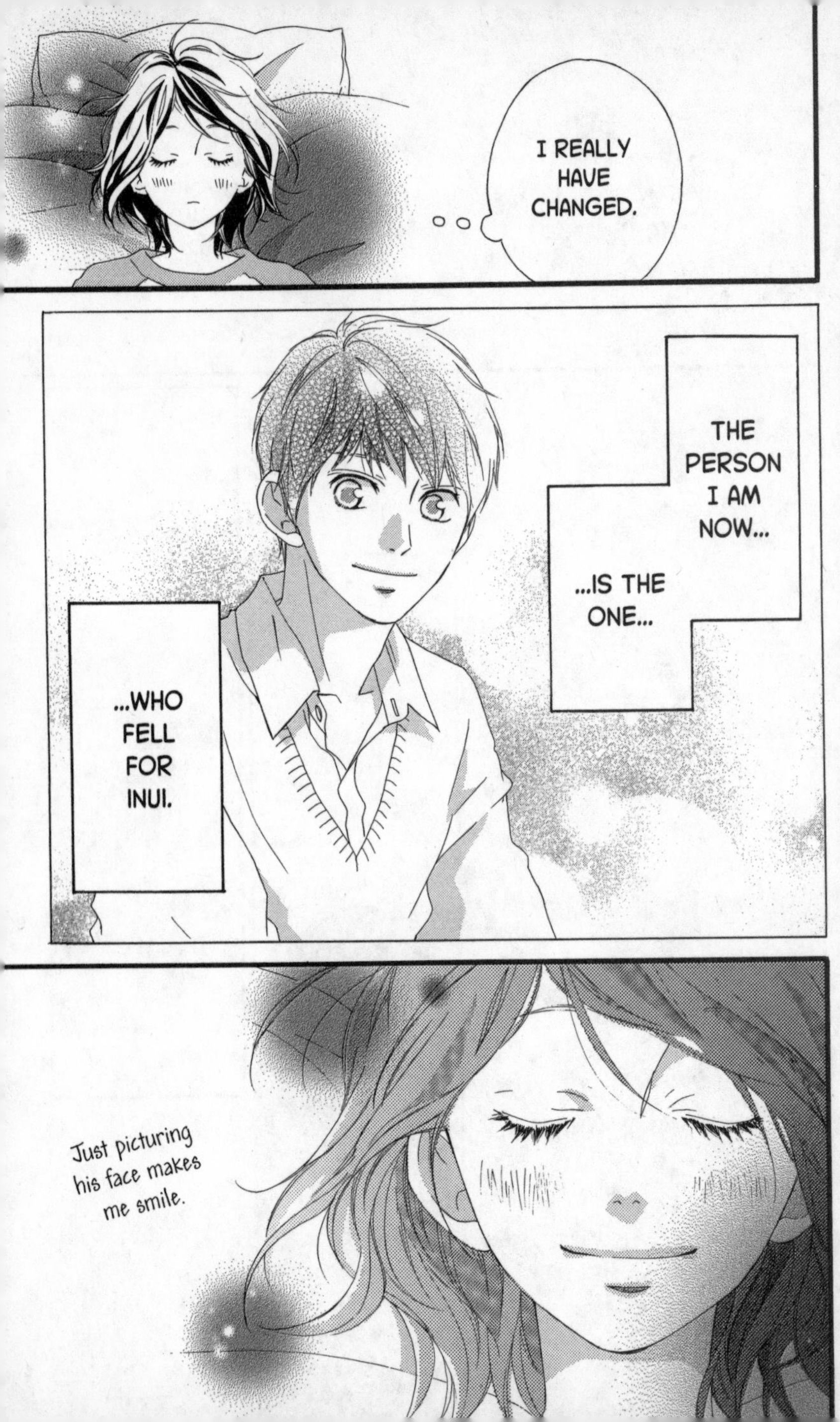
I REALLY HAVE CHANGED.
THE PERSON I AM NOW...
...IS THE ONE...
...WHO FELL FOR INUI.
Just picturing his face makes me smile.

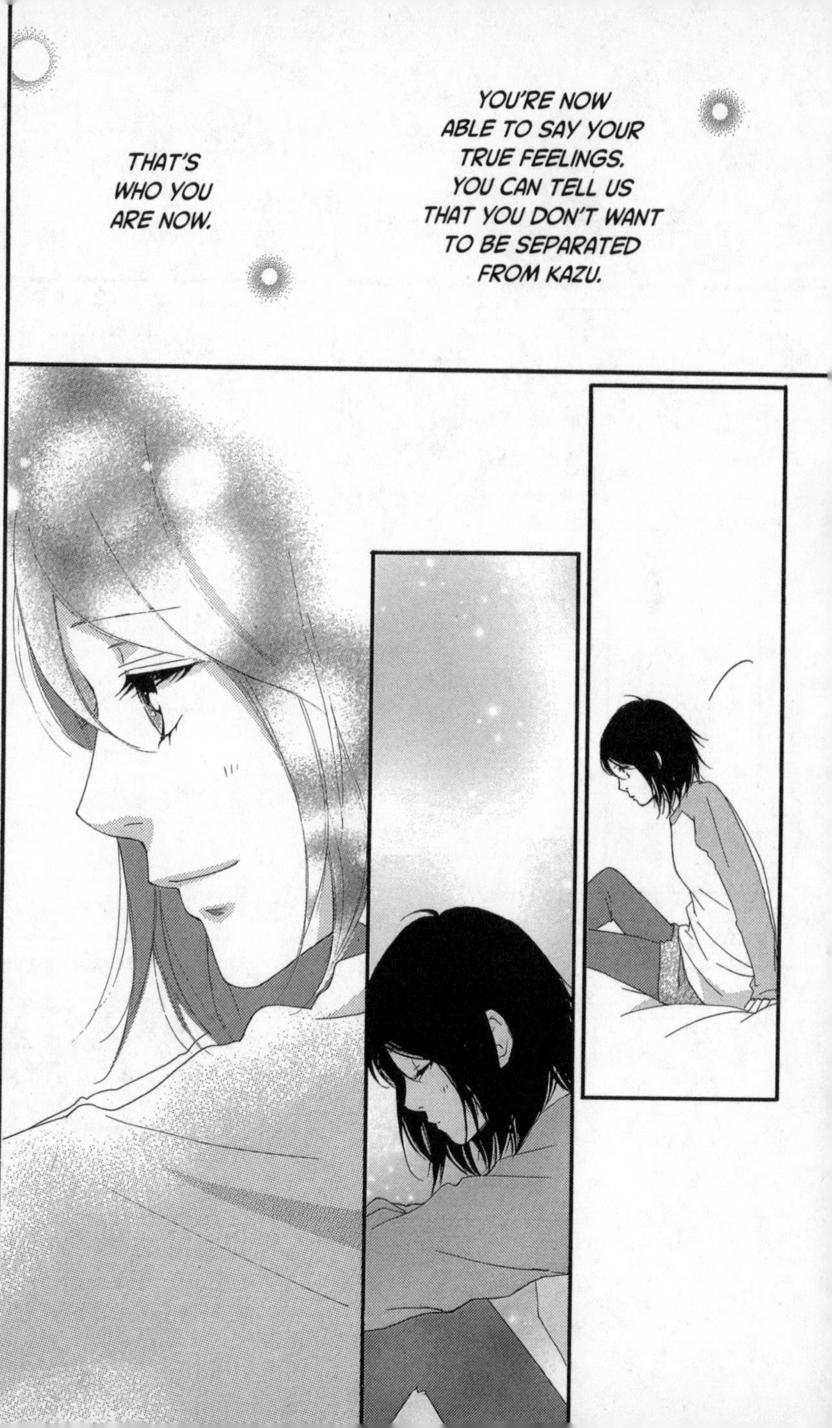
YOU'RE NOW ABLE TO SAY YOUR TRUE FEELINGS. YOU CAN TELL US THAT YOU DON'T WANT TO BE SEPARATED FROM KAZU.
THAT'S WHO YOU ARE NOW.

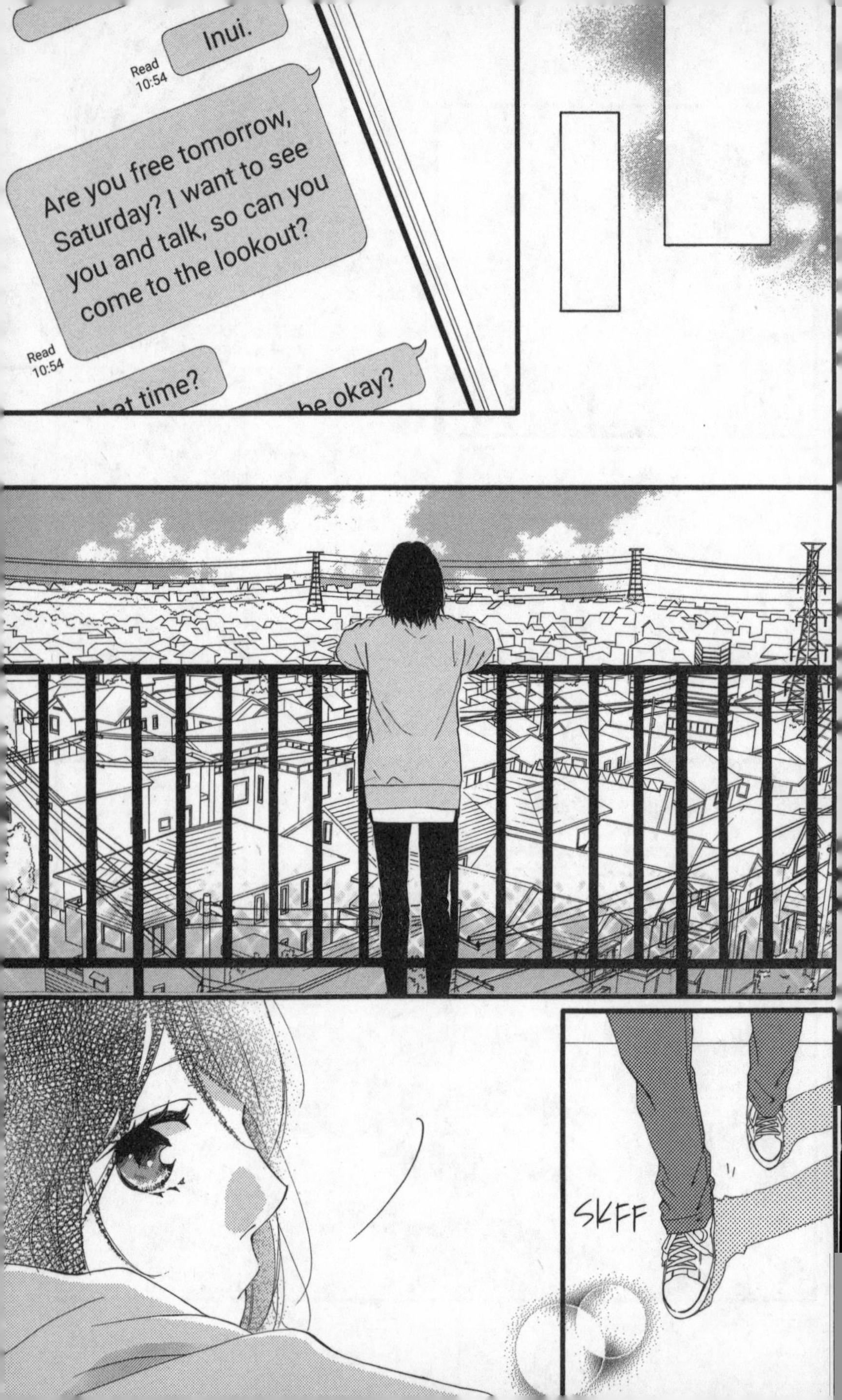
Inui.
Read 10:54
Are you free tomorrow, Saturday? I want to see you and talk, so can you come to the lookout?
Read 10:54
SKFF

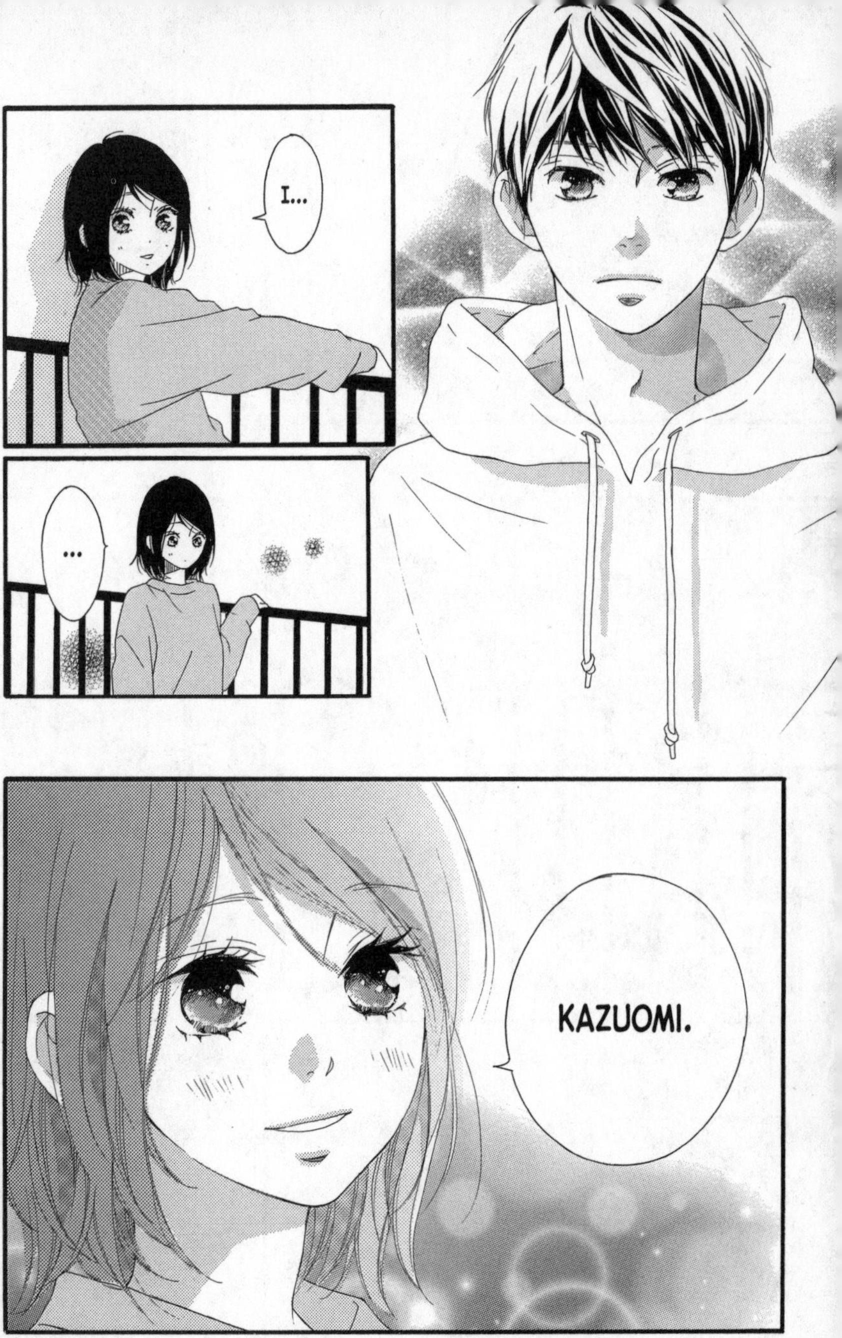
I...
...
KAZUOMI.

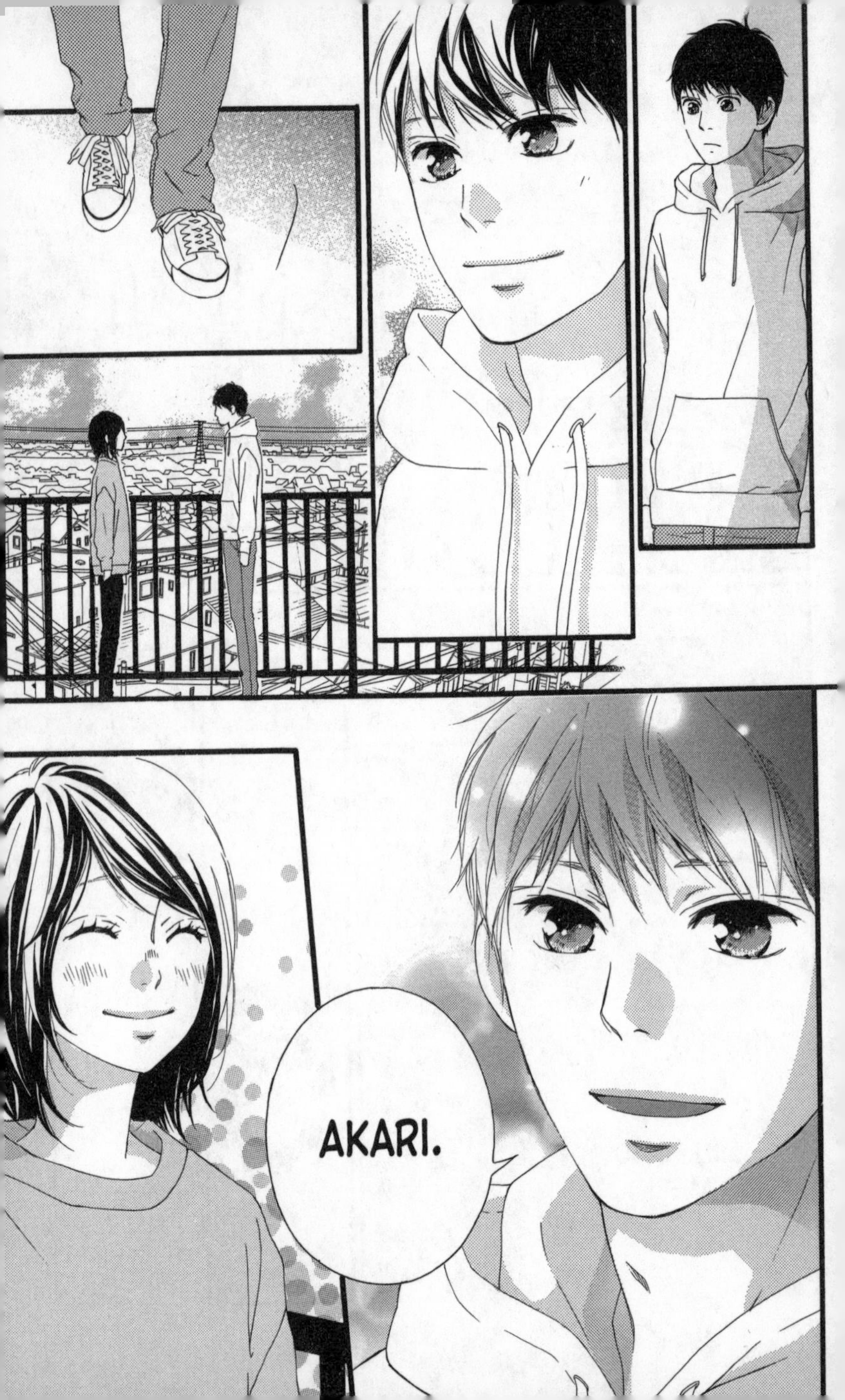
AKARI.

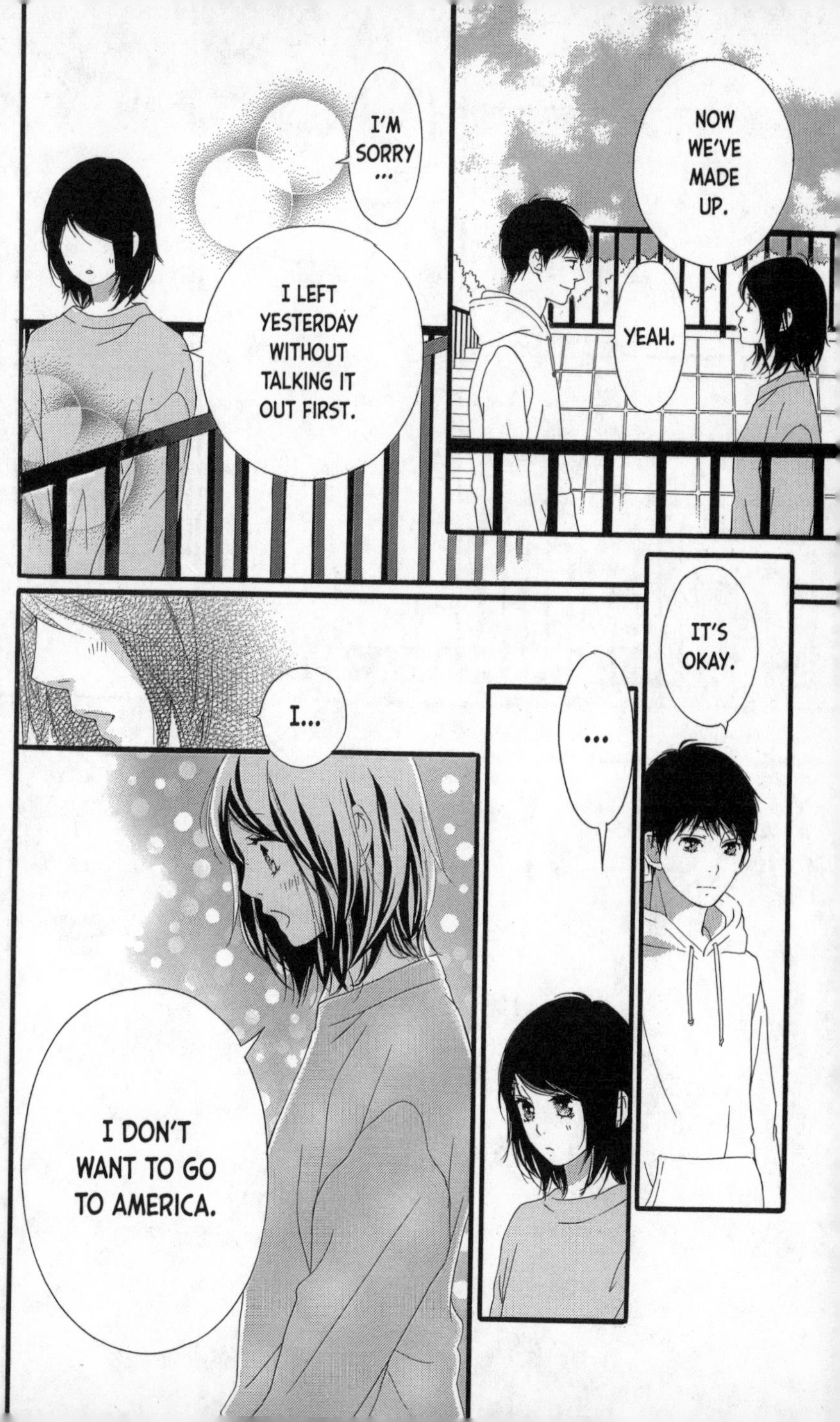
NOW WE'VE MADE UP.
YEAH.
I'M SORRY ...
I LEFT YESTERDAY WITHOUT TALKING IT OUT FIRST.
IT'S OKAY.
...
I...
I DON'T WANT TO GO TO AMERICA.

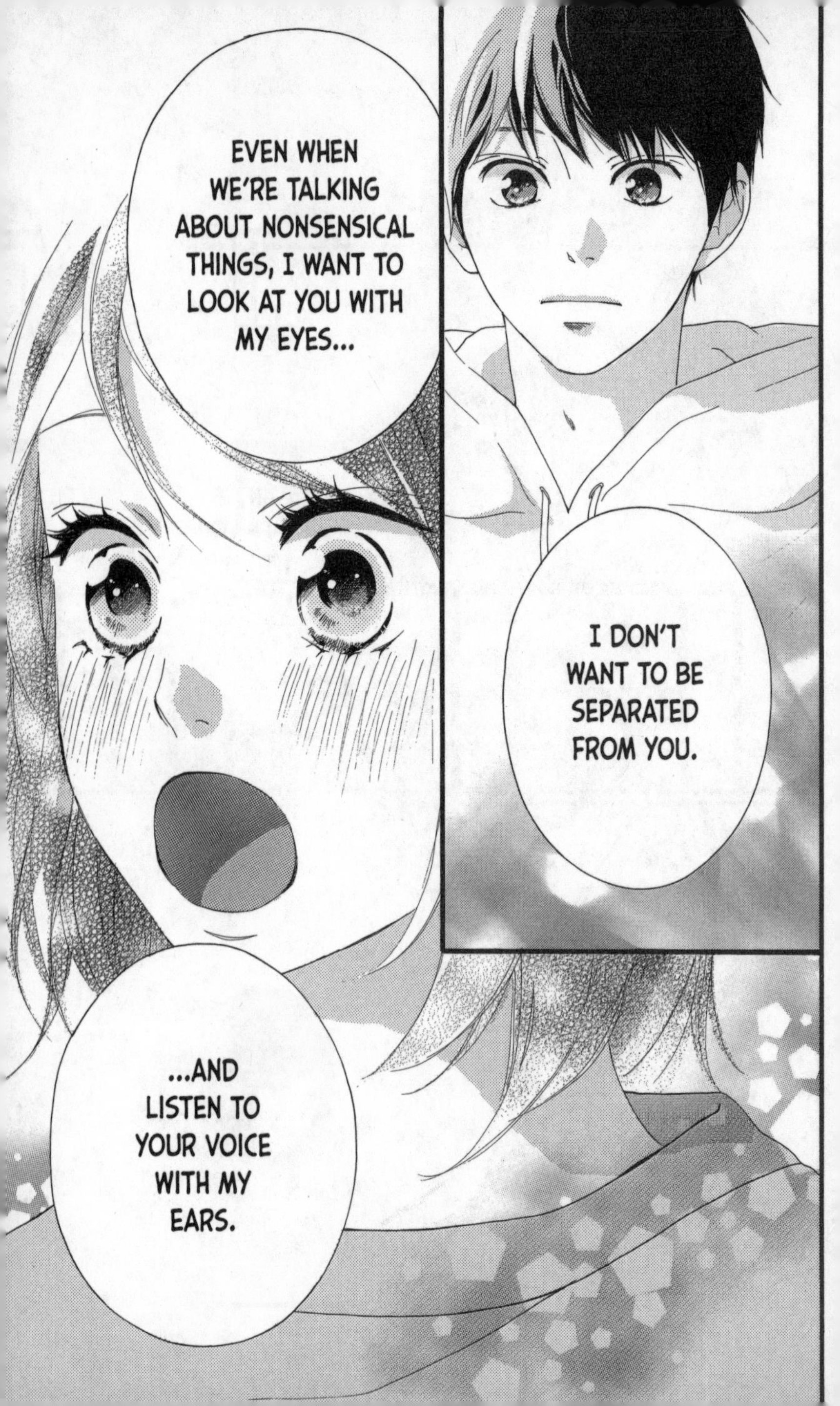
I DON'T WANT TO BE SEPARATED FROM YOU.
EVEN WHEN WE'RE TALKING ABOUT NONSENSICAL THINGS, I WANT TO LOOK AT YOU WITH MY EYES...
...AND LISTEN TO YOUR VOICE WITH MY EARS.

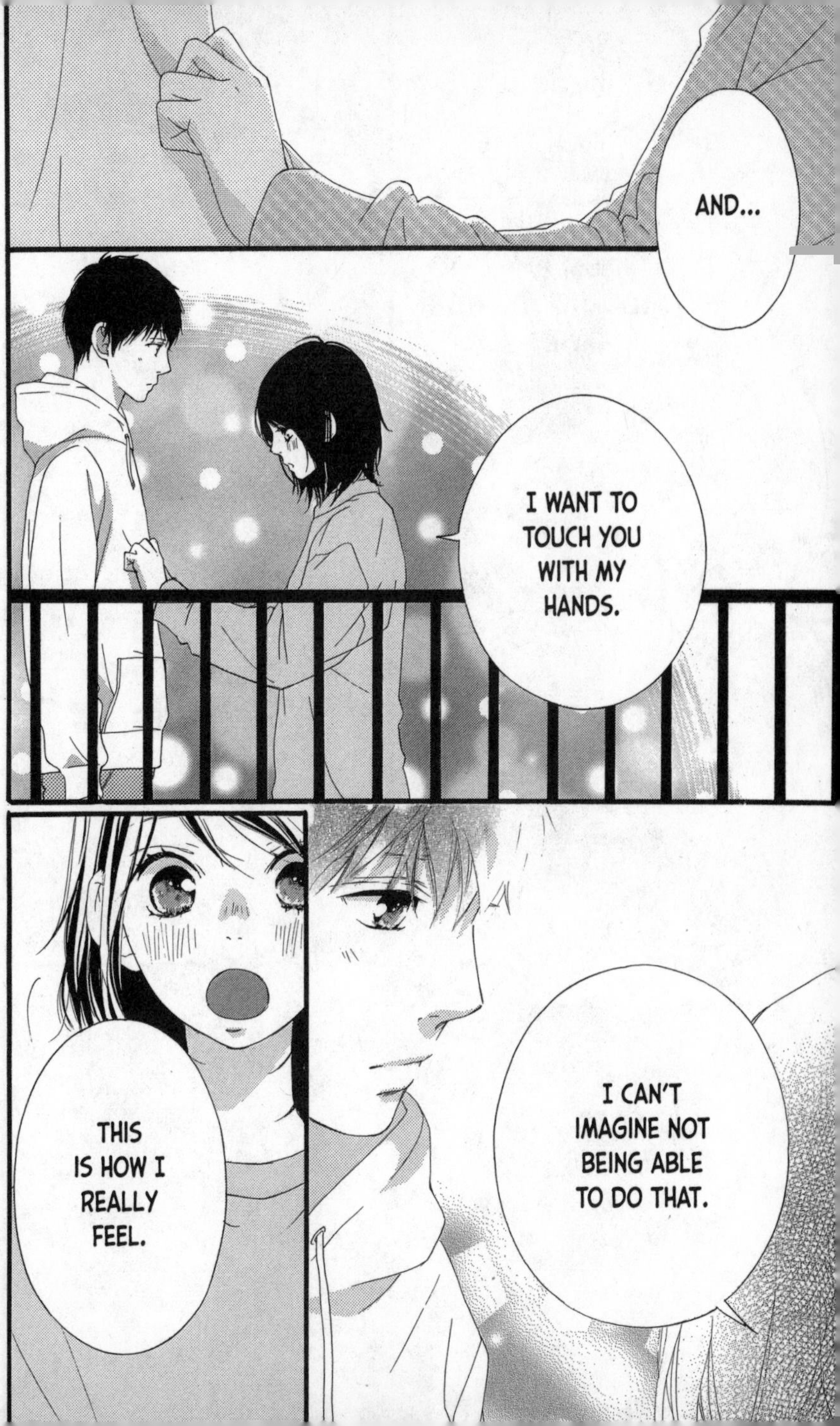
AND...
I WANT TO TOUCH YOU WITH MY HANDS.
I CAN'T IMAGINE NOT BEING ABLE TO DO THAT.
THIS IS HOW I REALLY FEEL.

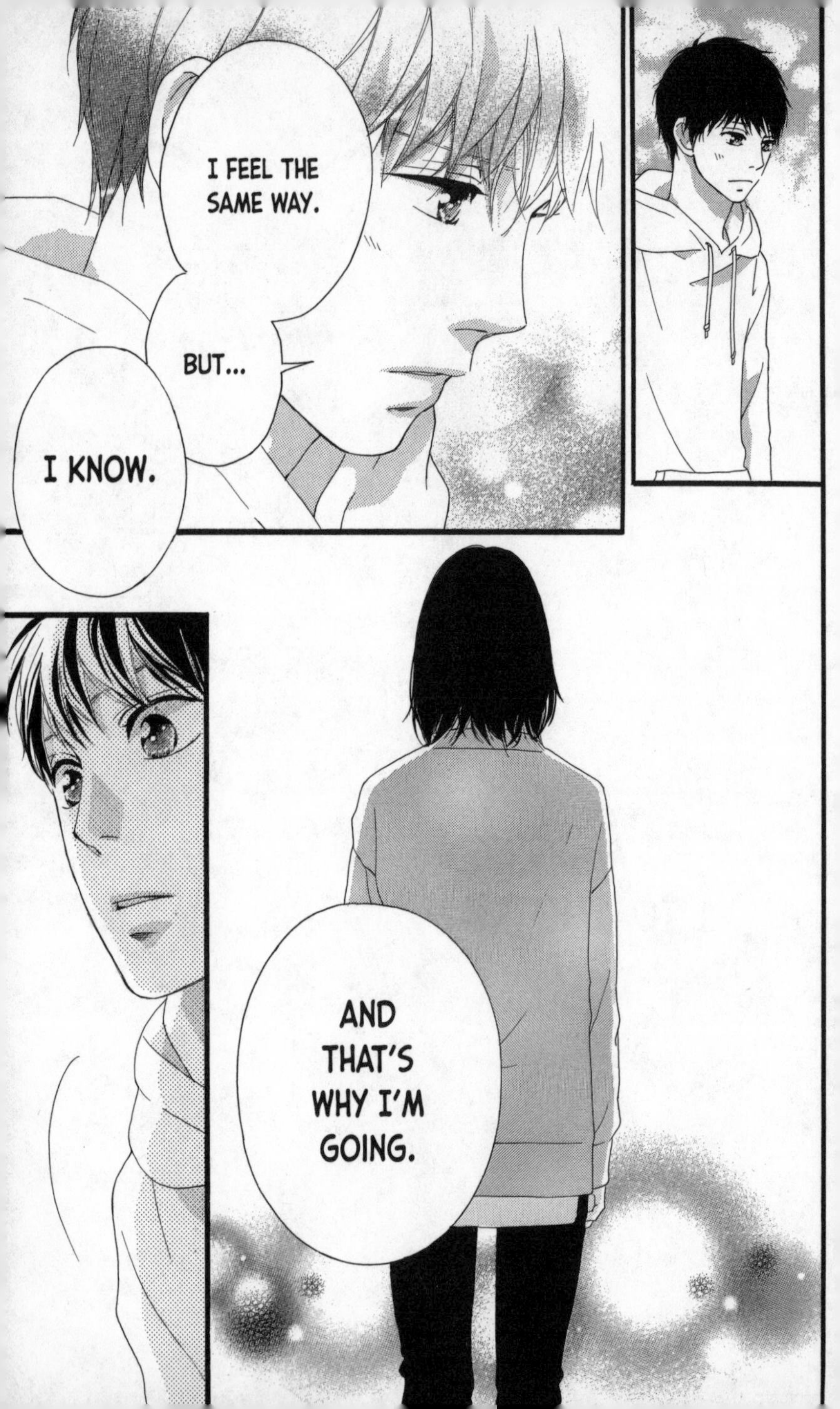
I FEEL THE SAME WAY.
BUT...
I KNOW.
AND THAT'S WHY I'M GOING.

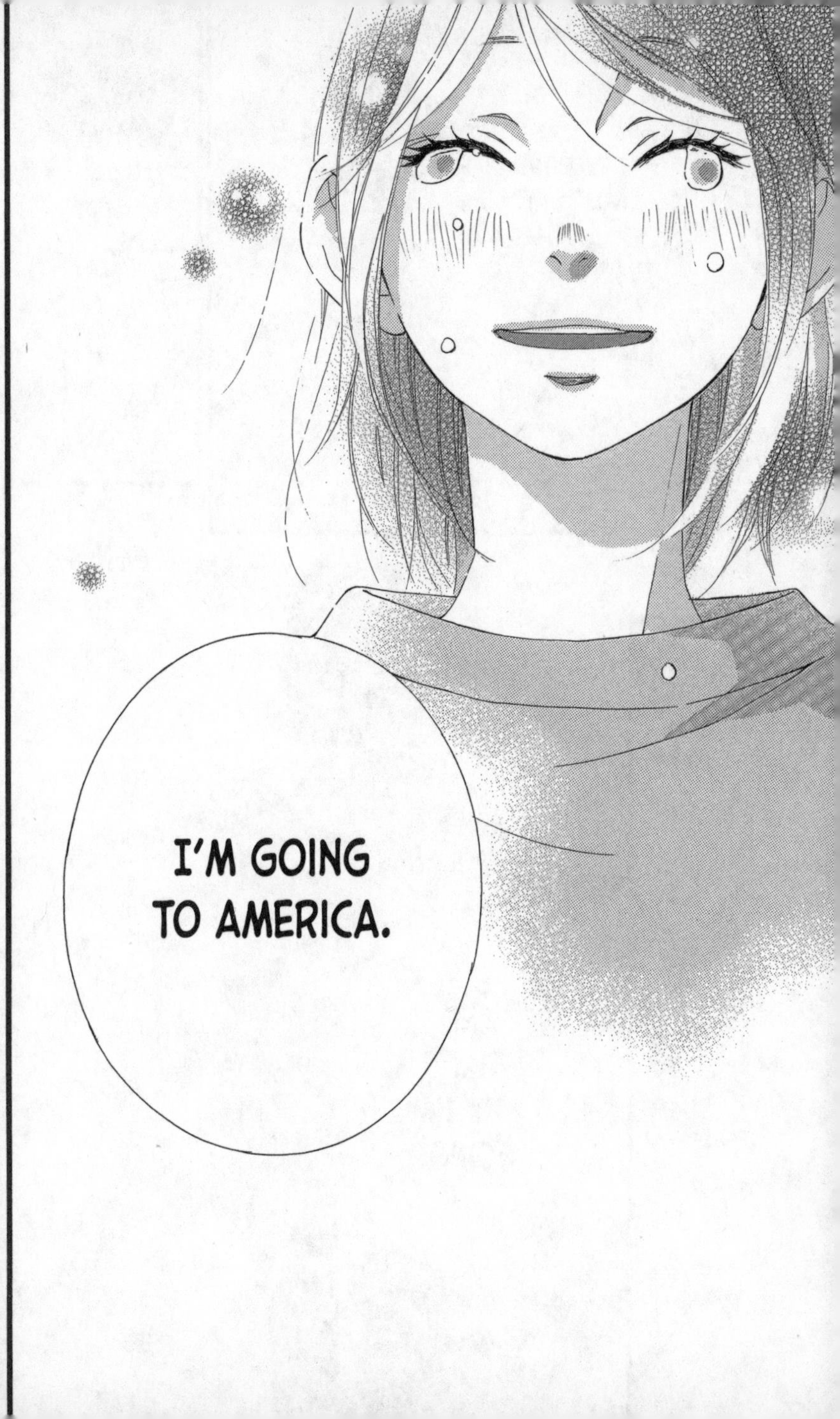
I'M GOING TO AMERICA.

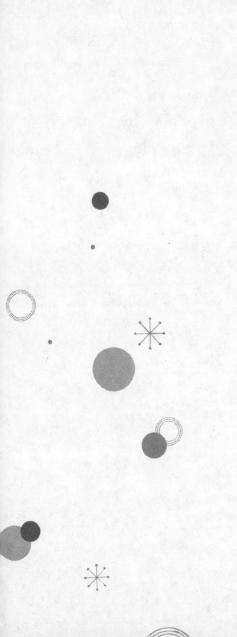

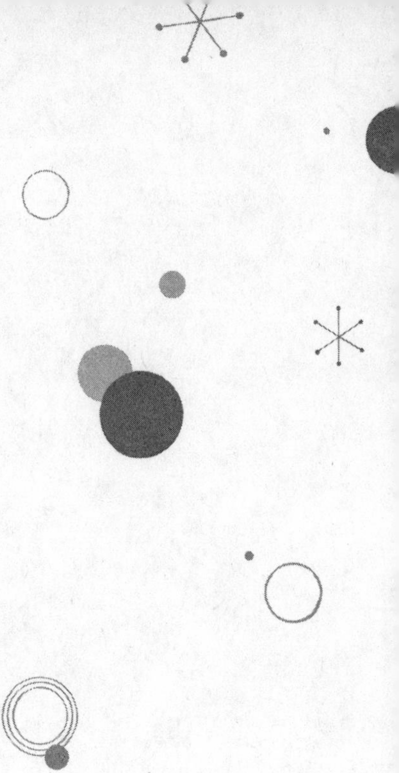

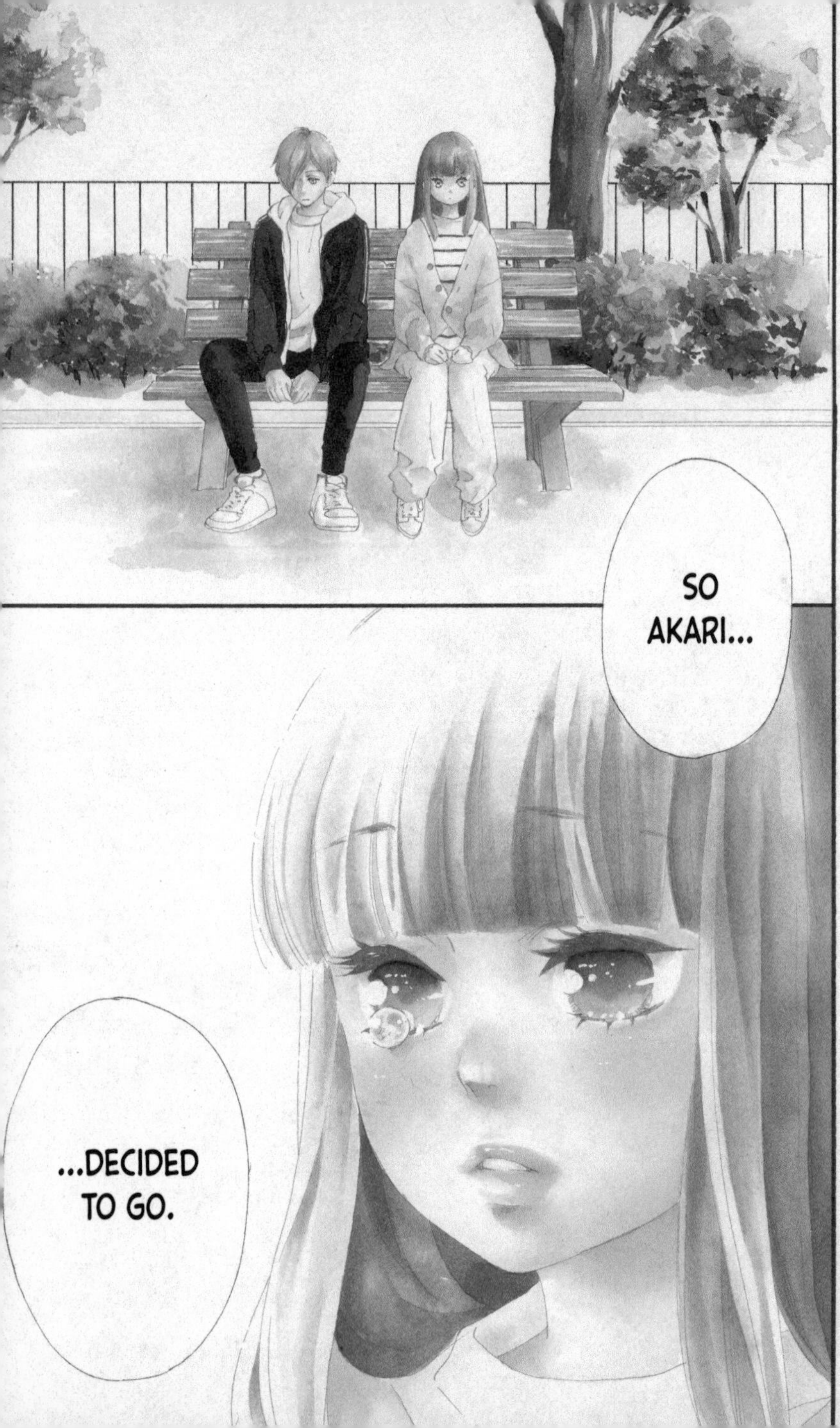
SO AKARI...
...DECIDED TO GO.

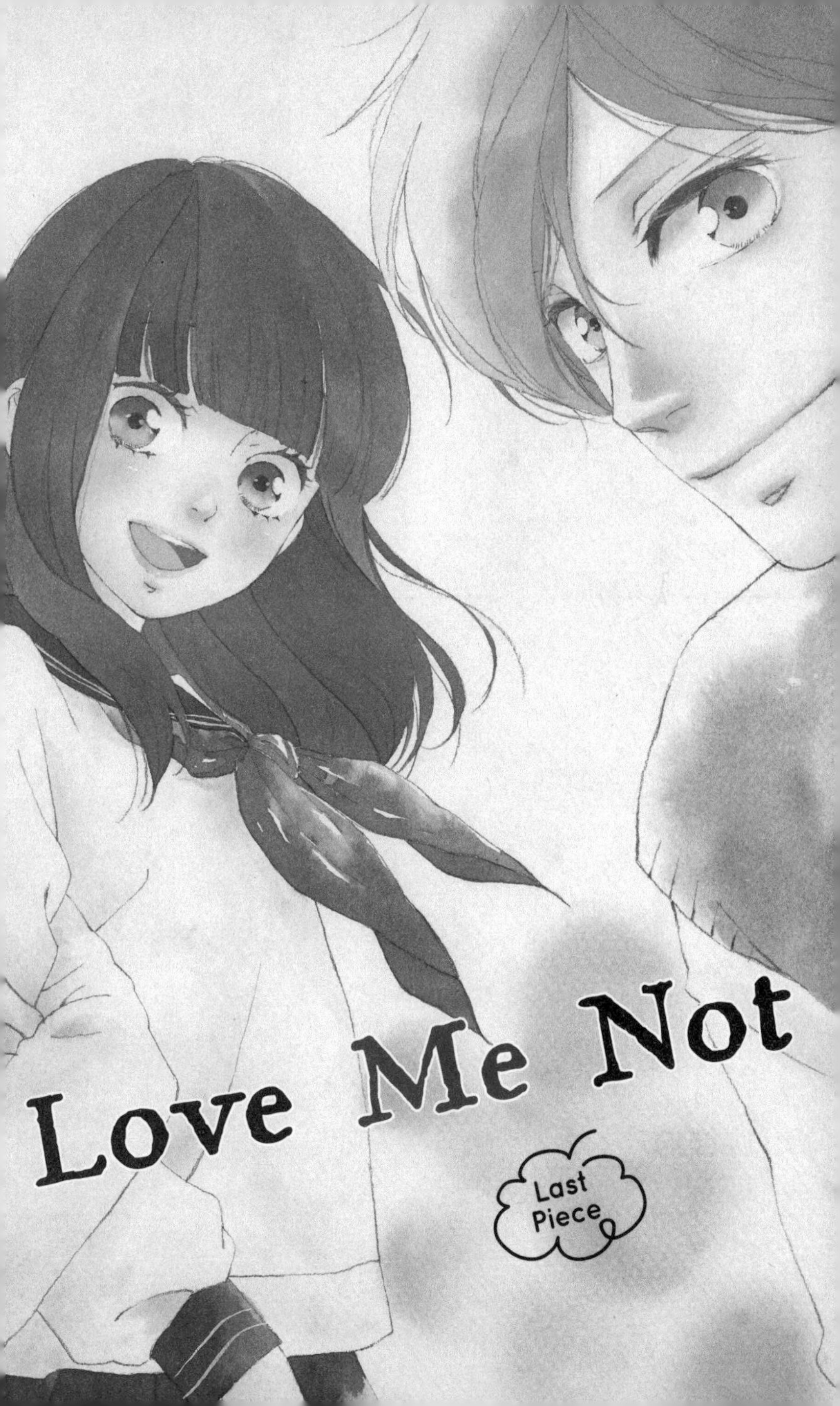
Love Me Not
Last Piece

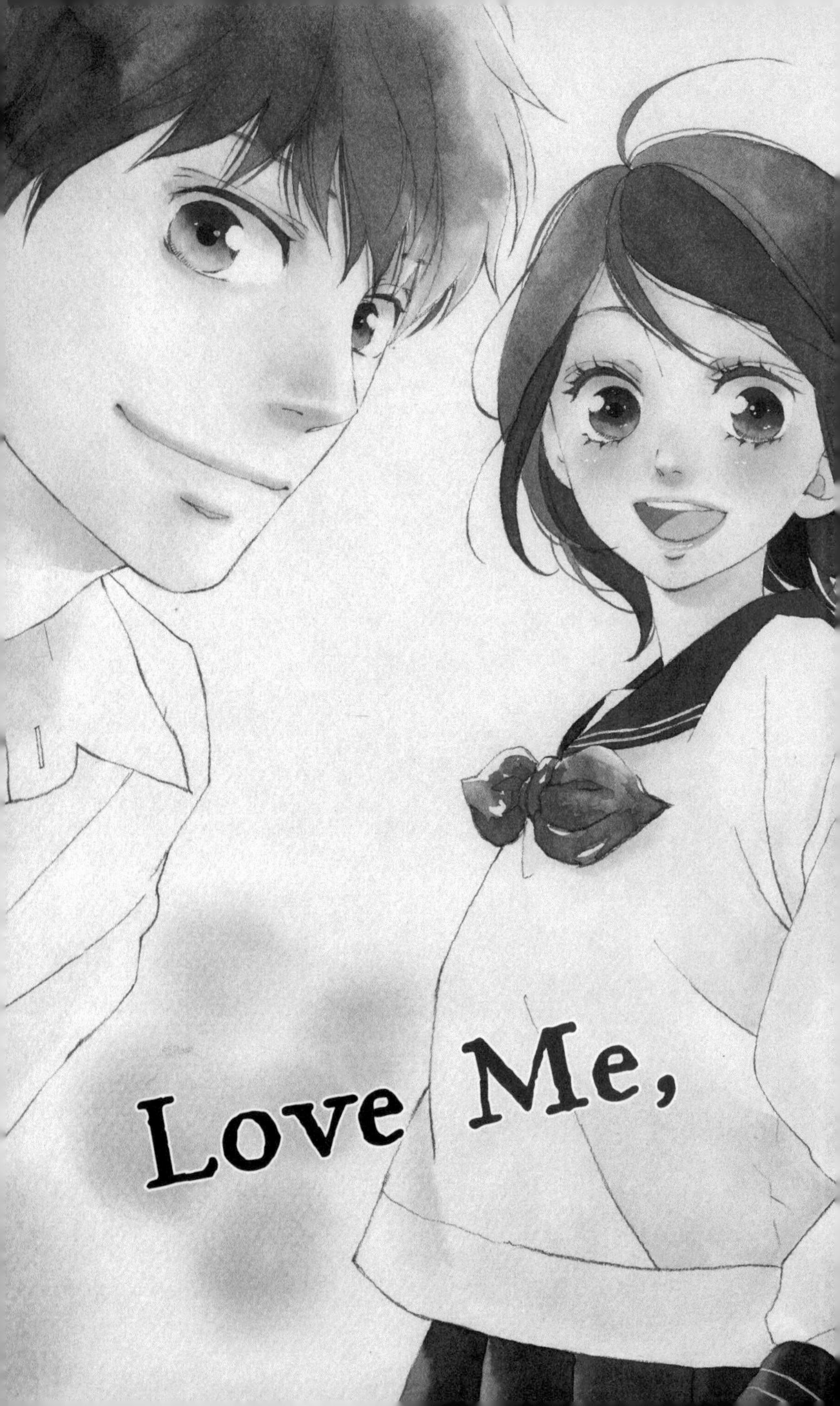
Love Me,

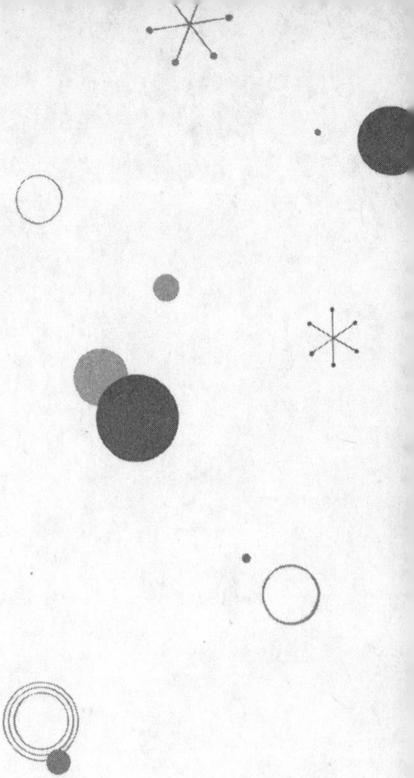

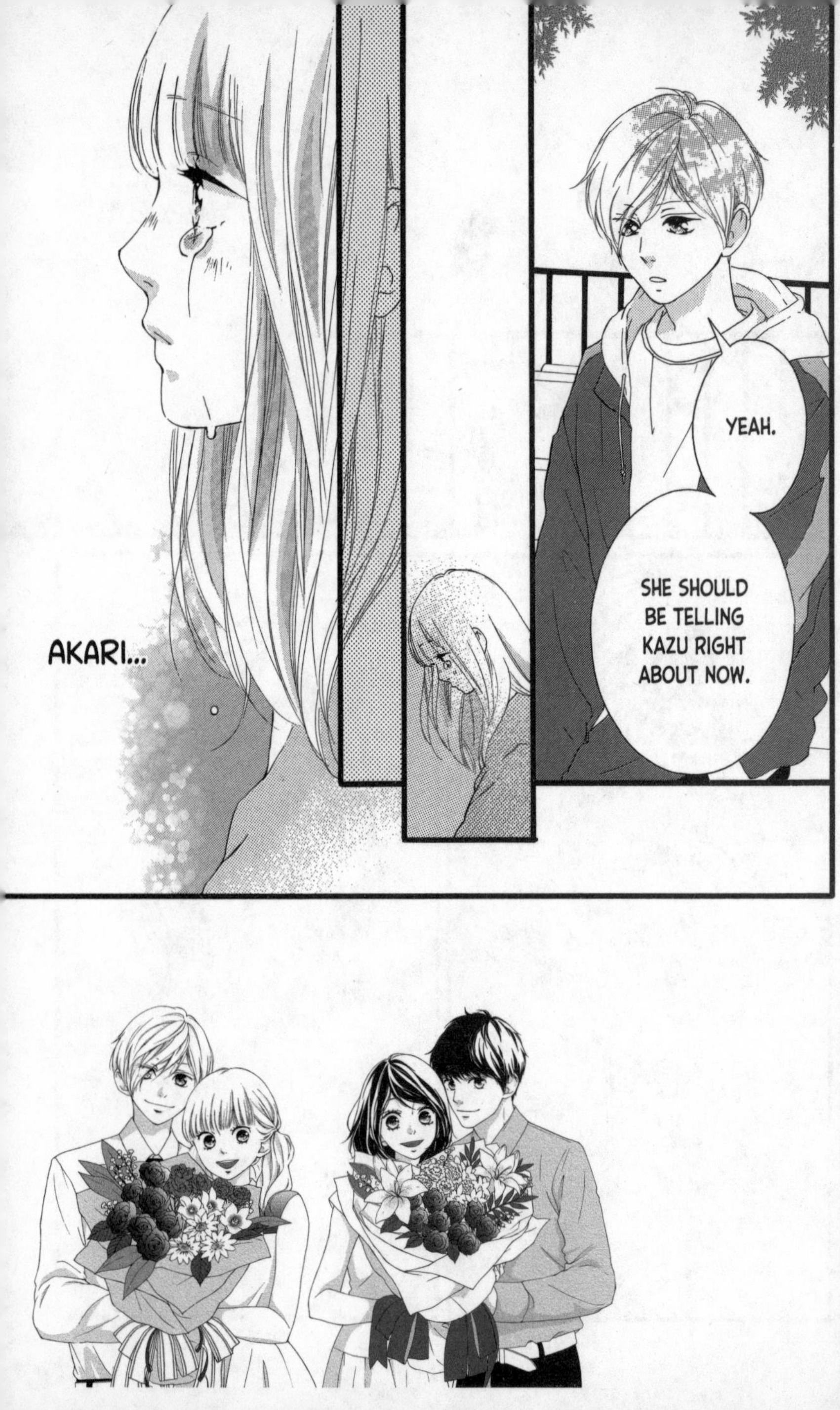
YEAH.
SHE SHOULD BE TELLING KAZU RIGHT ABOUT NOW.
AKARI...

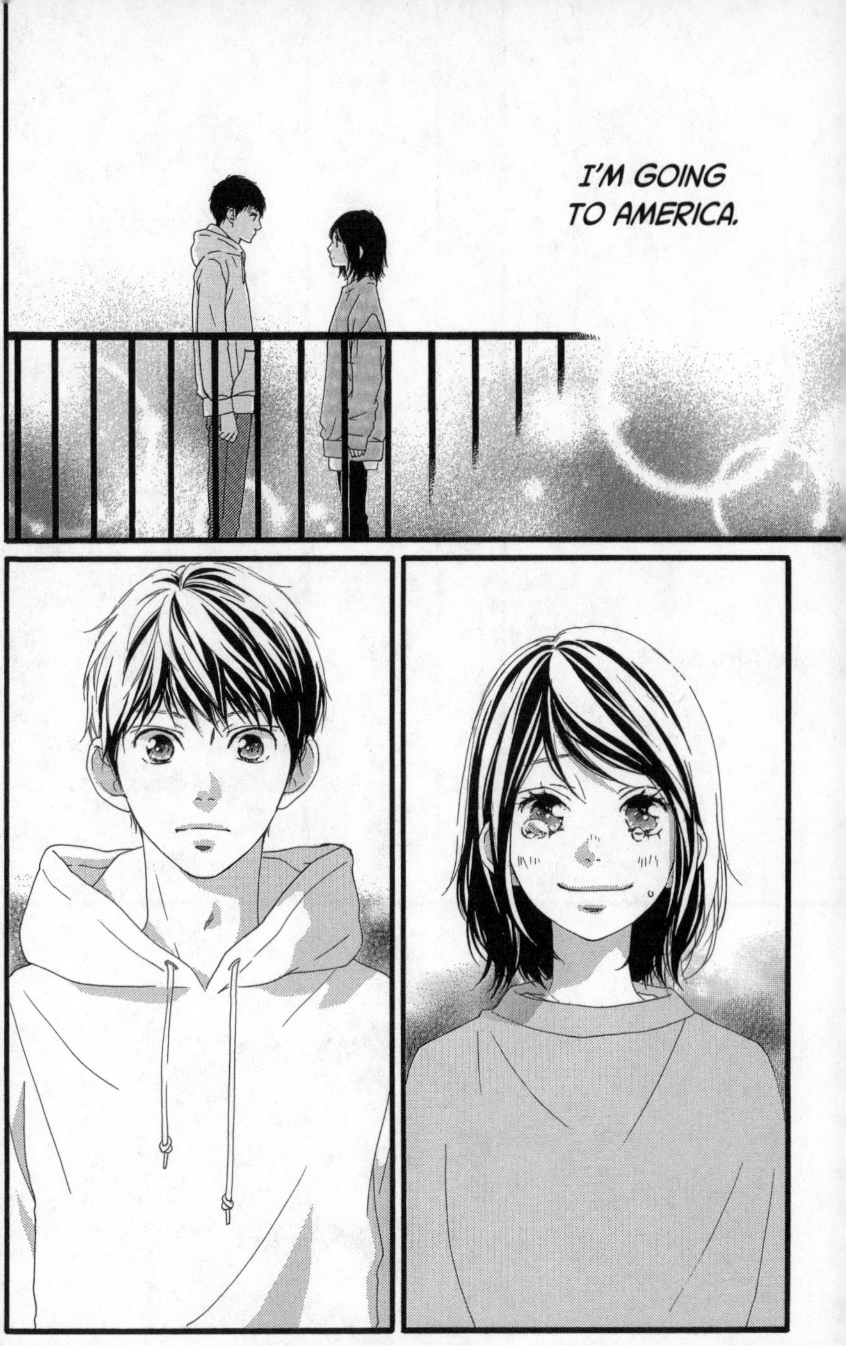
I'M GOING
TO AMERICA.

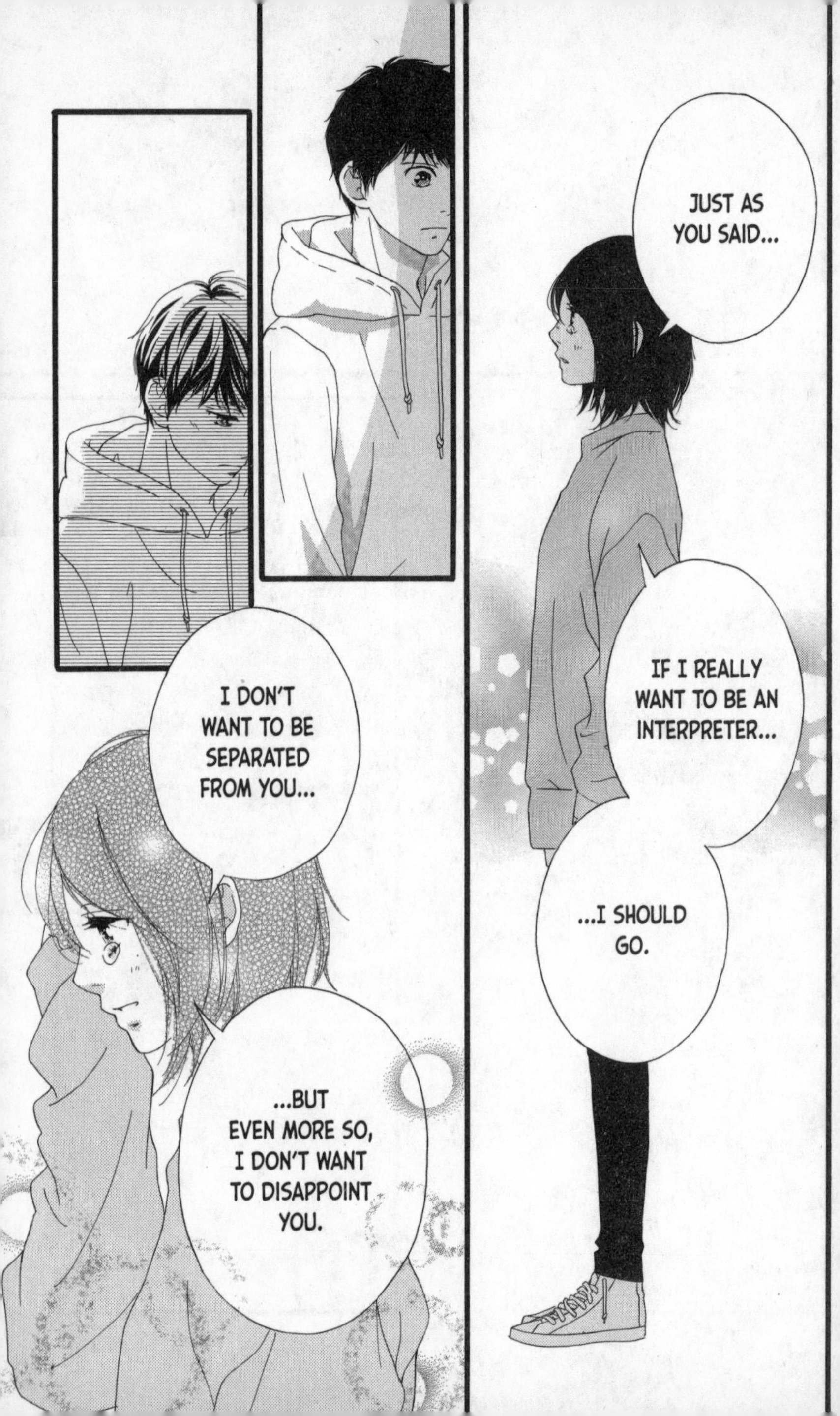
JUST AS YOU SAID...
IF I REALLY WANT TO BE AN INTERPRETER...
...I SHOULD GO.
I DON'T WANT TO BE SEPARATED FROM YOU...
...BUT EVEN MORE SO, I DON'T WANT TO DISAPPOINT YOU.

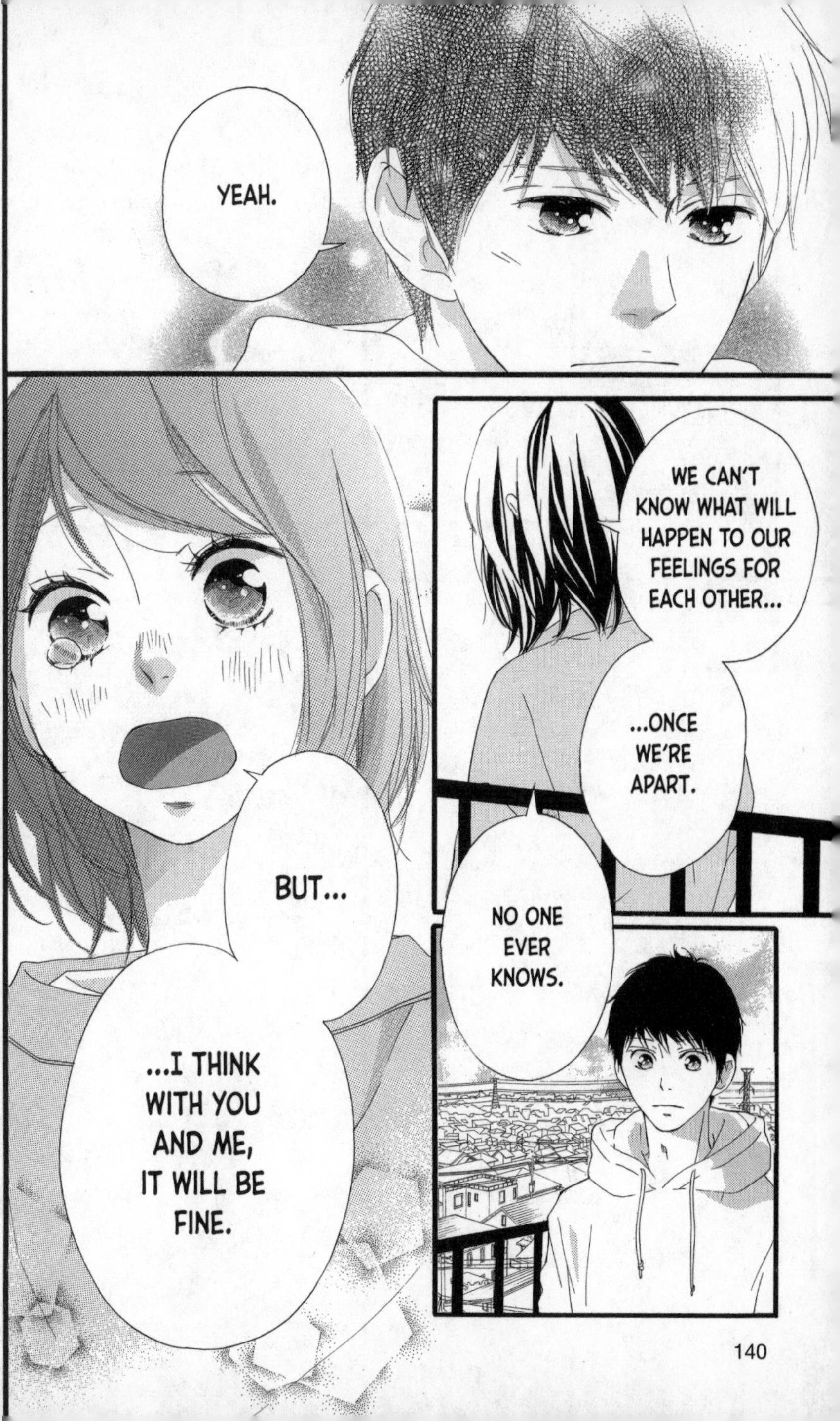
YEAH.
WE CAN'T KNOW WHAT WILL HAPPEN TO OUR FEELINGS FOR EACH OTHER...
...ONCE WE'RE APART.
NO ONE EVER KNOWS.
BUT...
...I THINK WITH YOU AND ME, IT WILL BE FINE.

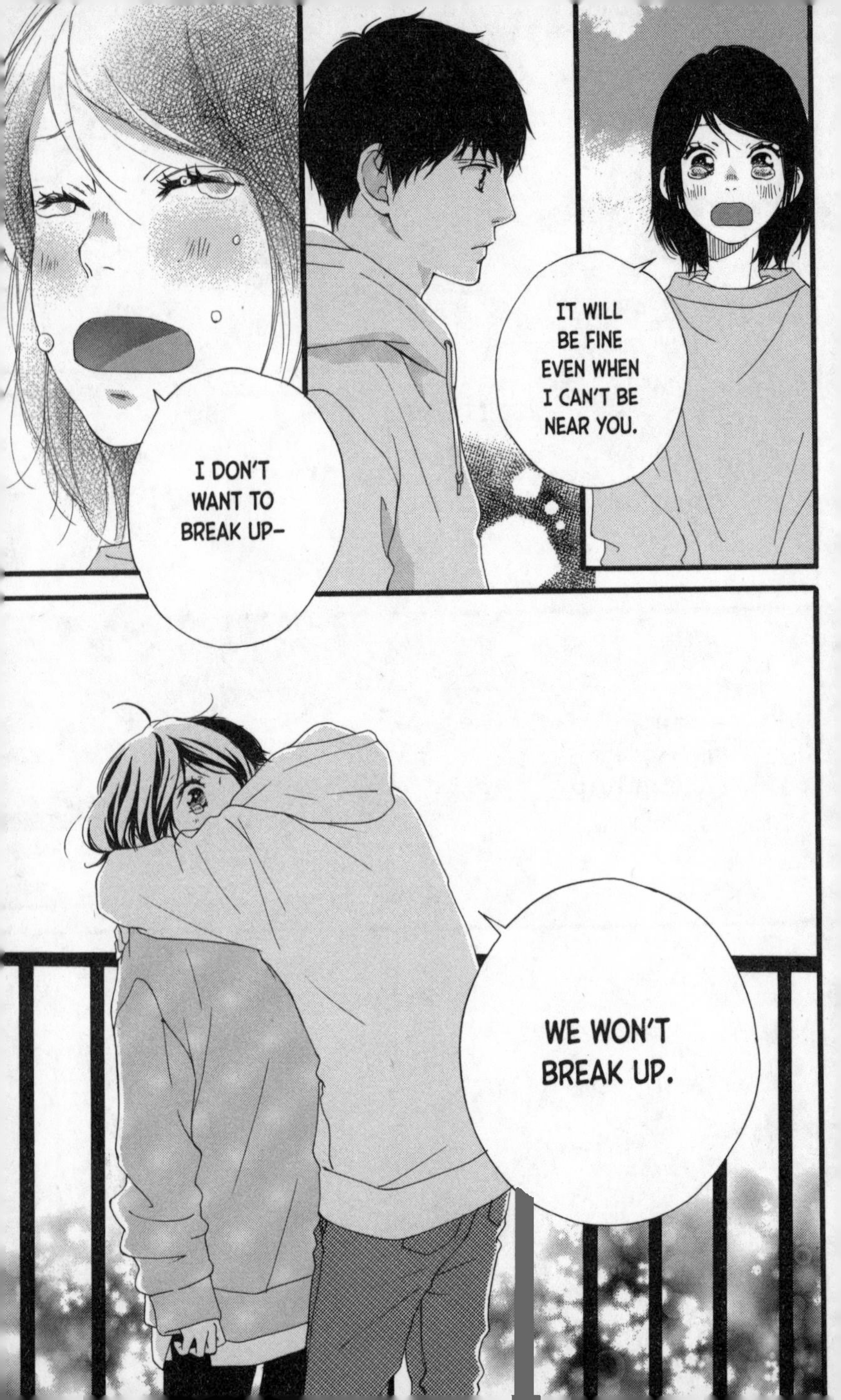
IT WILL BE FINE EVEN WHEN I CAN'T BE NEAR YOU.
I DON'T WANT TO BREAK UP–
WE WON'T BREAK UP.

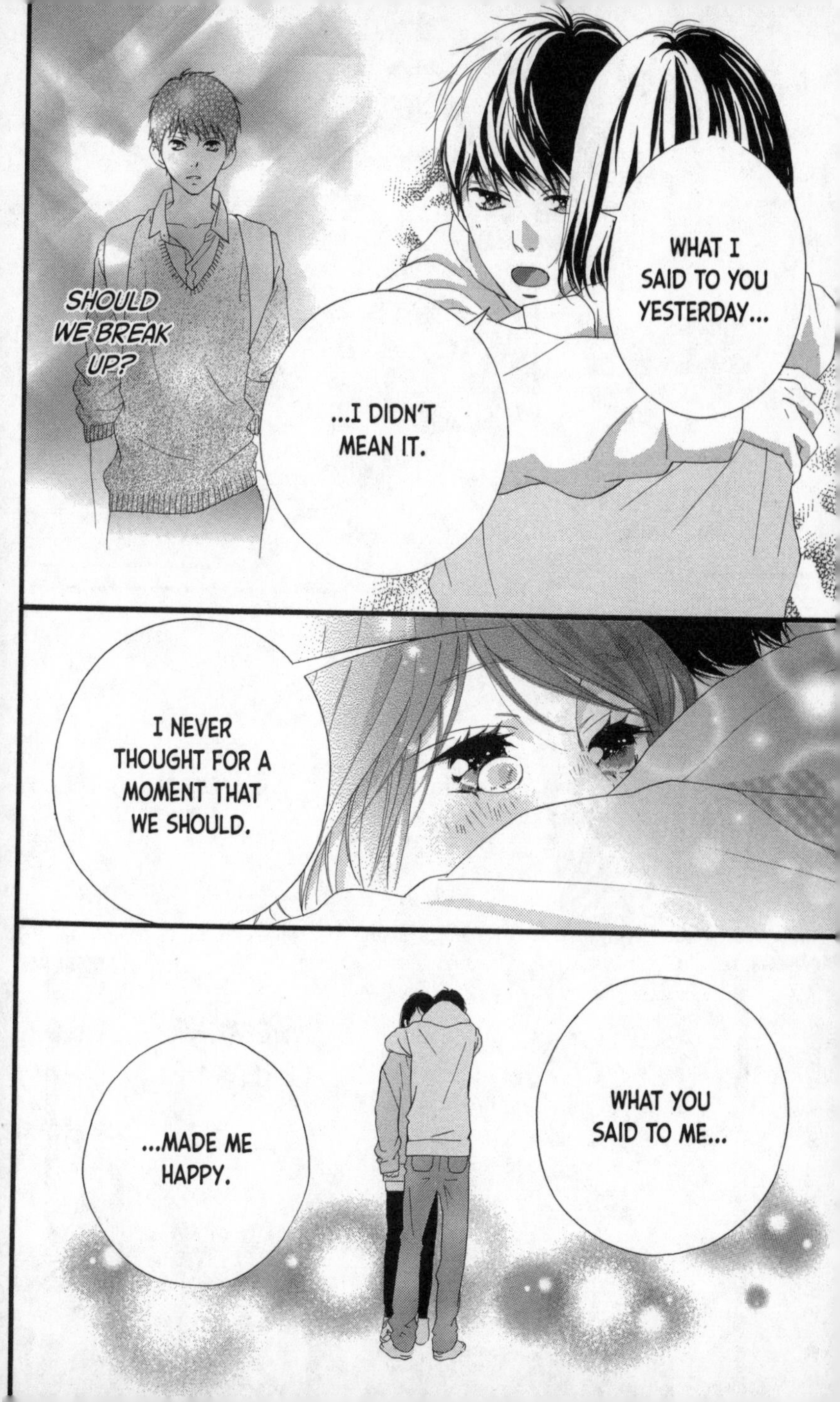
WHAT I SAID TO YOU YESTERDAY...
SHOULD WE BREAK UP?
...I DIDN'T MEAN IT.
I NEVER THOUGHT FOR A MOMENT THAT WE SHOULD.
WHAT YOU SAID TO ME...
...MADE ME HAPPY.

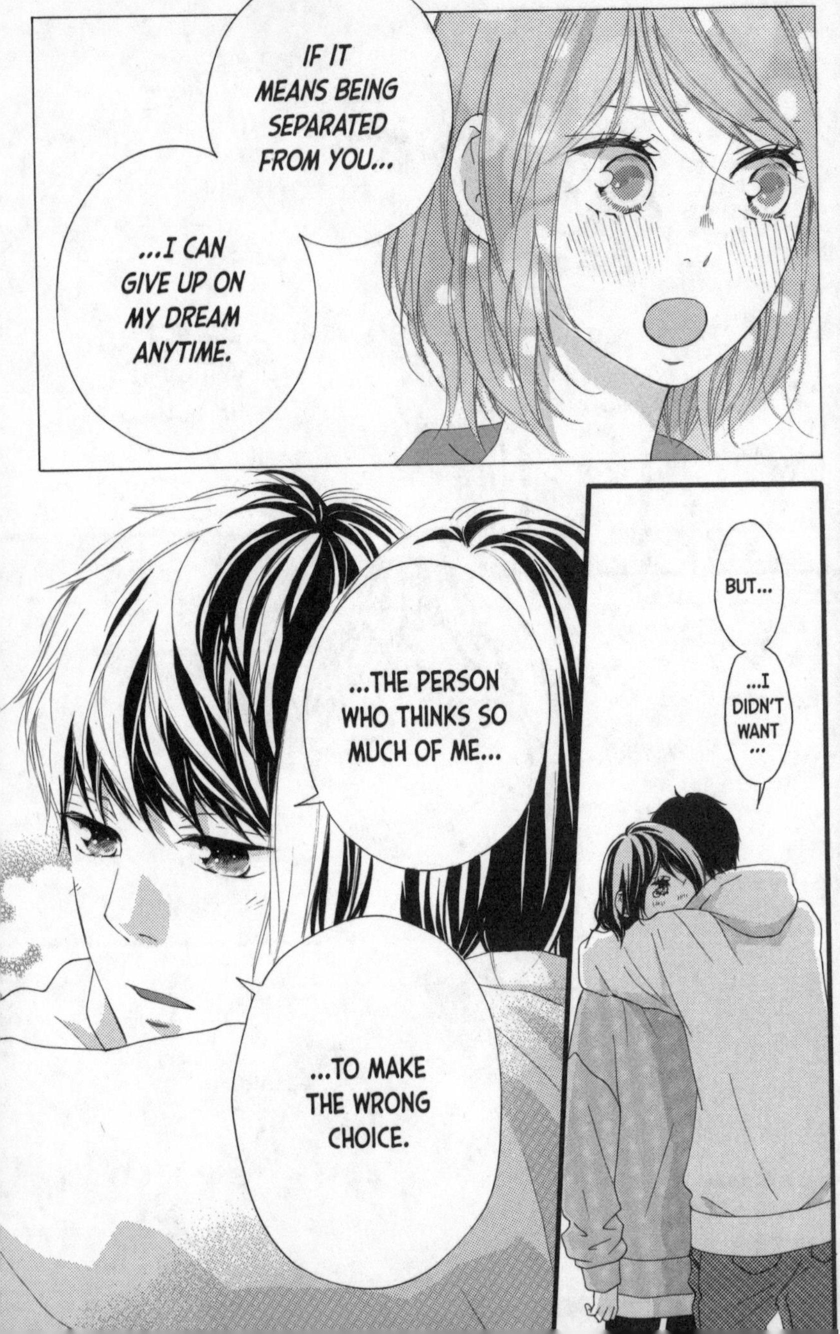
IF IT MEANS BEING SEPARATED FROM YOU...
...I CAN GIVE UP ON MY DREAM ANYTIME.
BUT...
...I DIDN'T WANT ...
...THE PERSON WHO THINKS SO MUCH OF ME...
...TO MAKE THE WRONG CHOICE.

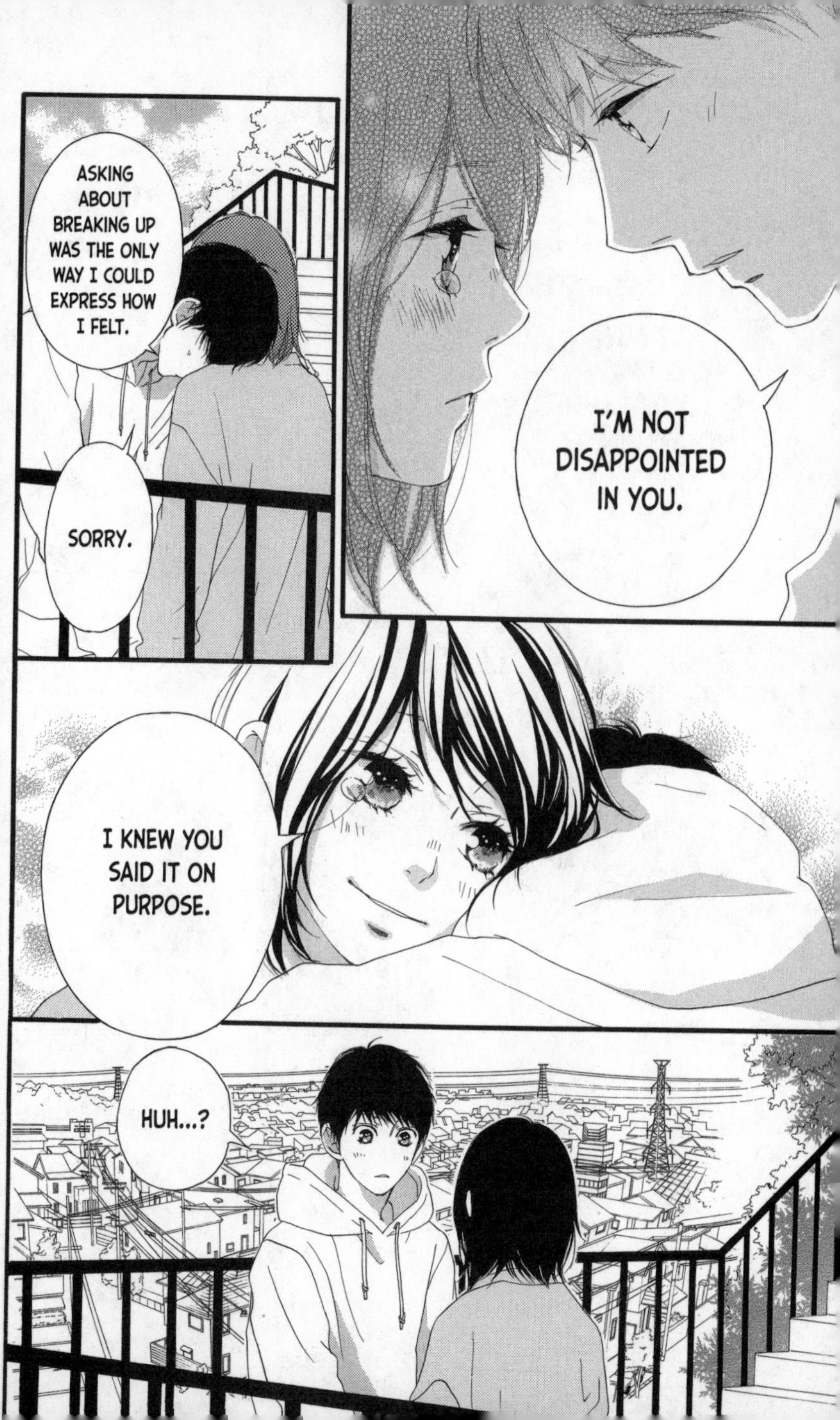
I'M NOT DISAPPOINTED IN YOU.
ASKING ABOUT BREAKING UP WAS THE ONLY WAY I COULD EXPRESS HOW I FELT.
SORRY.
I KNEW YOU SAID IT ON PURPOSE.
HUH...?

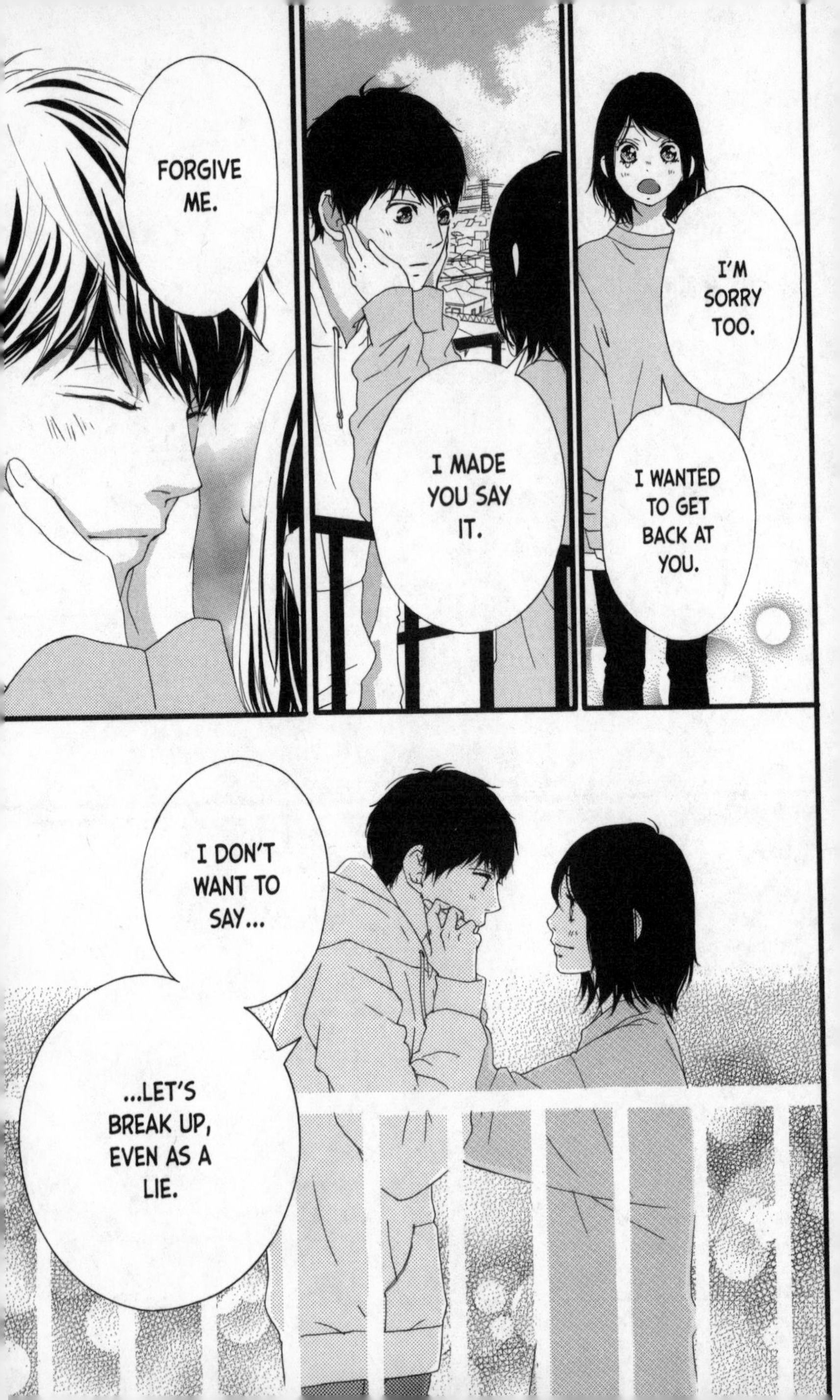
I'M SORRY TOO.
I WANTED TO GET BACK AT YOU.
I MADE YOU SAY IT.
FORGIVE ME.
I DON'T WANT TO SAY...
...LET'S BREAK UP, EVEN AS A LIE.

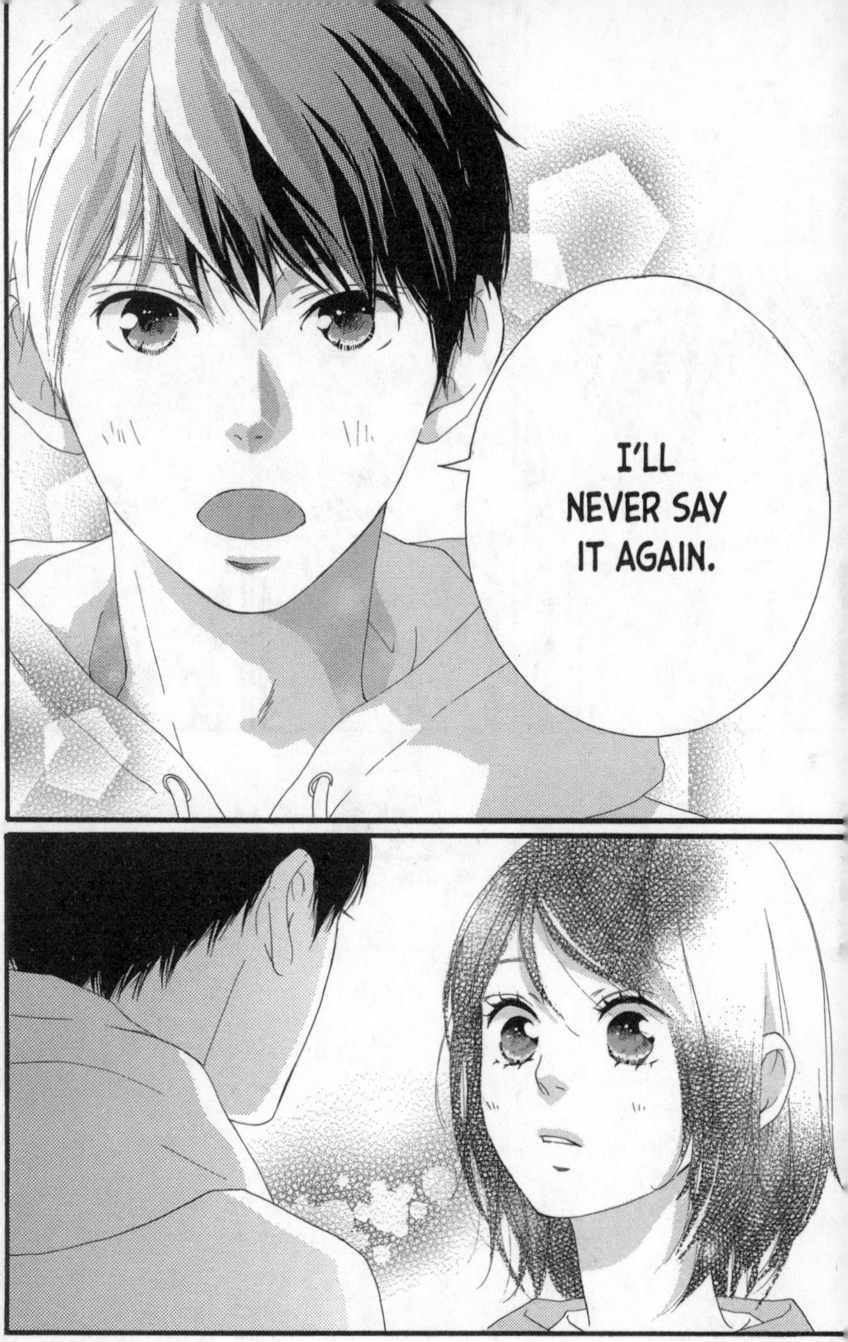
I'LL NEVER SAY IT AGAIN.

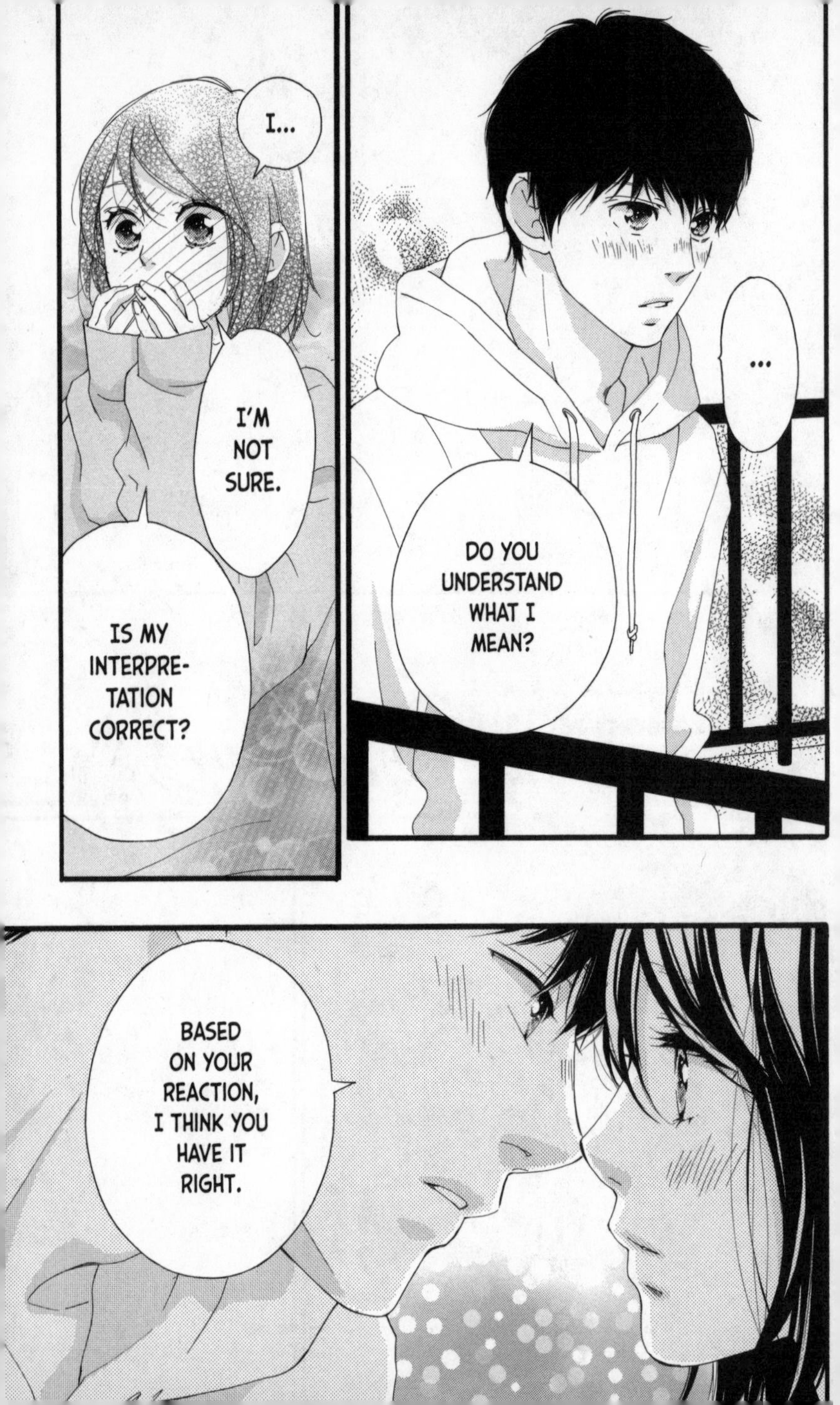
...
DO YOU UNDERSTAND WHAT I MEAN?
I...
I'M NOT SURE.
IS MY INTERPRETATION CORRECT?
BASED ON YOUR REACTION, I THINK YOU HAVE IT RIGHT.

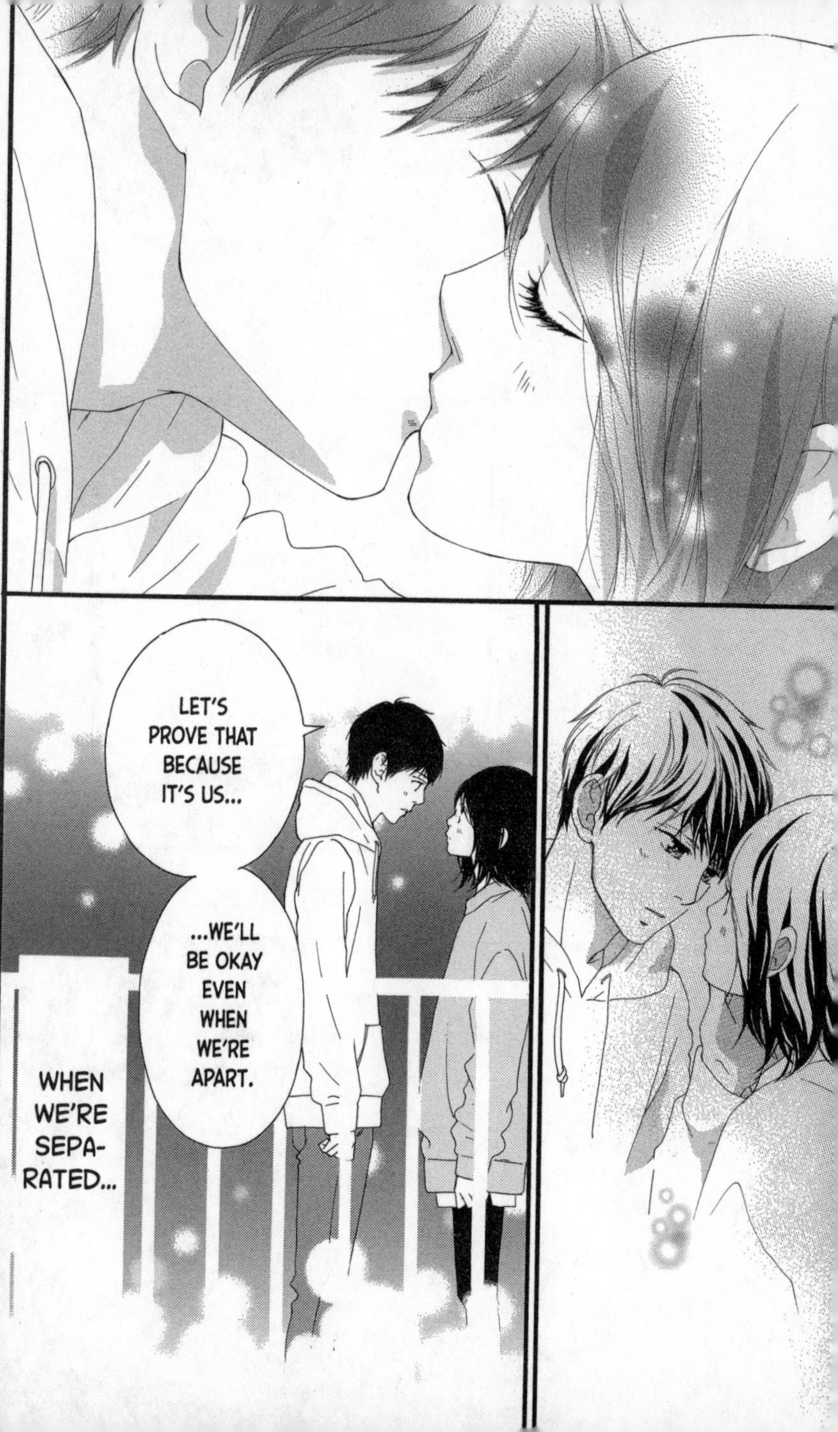
LET'S PROVE THAT BECAUSE IT'S US...
...WE'LL BE OKAY EVEN WHEN WE'RE APART.
WHEN WE'RE SEPA-RATED...

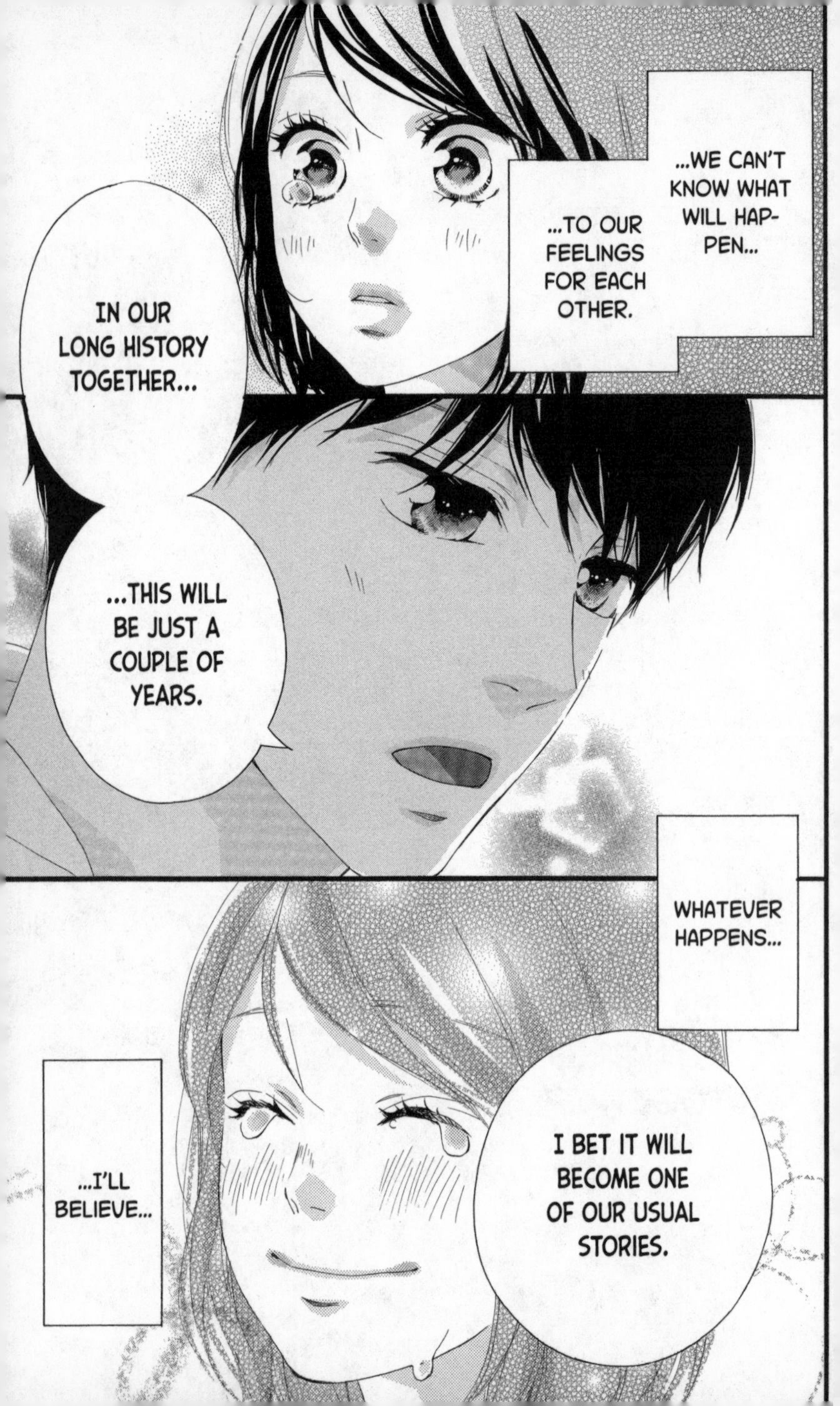
...WE CAN'T KNOW WHAT WILL HAP- PEN...
...TO OUR FEELINGS FOR EACH OTHER.
IN OUR LONG HISTORY TOGETHER...
...THIS WILL BE JUST A COUPLE OF YEARS.
WHATEVER HAPPENS...
...I'LL BELIEVE...
I BET IT WILL BECOME ONE OF OUR USUAL STORIES.

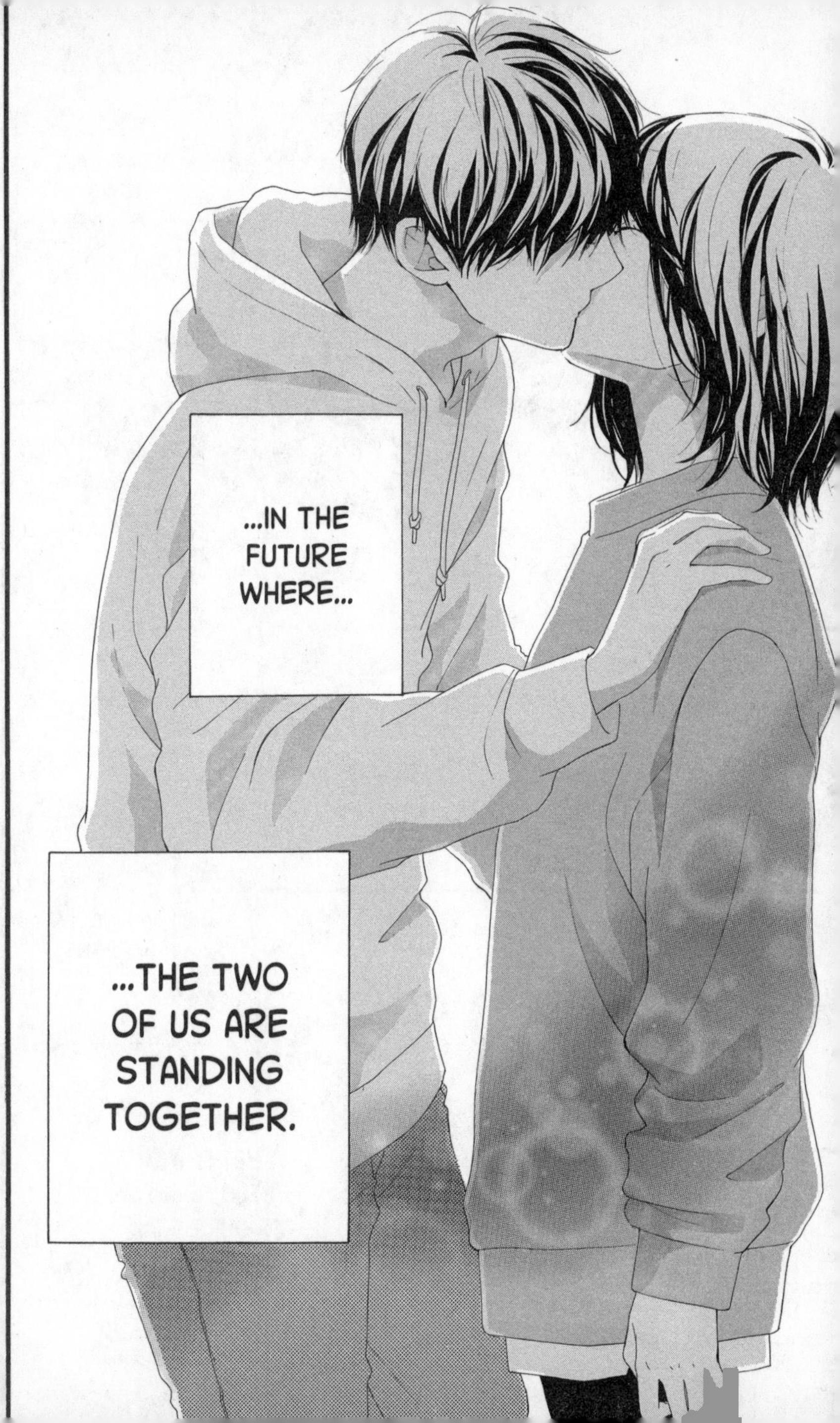
...IN THE FUTURE WHERE...
...THE TWO OF US ARE STANDING TOGETHER.

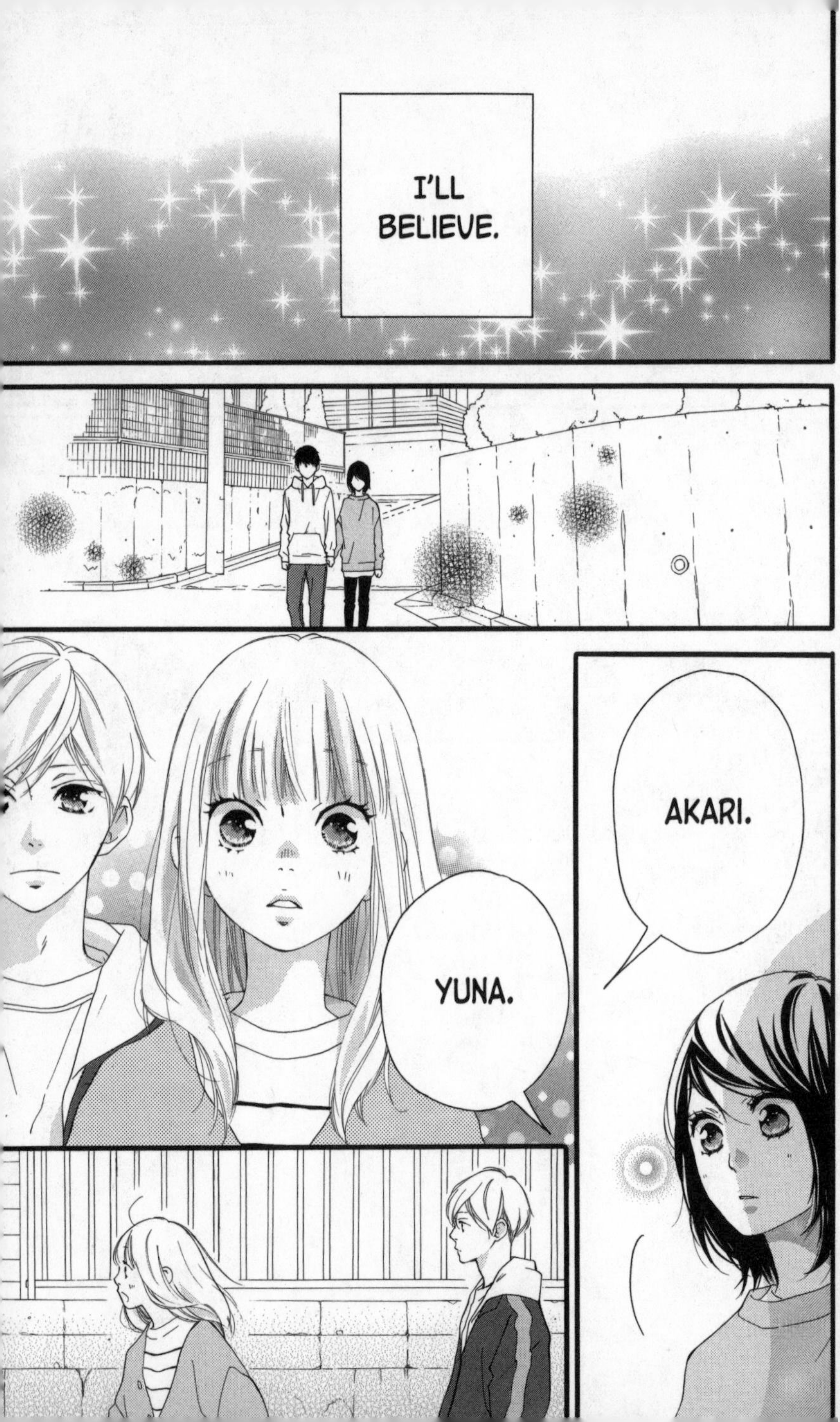
I'LL BELIEVE.
AKARI.
YUNA.

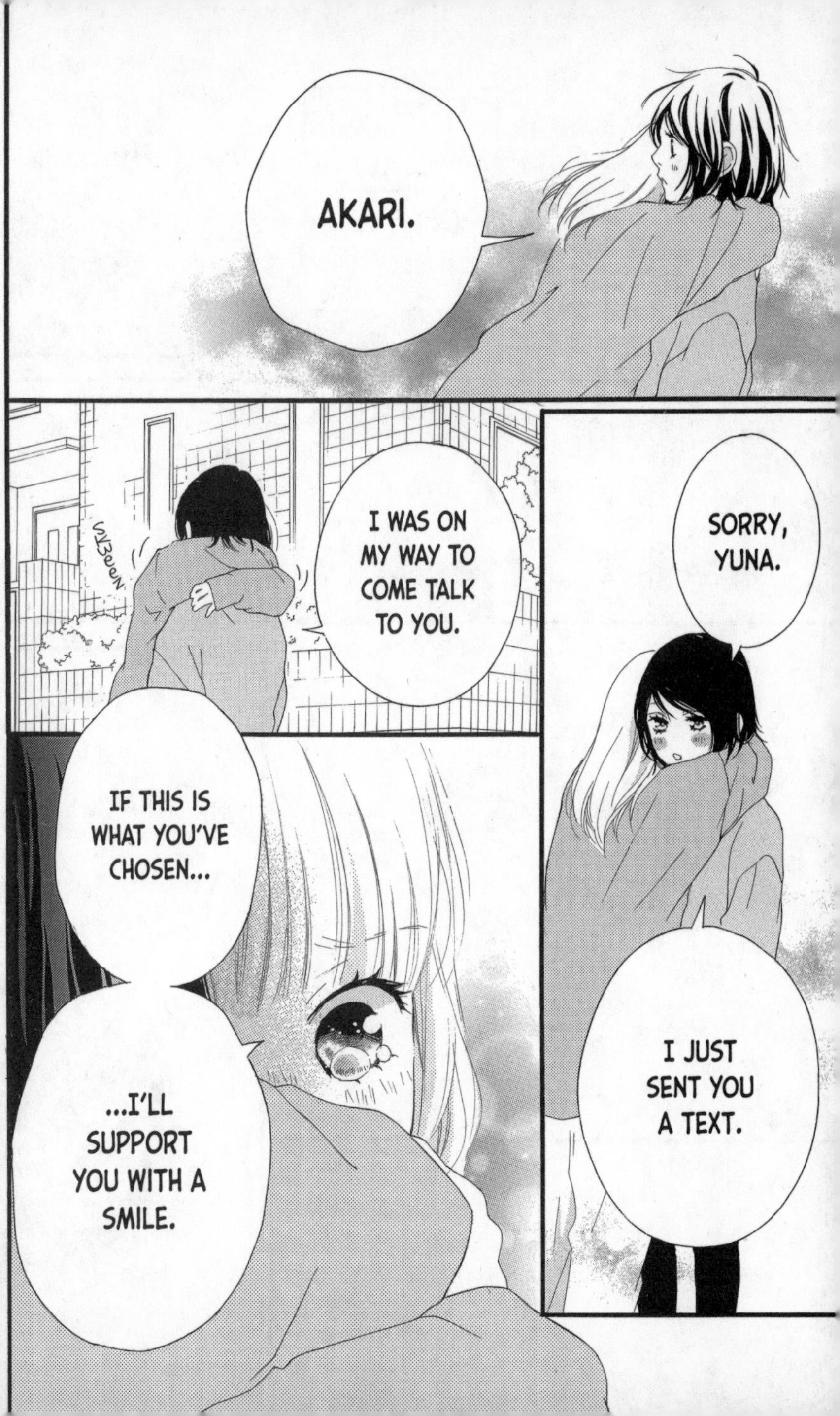
AKARI.
SORRY, YUNA.
I JUST SENT YOU A TEXT.
SQUEEZE
I WAS ON MY WAY TO COME TALK TO YOU.
IF THIS IS WHAT YOU'VE CHOSEN...
...I'LL SUPPORT YOU WITH A SMILE.

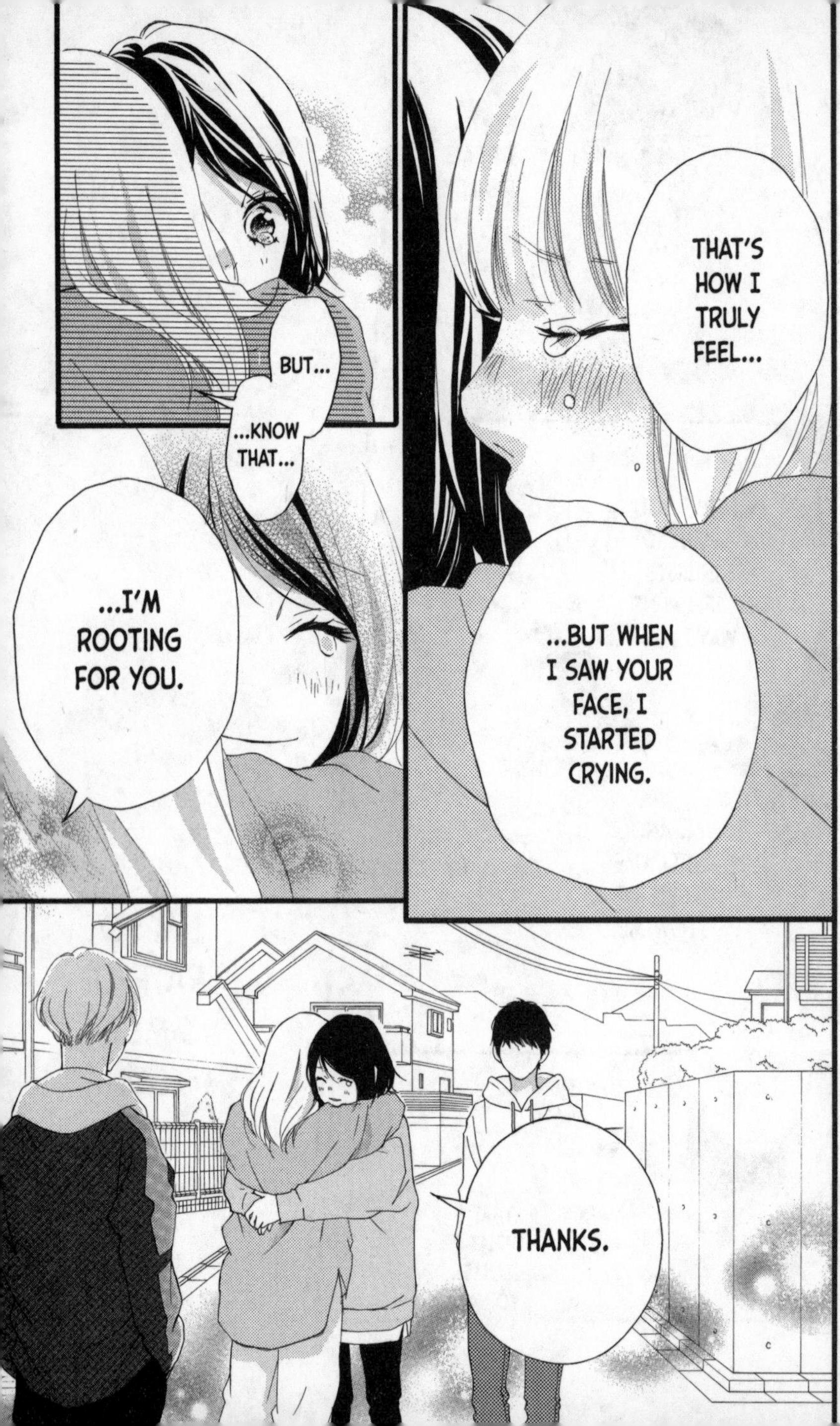
THAT'S HOW I TRULY FEEL...
...BUT WHEN I SAW YOUR FACE, I STARTED CRYING.
BUT...
...KNOW THAT...
...I'M ROOTING FOR YOU.
THANKS.

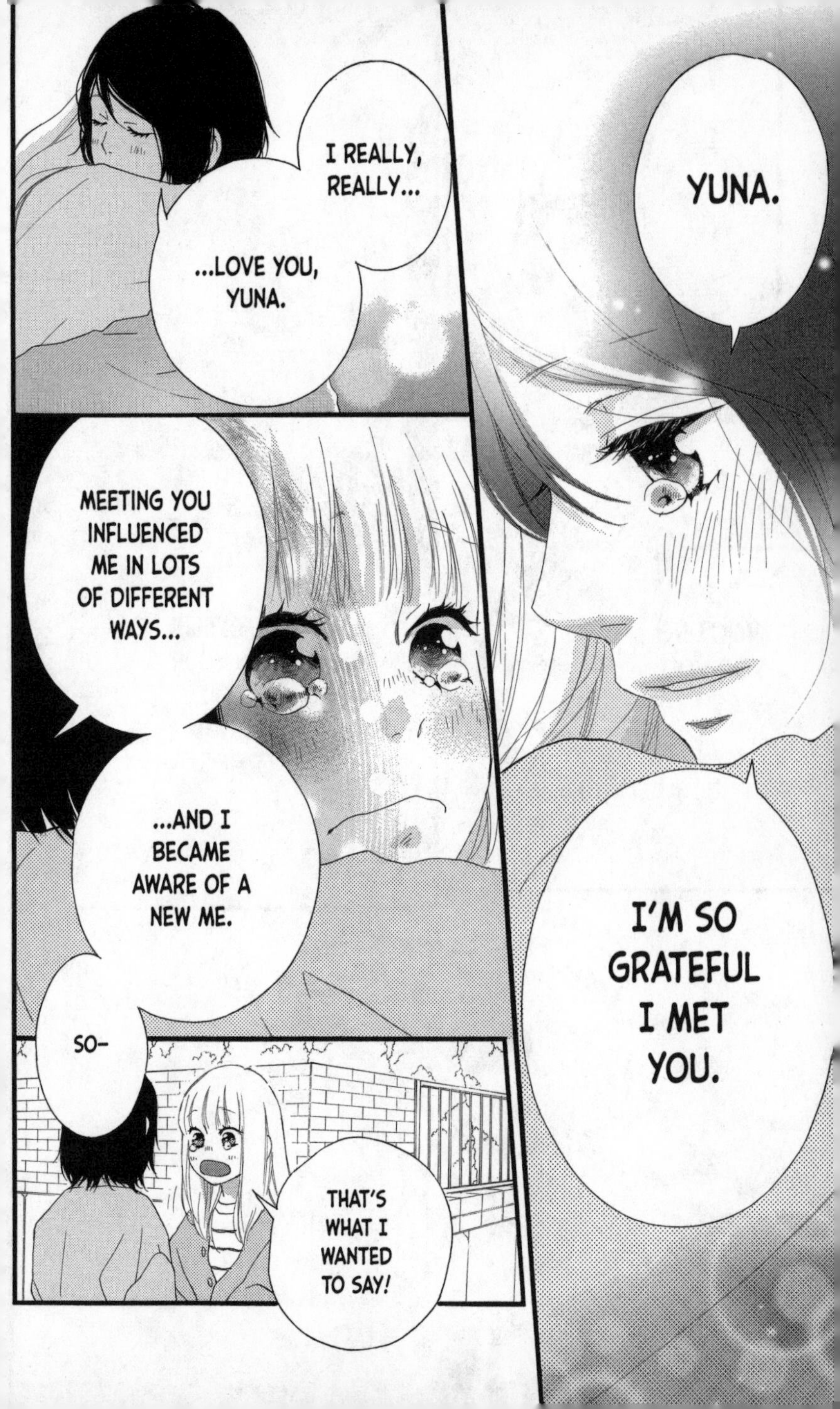
YUNA.
I'M SO GRATEFUL I MET YOU.
I REALLY, REALLY...
...LOVE YOU, YUNA.
MEETING YOU INFLUENCED ME IN LOTS OF DIFFERENT WAYS...
...AND I BECAME AWARE OF A NEW ME.
SO-
THAT'S WHAT I WANTED TO SAY!

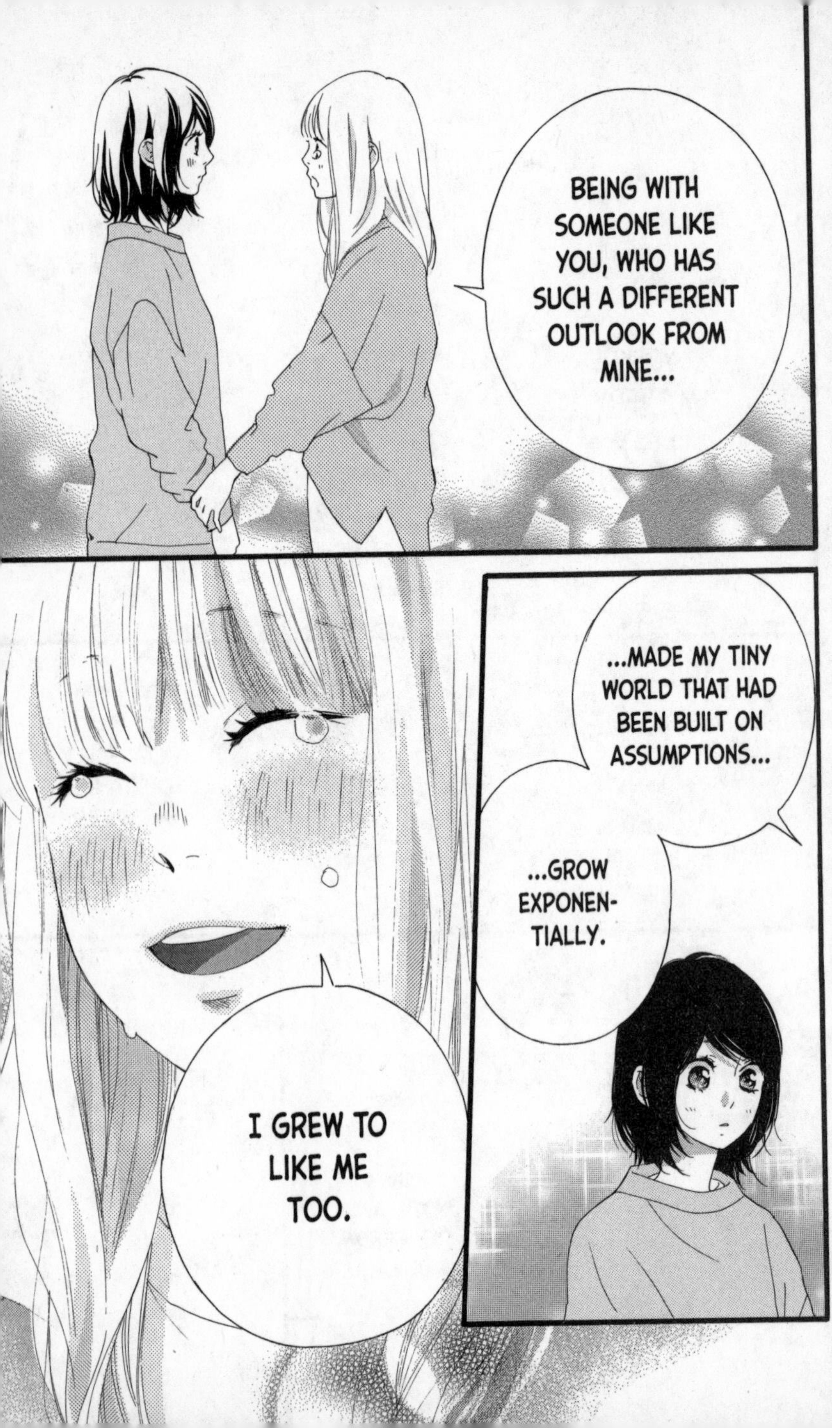
BEING WITH SOMEONE LIKE YOU, WHO HAS SUCH A DIFFERENT OUTLOOK FROM MINE...
...MADE MY TINY WORLD THAT HAD BEEN BUILT ON ASSUMPTIONS...
...GROW EXPONEN-TIALLY.
I GREW TO LIKE ME TOO.

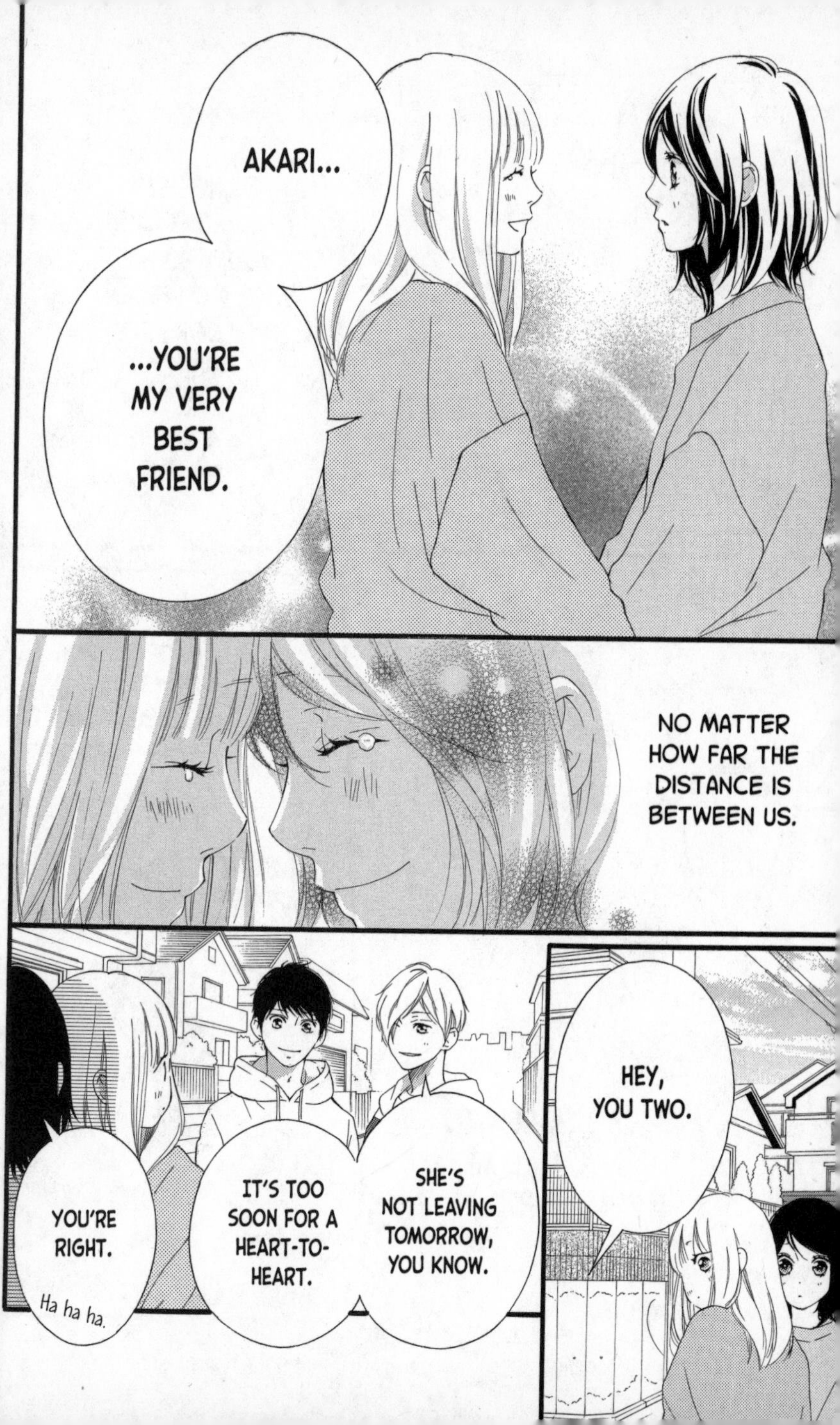
AKARI...
...YOU'RE MY VERY BEST FRIEND.
NO MATTER HOW FAR THE DISTANCE IS BETWEEN US.
HEY, YOU TWO.
SHE'S NOT LEAVING TOMORROW, YOU KNOW.
IT'S TOO SOON FOR A HEART-TO-HEART.
YOU'RE RIGHT.
Ha ha ha.

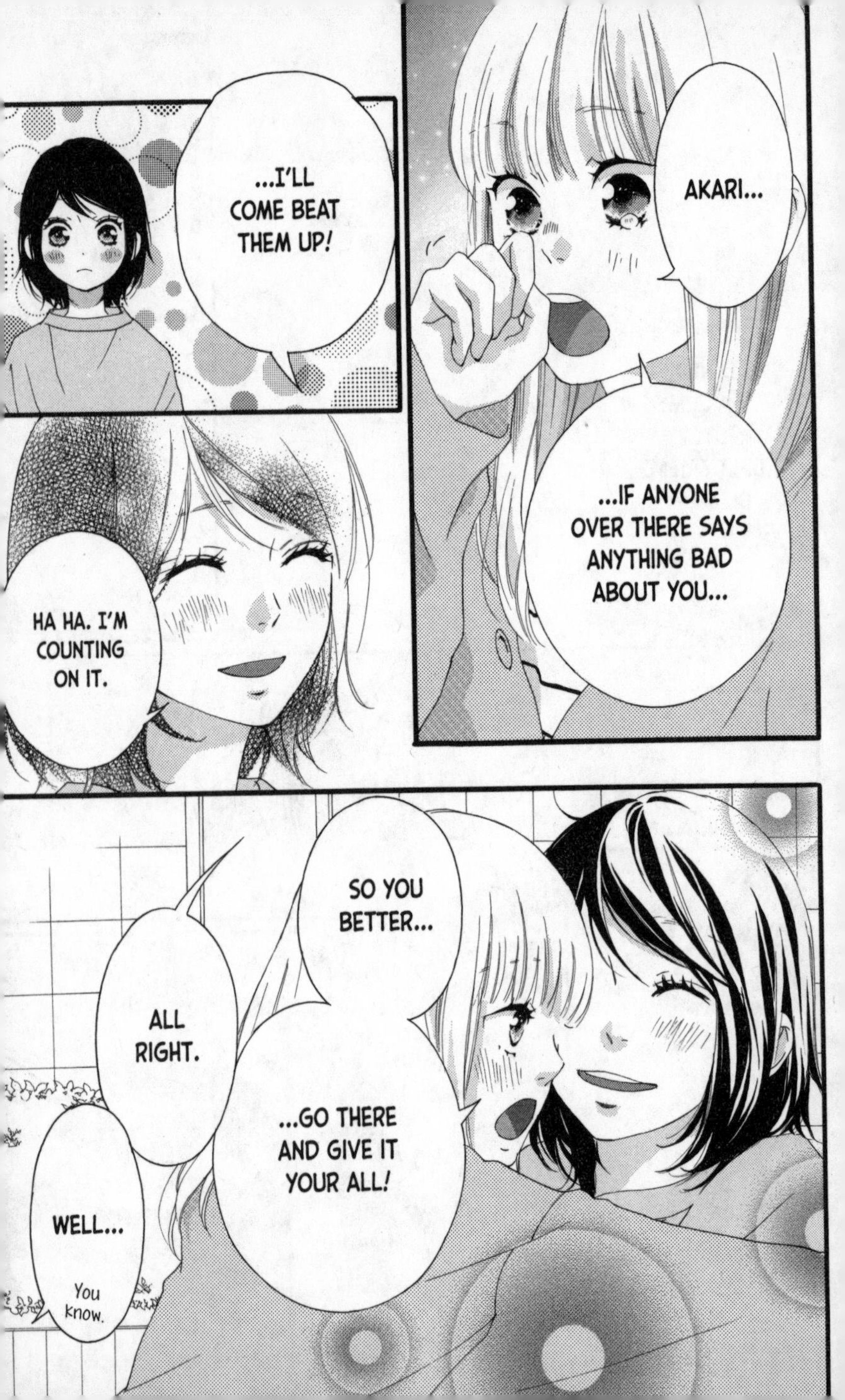
AKARI...
...IF ANYONE OVER THERE SAYS ANYTHING BAD ABOUT YOU...
...I'LL COME BEAT THEM UP!
HA HA. I'M COUNTING ON IT.
SO YOU BETTER...
...GO THERE AND GIVE IT YOUR ALL!
ALL RIGHT.
WELL...
You know.

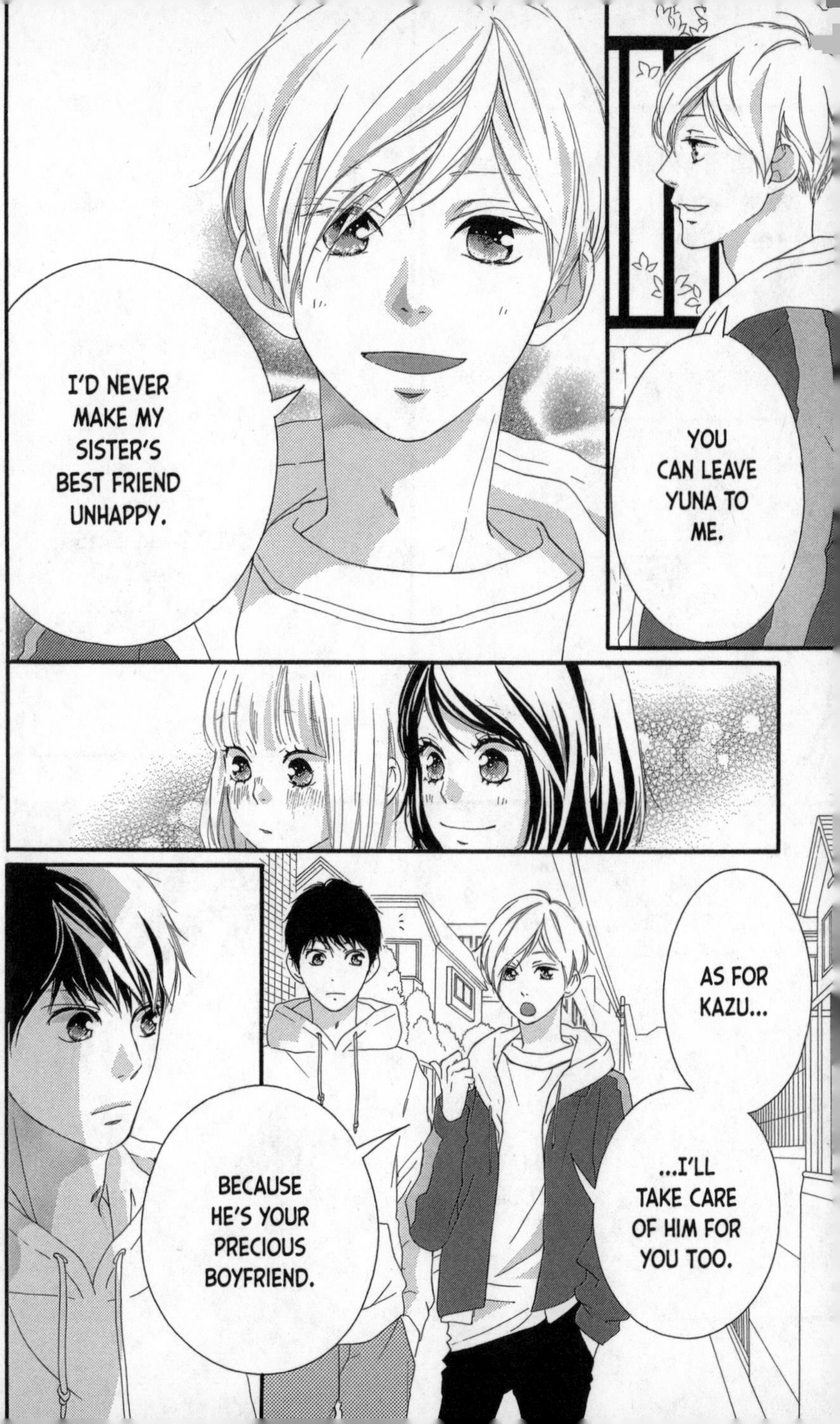
YOU CAN LEAVE YUNA TO ME.
I'D NEVER MAKE MY SISTER'S BEST FRIEND UNHAPPY.
AS FOR KAZU...
...I'LL TAKE CARE OF HIM FOR YOU TOO.
BECAUSE HE'S YOUR PRECIOUS BOYFRIEND.

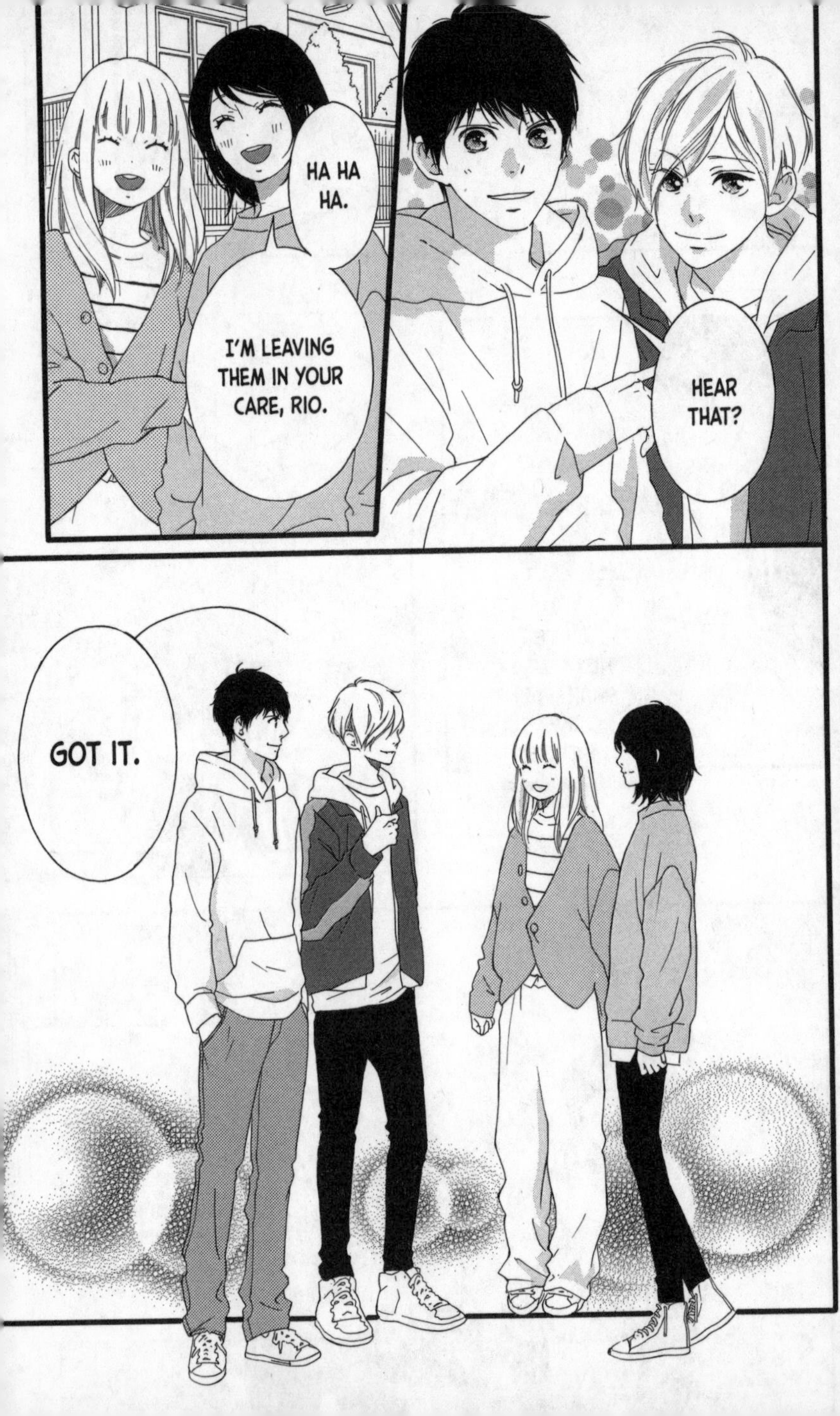
HEAR THAT?
HA HA HA.
I'M LEAVING THEM IN YOUR CARE, RIO.
GOT IT.

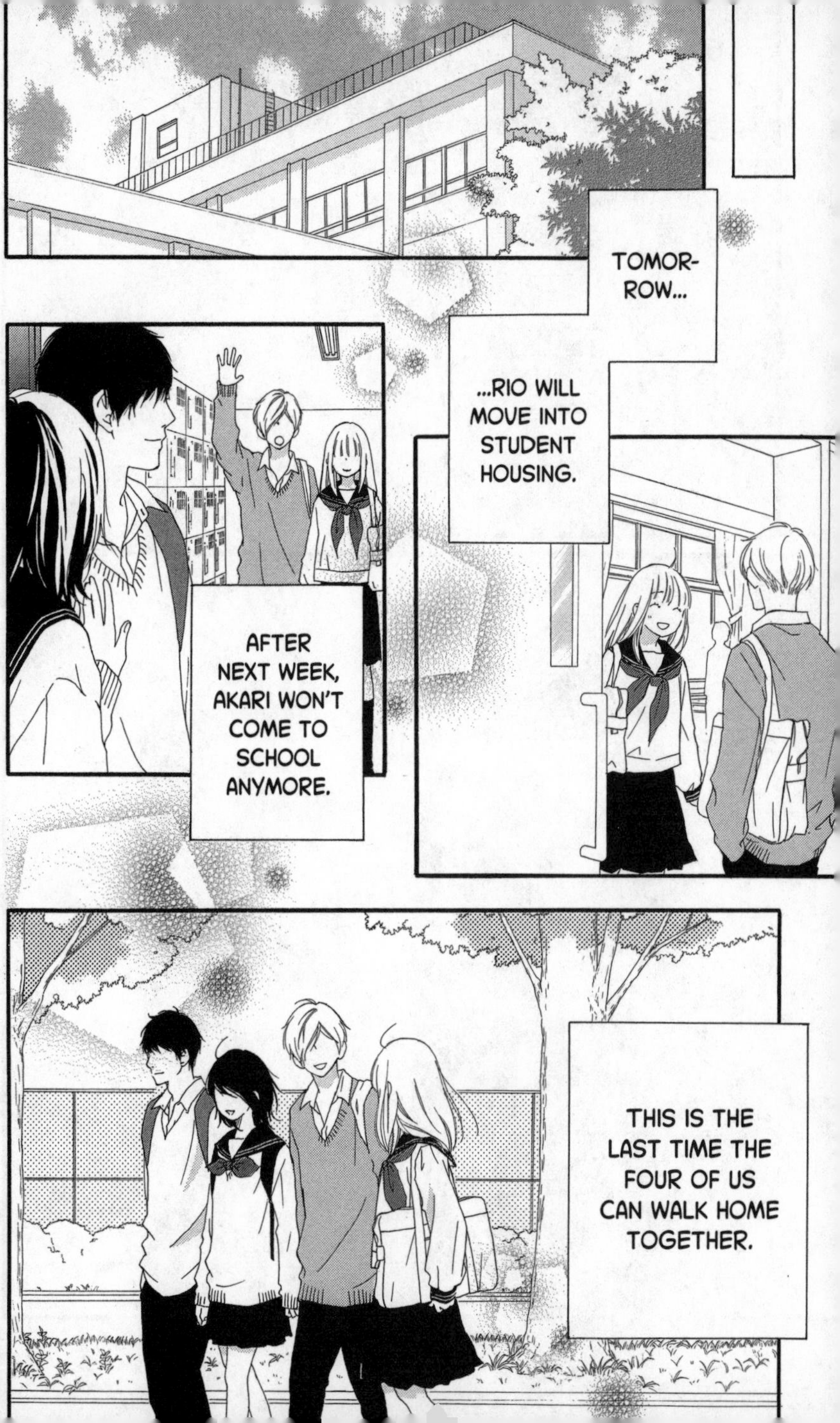
TOMOR-
ROW...
...RIO WILL MOVE INTO STUDENT HOUSING.
AFTER NEXT WEEK, AKARI WON'T COME TO SCHOOL ANYMORE.
THIS IS THE LAST TIME THE FOUR OF US CAN WALK HOME TOGETHER.

(Continued...) What a perfect surprise! Even the conversation on the way to the limo was staged. Everything was unexpected. Inside the limo, we watched a DVD the assistants had put together showing their color illustrations of *Love Me, Love Me Not* edited and set to music. The overall quality was amazing. There were also clips of the assistants at work, and one showed how to get from the station to my house. For some reason, they made a horror movie clip as well. They'd all been so busy themselves, and yet they'd put so much effort into it. I was so happy. While we were watching the DVD together, I was thinking that I must be the happiest person on earth at that moment. (*laugh*) Of course the dinner afterwards was delicious. It was the best wrap party ever. Thank you, everyone!!!

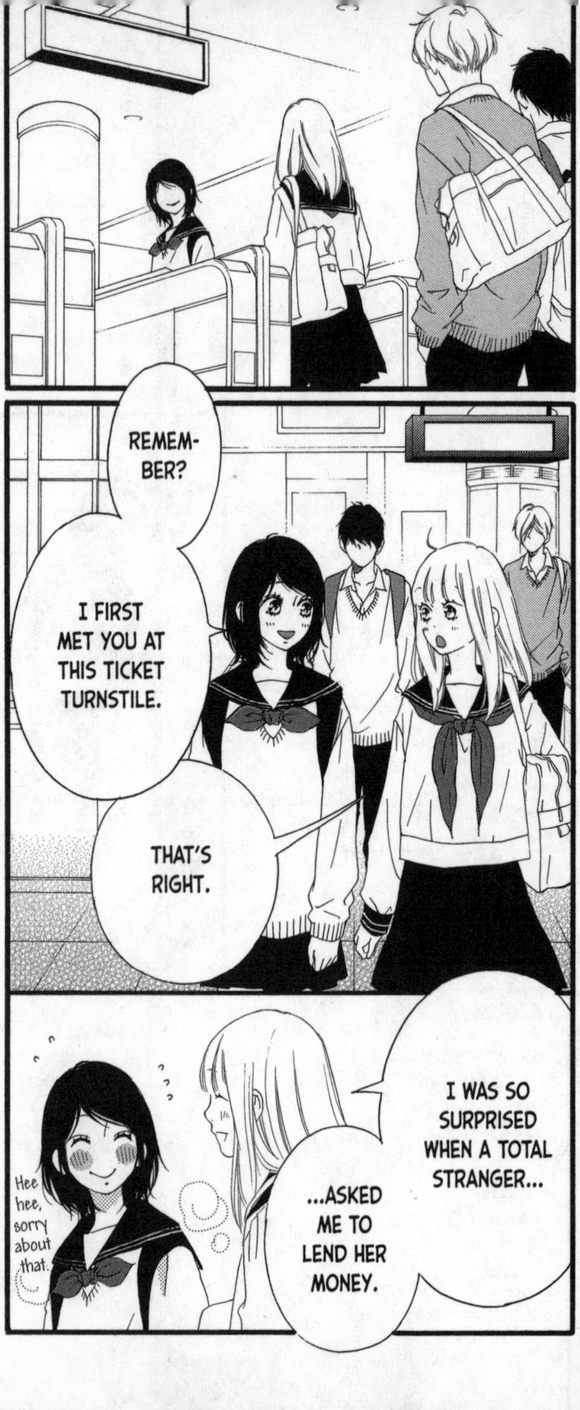
REMEMBER?
I FIRST MET YOU AT THIS TICKET TURNSTILE.
THAT'S RIGHT.
I WAS SO SURPRISED WHEN A TOTAL STRANGER...
...ASKED ME TO LEND HER MONEY.
Hee hee, sorry about that.

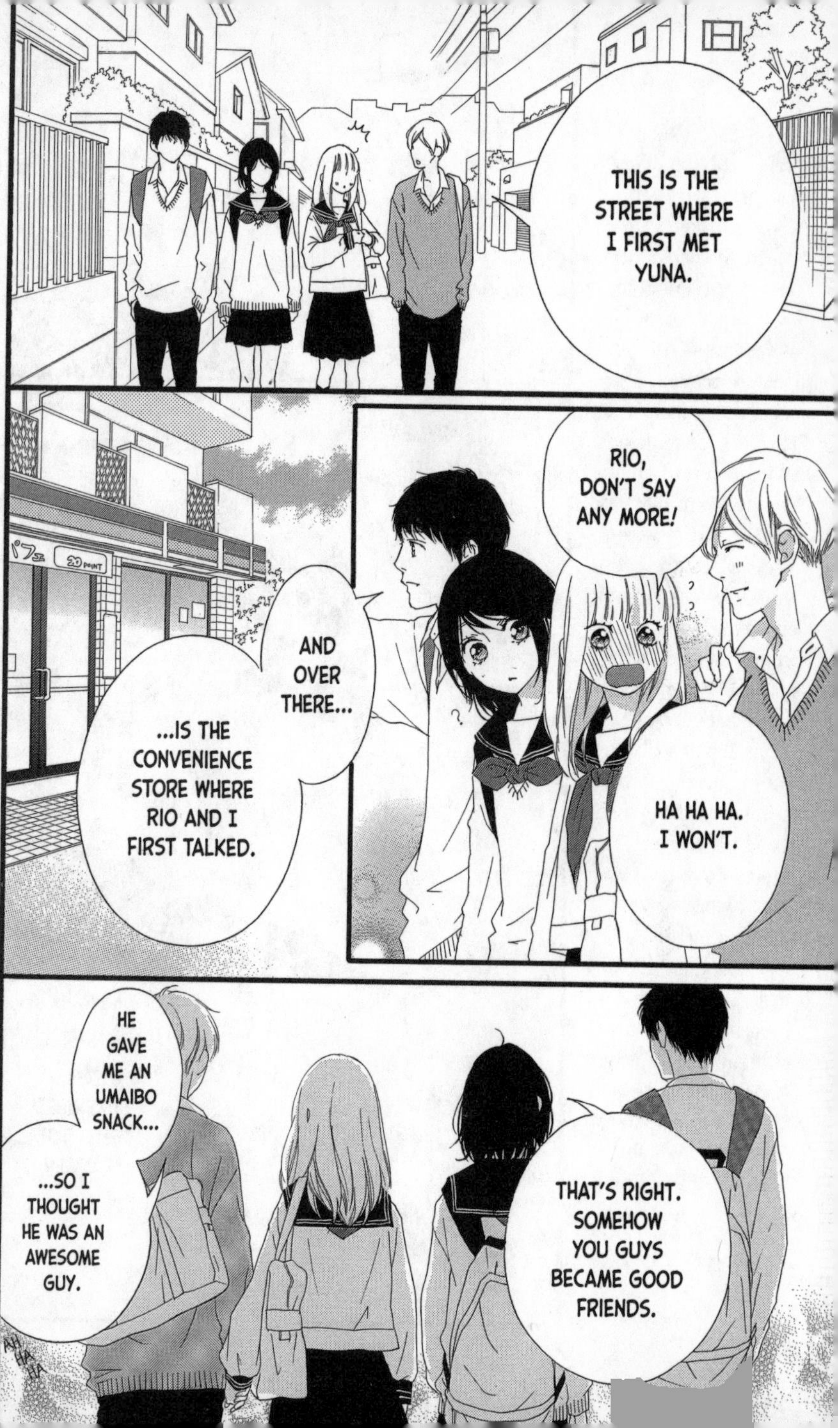
THIS IS THE STREET WHERE I FIRST MET YUNA.
AND OVER THERE...
...IS THE CONVENIENCE STORE WHERE RIO AND I FIRST TALKED.
パフェ
20 POINT
RIO, DON'T SAY ANY MORE!
HA HA HA. I WON'T.
THAT'S RIGHT. SOMEHOW YOU GUYS BECAME GOOD FRIENDS.
HE GAVE ME AN UMAIBO SNACK...
...SO I THOUGHT HE WAS AN AWESOME GUY.
AH HA HA

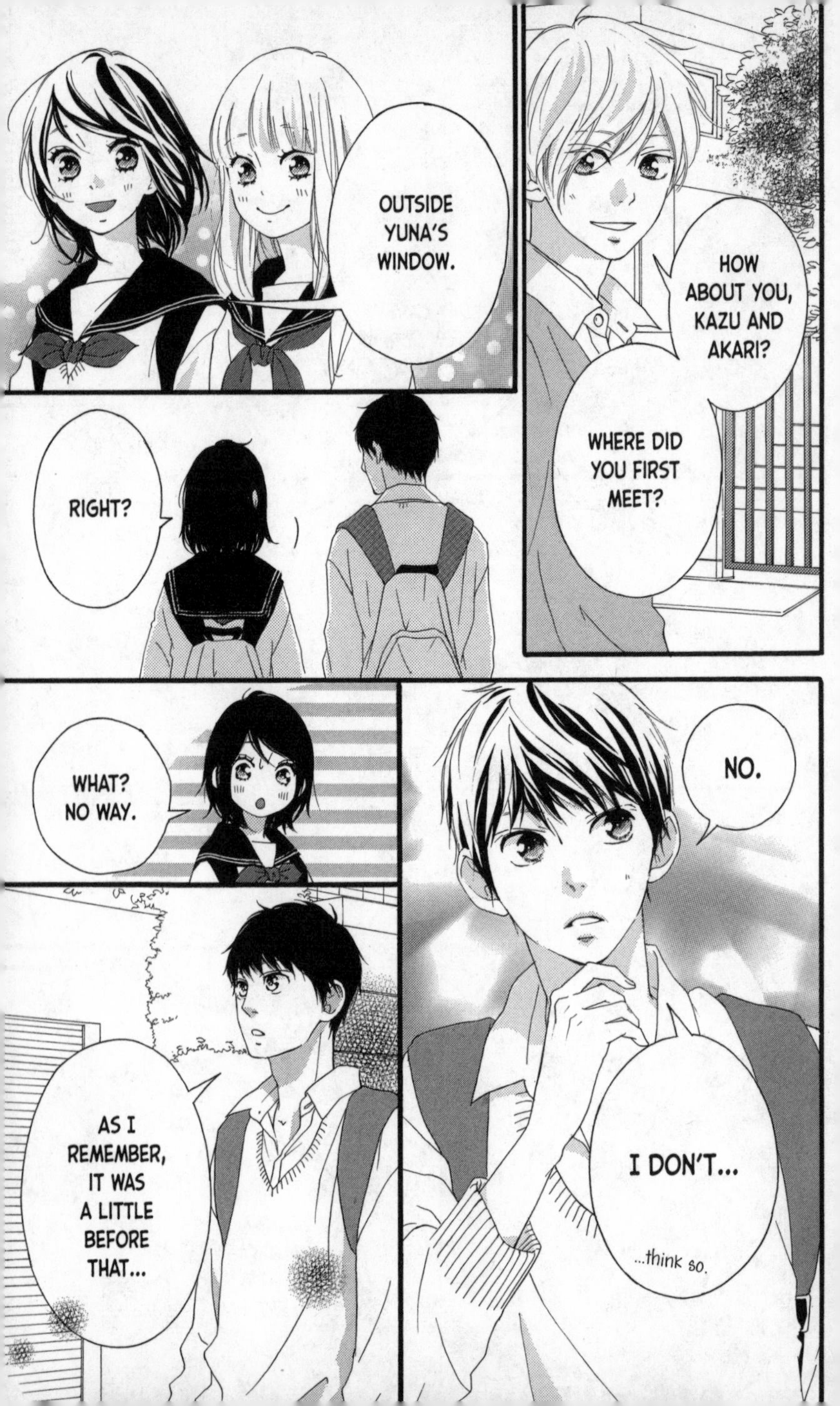
HOW ABOUT YOU, KAZU AND AKARI?
WHERE DID YOU FIRST MEET?
OUTSIDE YUNA'S WINDOW.
RIGHT?
NO.
I DON'T...
...think so.
WHAT? NO WAY.
AS I REMEMBER, IT WAS A LITTLE BEFORE THAT...

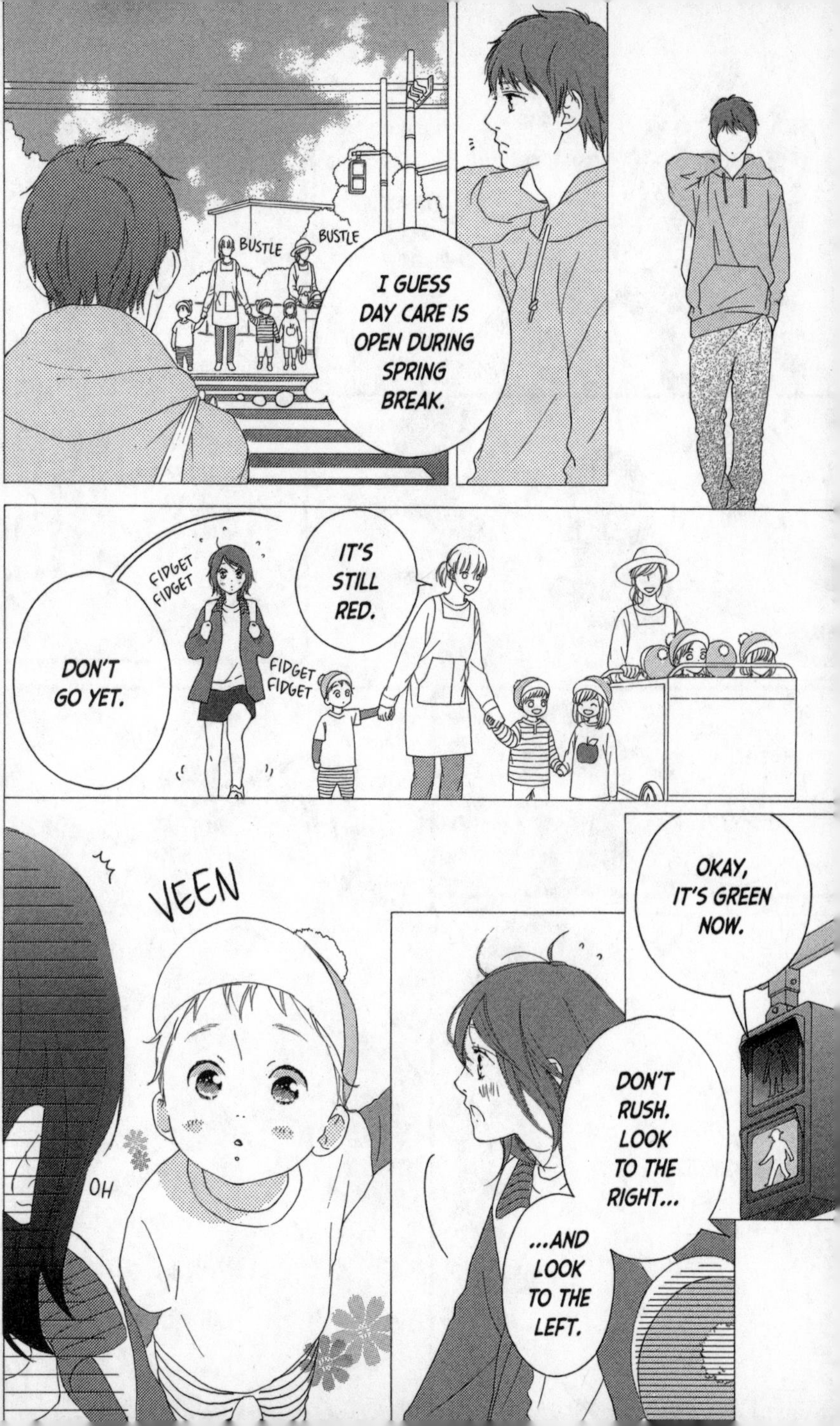
BUSTLE
BUSTLE
I GUESS DAY CARE IS OPEN DURING SPRING BREAK.
IT'S STILL RED.
FIDGET FIDGET
FIDGET FIDGET
DON'T GO YET.
OKAY, IT'S GREEN NOW.
DON'T RUSH. LOOK TO THE RIGHT...
...AND LOOK TO THE LEFT.
VEEN
OH

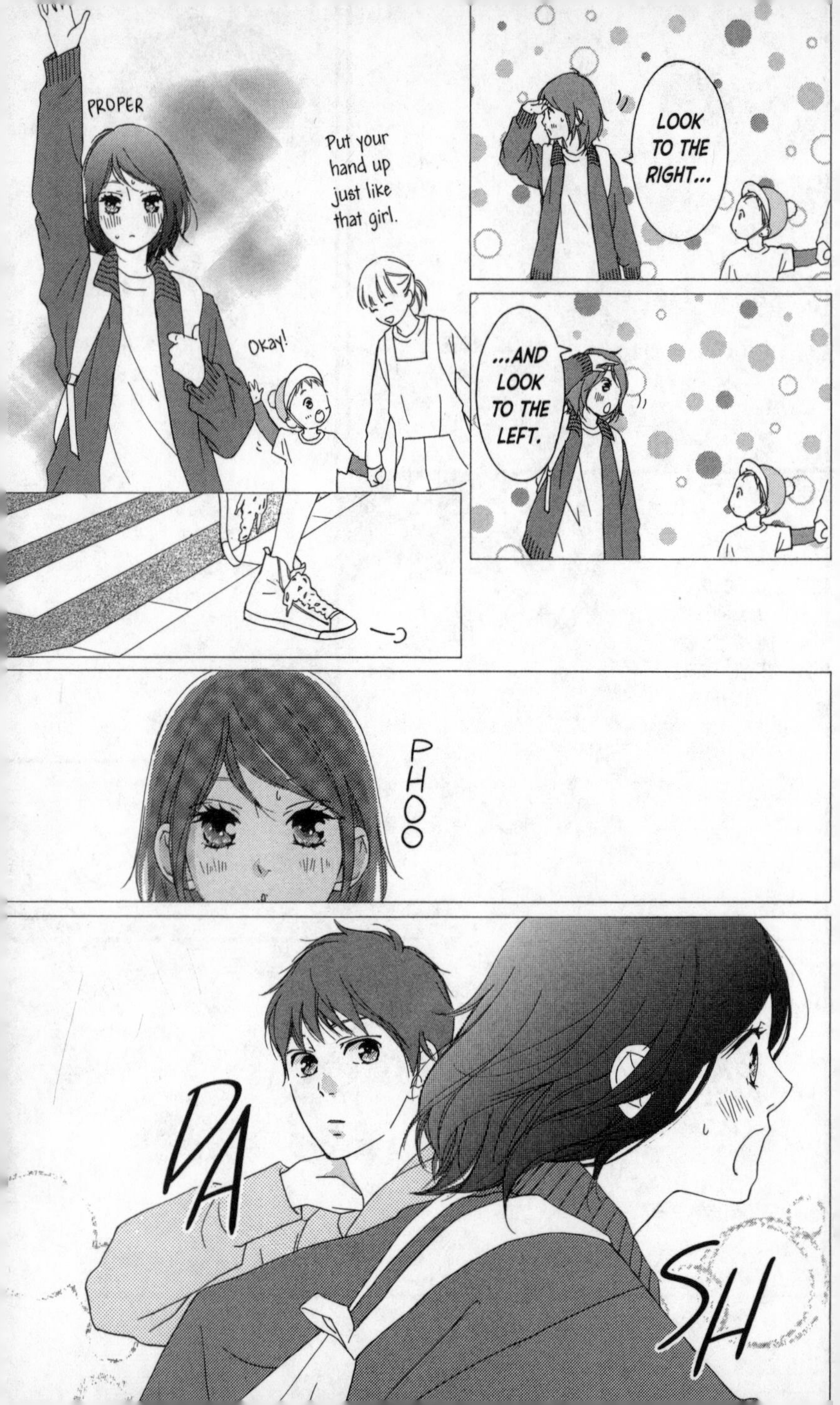
LOOK TO THE RIGHT...
...AND LOOK TO THE LEFT.
PROPER
Put your hand up just like that girl.
Okay!
PHOO
DA
SH

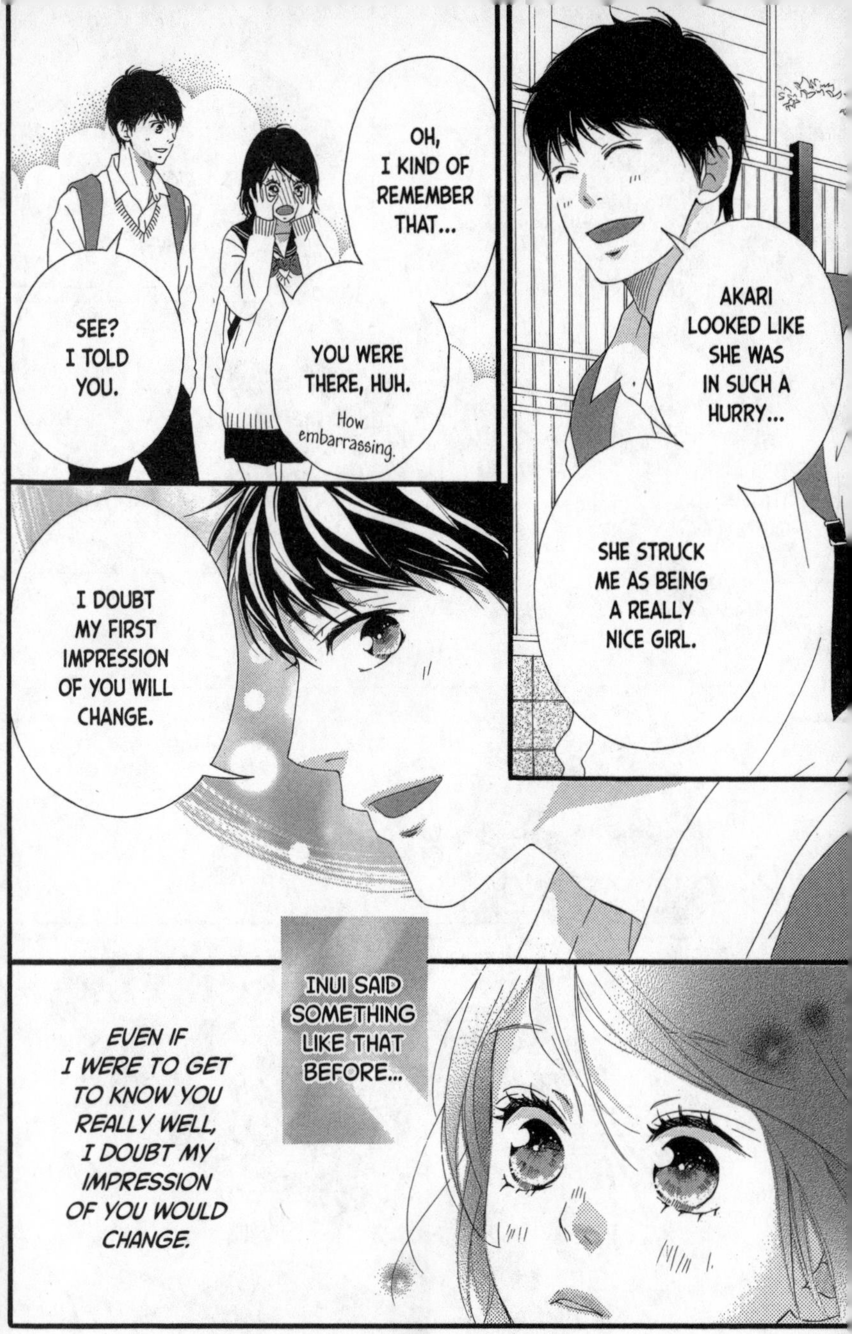
AKARI LOOKED LIKE SHE WAS IN SUCH A HURRY...
SHE STRUCK ME AS BEING A REALLY NICE GIRL.
OH, I KIND OF REMEMBER THAT...
YOU WERE THERE, HUH.
How embarrassing.
SEE? I TOLD YOU.
I DOUBT MY FIRST IMPRESSION OF YOU WILL CHANGE.
INUI SAID SOMETHING LIKE THAT BEFORE...
EVEN IF I WERE TO GET TO KNOW YOU REALLY WELL, I DOUBT MY IMPRESSION OF YOU WOULD CHANGE.

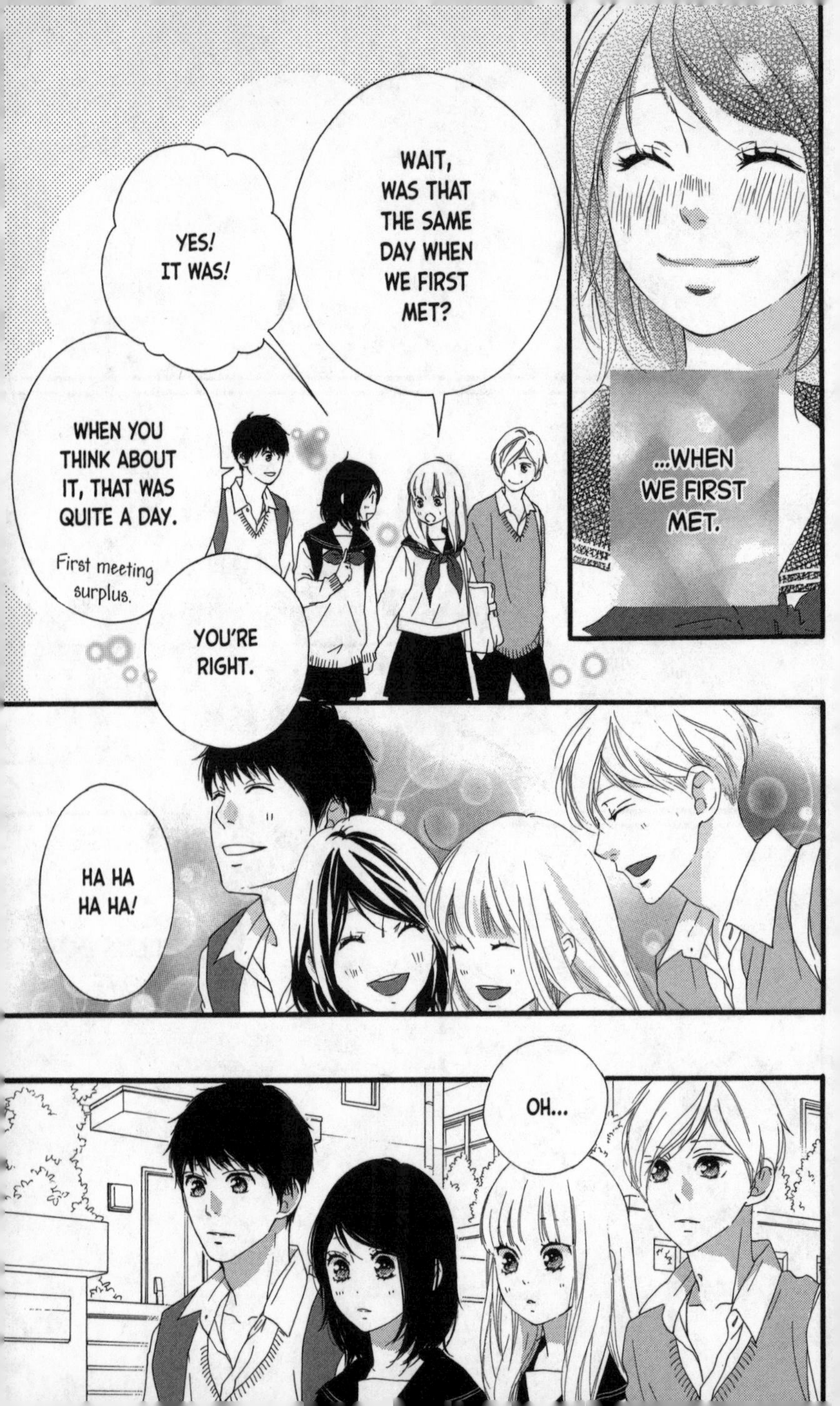
...WHEN WE FIRST MET.
WAIT, WAS THAT THE SAME DAY WHEN WE FIRST MET?
YES! IT WAS!
WHEN YOU THINK ABOUT IT, THAT WAS QUITE A DAY.
First meeting surplus.
YOU'RE RIGHT.
HA HA HA HA!
OH...

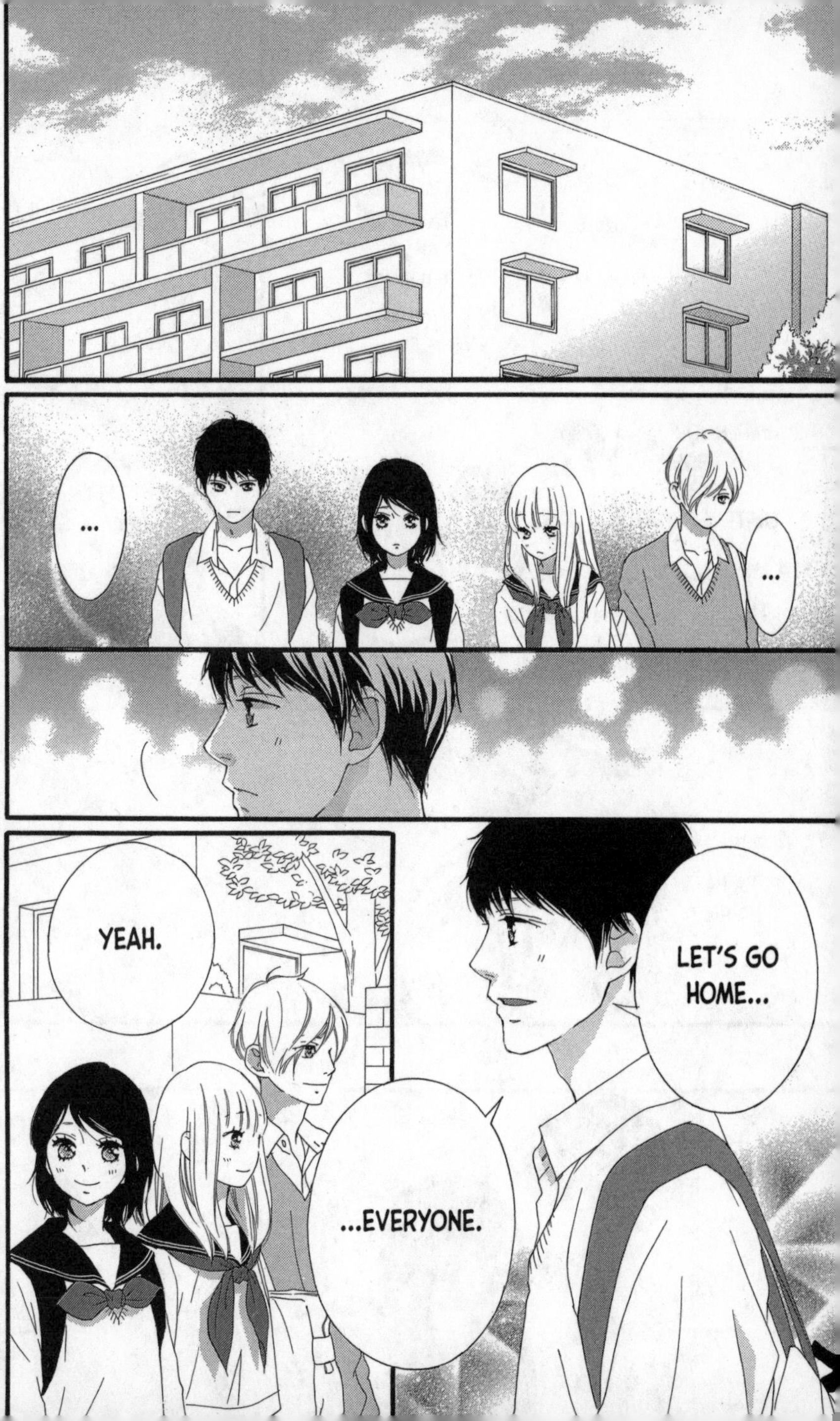
...
...
LET'S GO HOME...
...EVERYONE.
YEAH.

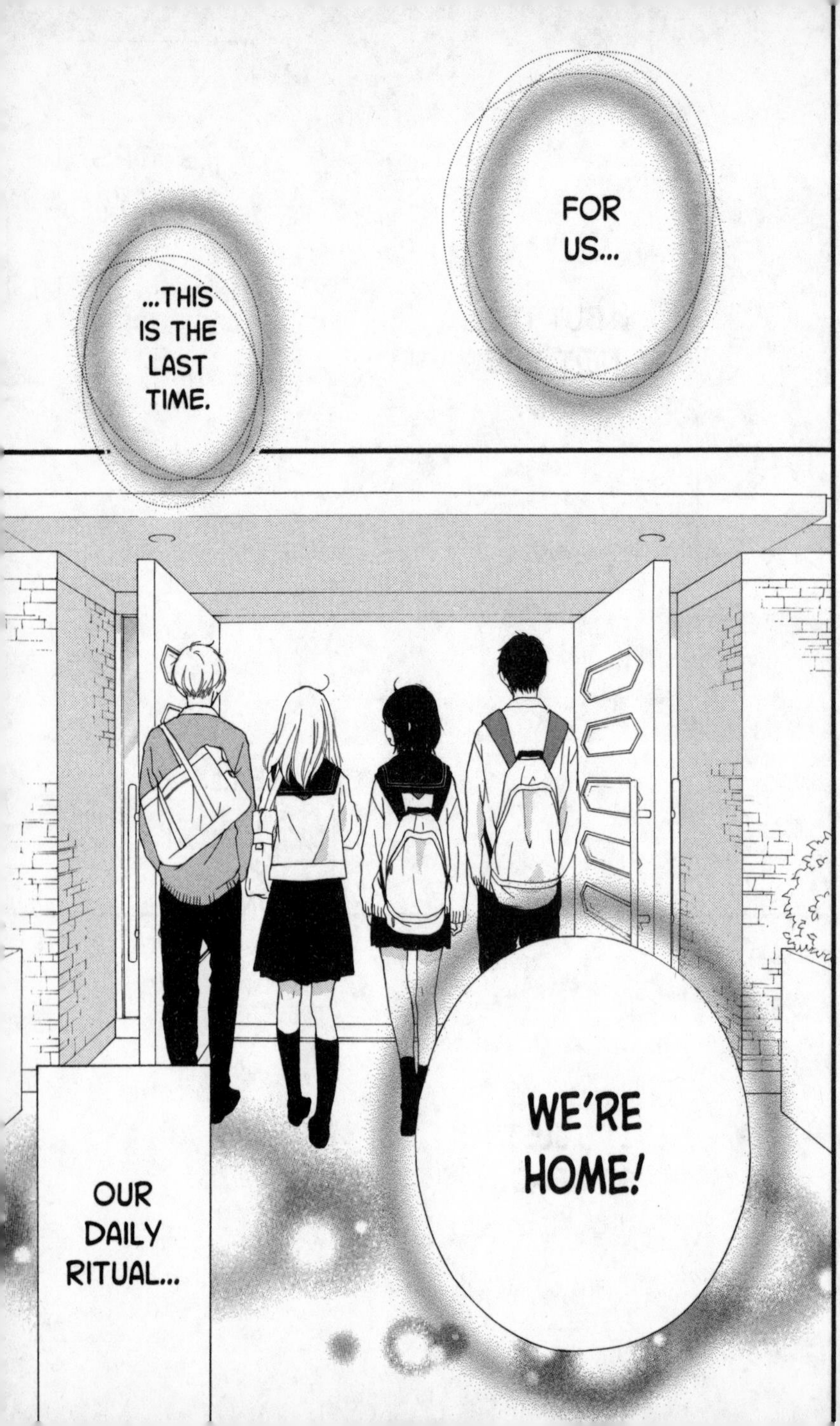

FOR US...
...THIS IS THE LAST TIME.
WE'RE HOME!
OUR DAILY RITUAL...

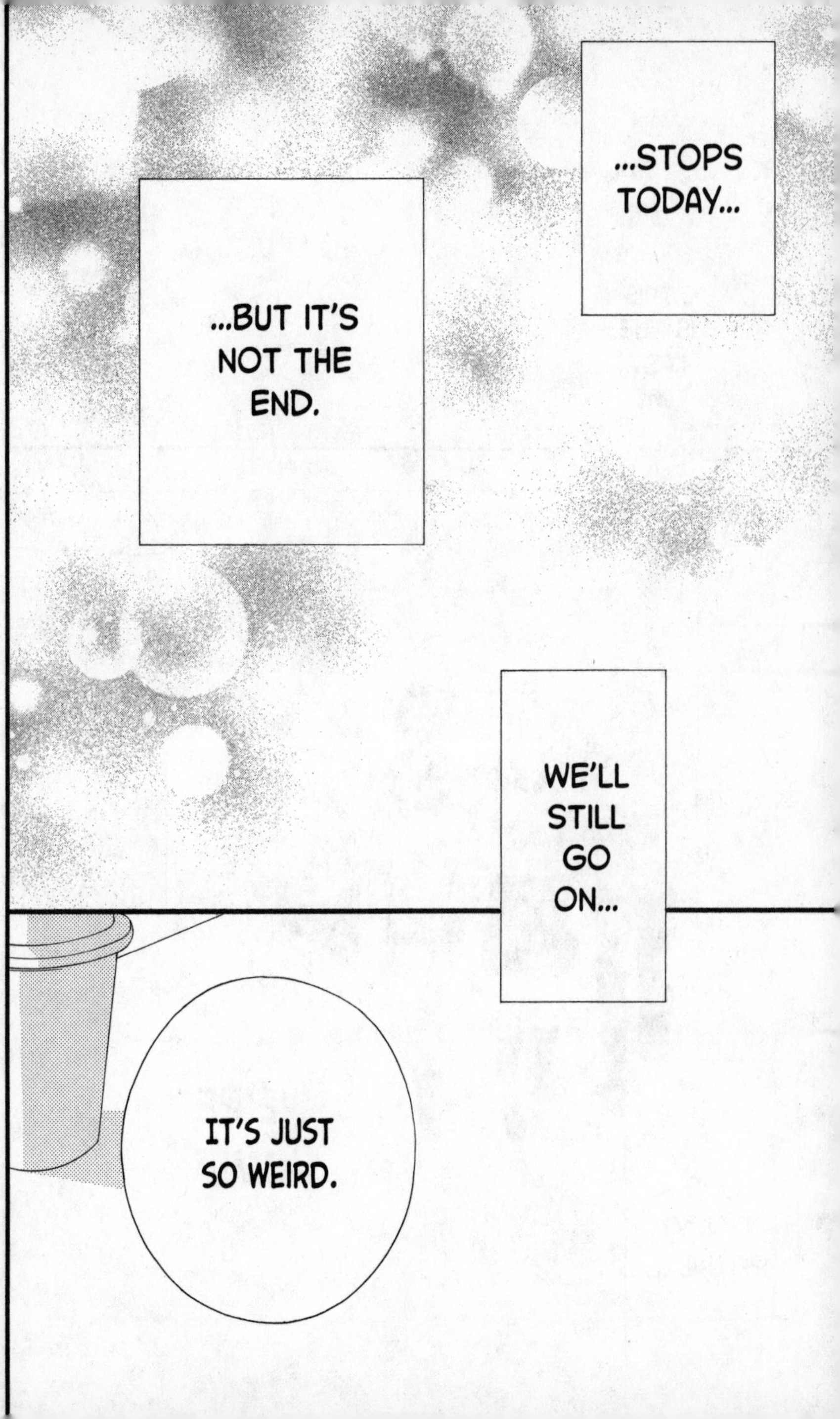
...STOPS TODAY...
...BUT IT'S NOT THE END.
WE'LL STILL GO ON...
IT'S JUST SO WEIRD.

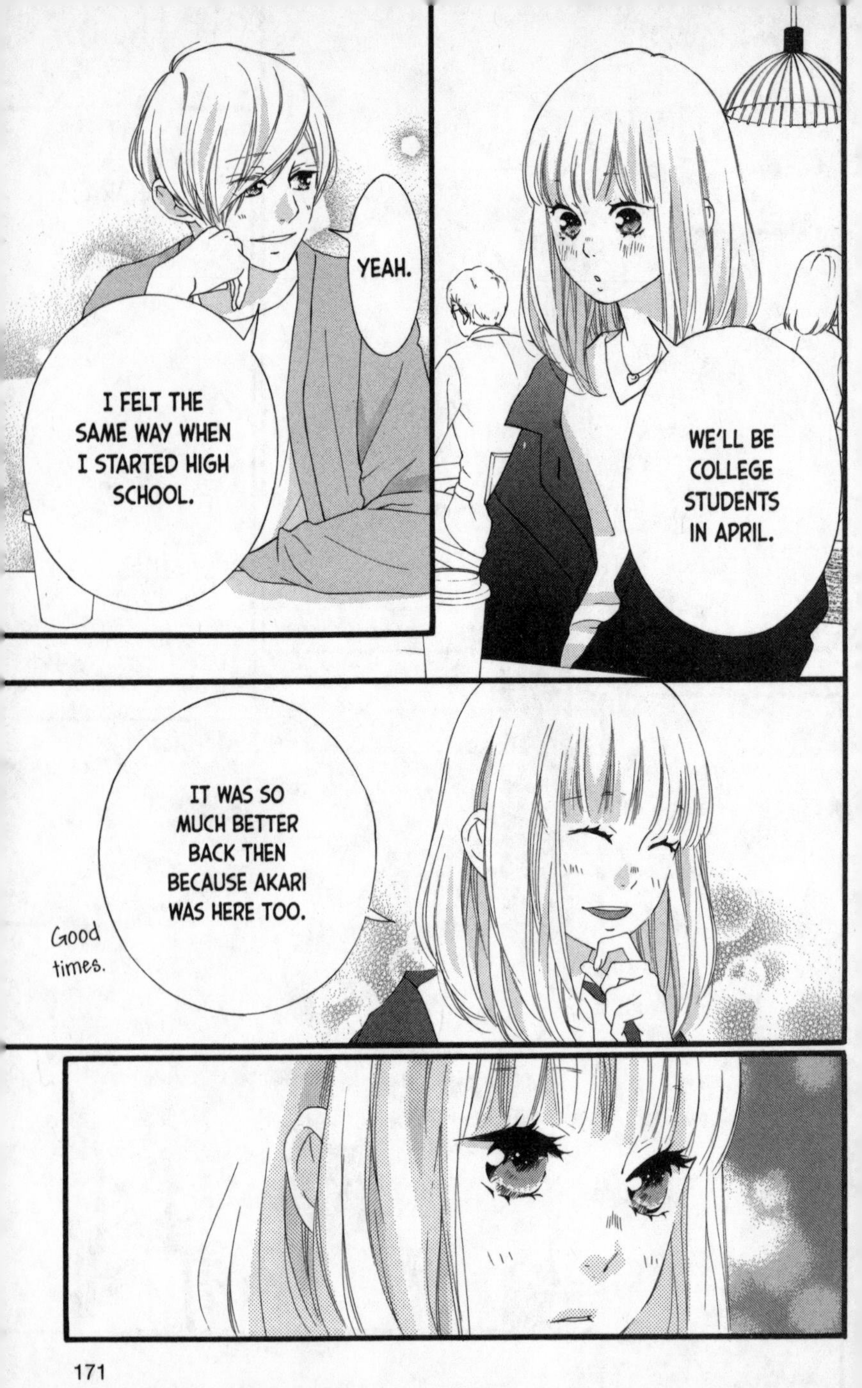
WE'LL BE COLLEGE STUDENTS IN APRIL.
YEAH.
I FELT THE SAME WAY WHEN I STARTED HIGH SCHOOL.
IT WAS SO MUCH BETTER BACK THEN BECAUSE AKARI WAS HERE TOO.
Good times.

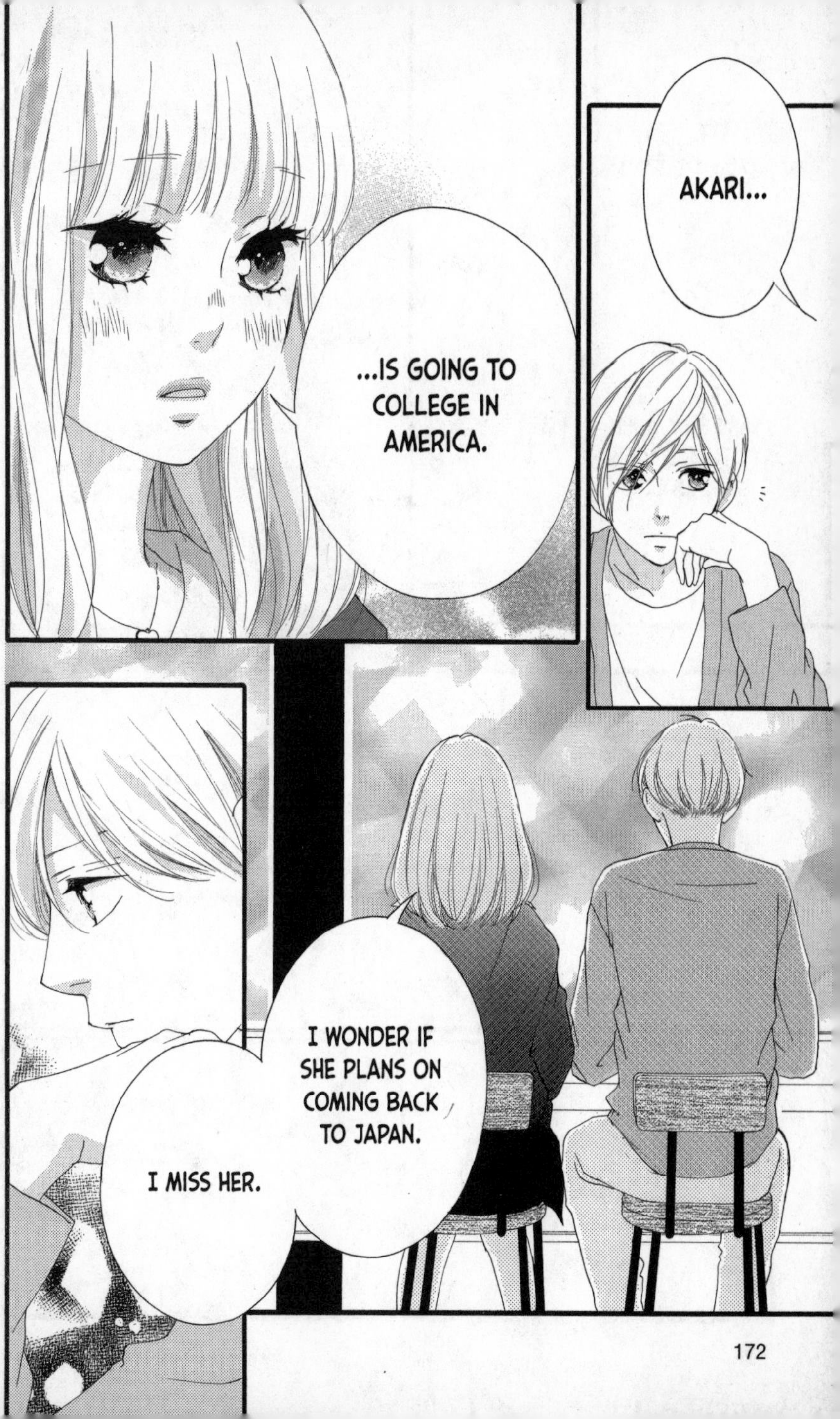
AKARI...
...IS GOING TO COLLEGE IN AMERICA.
I WONDER IF SHE PLANS ON COMING BACK TO JAPAN.
I MISS HER.

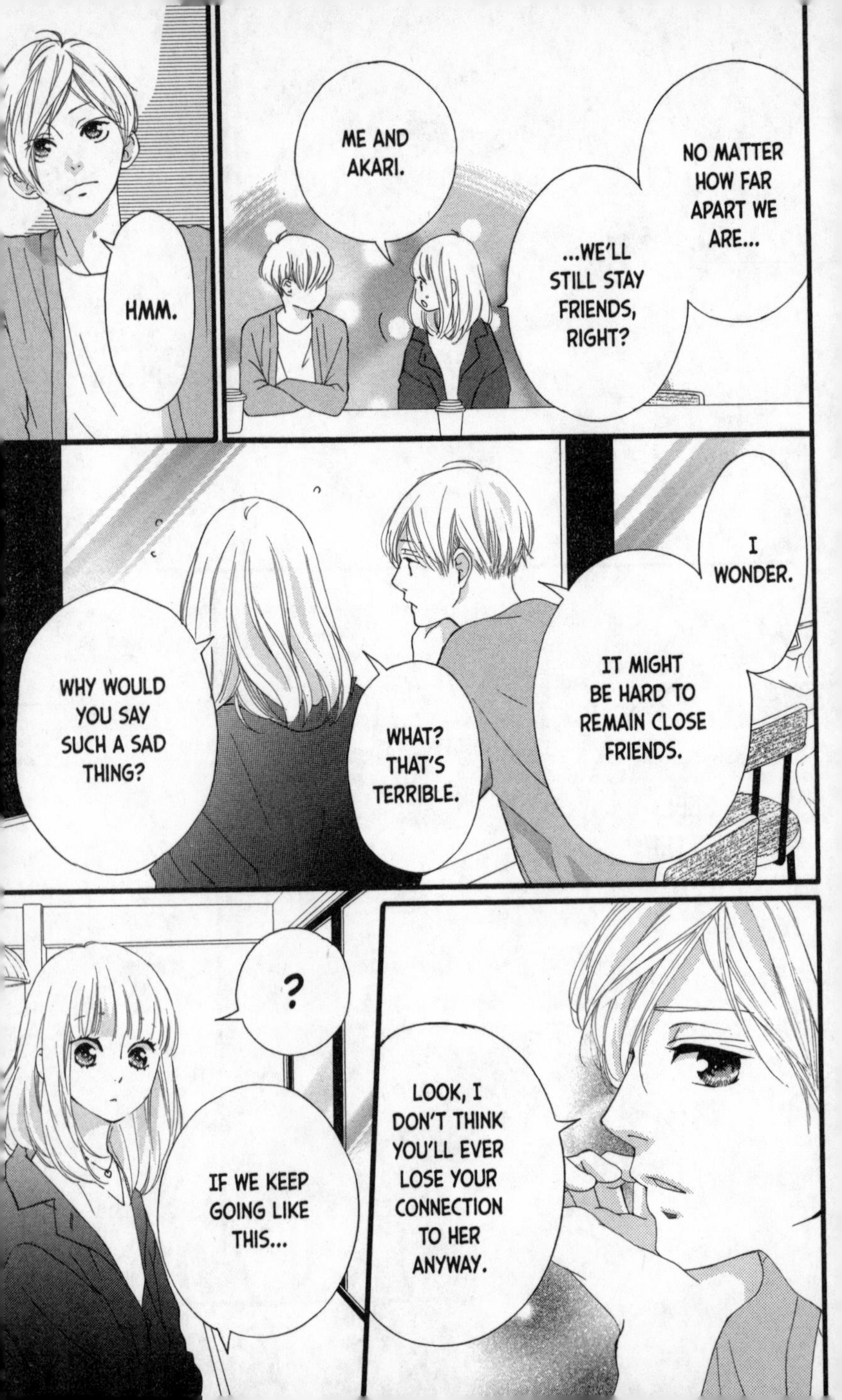
NO MATTER HOW FAR APART WE ARE...
...WE'LL STILL STAY FRIENDS, RIGHT?
ME AND AKARI.
HMM.
I WONDER.
IT MIGHT BE HARD TO REMAIN CLOSE FRIENDS.
WHAT? THAT'S TERRIBLE.
WHY WOULD YOU SAY SUCH A SAD THING?
LOOK, I DON'T THINK YOU'LL EVER LOSE YOUR CONNECTION TO HER ANYWAY.
?
IF WE KEEP GOING LIKE THIS...

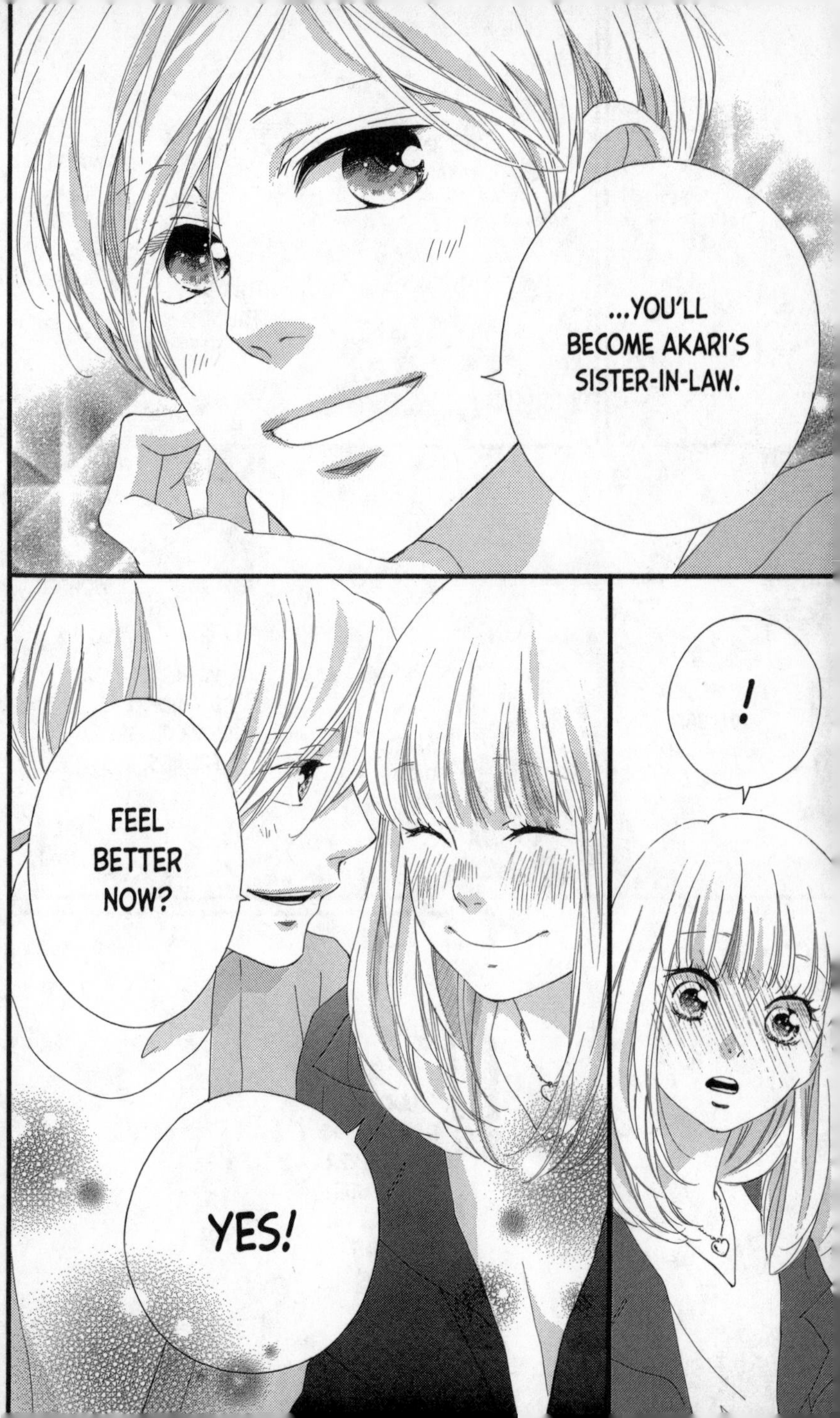
...YOU'LL BECOME AKARI'S SISTER-IN-LAW.
!
FEEL BETTER NOW?
YES!

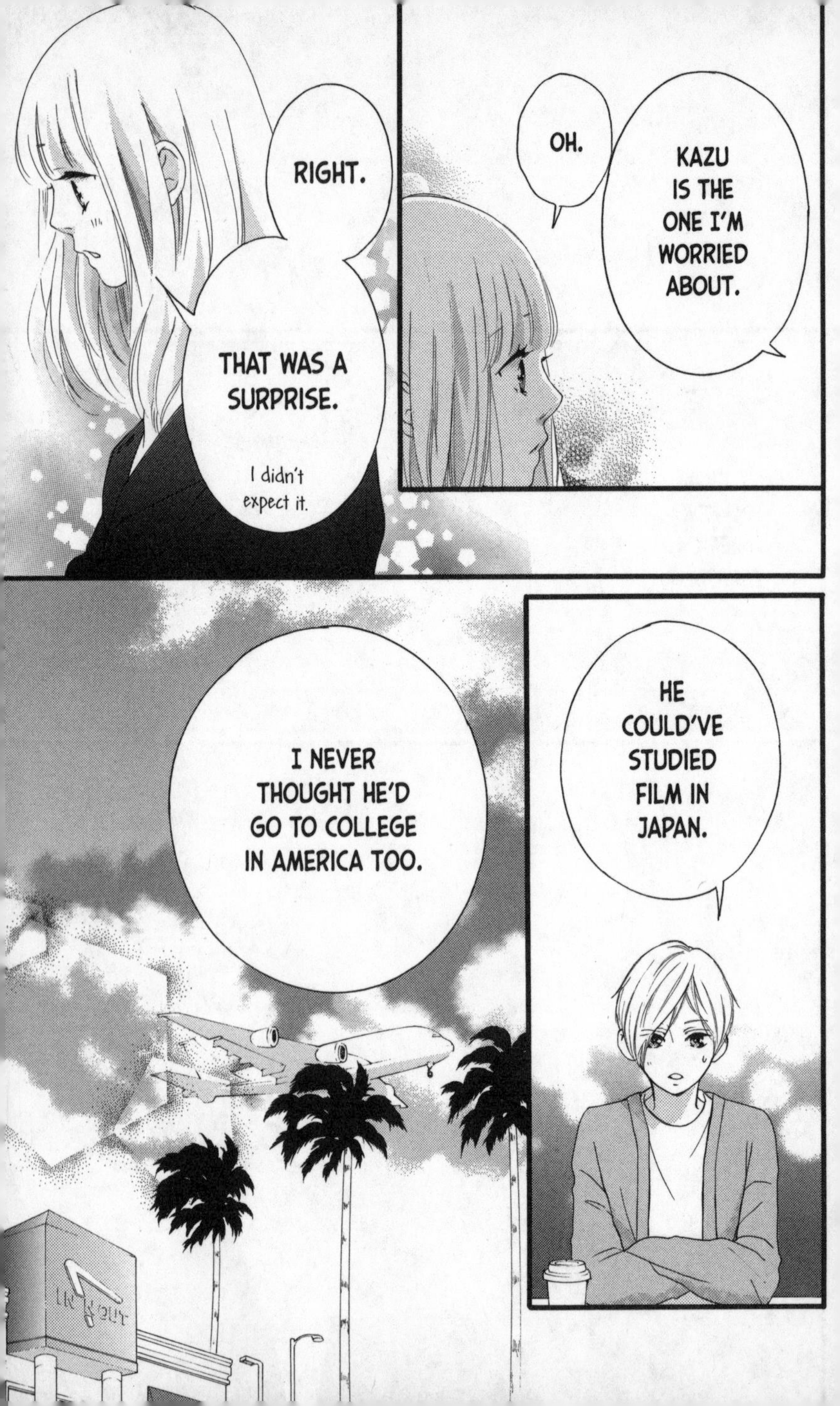
OH.
KAZU IS THE ONE I'M WORRIED ABOUT.
RIGHT.
THAT WAS A SURPRISE.
I didn't expect it.
HE COULD'VE STUDIED FILM IN JAPAN.
I NEVER THOUGHT HE'D GO TO COLLEGE IN AMERICA TOO.

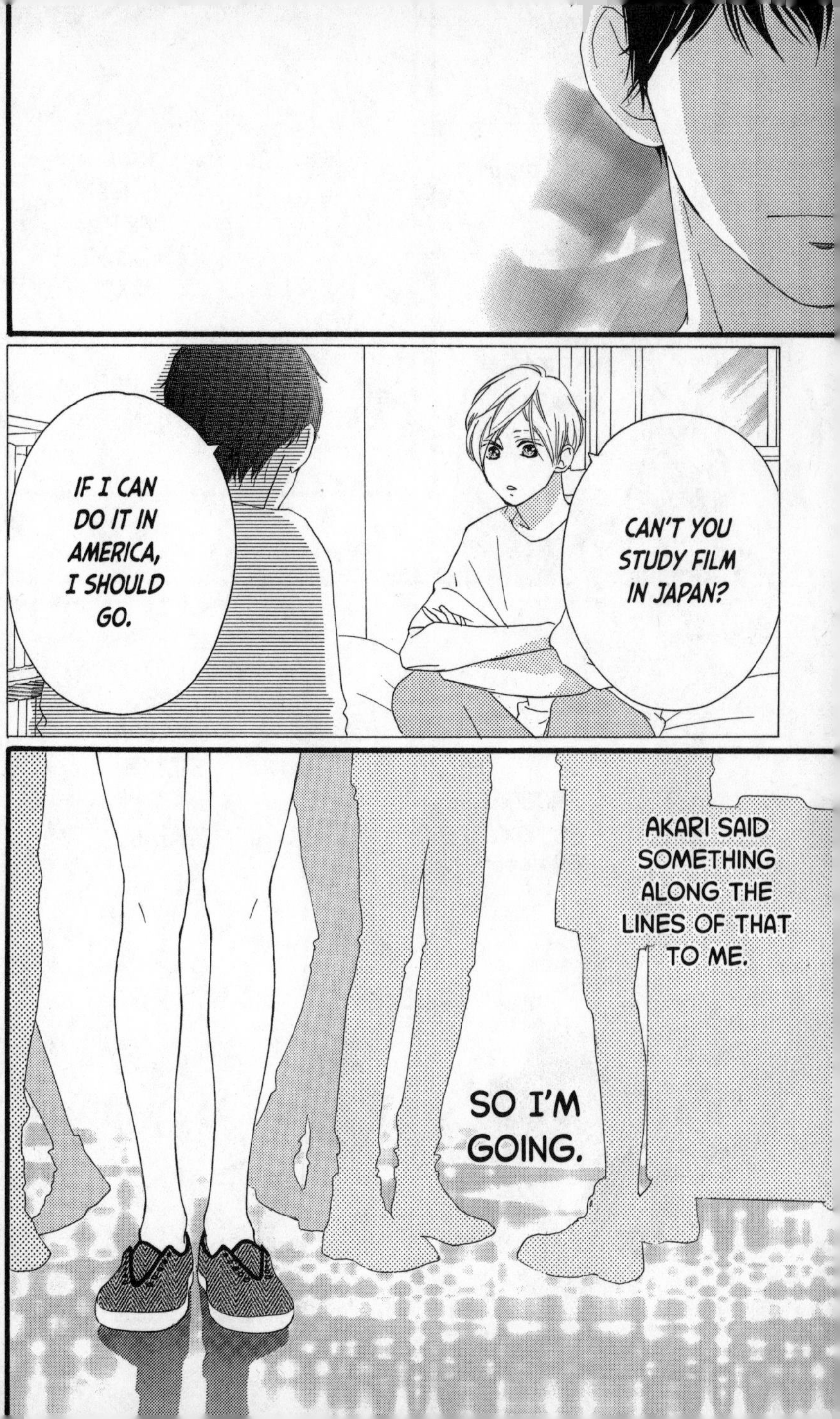
CAN'T YOU STUDY FILM IN JAPAN?
IF I CAN DO IT IN AMERICA, I SHOULD GO.
AKARI SAID SOMETHING ALONG THE LINES OF THAT TO ME.
SO I'M GOING.

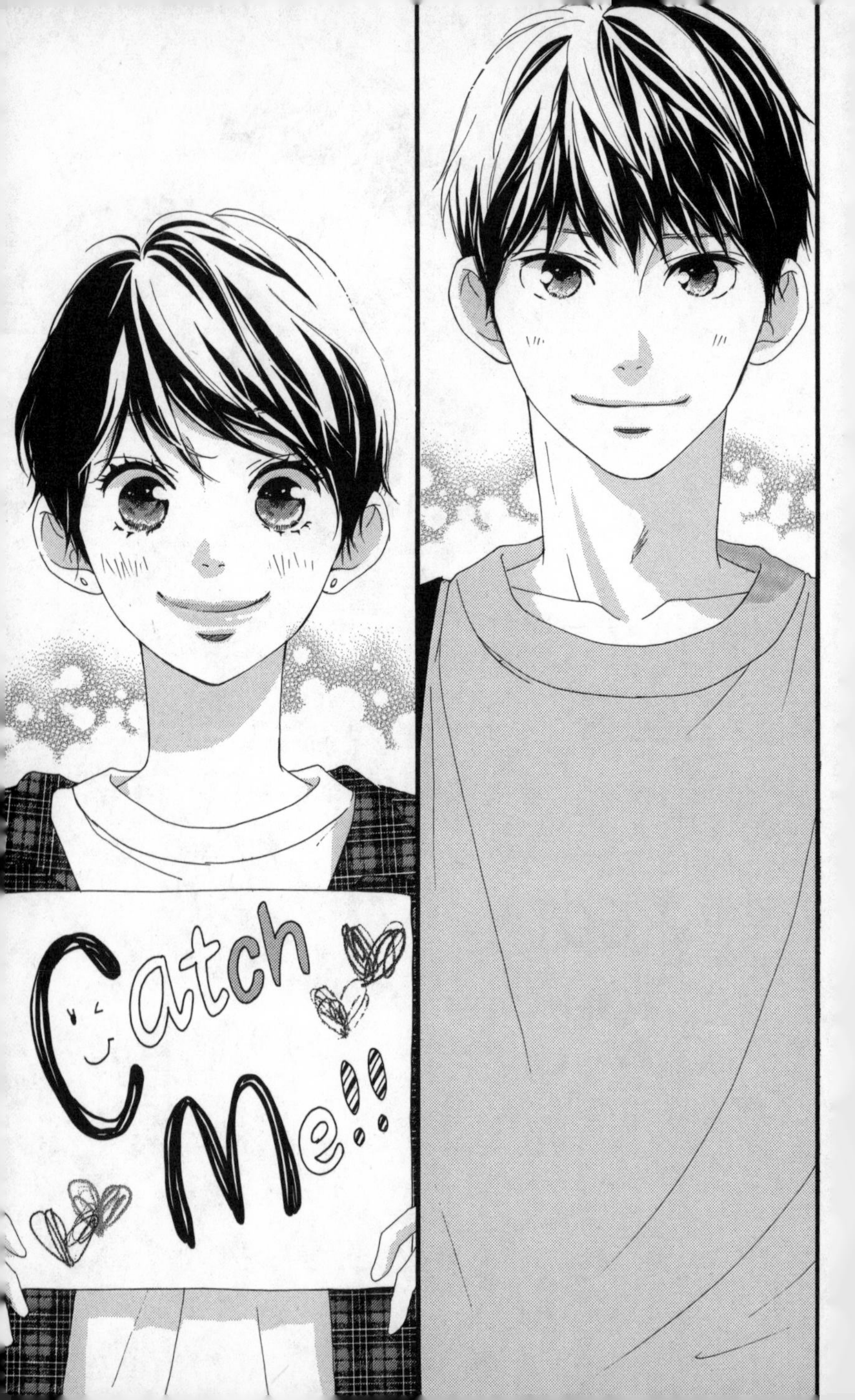
Catch Me!!

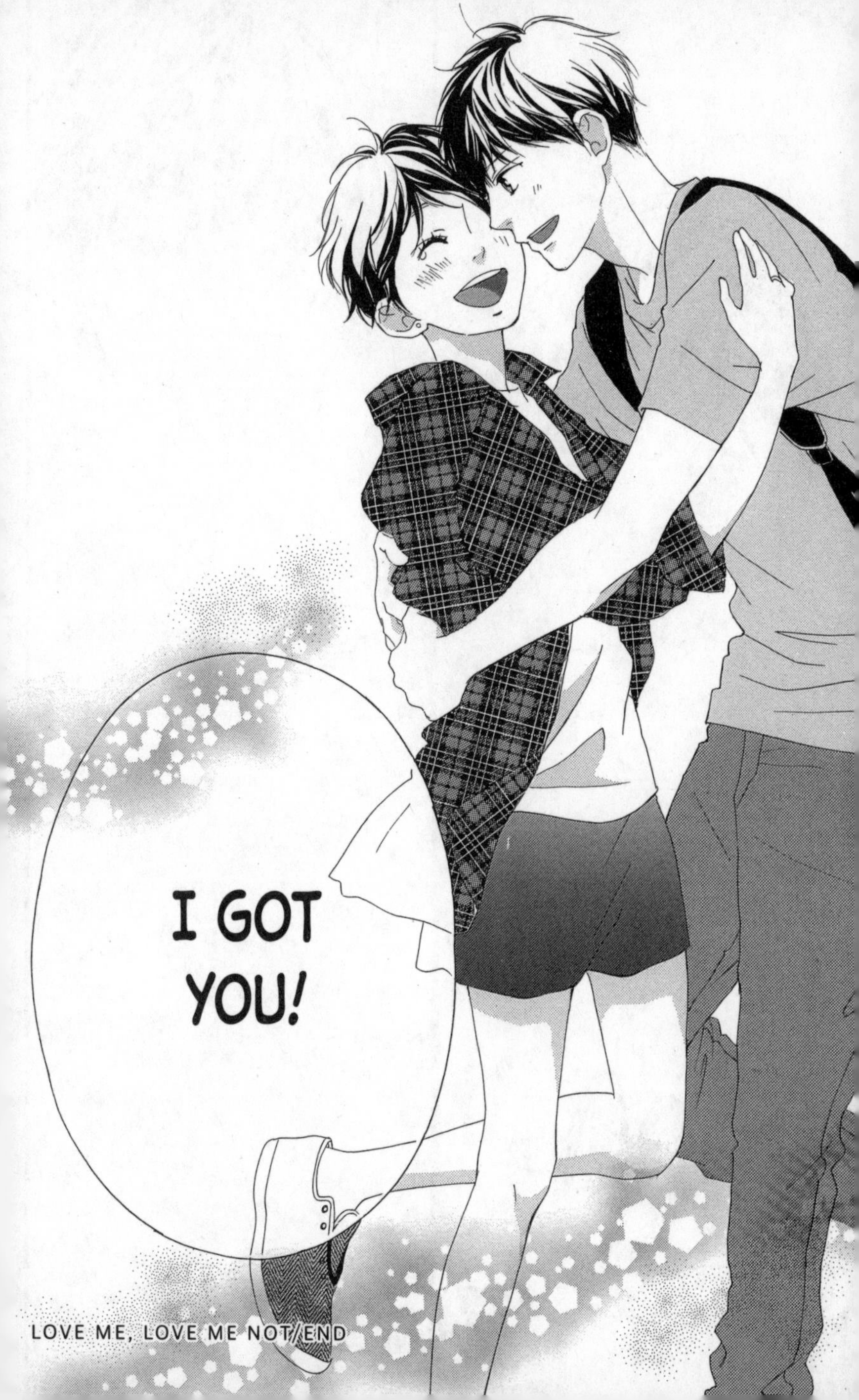
I GOT YOU!
LOVE ME, LOVE ME NOT/END

AFTERWORD

Thank you so much for reading
this series all the way to the end.

As I'm writing this, I have a terrible cold. Maybe it's something to
do with the sense of relief I have now that the series is over, but
it's been a while since I've had a cold that has dragged on for so
long. A little before I came down with this, I had a conversation
with one of my assistants who told me I'm always so healthy. I said,
"Yeah, I am. I only get the odd cold. I'm very hardy! Ha ha." Having
just had that conversation, I felt too awkward telling everyone I had
a mega cold, so no one knows I am quietly hanging out in my bed.
I'm feeling very fortunate that it happened after the series ended.
(I shudder to think what would've happened if I still had work due.)
I feel like maybe I wanted to be more sentimental about the end of
the series, but the *Love Me, Love Me Not* movie is being released
in 2020, so maybe there's no need for me to feel wistful. I'd be
very happy if you all felt the same way too.

I'm looking forward to seeing you again somewhere, sometime...

Io Sakisaka

Thank you so much for the past four years. It feels like they went by in a flash, but also that they took a very long time. I can only conclude that this series ran exactly the right amount of time. (*laugh*)

For everyone who read this all the way through, thank you so very much.

By the way—in the end, Ryosuke became my favorite character.

Io Sakisaka

Born on June 8, Io Sakisaka made her debut as a manga creator with *Sakura, Chiru*. Her series *Strobe Edge* and *Ao Haru Ride* are published by VIZ Media's Shojo Beat imprint. *Ao Haru Ride* was adapted into an anime series, and *Love Me, Love Me Not* was made into an animated feature film. In her spare time, Sakisaka likes to paint things and sleep.

Love Me, Love Me Not

Vol. 12
Shojo Beat Edition

STORY AND ART BY
Io Sakisaka

Adaptation/Nancy Thistlethwaite
Translation/JN Productions
Touch-Up Art & Lettering/Sara Linsley
Design/Yukiko Whitley
Editor/Nancy Thistlethwaite

OMOI, OMOWARE, FURI, FURARE © 2015 by Io Sakisaka
All rights reserved.
First published in Japan in 2015 by SHUEISHA Inc., Tokyo.
English translation rights arranged by SHUEISHA Inc.

The stories, characters, and incidents mentioned in this
publication are entirely fictional.

Printed in the U.S.A.

Published by VIZ Media, LLC
P.O. Box 77010
San Francisco, CA 94107

10 9 8 7 6 5 4 3 2 1
First printing, January 2022

viz.com   shojobeat.com

Shojo Beat Romances by IO SAKISAKA

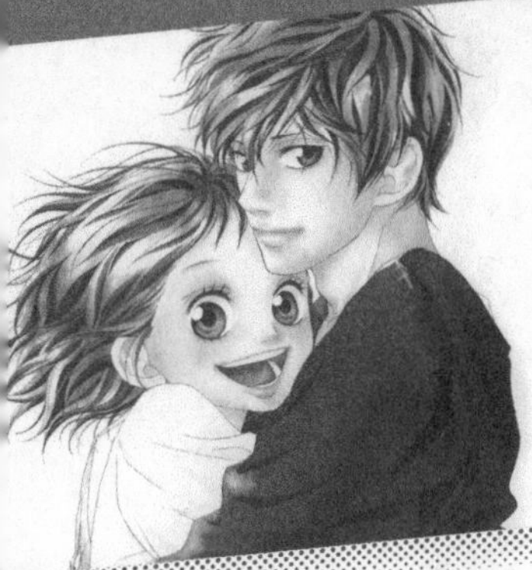

STROBE EDGE

When Ninako meets Ren, the handsome, enigmatic guy that all the girls worship, her life takes an unexpected turn. With just a few words and a smile, he changes her world...

Ao Haru Ride

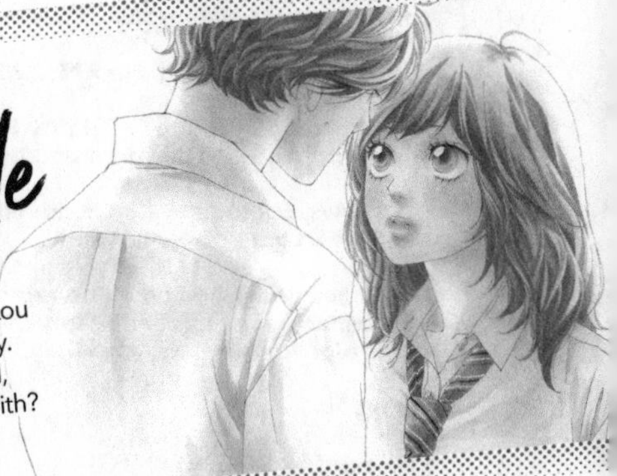

As soon as Futaba realized she really liked Kou in junior high, he had already moved away. Now, in high school, Kou has reappeared, but is he still the same boy she fell in love with?

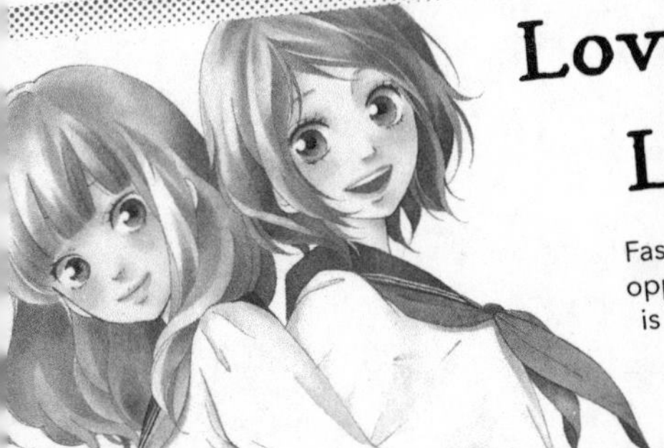

Love Me, Love Me Not

Fast friends Yuna and Akari are complete opposites—Yuna is an idealist, while Akari is a realist. When lady-killer Rio and the oblivious Kazuomi join their ranks, love and friendship become quite complicated!

RATED T TEEN

VIZ

DAYTIME SHOOTING STAR

Story & Art by
Mika Yamamori

Small town girl Suzume moves to Tokyo and finds her heart caught between two men!

After arriving in Tokyo to live with her uncle, Suzume collapses in a nearby park when she remembers once seeing a shooting star during the day. A handsome stranger brings her to her new home and tells her they'll meet again. Suzume starts her first day at her new high school sitting next to a boy who blushes furiously at her touch. And her homeroom teacher is none other than the handsome stranger!

HIRUNAKA NO RYUSEI © 2011 by Mika Yamamori/SHUEISHA Inc.

Stop!

You may be reading the wrong way.

In keeping with the original Japanese comic format, this book reads from right to left—so action, sound effects, and word balloons are completely reversed to preserve the orientation of the original artwork. Check out the diagram shown here to get the hang of things, and then turn to the other side of the book to get started!

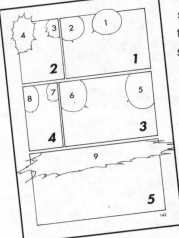